All

Politics

Is Local

Reflections of a Former County Chairman

William D. Angel Jr.

The Kent State University Press ⬛ Kent & London

© 2002 by The Kent State University Press, Kent, Ohio 44242
All rights reserved
Library of Congress Catalog Card Number 2001003961
ISBN 0-87338-728-7
Manufactured in the United States of America

07 06 04 03 02   5 4 3 2 1

Library of Congress Cataloging-in-Publication Data

Angel, William Daniel, 1947–
Not all politics is local : reflections of a former county chairman / William D. Angel, Jr.
p.   cm.
Includes bibliographical references and index.
ISBN 0-87338-728-7 (pbk. : alk. paper) ∞
1. Democratic Party (Allen County, Ohio)
2. Allen County (Ohio)—Politics and government.
I. Title.
JK2318.03 A54 2002
324.2771'06'0977142—dc21
2001003961

British Library Cataloging-in-Publication data are available.

For John Watts Hevener
1933–1993

The Governor had leaned across the table, bigger than life, stabbing at egg yolk, and put the idea to him: "Ain't no use fomentin'. Learned that long ago. Ain't no use 'cept in the last extremity. You want to overturn the existin' institution, that's fine. But you got to be sure you know how to build a better one."
—Billy Lee Brammer, *The Gay Place*

· Contents ·

• Preface •

In September 1984, I was managing state senator Steve Maurer's reelection campaign in Allen County, and a problem had arisen. Veterans groups were upset over plans for an October parade to celebrate the opening of Lima's brand-new Veterans Memorial Civic Center. One veteran told me that parade organizers had decided on a *1984* theme, replete with "Big Brother" and a retinue of storm troopers marching on Lima's town square. There was also something about simulating nuclear blasts. The vets wanted no part of this nonsense, no sir. They wanted me to call Maurer to express their displeasure and ask him not to appear in the parade. I obliged and phoned the senator's office, explaining the problem to Maurer's aide, Susan Gibler. When I got to the part about nuclear explosions, Susan giggled, stopping me in mid-sentence to ask incredulously, "Bill, what's in the water up there?" We both laughed, and a friendship started. By the way, the *1984* theme mercifully went away.

Shortly after the Maurer campaign ended, I began composing letters to Susan, recounting the goings-on in Allen County politics. I continued writing from 1986, when she moved to Fort Lauderdale, Florida, though 1988, when she returned to Columbus. At that point, my letter production slowed, as we communicated more regularly by phone and in person. Even so, between 1985 and 1989, I wrote over 120 letters to Susan. Some were quite long—fifteen or more handwritten pages. Others were written over a period of days and look like diaries. All the letters contained elements of personal information, and all offered detailed reflections on prominent events and personalities, as well as memorable conversations. I kept my own copies, seeing each letter as an avenue to my thoughts; consequently, the "Gibler Files" developed into a personal journal describing an intense period in my life. Written as events unfolded, the letters provide a clear window into the weekly (and sometimes daily) operations of the Allen County Democratic Party, particularly in moments of crisis.

My memory has always been good, but it is my letters to Susan Gibler that form the backbone of the narrative; without them, the analysis could not have been written. The "Angel to Gibler" citations indicate particularly accurate characterizations of events. Cited conversations appear as they were recorded in the letters. My interpretations may be open to question—people remember events differently—but the narrative is factual; wherever possible, I have confirmed my stories.

I am extremely grateful to Susan for reading my letters and for encouraging me to write them. Although we later drifted apart as our lives took separate turns, we remain friends.

I am also grateful to many others, especially those who contributed interviews for this book. Mary (Hevener) Kahal, Bev McCoy, Charlie Weidel, Marty Glazier, Tom Thompson, Howard Elstro, and Frank Winegardner all provided important insights into structure and activities of the Allen County Democratic Party before I became active in that organization. Mary's contributions and her reminiscences about her late husband John were especially enlightening and kindly given. I am particularly thankful to Dean French, Bob Routson, and Maj. Larry Van Horn, who supplied important information that sharpened my understanding of the tax-referendum controversy described in chapter 11. Also, Rochelle Twining was a constant source of information, contributing several interviews to help me clarify some of the less sharply rendered stories. In addition, Ida Kay Keller supplied important details regarding the Dumpbusters' organization and gave me a behind-the-scenes look into her county commissioner races of 1988 and 1990. Rick Siferd helped me recall events surrounding the nurses' strike at Lima Memorial Hospital in 1989. Finally, David Berger and Howard Elstro, together, gave me a clearer comprehension of the dilemmas David encountered in his 1989 mayoral campaign. I am equally indebted to Nancy Wyche, who helped me form a fresh interpretation of that election. Thanks to all.

Additional help came from a myriad of sources. The staff at the Lima Public Library, for instance, kindly helped me to relearn the intricacies of microfilm reading. Jim Krummel, editor of the *Lima News,* and Mike Lackey, a columnist for the newspaper, graciously helped me procure photographs. So did Anna Selfridge, curator of the Allen County Museum, which granted me permission to use *Lima News* photographs from the museum's archives. I also received photos from Marge Dornick, Bev McCoy, and Mary Kahal. Also, thanks to all who helped me locate photographs on my own. Finally, the Allen County Board of Elections gave me access to voter lists, election results, campaign finance reports, and minutes of board meetings. Thanks especially to Jan Maus and Ida Kay Keller. All this documentation was enormously helpful.

I am also grateful to Houston Mifflin for granting permission to use the passage from Billy Lee Brammer's *The Gay Place* that appears on the frontispiece. The excerpt from *The Gay Place*, copyright 1961 by B. L. Brammer, is reprinted by permission of Houghton Mifflin (all rights reserved). Thanks also to Rick Britton of Charlottesville, Virginia, who drew the map of Allen County.

Finally, I must thank all who have helped in the writing of this manuscript. I am especially grateful to The Ohio State University at Lima for granting me a special research assignment during the winter quarter of 1999; it allowed me to complete the first draft. I am thankful to all the deans under whom I have served—James Biddle, James Countryman, and Violet Meek. Dr. Meek was especially supportive of this project as it entered its final stages, but all my deans have kindly and graciously encouraged both my political activity and my scholarship. So has my department chair, Dr. Paul Beck, on Ohio State's Columbus campus. Thanks, Paul, for your support and encouragement.

I must also thank the Southern Humanities Conference for putting me on the program for the annual meeting at Eastern Kentucky University in February 1996. The paper I presented there was the seed that germinated into this book.

A few months after that conference, I sent a copy of my paper to John Hubbell, director of The Kent State University Press, inquiring whether the press might be interested in publishing a book-length version of it. He encouraged me in the project and shepherded it through to publication. My appreciation extends to John and to all at the press, including Joanna Hildebrand Craig, Erin Holman, Perry Sundberg, Christine Brooks, and Susan Cash, who helped with the editing, publication, design, and marketing of this book.

Thanks also to all who have read bits and pieces of the manuscript, especially my pal and colleague Roger Nimps. I owe particular appreciation to Dr. Sally Angel, professor of communications at Lima Technical College (and my wife), who read every page of the manuscript at least twice, recommended important editorial changes, and lovingly encouraged me to see the project through.

Not one part of this book could have been written, however, had it not been for the Democrats of Allen County, who generously allowed me to serve as their chairman for five years and who have continually made me feel welcome at party gatherings. Their heroic perseverance in the face of great odds provided a story that had to be told.

· Introduction ·
Reflections of a Former County Chairman

I'm a political scientist, but don't hold that against me. I learned a long time ago that political science has its limits. This is not to say that quantitative studies and model-driven analyses are unimportant. To the contrary—they are valuable. By profiling the electorate as a mass group, behavioralists can describe general tendencies that a more idiosyncratic approach, such as the one used here, might overlook. Samuel Eldersveld, for instance, does a wonderful job using aggregate data to describe the politics of local government in Ann Arbor, Michigan,[1] and yet the reader learns very little about the city's human culture, the day-to-day struggle that forms the bedrock of Ann Arbor and its politics.

Behavioral analyses of politics, like Eldersveld's, are too broad in focus and too narrow in technique. They are too broad in the sense that they don't get into the nitty-gritty of political life, barely considering the individual stories that create the wide sweep of analysis. The characters who form my story— John Hevener, Charlie Hauenstein, Rochelle Twining, Todd Hey, Cora Hamman, John Dornick, Leonard Boddie, and Steve Webb, among others—would have been overlooked by any behavioral approach. Similarly, by honing in on data and statistical indices, behavioral studies narrow the picture of culture's effect on local politics. They can describe what a culture looks like—what the citizens believe, and how they behave—but they are inadequate in explaining the culture's deeper implications—specifically, the wrenching impact it may have on the lives of individuals and on the politics they try to rouse. In this case study, voter surveys and modeled analyses of election data could have accurately and neatly mapped out Allen County's right-wing Republican culture; however, such aggregate data would have failed utterly to expose the messy tendrils of the area's deep-rooted conservatism, or to demonstrate how local conservatism constrains progressive action.

Isaiah Berlin put his finger on this problem: "Obviously, what matters is to understand a particular situation in its full uniqueness, the particular men and events and dangers, the particular hopes and fears which are actively at work in a particular place and at a particular time."[2] Berlin, of course, was writing about earthshaking events like the Russian Revolution. Still, my case study works along the same line, describing "the particular men [and dare I say, women], events, dangers, hopes and fears" that shaped political life in Allen County during the 1980s, especially during the time I led the Democratic Party there. For the general reader, this approach gives a gritty interpretation of how local parties function, the problems they face, and the fears they encounter as they confront overwhelming pressure from outside political forces.

The bottom line is that people form the foundation of political struggle. Intraparty fighting, such as that detailed here, supplies the lifeblood for any local party organization. When I first began writing this preface, the *Cleveland Plain Dealer* was reporting on an ugly feud between Cuyahoga county commissioner Jimmy Dimora, and the mayor of Cleveland, Michael White, over the location of a new county jail. There's nothing unusual about two local officeholders battling over turf, except that in this case both men are Democrats—and Dimora also happens to be chairman of the Cuyahoga Democratic Party.[3] Division, rivalry, feuding, and controversy enliven the local political scene; behavioralist studies, with their emphasis on aggregated data, give short shrift to this down-and-dirty side of politics.

It may seem odd to tell the story of a party organization that never won anything. It's true. The Allen County Democratic Party suffered an incredibly long losing streak, going twenty years (1976–96) without winning a single contested countywide election. The streak ended abruptly in 1996 when the party won a commissioner's seat and the county engineer's post.[4] But the struggle detailed in this book is one of an organization grappling to overcome its defeats and to prepare for a time when victory ultimately would come. Losing is a natural part of politics, and how parties cope with defeat and build from it is important. Even more important, losing parties provide opposition to the winners, creating necessary grist for the democratic process. It's an old part of politics in the United States—reserving a place at the table for minorities. By offering alternative voices and different views of local policy, losers keep the majority honest. Unless the opposition does its job effectively, governing parties succumb to arrogance and smugness, leading at best to mismanagement of the public trust, and at worst to downright political repression. In Allen County, the Democrats under my leadership offered a spirited, outspoken criticism of Republican officeholders, and if our accomplishments were mixed, we provided a forum that dissatisfied citizens could enter. There they could express their views and augment the county's "social capital," the societal glue that causes people to participate and work with each other in resolving local problems.[5]

Local parties, whether they lose consistently or win regularly, are important because they supply this social capital. They do more than recruit candidates and run campaigns; they create places where people can meet, discuss political issues, and hammer out ways of confronting community challenges. Indeed, during the time I chaired the Allen County Democratic Party, I saw Democrats, even those of us who were fighting one another, arouse broad civic responses to local problems.[6]

In this way, local parties supply the catalytic fuel needed to inspire public discourse. They plug people into the political process, and lay claim to the fact that politics is not a spectator sport, not the sole province of celebrity politicians on TV. No. People connect with the body politic through channels that local parties provide. Activists meet, discuss, organize, argue, plan strategy, talk to neighbors, and rail against injustice; as they do these things, they bring less active citizens into the loop, keeping alive the idea that politics is within the grasp of ordinary folks.

Yet local activism is frustrating, as this narrative of county politics shows. As a story of party organization at its most basic level, this book signals important and disquieting trends regarding the place of grassroots politics in the national party structure. At one time, county parties were dependable workhorses in the American party system, delivering the vote for slates of national, statewide, and local candidates. Politicians at the local level understood well the advice of George Washington Plunkitt, the loquacious Tammany Hall operative: "There's only one way to hold a district: study human nature and act accordin'. . . . To learn real human nature you must go among the people, see them and be seen."[7] That is, politicians talked with voters in their communities face to face, got to know them, worked the precincts one voter at a time during campaigns, and thereby connected their constituents to the body politic.

Today, voters have lost their former connection with political life, besieged by a barrage of "attack ads" and media-style candidates. State and national campaigns operate with minimal activity among grassroots loyalists, for the new politics holds that mass-marketing candidates is a more efficient way to reach the voters than mobilizing armies of volunteers to campaign door to door. Large-scale operations clutter the airways and overshadow the work of local campaigns, which see their messages lost amid the noise generated by the so-called big races. Average voters, as if heeding the advice of a newspaper editorial, "turn off their TV sets"[8] and turn away from politicians generally, local ones included.

Even when local politicians try to connect with the national or statewide organizations, they are given the "so what?" treatment; politicians higher up in the power chain act tone deaf to their efforts. Consider the story of "Al and Me." In July 1987 I met Al Gore. As one of eight candidates vying for the Democratic Party's 1988 presidential nomination, he had gone to Cleveland to schmooze at a convention of state party chairs.

I was there, still naive and optimistic in my second year as party chair and hoping I could offer some grassroots help to a presidential contender. At the opening-night cocktail party, I was roaming among the nondescript contenders—Bruce Babbitt, Joseph Biden, Paul Simon, the ones I knew didn't have a chance—when Jesse Jackson made his entrance. Immediately the whole room tilted to Jesse, grown men and women clamoring for a handshake as if he were a rock star or a professional athlete.

The shuffle left Al Gore alone, deserted and awkward, a sentry guarding a tray of cold shrimp. I approached, extended my hand, and said, "Senator Gore, I'm Bill Angel, and I chair the Allen County Democratic Party in western Ohio." Gore made polite eye contact, grasped my hand with a firm, politician's handshake, and responded crisply, "Good for you!" I hesitated a moment, expecting him to ask about political conditions in my county, but his eyes darted toward the Jackson partisans, who had swung like a conga line to the other end of the hall. Gore waved. He had obviously spotted someone more important than I. "Glad to meet you. Keep up the good work," he said, slapping me on the back as he hustled toward Jesse and his friends. I was left to defend the shrimp.

Al Gore and I are both members of the Democratic Party, but at that moment we occupied different circles within it. I had a following, but it was of little use to him. He needed an expert in campaign finance who could raise the millions in cash needed to pay for a presidential campaign, or a media guru who could mass-market his candidacy in several states at once. The Allen County Democratic Party was irrelevant to those priorities. So was I.

Local parties, however, are relevant to the people who work in them. They provide institutional frameworks where place-bound activists can connect with larger forces and perhaps use them to shape local politics. When I returned to Allen County following that 1987 encounter with Al Gore, I reported on the candidates, assessing their messages and chances, and prepared a preliminary list of volunteers for the 1988 presidential campaign. I even obtained candidate literature, which I placed in the party's booth at the county fair that August. So the party was plugged in to the national campaign, though the connection was mostly a one-way feed.

The problem is this: Politicians in the larger arena (e.g., Al Gore) are so focused on their problems and their campaign objectives that they overlook the cultural restrictions present at the local level. Attitudinal distance prevails; that is, politicians whose base lies in national or statewide politics either discount or ignore the counsel of Tip O'Neill, the late congressman and Speaker of the House: "All politics is local."[9] For instance, in the 1984 presidential primary, when I was coordinating the Mondale campaign in the Fourth Congressional District, a rep from the candidate's statewide organization, headquartered in Cleveland, made a request. "Could you drive up and down I-75?" he asked. "It runs through your district, right? And could you look for barns that front onto the interstate?"

"Why?"

"Well, we'd like to paint 'Mondale-for-President' signs on them. It'd be fresh paint, blue and white. Mondale would get the publicity. The farmers would get a fresh coat of paint on their barns."

I promised to do what I could, but I knew I'd do nothing with this harebrained idea. Most farmers would have pitchforked me right off their property. And even if I could have found some Democratic farmers, none would have been so foolish as to have their barns painted with the proclamation "Mondale-for-President" blazing long after the 1984 political season had passed. Farmers count votes, too.

As this anecdote shows, politicians in the larger arena often fail to comprehend the subtleties of county politics. It would seem they believe that not all politics is local, a perverse distortion of Tip O'Neill's dictum. O'Neill understood that the underpinnings of political life are found at the grass roots. Or, as a local politician once told me, someone has to spade the earth, plowing the way for future struggles.[10] In the grand scheme, county parties do the heavy lifting.

In part, this book is my story, a political memoir of sorts, but bear in mind that two Bill Angels are present in the narrative. There is Bill Angel the Storyteller, trying to come to grips with the truth behind events that occurred over a decade ago and to impart it to the reader. And there is Bill Angel the Sometimes-Confused Party Chairman, who often seemed more controlled by events than in control of them. In that respect, this book can be seen as a chronicle of political leadership, one man's struggle to discover what it takes to become a politician.

But it also is story of good people who cared deeply about their community, their state, and their country. Politics celebrates human struggle, the spirit of citizenship at the heart of any country and its political parties. Many different kinds of people give to their communities, but the most misunderstood perhaps are the battle-tested activists in the trenches of local campaigns. Although they could be regarded as partisan hacks and trouble-causing gadflies, in reality, they covet mostly the chance to see their party win an election, ideally more than once every twenty years. Most important of all, they want a voice in shaping the conditions of their everyday lives.

In my classes, we call that democracy.

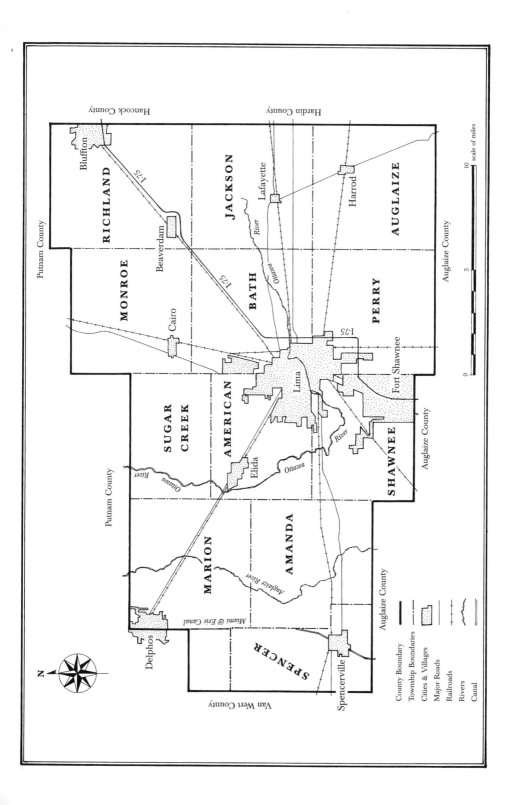

N

Hancock County

Hardin County

Putnam County

Bluffton

RICHLAND

Beaverdam

MONROE

JACKSON

I-75

I-75

Lafayette

Ottawa River

Harrod

BATH

AUGLAIZE

Cairo

PERRY

Auglaize County

Lima

SUGAR CREEK

AMERICAN

Fort Shawnee

I-75

Elida

SHAWNEE

Ottawa River

Auglaize County

Ottawa River

Putnam County

MARION

AMANDA

Auglaize River

Auglaize County

Miami & Erie Canal

Delphos

SPENCER

Spencerville

Van Wert County

scale of miles

10

5

0

County Boundary
Township Boundaries
Cities & Villages
Major Roads
Railroads
Rivers
Canal

Part One

The Real World

· 1 ·

Charlie, Mary, and John

March 12, 1986, Headquarters, Allen County Democratic Party
The fat man cradled a gavel in his right hand. Actually, it wasn't a real gavel but a toy mallet, the kind three-year-olds use to pound pegs into "Playskool" workbenches. The fat man was Charlie Hauenstein. Adorned in his best blue cardigan, he twirled the gavel as he waited, nervously letting it touch the desk every fourth spin. His normally tiny hand, unusually small for a man of his bulk, looked huge holding the whirling mallet.[1]

The costume and the prop were conspicuous. Charlie never dressed up for these meetings, and he never used a gavel. He ran the Executive Committee with heavy-handed informality, calling on immediate subordinates to deliver whatever information they had to impart. The rest of us were spectators, not expected to protest or offer insights. No one squawked, unless he or she wanted a verbal put-down by Hauenstein or one of his cronies.

It was Charlie's show that night, beginning with the roll call. Our secretary, Carol Falk, was ill, leaving Hauenstein to call out the names. It was an odd performance. He grew more and more agitated as he went down the list, jumping and squirming in his seat; by the time he reached the end of the roll, he was barking out the names, his voice much too loud for the cramped meeting space in party headquarters. Then he apprised us of correspondence and went over mundane business, taking his time, ratcheting up the tension in the room. Charlie's notice to Executive Committee members of the session's time and date had warned that it would be "an interesting meeting."[2] It would be the first formal gathering of the party since I had publicly announced my challenge to Hauenstein's leadership. In response, Executive Committee members had gathered like school kids on the playground, knowing a fight would break out and hoping it happened soon.

Finally, treasurer Vern Eley opened the main event, as it were, with a veiled attack on my management of a state senate race in 1984. Without mentioning

Charlie Hauenstein, 1975. *Lima News* photo from the archives of the *Lima News*.

my name, he questioned how someone who had directed a campaign to "the biggest defeat ever" could now present himself as a candidate for party chair. "I just don't understand it," Eley growled. Eley's setup allowed Charlie to proclaim, "That's right, Vern. The Executive Committee has come under attack! We've tried to get all kinds of people involved in the party, and now we've come under attack. Yeah, I don't understand it, either." On cue, several Hauenstein loyalists joined in mutual consternation at this supposed assault on the party.

I rose to my feet and began speaking: "Mr. Chairman, let's be clear. You're talking about me, right? I've organized a group to replace you as chair of this party, and yes, I will replace you after the May 6 primary, once the party is reorganized." Mutterings of "Bullshit!" countered this prediction, muffled by the cigarette smoke circling the room. "I've never attacked this committee," I persevered. "My concern is to make this party better, to bring new leadership. That's what I'm doing and what other folks are doing in support of our cause. I also understand we're all Democrats. Once this campaign is over and I'm sitting where you're sitting, I know we'll all need to work together." Hauenstein glared at me, now twirling the gavel with the velocity of an airplane propeller.

Todd Hey rose. As Hauenstein's adjutant and most loyal ally, Hey chaired the party's Central Committee, but more importantly, he did most of Hauenstein's legwork, circulating petitions, recruiting candidates, and lining up volunteers. "Charles, is it true this group filed criminal charges against me?" Hey asked, looking at the floor and speaking softly, like a teenager whose feelings had been hurt. Hauenstein answered him: "Yes, that's right, Todd. They protested your petition [as a candidate for central committeeman] and filed criminal charges against you."

I snapped at the bait. "Mr. Chairman, we did not file criminal charges against anybody. We protested some petitions in the Central Committee races, Todd's included. You know that!" Hauenstein, red faced and unable to contain himself, began yelling: "You asked the Board of Elections to file criminal charges against fellow Democrats! This is the real world, Bill! It's not college. You can't come in here, write on a board, and then erase it."

The real world. The rebuke contained gospel-like truth, the meaning of which was lost on most of us that night, a truth that nevertheless bears significance for anyone who has ever been involved in grassroots politics. Politics is not a cerebral exercise. It involves questions of power and who will exercise it. One can learn lessons about political struggle by reading books or sitting in college classrooms, but certain realities cannot be comprehended until they've been lived. It is this truth that Charlie Hauenstein spoke of that night, the night I joined him in the world of real politics.

I am not an activist by nature. In fact, when I first arrived in Allen County, in northwest Ohio, in 1978, fresh out of graduate school and trying to earn tenure at The Ohio State University at Lima, I stood on the political sidelines, voting and not paying much attention to local Democrats. But John Hevener, a colleague from the History Department, drew me out when he invited me to work on Dick Celeste's 1982 gubernatorial campaign. John and his wife Mary were coordinating the Allen County effort for Celeste, who that spring was fighting an uphill battle to win the Democratic Party's nomination for governor. The Heveners assigned me a precinct to work, introduced me to party activists, acquainted me with local culture, and gave me additional responsibilities within their organization. They were the ones who first encouraged me to run for party chair, even though they knew that my outsider status—and theirs, for that matter—might work against me.

The Heveners and I were outsiders in several ways. Sailing against the political winds, we backed the liberal Celeste over the more conservative Bill Brown; most county chairs favored Brown and saw him as the party's likely nominee for governor. An outspoken advocate of capital punishment and stern penalties for criminals, "Billy Joe" Brown had won his second term as Ohio's attorney general in 1978, the same year Celeste had gone down to defeat in a poorly run gubernatorial campaign against the aging Republican incumbent James A. Rhodes. Celeste had had his chance and failed, the chairs reasoned, and now it was the tough-talking Brown's turn.[3]

But the county regulars backed the wrong horse in 1982, setting up a perplexing situation when Celeste won the primary and eventually became governor. Because most county chairs had not backed his primary bid, important political matters, including patronage, went not to the chairs but to folks like John and Mary Hevener, who had been county coordinators in the Celeste campaign. This did not sit well with Allen County's Charlie Hauenstein, who had chaired the party in Allen County since 1972 and had been an outspoken advocate of Brown's candidacy.

We were also outsiders ideologically. "The Democrats here are antiwar Democrats," Hevener once told me in the deadpan accent of a native West Virginian. He paused a beat and let a smile crinkle across his face before adding the punch line: "Anti–*Civil* War."

This remark—which I later came to call "Hevener's Rule"—was more than the wry observation of a history professor drawing a link with the county's Copperhead past. It addressed the local manifestations of the fault lines and fissures that had split the national Democratic Party since the 1960s. The Heveners, the other Celeste supporters, and I were products of the civil rights movement, the women's movement, and the antiwar movement. We favored affirmative action, the Equal Rights Amendment, and nuclear disarmament. In contrast Hauenstein and the "old guard Dems" found their roots in organized labor. They were activists in affiliates of the United Auto Workers at the Ford Engine Plant, Clark Manufacturing, Airfoil Textron, General Dynamics, or the Teledyne Steel foundry. Liberal on economic issues—social security, the minimum wage, occupational safety, workman's compensation, and the like—they looked askance at the social agenda favored by "McGovernites," as Hauenstein contemptuously called us.

In part, these ideological differences reflected the different class backgrounds of the two camps. My pals and I were college graduates, worked in white-collar jobs, and while we generally sympathized with the goals of labor, we had neither walked picket lines nor physically stood up for our jobs and our families.

By contrast, Charlie's loyalists had lived though hard times, battled for union rights, and they looked with quiet suspicion on educated outsiders.

Today I understand that Charlie Hauenstein was not the ignoramus I once thought him, but I also know he wasn't much of a leader either. Standing about five feet ten inches tall and weighing over three hundred pounds, Hauenstein was an object of derision among most of the people who planned his eventual overthrow. He did not work crowds at party gatherings, choosing to sit at the head table, eye the crowd, and wait for supplicants to approach him for patronage or tidbits of gossip. He seldom made media appearances and grew to loathe reporters as trouble-makers and liars.

Hauenstein surrounded himself with a few trusted lieutenants, who did most of the administrative work associated with managing the party—and for the most part they did a minimal job of it. Records, including financial ones, were haphazardly maintained, funds were not systematically budgeted, and volunteer lists simply did not exist. But the most aggravating charge against Hauenstein was that Democrats had not tasted victory in a contested county election since 1976.[4]

Charlie did hold the party together during the grim years from 1975 through 1982, when James Rhodes was governor. Richard Celeste's gubernatorial victory aroused the expectations of "coattail" victories for Allen County Democrats, but we found ourselves as disappointed as ever. Even when enthusiastic candidates came forward, there was little hope of their winning: their efforts were undermined by a lackadaisical organization that did little to encourage voter turnout, help with fund-raising, or carry the Democratic message. Meanwhile, Hauenstein exploited his chairmanship primarily to muster whatever patronage he could gather, rewarding members of his family and his loyal followers with state jobs.[5]

Still, that 1982 Celeste campaign dramatically altered the party's internal culture. Specifically, it activated dormant Democrats, myself included, who had wanted to participate further in party politics but resented the clubby ineptitude of Hauenstein and his cronies. Charlie and the old guard distrusted us "intellectual, McGovernite" liberals and felt shadowed by the Celeste organization. The old-timers in Allen County hunkered down. Having withstood previous challenges to Hauenstein's leadership, they discounted any threat we "schoolteachers" represented. Hubris set in—they denied themselves the opportunity to assimilate the newcomers.

By 1986 Charlie Hauenstein had been worn down by personality struggles within the party, by inability to recruit volunteers, by abusive (in his eyes) treatment from the media, and by the frustration of knowing that few people in Allen County took the Democrats seriously. The time for change had come, but he didn't realize it.

Hauenstein's political world was a feudal one. County chairs were expected to work loyally on behalf of the state party and of state officials, soliciting funds, supplying volunteers for campaigns, and communicating the Democratic message to local voters. Through the party's higher-ups, chairs might award patronage, recommend local loyalists for state jobs, help a neighborhood tavern get a lotto machine, or promote a local businessman for a state contract. Party members who received such "perks" understood their end of the bargain: Remain faithful to their chairs and help in the party's campaigns at election time—staffing phone banks, erecting yard signs, walking door to door for candidates.

By 1986 this world was crumbling. For one thing, during the years when Jim Rhodes held the governorship, the Ohio Democratic Party had begun raising funds independently of the county organizations, building up its treasury for statewide races. As for campaigning, most statewide candidates adopted the Celeste model and built personal organizations, independent of the party apparatus. County chairs were contacted primarily out of courtesy; candidates lined up their own volunteers. Also, television and radio became more efficient means to secure votes; the armies of volunteers in the eighty-eight counties became tactically less essential.

As for patronage, party chairs found themselves with less and less to distribute. In Allen County, Hauenstein had little influence in getting local Democrats into openings at the Lima Correctional Facility or the Oakwood Forensic Center, even though a Democrat held the governor's office. A few opportunities remained to select people for positions with state liquor stores or the Ohio Department of Transportation, but these were usually entry-level jobs or part-time and seasonal.[6]

The passage of Ohio's Collective Bargaining Law in 1983 further undermined patronage by making it illegal for state workers to do political work. Consequently, county chairs who successfully endorsed loyal followers for state jobs lost their appointees' political services. Also, job openings had to be posted and filled competitively, giving internal applicants the first opportunity. Under such a system, party chairs lost their voice in most hiring decisions and had no influence whatsoever in internal hires and promotions. Furthermore, hounding after patronage threw county chairs into competition with each other, as they chased fewer and fewer jobs, taxing their energies and leaving little to show for their efforts.

Nonetheless, many county chairs—and Hauenstein was one of these—believed that a vigilant and aggressive chair could still massage the process, keeping an eye on job postings and using informal pressure to secure jobs for supporters. In Charlie's world, party leadership was driven by this formula: Go after the patronage, reward loyal followers, and build up the party's base. His base was the county Democratic Party Central Committee, which consisted of representatives of most of the county's 169 precincts.

Ideally, this organization should constitute the core group of party activists. Committee members, who are elected during partisan primaries held in even numbered years, serve as the party's eyes, ears, and legs within their precincts, informing party cadre about the needs of the neighborhood, canvassing the precinct on behalf of candidates, selling tickets for fund-raisers, and turning out the vote at election time.

But central committees seldom operate so efficiently. A few committeemen and committeewomen take their jobs seriously, but many pay minimal attention to party requests. As we've seen, there's little the party can do for them in the form of patronage; if the best they can get is a pledge of "good government," many will let pass the chance to work for the party. Realistically, a party chair is lucky if one-third of the Central Committee representatives work hard for the party, and if half will work occasionally. In fact, most county parties rely upon volunteers who are not part of the formal structure but will perform important chores for the organization and its candidates.

The organization's most important duty is to choose party leadership. After the primary results are certified, the newly elected Central Committee members meet and choose a Central Committee chair from among their number. If the Central Committee is fairly large (as it was in Allen County), it selects an Executive Committee, initially consisting of thirty or so Central Committee representatives. The Central Committee then delegates to this smaller group authority and responsibility to direct party operations. In time, new members will be added to represent important constituencies within the party, and subcommittees will be organized and filled. Once the new Executive Committee assembles, it elects its own chair, who becomes, in essence, the leader of the county party, the County Chair. The chair's power, therefore is tied directly to the Central Committee; if the chair is to stay in office, that Central Committee, along with its own chair, must be loyal and trustworthy.

From 1972 to 1986, this was how the process functioned in Allen County, where Hauenstein commanded the party, and where Todd Hey, Charlie's alter ego and heir apparent, was Central Committee chair. Both men were from Bluffton, a Swiss Mennonite community on Allen County's northern edge. Both worked at the Ford Engine Plant and were members of UAW Local 1219. Theirs was a mutually supportive relationship. Hauenstein held his position because

Hey was loyal and kept the Central Committee in line, ensuring majority support for the Hauenstein-Hey team. In return for Hey's fealty, Hauenstein directed certain rewards in his direction, the most important of them an appointment as deputy registrar for one of Allen County's three license bureaus.

The early 1980s notched the high-water mark of Hauenstein's power. In 1982 he crushed a haphazardly organized attempt to overthrow him. One of the ringleaders of that effort was Denny Mault, an unemployed UAW member and former officer in its Clark Equipment Plant local before the plant closed down. Mault was also running for state representative, creating a situation that so aggravated Charlie that he orchestrated all sorts of "dirty tricks"—including, some thought, suggesting to Mault's wife that Denny had a girlfriend on the side. Hauenstein finally pulled strings with the UAW to secure a job for Mault at the Lima's General Dynamics Tank Plant, where Denny's duties would demand so much time that he could neither run for public office nor serve as party chairman. Then, in a shameless attempt to sow dissension among Denny's associates, Charlie began mongering a rumor that Mault had started the revolt simply to push Charlie into finding him a job.[7]

As it turned out, Hauenstein needn't have bothered. That 1982 spat was torn by infighting and absurd tactical ploys. On one occasion, the conspirators plotted to overthrow Charlie when he was out of town; they would call a special meeting of the Executive Committee and replace him. Mary Hevener, who attended the session where this scheme was discussed, opposed the whole concept, declaring it "sneaky and underhanded."[8]

Ultimately, the special meeting never happened, and Hauenstein's opponents turned to planning a takeover when the party reorganized in the spring. But they couldn't determine who would run for chair to replace him. Mault, with his newly acquired job, was out. Then Gerry Tebben, the party's candidate for Congress in 1980, was the nominee, but she became angry at something a fellow dissident had said about her and removed her name from consideration. Tebben, in turn, showed up on the Heveners' doorstep one Sunday morning in mid-May and pleaded with Mary to let the dissidents nominate *her*. She caught Mary at weak moment. Mary had just returned from a nuclear-freeze rally in New York City; she had driven all night with a group of fellow activists and was a bit bleary eyed when Tebben appeared with her proposal. Mary agreed, much to her later regret. The effort failed; Charlie won overwhelmingly.[9]

Seemingly, then, Charlie Hauenstein had little to worry about. The dissidents had been scattered, and his hold on the party was secure, at least through the 1984–86 term. In fact, the Central Committee elected in 1984 (the one our organization now wanted to replace) was deeply loyal to him, choosing Hey by acclamation and nominating an Executive Committee dominated by Hauenstein loyalists.

Furthermore, Democrats held all statewide elected offices, riding on the coattails of Richard Celeste's victory in the 1982 governor's race; the party maintained a 60 percent majority in the Ohio House of Representatives and a seventeen-to-sixteen edge in the state senate. The success at the state level seemed to signal greater opportunities for the local party to disburse patronage and accumulate funds, or so Hauenstein believed.

It grated on Hauenstein that he had to check with the Heveners before he issued a patronage recommendation, but the governor had instructed all party chairs to secure the approval of Celeste coordinators before endorsing patronage requests. Celeste's dictum included the appointment of deputy registrars, the most significant patronage "plum" a county chair could still offer. Until 1988, deputy registrars (DRS) were political appointees who ran the state's driver's license bureaus, receiving a $1.50 "registrar's fee" for each transaction processed by their respective facilities. With hundreds of transactions going through each facility every month, these fees ensured a sizeable flow of money directly into the pockets of the DRS.

Of course, the Ohio Democratic Party kept track of the business that went through each license bureau and billed the county parties a monthly assessment, which amounted to 3.3 percent of the registrar's fees received by the DRS. The parties, in turn, relied upon the generosity of the DRS to pay assessment and supply an extra amount to the county party treasury. Allen County's DRS cooperated with this arrangement, generally donating 10 percent of their monthly fees to the local party.[10]

The DR system, then, was a cash cow for county parties and for those fortunate enough to win appointments as deputy registrars. Although many statewide and local candidates made monetary demands on the DRS, anything left after they'd made the requisite contributions was theirs to keep. This setup provided exceptionally good income for what was part-time work at best, exceeding twenty-five thousand dollars annually;[11] it was for this reason that license bureaus were the most sought-after of all the patronage "perks" a chair could distribute.

Charlie Hauenstein's demise can be traced to his handling of these appointments in Allen County. Following Celeste's 1982 victory, the Heveners tangled with Hauenstein over the naming of two of the county's three DRS, to replace the Republicans appointed in the Rhodes era.[12] Hauenstein wanted to award the two Lima bureaus to Todd Hey, but the Heveners said "No"; they wanted Ron Rose, a former Executive Committee member, to head both Lima agencies.

The very mention of Rose gave Hauenstein a headache. First of all, it was the Heveners who nominated him, and Mary's participation in the 1982 overthrow attempt still stuck in Hauenstein's craw. He had not forgiven—nor would he ever forgive—Mary for her role in that effort.[13] Furthermore, Rose himself was disloyal, in Hauenstein's eyes. In the mid-1970s, the party had organized a concert by the band Blood, Sweat, and Tears as a fund-raising event. To underwrite the cost of bringing the group to Lima, the party had to borrow from a local bank, and all Executive Committee members were asked to sign the note. Rose refused. The concert was undersold, the party lost a huge sum of money, and the signatories of the note, meaning the Executive Committee members, were stuck with the bill. All except Ron Rose. "If he couldn't give money to the party then," Hauenstein protested, "why should he take money from the party now?"[14]

But the Heveners pushed the Rose nomination anyway. "He bitterly objected to Rose," recalled Charlie Weidel, who witnessed Hauenstein's ranting about the trouble the Heveners were causing him. "Charlie prized loyalty," Weidel remarked. "If you were loyal to him, then he'd do anything for you, but if he thought you were disloyal, then watch out. He'd fight you with all his power."[15]

So pressure mounted on Mary Hevener, who had to handle a barrage of telephone calls the day before a meeting of the Executive Committee, sometime in early 1983, at which the decision would be settled. The first call was from Beverly McCoy, a black schoolteacher and one of Mary's best friends. "Mary, you'll never believe what just happened. Charlie Hauenstein called me, and you know what? He offered me a license bureau. Now, Mary, what's going on?"[16]

Mary Hevener was dumbfounded. And angry. "I was never so mad at Charlie Hauenstein, as I was then. I could hardly speak," she later declared. "It was so Machiavellian."[17] It is doubtful that Hauenstein seriously entertained the prospect of making McCoy a deputy registrar. Ever the crafty politician, he was playing the divide-and-conquer game, pitting Mary against her dear friend Bev McCoy and placing the Heveners in the uncomfortable position of opposing the award of a license bureau to a prominent member of Lima's African American community.

Moments after Mary finished her conversation with Beverly McCoy, the telephone rang again. This time it was Jim Ruvulo, chair of the Ohio Democratic Party. Ruvulo was testy, unwilling to hear Mary's side of this story. He curtly announced that Todd Hey would be appointed to take charge of one license bureau and commanded Mary and John to come up with the name of another appointee. Any recommendation of Ron Rose would be rejected.

Seconds later, Hauenstein himself called. Although he needed the approval of the Heveners for the deputy registrar appointments, he was not in a placating mood. Instead, knowing that Ron Rose's name was no longer on the table, he tried to bully Mary Hevener into letting him appoint Hey to be the DR for both bureaus. "John and I won't go along with that," Mary bristled. "I'll go to the mat with you on this one, Mary," Hauenstein threatened. Mary refused to submit. Shaking with anger, her fury mounting, she told John about Hauenstein's threat—"I'll go to the mat with you." John eyed his wife's five-foot frame. "I certainly hope Charlie falls first," he deadpanned.[18]

Ultimately Hauenstein relented, but so did the Heveners. The forces aligned against them—Ruvulo's support of Todd Hey, Charlie's Machiavellian offer to Beverly McCoy, and the wearing tension each phone call had produced—were too much. They went along with Hauenstein's appointment of Hey to the lucrative bureau in the Lima Mall, which they had opposed, and nominated Frank Winegardner as a compromise appointee to the other bureau. Hauenstein reluctantly approved Winegardner—who attended the same church as the Heveners and who had been a Celeste volunteer—but not without publicly berating Mary in a long tirade at the Executive Committee meeting where the final arrangements were worked out. He never absolved the Heveners, taking out his anger on Mary, whom he bullied and insulted in one Executive Committee meeting after another through the 1983–84 term.[19]

One April afternoon in 1983, John Hevener approached me in the faculty lounge, exasperated by yet another confrontation with Charlie Hauenstein. Hevener had often entertained me with tales of Hauenstein's chicanery, but this time his tone was different—more serious, subdued. "We need new leadership, Bill," he explained. "Mary and I were impressed with the work you did for the governor, the way you worked those two Republican precincts on Lima's west side and carried them for Celeste. We think you'd be the right man for the job."

"What job?"

"To replace Charlie . . . as county chairman."

Flabbergasted and somewhat flattered, I demurred. "Not yet. I haven't paid my dues. I lack experience."

"Well, keep thinking about it," Hevener replied, smiling. He liked to fly-fish the trout streams near his boyhood home in Pocahontas County, West Virginia, and knew that he'd made only his first cast into these particular waters.

John and Mary
Hevener, circa 1989.
From the collection of
Mary (Hevener) Kahal.

John Hevener was a patient man. He had to be. Struck down as a teenager by
polio that left him bedridden and paralyzed for several months, and then
severely debilitated on the right side, Hevener had suffered physically throughout his life. Furthermore, he understood the stress a career in academe can
bring, public perceptions notwithstanding. After he earned his Ph.D. in history at Ohio State University, he received tenure twice but also lost it twice—at
Whitewater State University (Wisconsin) and Mankato State University (Min-
nesota), respectively. Both institutions experienced financial problems and
eliminated his position. He finally landed at Ohio State University/Lima Campus, earning tenure there but knowing that tenure, much like life itself, never
entitles one to security.

Hevener could tolerate superficially rude behavior with unusual grace, by
viewing matters from the other person's perspective. A labor historian who studied the battles to organize coal miners in Appalachia, he once visited a small
public library in the Kentucky coal fields, to investigate microfilm copies of
local newspapers. Within an hour after Hevener began work, the head librarian

strode into the room where he was staring at the film reader. She "harrumphed" and left. Fifteen minutes passed. The librarian returned, fidgeted, and left again. Finally, she entered the room a third time and abruptly turned the machine off. "It'll get hot if you use it too much," she huffed, turned on her heel, and spun out of the room.

John allowed the reader (and the librarian) to cool and took a break, figuring he needed one anyway. He never said anything to the librarian. It wasn't her fault, he reasoned. She just wasn't used to scholars coming in and using the equipment.[20]

On a different occasion, Hevener and I held a "skull session" with Steve Webb, a labor representative for public employees' unions. We were in Webb's dining room. The family dog was loose under the table, looking for attention before eventually camping at John's feet. As the meeting concluded and we all got up to leave, John felt something wet near his shoe top; looking down, he saw that the pup had shredded his pant cuffs into a chewed-up tangle of thread. Webb was aghast and offered to buy John a new pair of trousers, but Hevener replied that it wasn't necessary. "I should have been paying more attention," he said.

Hevener had a chiseled face and expressive eyes that twinkled whenever he listened to a good story, or told one himself, such as the one about his encounter with the librarian. The eyes could also cloud over when he was angry, which didn't happen very often, but often enough that one didn't want to get on his "fightin' side."

People miscalculated if they saw indecision in John's polite demeanor or weakness in his physical handicap, or concluded that he was someone who could be easily bowled over. Hevener never did anything he didn't want to do, and he possessed a strong moral compass. He had a well-defined understanding of what was ethical and what was unethical, what was tolerable and what could not be endured. While he was forgiving of most human weaknesses, he maintained certain boundaries that one dared not cross if one didn't want to risk his anger. He viewed politics in terms of morality: virtue on one side, wickedness on the other. As Mary Hevener later observed, "John was a Calvinist at heart. He might have discarded a little of that from his intellect, but it was in his bones."[21]

I later found this out the hard way during the spring of 1988, when we were trying to counter efforts by the old guard to regain control of the party. I had become exasperated by reported defections to Hauenstein's camp, and at one planning session I suggested that we draw up a declaration of party accomplishments and ask every Central Committee and Executive Committee member to sign the statement. "That's a good idea," someone chimed in. "That way we can find out who our enemies are." Hevener voiced concern that the move was an overreaction, and he later became quiet as I hammered on the theme of "loyalty" and proceeded with plans to draw up the statement. When we adjourned, John quickly packed up his briefcase and headed for home; he did not join us for beer afterward, his normal custom.

A few days later, Mary Hevener phoned to tell me that John was upset about "this business with the statement." In John's view, it was nothing more than a loyalty oath, she warned, and it troubled him when folks started talking about loyalty. He believed that people should be free to make up their own minds and that matters of personal commitment should have no place in their decisions. I thought over what Mary had said and quickly met with Hevener to apologize. He understood the pressure Hauenstein was applying to our organization, but he stressed that we could only hurt ourselves if we concentrated on issues of loyalty. "Bill, if you expect party members to support you because of some 'loyalty principle,'" he stated, kindly but emphatically, "the party'll be no better than the one Charlie led." In the end, we scuttled idea of a signed statement.

Charlie Hauenstein never understood this side of John Hevener. Long after Charlie had lost his position, he could not accept the fact that it was John—not Mary—who had orchestrated his downfall. As late as 1989, he continued to think of John as "Mary's innocent victim," who had simply gone along with her because she "ran the house."[22] Hauenstein could not see beyond Hevener's physical infirmity, nor could he understand that with every jab and jibe at Mary, he had transformed John into an unyielding enemy.

In fact, Mary Hevener was an uncertain opponent, much less resolute than her husband. Mary Hevener hated conflict—not a helpful characteristic for a prospective politician. She considered most of the criticism directed at Hauenstein to be mean spirited and misdirected, especially comments about Charlie's massive weight, crude grammar, and fumbling public persona. She had gotten suckered into the 1982 overthrow attempt, she believed, unwisely allowing her name to be put forward as a dissident candidate for chair and thereby inhibiting her ability to work effectively within the party. Knowing the emotional and political cost, Mary wasn't sure now she wanted to be part of yet another coup attempt. Even in the face of Hauenstein's verbal assaults and personal attacks, Mary doubted the wisdom of forcibly removing him. As long as she could work on campaigns, donating time and energy to specific candidates, she could live with Charlie Hauenstein as the party chair.[23]

For John Hevener, however, the road to outright opposition began during that 1982 campaign. As a Celeste coordinator, John had sat through interminable meetings of the so-called Coordinated Campaign Committee, chaired by Hauenstein. Ordinarily, these meetings provided opportunities for local campaigns to touch base with each other, sharing plans and expertise and coordinating activities, but under Hauenstein's direction they always were laced with petty sniping at Dick Celeste and the perceived foibles of his campaign. John wrote off these sessions as inconsequential to what he was trying to do. Besides, 1982 was Celeste's year, and Charlie's grumbling could do nothing to impede the inevitable result.

After Celeste won, John poured over the Allen County results, examining the numbers precinct by precinct and comparing them to the tallies from previous gubernatorial elections. Hevener noticed that Celeste had won some precincts where a Democrat had never done well before, especially in Lima's overwhelmingly Republican Fourth Ward. These results, he figured, portended well for the Democrats, if only they could build up their strength in these Republican strongholds.

He took his findings to the postelection meeting of the Coordinated Campaign Committee, but Charlie paid no attention to them. Todd Hey had already put together a summary—or at least, he had asked "one of the girls" to compile the results precinct by precinct, as John had done. Todd's helper, however, had done a sloppy job, transposing the numbers and producing an impression exactly opposite to what Hevener was arguing. When John persisted, politely but firmly, Hauenstein waved him off with a "Whatever, John," and turned to the next item on the agenda. At that point John realized that the party's situation was hopeless. Its chairman could not listen to new viewpoints, even when they were uncontentious and presented in a conscientious and forthright manner. If the party could not correctly interpret election results and allow for adjustments in course even to reinforce success, he realized, there was no possibility the party could ever win anything locally.[24]

John Hevener's opposition to Charlie began to build over the next six months as he watched Hauenstein and his gang bully Mary, insult Governor Celeste, and demean the governor's allies within the party. The turning point came at an Executive Committee meeting at which Hauenstein went too far in attacking his opponents—both the real and the imaginary.

Executive Committee meetings under Hauenstein appeared disorganized, almost thrown together, but in reality they were carefully orchestrated, especially if Charlie had a personal agenda. On such occasions, his lieutenants would arrive early, taking seats in the back of the room. Charlie would start a harangue, complaining that the governor's tax hike was too high, that he was unwilling to help with patronage matters, or that he had a low regard for party chairmen.

When Mary Hevener would respond—predictably—to defend the governor, she would be caught in a cross fire from Hauenstein's cronies, who matched Charlie's shots with salvos of their own.[25]

At this particular meeting, not only did Charlie question Governor Celeste's competence, but he and his comrades were particularly harsh in attacking Mary when she rose to the governor's defense. Long after Mary had sat down, Hauenstein persisted in his diatribe, causing party members who witnessed his performance to wince, wondering, "What's Charlie picking on Mary for?"[26] When Hauenstein finished with Mary, he aimed his invective at other targets, laying about him a swath of insults, declaring he was not about to listen to "a bunch of school teachers and college professors." John, who had accompanied Mary to this meeting, grew livid as he listened to Charlie's verbal onslaught and left the meeting shaking with anger. "That's it!" he muttered to himself. "Charlie's out of here. We're getting rid of him."[27]

The next morning, Hevener visited the Board of Elections and requested the poll workers list, which showed the names, addresses and telephone numbers of all Democratic poll workers and Central Committee members. That very afternoon, he asked me to run for county chair. He knew it might not happen right away, but he believed it would happen. For John Hevener, there would be no turning back. He had made up his mind.[28]

Charlie Hauenstein had a reputation as an intelligent, tactically skilled politician, but he had seriously blundered in dealing with the Heveners. Had he tried harder to get along with John and Mary, had he been more accepting of their role as Celeste coordinators, he would have stayed on as party chair, and perhaps there would have been an orderly succession by Todd Hey or another associate from the UAW. The Heveners did not particularly like the informal way in which Hauenstein managed the party, nor did they like his tendency toward cronyism, but until Hauenstein began making his attacks personal, implying that their activism was not welcome, John and Mary—especially Mary— were uncertain in their resolve to challenge his leadership. But by the spring of 1983, the time had passed for reconciliation. John Hevener had become Charlie's enemy and was formulating a strategy to oust him as party chair.

· 2 ·

Power of the Chair

February 9, 1984

The UAW hall is a homely building, a rusted brick island surrounded by asphalt and American-made cars. From its arched roof, green neon radiates the letters U-A-W, shining like a beacon for southbound cars on Interstate 75, only a football toss from the front door. The main hall is a huge cavern, resembling a high school gymnasium with bleachers folded into the wall. Hanging stage-left, an eight-foot photograph of a young Hubert Humphrey beams on the workers below. But on this night, they weren't beaming back. They were frustrated and angry that I was making them stay longer than they had planned.

Throughout Ohio, presidential caucuses were meeting, choosing delegates for the May primary.[1] Charlie Hauenstein and the other party regulars were supporting the favorite-son candidacy of John Glenn; I had landed the job of managing Walter Mondale's campaign in the Fourth Congressional District, and my immediate duty was to chair the Mondale delegate caucus and preside over the selection of four delegates, two male and two female, as prescribed by rules of the Ohio Democratic Party. A week earlier it had seemed a fairly routine task. I had collected a list of nominees, Democrats who had filed affidavits declaring their allegiance to the former vice president. All I had to do was introduce the various nominees, allow them time for some brief remarks, and then the caucus would vote. Simple. And naive.

Two nights before the caucus, Mary Hevener had phoned. It was after 11 P.M., and her voice was agitated: "Did you know that Bob Gehr and other labor leaders are screening delegates and picking a 'Labor slate' for Thursday's caucus?" I did not. However, Bob Gehr, the UAW CAP Council president and my main liaison with organized labor, had told me over lunch that Mondale was labor's candidate and that the unions expected to influence the selection of delegates.[2] "We want our people elected," he had declared. He had said nothing about a labor slate. "It was simply awful," Mary continued. "Bev McCoy and I went out to the UAW hall to be interviewed. Actually, I think they were more interested in Bev than me. She made it. I didn't. Bob Gehr and Ed Finn say they're going to push through the slate regardless what anyone says."

"That can't happen," I answered. "The rules say, 'Caucus members will vote from a list of candidates.' I've planned on letting all the nominees speak and be voted on by secret ballot."

"Ed says they're going to 'force' a vote on the slate—and only the slate."

"But what about nominees who aren't part of a union? They support Mondale, right? If we vote on just the slate, they won't have a chance to be heard."

"I know, Bill. They were getting pretty nasty, though. They kept talking about 'playing hardball.' It was awful."[3]

Finn, who was the CAP council's international representative, and Gehr believed—erroneously as it turned out—that Mary and Bev would "deliver" their friends to support the labor slate, but they never clearly communicated this expectation to the two women.[4] In fact, Mary's late-night call to me produced the opposite effect.

The next morning, I phoned Chris Hagan, a Clevelander who was handling Mondale's field volunteers, and apprised him of the situation. Hagan was dismayed at labor's plan to push a preselected slate. He confirmed my understanding that anyone who wanted to become a delegate for Walter Mondale had the right to be voted on. But he also observed that if the unions mobilized their troops, I would be at their mercy. With this cryptic assurance, I pursued the matter locally, phoning Bob Gehr to inquire about "the business of a 'labor slate.'" He tersely confirmed Mary Hevener's story, emphasizing the unions' intention to elect their nominees without opposition. I objected, arguing that the caucus's rules clearly called for a secret ballot, with caucus members voting from a list of nominees, but Gehr was not impressed. "You do what you have to do, Bill, and we'll do what we have to."

Bob Gehr and the UAW had drawn the line—we and you, labor and nonlabor, good guys and bad guys. He did not ask me to "deliver" support for the unions' nominees, nor did he imply that any sort of deal had been reached with Bev McCoy about endorsing a labor slate. He apparently believed the unions could muscle their way through the caucus and that there was nothing I could do to stop them. In his estimation, I was superfluous. My job was to chair the meeting and stand back while the labor tide rolled. Gehr figured I wouldn't cross the line and that labor would elect the slate he intended.

Our conversation confirmed what I had already begun to suspect. Upon convening the caucus, I could expect a motion offering a slate of labor-endorsed delegates for Walter Mondale. This motion would be seconded, and the caucus would vote to elect the labor-endorsed delegates as a slate. No speeches. No voting on individual candidates. No secret ballot. The rules of the caucus would be sacrificed to the rules of power and expediency.

I had other ideas. On February 9 I arrived early at the UAW hall, nervously eager to get the session under way. Although it was forty-five minutes before the caucus was to start, buses and cars had already filled the parking lot. Folding chairs had been set up in the main hall, arranged in two large blocks, separated by an aisle. As I grabbed a seat in the back, Ed Finn was explaining labor's strategy to a hundred or so union activists grouped in the seats on stage-right. "We will elect the delegates as a slate," he intoned, staring me straight in the eye, glowering and placing emphasis on "will."

The activists were wearing small signs, handcrafted out of construction paper, that read, "I'm voting the labor slate." When I mounted the podium to begin preparations for the meeting, I looked up and noticed all the union members were sitting to my right, "Labor slate" signs pinned to their lapels. They were talking only to each other and casting occasional sideward glances to the opposite side of the aisle, where considerably fewer nonunion friends of Walter Mondale were sitting. Labor had mobilized the troops. By the time I called the caucus to order, word of the impending confrontation had swept the hall. The atmosphere to my right was boisterous and noisy, sunny with the confidence of certain victory, while to my left all was comparatively still, yet roiling dark with consternation and resentment.

Labor's scheme was already at work. The original list of nominees dwindled as one by one the unendorsed union candidates withdrew their names. Only the four members of the labor slate and a few nonunion candidates remained. The latter group consisted of white-collar workers, liberal Democrats who had traveled long distances, several from as far away as Mansfield, a two-hour drive from Lima. Although they did not have the votes to win, they deserved a chance to be heard. Instead, the unions intended to push them aside, intimidate them into silence, and end the caucus early. This was labor's show, in labor's house, and labor would win—so the unions believed.

I called the meeting to order and was starting to explain the rules of the caucus when Bud Hullinger, an activist with a public employees local, rose—as choreographed—to challenge me. "I move election of the following slate—Jack Obenour, Ste——" I cut him short. "That motion is out of order. The rules of the caucus provide the election will be held by secret ballot, and the delegates will be voted upon as individuals and not as a slate."

Growling surged from the right side of the hall. Several union activists raised objections. Tom Thompson, the UAW's liaison with the United Way Board, paced along the side aisle, declaring that I was out of order but stopping short of formally challenging my ruling. Steve Webb also rose to his feet, to proclaim his ringing opposition. Steve was chief negotiator for the American Federation of State County and Municipal Employees. I had met him during the 1982 Celeste campaign and had considered him genial and easygoing. Not so tonight. Huffing that my ruling was improper, he objected to my effort to force a ballot on the grounds that it would only prolong the meeting.

Although I didn't know it at the time, John and Mary Hevener, Beverly McCoy, Frank Winegardner, and few others were quietly cheering me on from their seats on the nearly vacant left side of the hall. "Get 'em, Bill. . . . Get 'em," whispered McCoy. Snarls, shouts, and insults continued from my right, but I held firm. "No! The rules provide that delegates will be elected individually. I checked with the Mondale organization this morning and was told that's what we should do. And that's what we're going to do. The motion is out of order. We're going vote by secret ballot."

More grumbling swelled as I introduced the nominees. Quiet muttering persisted as contenders delivered speeches, some carefully prepared, explaining why Walter Mondale should become the next president of the United States. After the speeches, the tellers distributed and collected ballots, and I declared a recess while the votes were tallied. The storm subsided.

As I strolled among the caucus members, a few labor activists nodded in a friendly way. Tom Thompson tried to scold me, but at least he was talking. Steve Webb, puffing on cigarette, smiled a crooked sort of smile, as if he hadn't meant to smile at all. "How you doin'?" he asked. "So we're still speaking?" I responded, smiling and sticking out my hand. "Sure. You just did what you had to do," he replied, accepting the handshake. Others were not so quick to forgive. Several turned their backs as I ambled past, and I heard one man say, loud enough for me to hear, "Who does he think he is? Some college 'perfesser' telling us what to do."

Of course, the labor slate won overwhelmingly, but selecting delegates wasn't the sole purpose of the caucus, a point I emphasized just before we adjourned. "We are the Democratic Party," I explained. "That's the *democratic* party. This caucus included people who came from Mansfield, Carey, Galion, Dola, and Bucyrus, and they wanted to be heard. It was only democratic that we give them that chance." Applause rose from both sides of the hall, more in response to the impending adjournment than to the content of my remarks. Not everybody was happy. A number of Mary's and John's pals groused about the way the unions had tried to railroad the nomination process. One of them, Phil Kahal, was so "ticked off" that he muttered to Frank Winegardner on their way out the door, "If the unions can win elections by themselves, more power to them." Others were so angry that later they deserted Mondale altogether and jumped to Gary Hart. "Labor lost a lot of good will that night," Mary later reflected.[5]

There was not much joy in the union camp either. As Mary Hevener was leaving the UAW hall, Ed Finn approached her and observed acidly, "I can't understand how [McCoy] got so many more votes than the others."[6] Finn felt he had been double-crossed. In his view, Bev and Mary had not provided support for the labor slate gambit; instead, they had used union votes to get Bev elected without delivering any white-collar votes for the rest of labor's candidates.

Actually there was nothing conspiratorial about the outcome. McCoy's total reflected the combination of Mondale supporters from Lima who did not vote for anyone else on the labor slate and the votes supplied by the unions. In fact, this result was a predictable consequence of the process Ed Finn and Bob Gehr had fostered. They had had the votes to win without "playing hardball." But they did anyway, and in doing so they offended potential supporters of Walter Mondale, folks who were their natural allies. Furthermore, Finn and Gehr were publicly embarrassed, done in by a college-educated, novice politician who had stood up to labor on its own turf. They seethed as they watched our smirking faces and joyous handshakes, our exultation at having denied labor a complete victory.[7] Their anger would linger for years.

But for the time being, I took pleasure in accepting congratulations from the Heveners, Beverly McCoy, and Janet Quinn, among others. Quinn had strong labor ties, having been secretary for Local 106 at the old Clark Equipment Plant. "You showed 'em," she remarked, smiling. "You looked 'em right in the eye and told 'em, 'Go to Hell.'"

"Yeah, I know," I replied. The moment was sinking in. "But they could have challenged my ruling. They had the votes. Why didn't they?"

"You were the chair," she said. "They respect the power of the chair."

Mondale would lose the Ohio primary, and he would get creamed in the Fourth Congressional District, which would send but one Mondale delegate—Bev McCoy—to the national convention. Still, that presidential primary whetted my appetite for political struggle. In late May, state senator Steve Maurer asked me to coordinate his reelection bid in the Allen County portion of his district. I accepted immediately.

A Vietnam veteran, Maurer carried the square-jawed, broad-shouldered look of the Bavarian farmers who had settled Shelby County, his home place in the southern end of the Twelfth District, which he represented. He spoke German fluently and often peppered Deutsche sayings into his speeches, and his older constituents, who had learned the language on their grandparents' laps, nodded approvingly. But Steve Maurer was a doomed candidate. He had barely won office in 1980, squeaking by the incumbent Dick Ditto with only seventy-eight votes to spare. More critically, he had "walked the plank" for Governor Celeste in 1983 by voting for the governor's so-called 90 percent tax increase; Maurer's vote for that tax hike would become the central issue in his reelection bid.[8] His opponent was the Allen County commissioner, Bob Cupp, a rising star in the local Republican Party. Cupp would spend the campaign pounding Maurer on taxes.

But in the summer of 1984, I wasn't thinking about Maurer's difficulties. As the senator's local manager, I was appointed to the party's Executive Committee, where I had the opportunity to witness the organization's troubles firsthand. I quickly allowed myself to become an object of suspicion of the party chair—Charlie Hauenstein.

When Charlie had recruited that year's local candidates, he had promised them monetary support, yet as summer turned into fall no one had received a single dime from the party. Hauenstein stonewalled the candidates' repeated requests for financial help, claiming that he wasn't sure how much money the treasury held.

In fact, he probably didn't know; the accounting was so Byzantine that no one knew the party's financial condition. Hauenstein appointed a committee to audit the books, but the committee could not do its work; according to one member, "The books were a mess." The monthly statements that the treasurer, Vern Eley, gave the Executive Committee were of little value. He would read his "report" from the party's checkbook, scratching his head and muttering, "Well, Charlie, . . . we paid some bills and now have about . . . oh, I'd say about a hundred fifty dollars and some-odd cents." The treasury always showed a low balance, despite the contributions coming in from the county's three deputy registrars.

Of all the local candidates, John Coplen was perhaps the most upset about the lack of financial support. Coplen was trying to retake the commission seat he had lost in 1980 and desperately needed a cash infusion to pay for television advertising. Steve Webb, who had confronted me the night of the Mondale caucus, was now Coplen's campaign manager. A fierce Coplen loyalist, Webb genuinely believed that a Coplen victory was possible, and he resented Hauenstein's insinuations that the party's treasury was low. The party had to have more money, Webb reasoned, and with my help, he hatched a scheme to wrestle some of it away.

On September 5, 1984, the Executive and Central Committees held a combined meeting at the UAW hall with the Ohio attorney general, Anthony Celebreeze, as the guest speaker. Beforehand, Webb circulated among the candidates and their coordinators, grumbling about Hauenstein's unwillingness to release party money to the candidates.[9] He grabbed a seat across from me, lit a cigarette and muttered about the weak financial status of the local campaigns. Finally, he poked out his cigarette and, looking directly at me, suggested a plan to get Charlie to take action: "Someone needs to ask Charlie when he's going to get off his butt and give the candidates some money. Make a motion—I can't—I'm not a member of the Executive Committee. Move that the party donate say . . . $2,500 to each of the candidates. That'd be . . . oh . . . $15,000 all together for John and the other candidates."

"But Charlie'll just say, 'We don't have the money,'" I responded.

"So what? You get the motion out there, and the party has to vote on it. We'd look pretty stupid turning down a motion with Tony Celebreeze sitting up there. And if Charlie says we don't have the money. . . . Well, we can borrow it. We got all those contributions coming in from the license bureaus. Just borrow the money against future revenues. Just like buyin' a car." It was clear to me that Webb was asking me, the new kid, to make the motion. "Fine," I said, "I'll do it."

"Pickle" Felter, who was listening nearby, agreed to supply a second. Pickle was a child of the sixties, an ornery Kent State grad who was always up for a bit of mischief. This wouldn't be like occupying the ROTC building, but it was close enough.

The attorney general gave his speech, a "September homily" about the need for hard work, unity, and self-sacrifice in a crucial election year. Hauenstein followed with some procedural matters. He ended by asking, "Is there any more business for the Executive Committee?"

I stood up and, with the attorney general of the state of Ohio looking on, I declared, "Mr. Chairman, in view of what Mr. Celebreeze just said about the need for energy and sacrifice, I move that the Allen County Democratic Party donate $15,000 to our local candidates, including Steve Maurer, the money to be divided equally among them." Dead silence. The color drained from Hauenstein's face as he gripped the podium and asked, "Is there a second to motion?" He was hoping against hope there would be none. Sitting at the back of the hall, Pickle grinned wide and waved his hand. The proposal was on the floor.

Vern Eley leaped to Hauenstein's defense. "Charlie, we don't have the money for this. If Bill Angel has some bright ideas about how we can raise some money, maybe he can tell us." I borrowed Webb's slant: "Look, we don't need the money in November; we need it now. Why can't we just borrow the money and pay it back with future revenues?" Citing the "Blood, Sweat, and Tears" story, Hauenstein responded, "We tried that once. The party got deep into debt and took a long time to get out." Bill Johns, Todd Hey, and Paul Prater added their support for Hauenstein's misgivings, and Vern Eley moved to table the motion, referring it to the party's finance committee.

I asked, "Will you have a report at our next meeting?"

"Yes," Hauenstein said, replying through his teeth.

My behavior that night was both impudent and imprudent. I had blindsided Hauenstein, acting only on Steve Webb's appraisal of the matter, and I had embarrassed our chairman and the party in front of a state official. Furthermore, I had not lined up the votes need to pass the motion. Finally, the motion didn't ultimately produce the money, not as much as the campaigns needed. When the recommendation finally came from the finance committee, it was for considerably less than what I had called for: The party would borrow five thousand dollars—not fifteen thousand—and divide it equally among the Allen County candidates only. Maurer was left with no contribution, a payback for my impertinence.[10]

Yet it was right for me to issue my audacious proposal. The candidates wanted money from the party, but no one wanted to challenge Charlie. So I stepped up. And suffered the consequences. Hauenstein's attitude toward me hardened, and he took it out on Steve Maurer. The snub of not giving a contribution to Maurer's campaign was followed by actions toward me that bordered on hostility. I asked for a list of party volunteers and never received it. I requested the name of someone to help coordinate Maurer's appearances in Allen County, but Hauenstein couldn't "think of anybody." This attitude extended to Todd Hey. When I invited Hey to sell tickets for a Maurer fundraiser at which Governor Celeste was to be the featured speaker, he never tried—although he did buy ten himself, a hundred dollars' worth.

I also came under vocal criticism from Hauenstein and his cronies. I received the "Mary Hevener treatment" in Executive Committee meetings, becoming a target whenever I raised my voice. In the September committee meeting I asked Hauenstein why Maurer had been left out of the party's disbursement to candidates; he sneered that Maurer didn't need any money from the Allen County Democratic Party, not with all money he was receiving from political action committees. I also caught verbal barbs for not promptly erecting the red-and-white "Reelect Steve Maurer" yard signs that my volunteers and I had assembled and stored at party headquarters. We eventually posted the signs, but not without enduring sniping for being slow about it. When I sent Maurer volunteers into Bluffton to do some door-to-door canvassing in Charlie's hometown, Hauenstein blew a gasket, complaining that I had violated protocol by not inviting him to orchestrate the effort.[11]

In late October, Bob Johnson—the Heveners' contact in the governor's office—arrived to ease the tension that had developed between me and Hauenstein. In 1982, Johnson had been Celeste's coordinator in Franklin County (Columbus), securing a surprising victory for the governor there. Now, he was troubleshooting in Allen County, where the party's lethargic approach to the campaign was causing alarm among officials in the Celeste administration. Celeste felt a particular obligation to Maurer because of the vote he had cast in favor of the 1983 tax bill. Johnson knew that Maurer's chances hinged upon a high turnout; his assignment was to prod Hauenstein and Hey into action, assess the party infighting, and motivate the factions to work with each other.

Charlie Hauenstein was immediately suspicious of Johnson's mission. He didn't like interlopers arriving uninvited to tell him what he should do, and he was particularly mistrustful of Johnson, an emissary from "Camp Celeste." He gave Johnson little help, let him find his own place to stay (with the Heveners), and provided him no work space in party headquarters.

As for problems with the Maurer campaign, they were my fault, Hauenstein explained; I was not "a team player" and had "no sense of protocol." Johnson inquired when the party was going to install phone banks. "Ask Bill Angel about that," Charlie snorted; he went on to declare that the treasury could not afford a phone campaign, because I had pressured the Executive Committee into making contributions directly to the candidates, thus leaving the party short of money.[12]

Johnson moved immediately, using his contacts with the "Governor's Committee," the fund-raising arm of the Celeste campaign, to secure telephones and to infuse the party with cash to help with other "get out the vote" (GOTV) activities. Even so, the party was unprepared for election day. On Tuesday, October 30, Hauenstein called a special meeting of the Executive Committee to arrange the final push.[13] We had assembled in the headquarters, a dingy, uncomfortable storefront on Spring Street, not far from Lima's downtown. Todd Hey distributed stacks of precinct lists, each with voters' names and addresses. Hauenstein was barking out instructions, commanding us to take one or two of these lists, fill in the phone numbers beside the names, and return the lists to headquarters no later than the day before the election.

As far as any of us could tell, the distribution of the lists was random; Hauenstein had not prioritized the precincts in any order of importance. Additionally, the timing for this project was bad. It was a week before election day, and the candidates needed our help to put up yard signs and canvass targeted precincts. Here we were, being ordered to do clerical work that should have been completed weeks before. When several of us objected to this eleventh-hour assignment, Hauenstein blustered, "That's the way it always is! We ask Executive Committee members to do something, and all we get are excuses." He then brusquely ordered us to get to work filling out the lists.

The diatribe silenced Charlie's critics, and as the grumbling subsided, Otha Harris took the floor. Harris was president of Lima's chapter of the National Association for the Advancement of Colored People and Hauenstein's broker in the black community. He was a burly man whose eyes held an expression that was at once imploring and calculating. When he moved to speak that evening, we all knew what he wanted—"street money." We had heard this pitch before, and it went something like this: "I got deep pockets, but tonight my pockets are empty. Now y'all expect people to vote, but some folk don't have enough money to get to the polls. Why, I know men who can't even take off work to vote. You want helpers? Well, helpers need money . . . for gasoline, maybe a sandwich and a Pepsi. I need to know if my pockets are going to stay empty, or is somebody gonna fill 'em?"

Hauenstein responded that the party could not help, because its treasury was dry. Staring toward Bob Johnson, who was standing near the doorway, he suggested that perhaps "our man from Columbus" could come up with some assistance. Johnson said he'd do what he could, but he was furious that Hauenstein had put him on the spot.

Afterward I met him at the law office of our candidate for state representative, Tim Hamman, where he had set up a desk during his stay in the county.[14] He was drinking a beer and venting his rage long-distance to Kathy Tefft-Keller, of the Governor's Committee. Bob's end of the conversation went something like this: "Do you know what Hauenstein did tonight, TK? He handed out precinct lists and wanted people to fill in the phone numbers. Can you imagine? This should have been done in September. . . . And there's nothing going on in the black community. Otha Harris wants street money, and we need to get him some. What? . . . Yeah, Charlie insists we work through Otha and nobody else. I'm not sure we have any choice, but I'll meet with some ministers and others black leaders and see what I can do. *Man*, things are really a mess up here."

Finishing his call, Johnson offered me a beer. He was still fuming at the way Hauenstein and Harris had set him up. Before turning to the issue of street money he asked, "When are you guys going to do something about Charlie Hauenstein?" Bob's attitude toward street money was pragmatic, an attitude he shared with many white politicians in the Democratic Party, who perceived street money as an efficient mechanism to turn out the black vote, particularly in counties where the black population was highly concentrated. Allen County was one of these: 11 percent of the population was African American, much of it (89 percent, to be exact) in the city of Lima.[15] Party officials would throw cash into the pockets of a minority politician like Otha Harris, hoping that it would be spent effectively enough to make the vote in black precincts higher than it might be otherwise. The money was supposed to go to workers who canvassed precincts, worked phone banks, or distributed sample ballots in front of polling places, or to subsidize expenses for food or gasoline; allegations always surfaced, however, that it sometimes crossed the palms of voters themselves. No one knew for certain. A figure would show up on the campaign finance report showing a disbursement for "GOTV expenses," but nothing else. No one knew exactly how the funds were spent. No questions were asked. The money would be delivered shortly before election day, and the votes would follow. At least, that was the idea.

If street money came into Allen County, it didn't do much good.[16] By mid-afternoon on election day, turnout in the minority precincts was only 25 percent, and Bob Johnson was seething. Maurer would be dead, he warned, unless southside voters started producing. At four o'clock, he dispatched me to verify turnout in Lima's Fifth and Sixth Wards, which included the county's most crucial minority precincts. After doing that, I was to find Otha Harris and instruct him to get his volunteers out on the street and send the folks who hadn't voted to the polls—"We paid for 'em," I recall Johnson saying.

By late afternoon, turnout in the city's south side was barely approaching 40 percent. After checking the polling places, I headed for the Eleventh Street Missionary Baptist Church, where Otha Harris was a member; it was serving as his GOTV headquarters. I entered the recreation hall in the basement and found Reverend J. D. White, the pastor; Sixth Ward councilman Henry Horne; Ted Davis, Harris's sidekick; and a couple of other, older black men. They were sitting around a table, drinking coffee and talking high school football.

"How's it goin'?" I asked, sizing up the situation and figuring what to do next. "Oh, fine, fine, fine," one of the men replied. "People are votin', and things are runnin' good." The others nodded their "amens" to this assessment. "You think so? I'm not so sure. Turnout is really down in the precincts around here." They all disputed my appraisal, but I interrupted. "Look at these precinct lists— 6A, 6B, 6C, 6D, and these in the Fifth Ward. We have 35 to 38 percent turnout in most of these. None is above 40 points."

"Let me look at those," said Henry Horne. He scanned the lists and turned to the others, still seated around the table: "Well, I see what Bill means," he observed, pointing out the names that I hadn't crossed off. "These are the ones who haven't voted, and yeah, there are a lot of 'em left."

I pushed on. "Does anyone know where Otha is?" No one did. "You may find him up on Fourth Street," Horne suggested, before volunteering, "If it's all right with you, Bill, I'll keep these lists and work on 'em." I thanked him and went looking for Harris. I never did find him, not that it would have done any good. I couldn't do much, and neither could Otha Harris or Henry Horne; the party had no plan for "a body pull"—a door-to-door blitz cajoling nonvoters into action.

While I was on my foray into the Sixth Ward, Beverly McCoy and Steve Webb were riding around Lima's south side in a sound truck, Webb at the wheel and McCoy announcing the party message: "Today's election day. Mondale needs you. So do all the Democrats. Vote! Please Vote!" The streets were deserted, however, and Webb grew more and more disgusted as the afternoon went on. "This is so stupid," he declared. "No one's out, and no one here is going to vote. What a damn waste of time!"[17]

Back at headquarters, GOTV was staggering to a close. Volunteers had spent the afternoon calling voters whose names appeared on the precinct lists that had been turned in. But no one had targeted precincts for priority calling, and the most crucial lists, those containing a sizeable number of Democratic households, did not exist. Runners were available to verify turnout in important precincts, but there was no plan for canvassing neighborhoods where turnout was low and pulling nonvoters to the polls. Furthermore, volunteers had gone home, leaving no one to drive voters to the polls, and as I had already discovered, coordination between the party's operation and that of Otha Harris was practically nonexistent.

The results were predictable. Maurer lost, gaining only 37 percent in Allen County and barely 40 percent districtwide. Mondale, who had only 27 percent support himself, dragged the ticket down; all the local candidates lost. Among the latter group, John Coplen did the best, gathering 46 percent of the votes in his race; he might have won, had Democratic turnout been higher.[18]

Late on election night I arrived at Maurer's "victory party"—more of a wake, actually—to pay my respects to the candidate and to commiserate with friends I'd met that fall. Maurer greeted me warmly and handed me a beer. He understood the difficulties I'd encountered working with Charlie Hauenstein, and he was equally aware of the lackadaisical effort the party in Allen County had shown his campaign. "*Vielen dank.* Thanks for the help, Mr. Chairman," Maurer said, a wry smile sliding across his face. "Now, when are you going to do something about that party of yours?"

· 3 ·

Democrats for an Effective Party

February 1986

Rochelle Twining was floored the moment she arrived at her first meeting with Democrats for an Effective Party (DEP). She found bedlam—a gaggle of us "DEP-ers" pinwheeling in conversation and poring over voter lists.

"Who's this Willie Mae Thornton?"

"The blues singer? She's dead."

"Be serious. The one in Perry North. Anybody know her?"

"Yeah. Her husband owns that hog farm out on Bowman Road."

"Naw, she works at Ford . . . a friend of Todd's."

"Uh uh, it's her brother that works at Ford. Her husband owns the hog farm."

"Think she'll go with us?"

"Not if she works at Ford."

"What about her brother?"

"Ah, I know her from South High. . . . Want me t' feel her up?"

"Feel her out."

"Right."

On it went. We were looking for Central Committee candidates and happened to be riveted on the Perry North precinct before moving on to a different one. "Man, I thought you guys were crazy," Twining later reflected. "You weren't going precinct by precinct. You were going voter by voter, and you had been meeting like that for months. I thought, 'This is insanity. I want out.' But I also saw how committed you guys were and knew I wanted to be part of it. So, I stayed."[1]

Twining was right. We were insane—and we were focused on taking over the Allen County Democratic Party. She had walked into the core element in our strategy—finding Central Committee candidates who would support a change in leadership. With the filing deadline less than two weeks away, we had ninety-five recruits committed to our cause but needed at least forty more. We had a right to be crazy.

David Berger didn't attend many gatherings in which we formulated strategy to take over the party. In fact, Berger wasn't terribly inspired by partisan politics. As director of the Rehab Project, a nonprofit organization that rebuilt residential housing in Lima's south end, he had developed skill as a negotiator who could encourage neighborhood residents to work together. Because he needed grants and funding from government at all levels, Berger was cautious not to wear his partisan sympathies too openly. But he was still a Democrat, and he found himself at one of our meetings, sometime in March 1985, dragged there by his friend and deputy Howard Elstro.

Berger listened for a spell as we compared several tactical schemes, and when he finally spoke, his eyebrows arched with polite disdain. "There has to be more to this effort than simply 'getting rid of Charlie Hauenstein,'" he declared. He warned that unless we could articulate a vision of what we wanted to accomplish, we would produce a party not much different than the one led by Charlie and his pals.[2]

In fact, all of us there agreed that Hauenstein needed to be replaced, but none of us had spelled out why we wanted to undertake this extraordinary action. We immediately set to work defining our movement, choosing the name "Democrats for an Effective Party," or DEP—for symbolic effect—and settling on a statement that delineated our goals. Simply put, we declared that a change in leadership was needed to accomplish three important objectives: elect Democrats to countywide offices, supply a vocal and visible opposition to local Republicans, and strengthen the party's grassroots base.

The first objective—electing candidates—had obvious appeal. The 1984 campaign had been an especially humiliating experience. Despite all the energy we had expended trying to help our candidates, we felt pulled down by the negativism in the party apparatus. Particularly dispiriting was the way the party had run away from Walter Mondale. It had minimized his significance as the Democrats' presidential candidate to the point that he did not exist—no Mondale yard signs, no literature drops for Mondale, no public events touting his candidacy. Mondale had limited appeal in Allen County, but we still believed he represented the primary way to stimulate Democratic turnout—he headed our ticket, after all.

Equally troubling was the party's passive response to President Ronald Reagan's whistle stop in Lima. Reagan had arrived in the same Pullman car that Harry Truman had used when he campaigned here in 1948, a symbolic swipe at all Democrats, but Hauenstein had said nothing. At the very least, he could have protested the use of county workers—and taxpayer money—to fix the railroad station and to improve the roadbed just in time to be used by Reagan's train. He also could have criticized the school superintendents in the county who had sent their marching bands to participate in a partisan political event. But Hauenstein had kept his mouth shut, and the visit had gone unchallenged.

Of course, this explains our second objective—to provide an oppositional voice to the Republicans. Charlie Hauenstein never trusted or liked the media; he shunned any kind of public exposure for himself. But he never allowed anybody else to speak on matters that were important to the Democratic Party, either. Once Pickle Felter suggested that the party hold monthly press conferences to tout the Democratic message. Hauenstein derided the proposal: "We already tried that. It didn't work. We'd call a press conference. The news media would say they'd be there, and then no one would come."

However, I had started to curry a relationship with the media. Because I was a political scientist, television and radio reporters would call on me, asking for analysis of some political development or other. For instance, I had attended the Reagan whistle-stop rally as a political analyst for WCIT radio, and on election night I had shared my insights with John Garlock, the news anchor for WLIO TV. Also, I was developing the ability to speak in sound bites, giving quick and cogent assessments of news stories. None of this went down well with Charlie Hauenstein, but I figured that as long as I wasn't presenting myself as a spokesperson for the party, it wouldn't matter. Still, the fact remained that because of Hauenstein's chilly relationship with media, the Democratic Party was invisible in newsprint and inaudible in the airwaves unless outside officials, such as state treasurer Mary Ellen Withrow or auditor Thomas Ferguson, came to town and engaged in public relations on their own.

The third objective—building a stronger grassroots organization—underlined a conspicuous need. Those of us who had managed campaigns had done so with little or no help from the county Central Committee. Most of the incumbent members were "encumbrances," to borrow a malaprop suggested by a DEP activist. Few would work their precincts for candidates or carry out such essential tasks as finding yard-sign locations, helping with voter registration, and distributing candidate literature door to door. This objective, therefore, had a twofold purpose: to create a Central Committee that would both elect new leadership and energize the party's grassroots base.

Beneath these objectives was a subtext, however, a message that all of us understood but didn't express outside our meetings: The party was a joke, an embarrassment. Our party chairman was so fat he couldn't sit in a folding chair without spreading his legs wide and placing his palms over his knees, his elbows swinging outward, for balance. Hauenstein's obesity should have generated sympathy, but most of us—stung by his insults and his barely concealed contempt—were beyond feeling sorry for him. His chief lieutenant, Todd Hey, was friendly enough but in a seedy sort of way. He'd toss money to candidates, pulling out bills or writing checks on-the-spot, then smile through crooked, tobacco-stained teeth and say something like, "This is the way the game is played." Otha Harris—the party's only link with black neighborhoods—ran the local NAACP out of the back seat of his beat-up, pea-green Cadillac and gave little thought to the social mission of that organization. His demands for street money only affirmed racial stereotypes in a community riven by animosity toward African Americans. Then there were the party meetings; they smelled of ripe onions and stale beer, and they reeked with defeatism and complaints: "If Celeste won't help us—then goddammit, git rid of the sonuvabitch," Paul Prater once proclaimed. Finally, none of us knew how much money the treasury held, and so we all suspected that Charlie and his gang were helping themselves. Charges of corruption were rampant. But we didn't say these things publicly, only among ourselves, convincing each other that we were doing the right thing—that the only way to save our party was to split it.

Of course, Charlie Hauenstein and the old guard had the same low regard for us. We were "Yuppie scum," "Celestials," McGovernites, liberals who were trying to tear down the party and slight its accomplishments. Furthermore, we were trying to do something Charlie had vowed would never happen—take the party from labor. In 1970 Hauenstein and Bob Gehr had orchestrated an overthrow of their own, seizing the party from a group of lawyers headed by Bob Kuhn, Harry Meredith, and Willis Siferd. The party had been in labor's hands ever since. Now, Charlie Hauenstein, Todd Hey, Paul Prater, Bill Johns, Vern Eley, and others in their circle were not about to let the party fall to schoolteachers, lawyers, pseudo-intellectuals, or anyone who didn't earn a living in a factory.

A political campaign commonly produces a "ripple effect." That is, organizers begin by recruiting a "cadre," a group committed to the campaign's cause. These "true believers," in turn, ask others to join. As the process continues, the campaign's circle grows, much like the ripple produced by a pebble tossed into a calm lake.

On that April afternoon in 1983, John Hevener had heaved a boulder when he asked me to run for party chair. Following the 1984 election, the circle grew as Pickle Felter, John Coplen, Steve Webb, Janet Quinn, Beverly McCoy, Howard

34 · *The Real World*

Elstro, and others joined us to begin laying the strategy for a "takeover." Essentially, we had to convert the Central Committee—that is, bring it around to accepting new leadership. But most of the incumbent Central Committee members were in the Hauenstein camp, firmly committed to the old regime. The only way to produce a change in leadership was to find new committeemen and committeewomen, to replace the old guard with a new set of activists.

It was a convoluted process, one that we barely understood ourselves. Allen County had 169 precincts, and we reckoned we could count on no more than fifteen incumbent committee members to support our cause. Another twenty or so were so entrenched in their neighborhoods that it would have been foolish to try removing them. That left 134 precincts, and there we would have to recruit candidates to try to unseat Central Committee members. Once the recruiting phase was done, our candidates would have to wage a voter-to-voter campaign during the primary; after the primary, we—the cadre who had started this effort—would have to lobby victorious Central Committee candidates to vote for a new Central Committee chair.

We set out to win a minimum of eighty-five votes. The most essential step was to recruit candidates to run in as many precincts as possible, but a related issue seized our attention straightaway. Once our candidates won their respective races, they would have to vote for a Central Committee chair, and that vote would be the culmination of our effort, signifying victory or defeat. The first order of business would be to topple Todd Hey. I would never become chair of the Executive Committee, and hence, party chairman, unless the Central Committee first chose a DEP supporter to replace Todd. Once DEP commanded a majority of the Central Committee, it would form an Executive Committee of DEP loyalists, folks who would be expected to vote for me. Choosing a candidate for Central Committee chair, therefore, would be the most important decision DEP would make. We required someone who could work with me, but we also needed a candidate who could appeal to groups that I could not win over on my own.

This meant our candidate had to come from organized labor. The Democratic Party's base in Allen County lay in blue-collar households: Most of the party's voters worked in the factories or were members of union families. Also, a candidate from labor's ranks would disarm an important argument that Hauenstein/Hey would level against us—that we were stealing the party from labor.

We settled on Steve Webb. Webb was the regional representative for the American Federation of State County and Municipal Employees (AFSCME), a member of the executive board of the Allen County AFL-CIO, and a member of the Allied Labor Council. He was a shrewd and tireless negotiator, loved to talk, and he especially liked casual meetings—at lunch counters or in peoples' offices—particularly if a bit of conspiracy was involved.

During one September morning in 1984, he and I sat in the office of Allen County auditor Dean French, a Republican, asking French about the county's financial condition. Both of us were hoping to turn up some incriminating data that might help the candidacies of John Coplen and Steve Maurer. I was struck by Webb's boldness, walking into French's office with me in tow and asking "if the county was goin' broke." His conversational tone was that of someone who was at once a country bumpkin "just wonderin' about somethin'" and the city wiseacre, "lookin' for dirt."

Webb talked and talked to French that morning—three hours altogether—joking with him one moment and challenging him the next; the men exchanged stories and borrowed cigarettes from each other. Eventually, Webb got French to admit that the county was indeed in financial trouble; in fact, it would have to delay December's payroll and other bills until January, when a new fiscal year began. It was quite an admission but one that didn't stick. We had no figures, other than the ones French had kindly given us, and accountants from the state auditor's office found those inconclusive at best. Still, Webb displayed guts that morning, walking brazenly onto Republican turf and with unabashed charm standing up to a county official.

We would present ourselves as a team, "Angel for Party Chair and Webb for Central Committee Chair." He and I were both in our late thirties, and we shared a disdain for Charlie Hauenstein. I would speak for the movement, articulate our message, supply direction and vision. Webb would be the smooth-talking street fighter who would charm people into running for Central Committee or into voting for him as Central Committee chairman. Webb and I together fashioned a coalition that combined the "Celestial" wing of the party, with its working-class base. Our movement was an alliance between liberal, white-collar professionals and labor Democrats who deeply resented the fact that the party's direction came from a small faction within the UAW.

The goal that united this coalition was a desire to "get rid of Charlie Hauenstein," and we papered over the philosophical differences that separated us. One of the most significant tensions was class based. A number of us—white-collar types like me, the Heveners, Beverly McCoy, and Howard Elstro—viewed politics as an activity in which citizens participated selflessly to promote the public good. An elitist, somewhat aristocratic tone permeated this philosophy, and that tone sometimes strained relations with the blue-collar members of our movement, who talked very much like Charlie Hauenstein's followers. Although blue-collar activists like Steve Webb and John Coplen accepted the critique of the party as outlined in our list of objectives, they were absorbed with issues of patronage, much more than was DEP's white-collar element.

Specifically, they resented Hauenstein and his associates for selfishly using control over the patronage to benefit themselves, their families, and their most loyal supporters, while closing out others. Our movement's labor side wanted a piece of the action, too. Steve Webb and John Coplen, who represented this wing, expressed their concerns at various phases in the process but most clearly during the spring of 1986. They began staking out patronage turf, and in a way that raised ethical concerns. Webb made it clear that he was looking to take over Hey's license bureau, and there was talk of "cleaning house" in the Ohio Department of Transportation's district offices once Hauenstein was gone.

These tensions became especially apparent when we began to solicit financial donations. John Coplen, who enjoyed numerous connections with the local business community, spearheaded DEP's fund-raising campaign. When he reported the results of his efforts to a DEP meeting in late February 1986, he issued the rather daunting observation that when his contacts donated money, they expected "something in return." When pressed as to what this "something" meant, Coplen replied, "You know, things like license bureaus, lotto machines, state leases, that kind of stuff."[3]

Afterward, Howard Elstro and Stan Carder pulled me aside. They had been assigned to work on DEP's finance committee along with Coplen and Bob White, a Westinghouse employee and a labor representative with the electrical workers' union. Clearly troubled by Coplen's style, Elstro bought me a beer and said, in his deliberate, grainy voice, "You know, if we win this thing, we're going to have trouble keeping you honest." He expressed his exasperation at dealing with Coplen, who, in Howard's eyes, was making deals that would mire me in quid-pro-quo sleaze.

Carder nudged him and said, "Tell him about Bob White." Elstro took a swig of his beer and told me about a side meeting he and Carder had had with Coplen and White earlier that evening. Starting off as an update on Coplen's fund-raising forays, the session had degenerated into a confrontation when White proclaimed in a display of bravado, "Now, you boys just leave the fund raisin' up to John and me. If certain people found out how we collected this money, you could find us face up in some pond, and it wouldn't be our peckers stickin' up."

"Jesus Christ," I muttered, "What the hell does that mean? We're only trying to raise about two thousand dollars. Shit, we could raise two thousand dollars among ourselves! No need for deals. What kind of game are White and Coplen playing anyway?"

"I don't know. Just watch 'em," Elstro emphasized, and Carder nodded in agreement.[4]

At the next DEP meeting I acknowledged Coplen's effort but also stated rather strongly that no political commitment was attached to any financial donation. Coplen listened politely to my statement, then smiled wryly and shrugged his shoulders as if to say, "Okay, if that's the way you want it." We left the matter there.

But money kept coming in. Coplen and his committee raised $2,691—over one-third of it as cash contributions, in twenty-five, fifty, and hundred-dollar amounts.[5] I didn't question this procedure. None of us did. We were grateful for the money and for John Coplen, who brought it to us. The object was to win.

You'll find The Alpine Village Restaurant tucked into Lima's western edge, kitty-corner from the Catholic cemetery. It's a Democratic watering hole, host to fund-raisers, election-night parties, and conspiratorial intrigue. You enter through the lounge, where a few regulars are gathered around the bar, watching CNN. "Little Joe" Guagenti, who owns the place, turns from his coffee cup and asks, "How's it goin'?"

Before you can reply, he's on his feet, shakes your hand, and begins escorting you around the corner of the bar. "Man, business is slow tonight. . . . The others are in the back. Say, you need anything?"

Little Joe guides you through the restaurant's dining area, a long, dark, leathery room freshened by the fragrance of marinara sauce and warm Italian bread. Then, pointing toward a door near the main entrance, he says, "They're in there. Go on in and I'll send one of the girls back for your order."

You enter a conference room. No smells of marinara sauce here, just cigarette smoke, spilt beer, and very old coffee. It's a well lit, austere space. Sketches of the White House and the U.S. Capitol line the walls.

John Hevener presides. He's reading down a computerized list, which he appears to have committed to memory. In his coarse Appalachian voice he declares, "Now, Delphos is still a problem. Can't find anyone to run there. Maybe the incumbents will be okay. They could vote for us, I guess. Ah, we'll have to work on that. Now, Lima, precinct 1A. Rose Rita Gorman's the incumbent. Says she'll go with us. 1B . . . Carolyn Baily. She's one of Charlie's people. No way she'll vote for Steve. Looks like we have three names, though. Anybody contact these?"

Hevener continues down the list, collecting feedback as he goes. Others in the room fill him in on potential recruits and news of neighborhood politics. At this point you're stunned by the detail these people are bringing to the job, yet they are enjoying each other immensely. As you look at your watch, you realize the meeting still has a long way to go.

You've walked into a meeting of the "DEP Recruitment Task Force, John Hevener, Chairman." Hevener concludes the roll call of the precincts and begins passing out voter lists—the names, addresses, and partisan affiliations of every registered voter in particular precincts. He looks at you, smiles a crinkly half-smile, and says, "Tonight we'll do Bath and Perry Townships. Just grab a list and holler if you know anybody on it."

"How'd you get these lists without Charlie finding out?" you ask.

"Well, that was a problem. None of us could've waltzed into the Board of Elections and ask for 'em. That's for sure. Charlie would have found out before we'd even left the place. So, we asked Phil Kahal. You know him? Teaches at Ohio Northern. Well, Phil went in and got 'em for us. Said he was doin' a public opinion survey."

"What do you do with these names you come up with?"

"Well, they're prospects. One of us talks to 'em, sizes 'em up, and asks if they'd like to join us, to run in their precinct. If they say 'Yes,' then we have to get 'em on the ballot."

"How?"

"Well, Pickle's in charge of that end of the operation, aren't ya', Pickle?"

"What? Oh, yeah." A boyish-looking man with long hair and wire-rimmed glasses looks up, his round face reminding you of John Denver. "Pickle runs a blacktop-sealing business," Hevener explains. "Has a lot of downtime during the winter. So we put him in charge of the petitions."

"Yeah, man, I'm the petition man," Pickle says proudly. "First thing I had to do was get petitions for us to use. Couldn't just walk into the Board of Elections and say, 'Gimme a hunnert 'n fifty of them suckers.' So, I got one for myself, and we've been squeezing 'em out on Steve Webb's copier.

"We have what we call a hens-and-chicks strategy," Pickle continues. "When one of us recruits a candidate, that person becomes sort of a 'mother hen' to that candidate. You see? Each one of us makes sure our recruits—our 'chicks'— get their petitions, fills 'em out correctly, circulates 'em, and gives 'em back by February 19. That's the day before we have to file. Man! I can't wait to see Charlie's face when we show up with all them petitions."

Pickle looks up. The waitress arrives with a tray full of beers, passes them out, then turns to you, the newcomer: "What'll you have?" You place your order, feel immediately at ease, and begin going down the names on the list Hevener has handed you.

"Who's this Willie Mae Thornton?" someone shouts.

It went like that—weekly sessions mostly—throughout the fall of 1985 and early winter of 1986. By early February, though, our effort was running out of steam. Although we had received firm commitments for candidates in fifty-three precincts, that seemed to be our limit; we were reeling in few additional recruits.

The ripple effect saved us. As our task force enlisted new candidates, the newcomers reached out to enroll still others. Consequently, the project acquired additional energy, just when Hevener, Webb, the others, and I had exhausted our personal lists of friends and associates. For example, Hevener recruited Tom Sciranka, a conservative, young Democrat who lived in Lima's north end, to run against Carol Falk in precinct 2G. His would be a tough race. Falk was the party's secretary and was a clerk at the Board of Elections. She was a gentle woman, well liked by all who knew her—even us DEP-ers—but we weren't going to let any of Hauenstein's close associates have a free ride. In the end, Falk defeated Sciranka in the primary, but three candidates he recruited would win their races.

Then, more fresh blood infused our movement. One of the most valuable of our new activists was Bryan Hefner, a sixty-nine-year-old farmer from east of Lima. Hefner was a relentless Democrat who possessed erratic and unbridled energy, the kind that often had to be channeled. After the 1982 campaign he had mysteriously disappeared from political life, not even running to keep his committeeman's post in Jackson Township. But when Coplen and Webb approached him about becoming a DEP-sponsored candidate, he not only agreed to run for his old seat but helped recruit fourteen or so additional candidates.[6]

There were others. The south end of Lima was Otha Harris's turf. Our recruitment effort had stalled in Lima's Fifth and Sixth Wards, simply because we didn't know many people in those neighborhoods. All of us, with the exception of Beverly McCoy, were white, and although McCoy was of some help, she was originally from Cleveland, was not a native southsider, and lived in Lima's west end. Her contacts were limited, confined mainly to the teaching community, and we had been having extreme difficulty finding candidates to run in the minority precincts.

Tom Doyle helped us in Lima's south side, not by recruiting candidates himself but by bringing in Leonard Boddie. Doyle was a social activist, a participant in a number of liberal causes, including the National Abortion Rights Action League, the nuclear-freeze movement, and the Witness for Peace program. His activism had brought him into contact with Boddie, the associate pastor at the Shiloh Missionary Baptist Church in Lima and director of the Salvation Army Community Center. Boddie's church and community connections helped us fill most of the slots in the black precincts. Leonard had a personal agenda: He wanted to run for city council against Henry Horne, the Sixth Ward incumbent, and he knew that he was most likely to win if there was a change in party leadership, one that would lessen Otha Harris's influence in the south side. He signed on with this objective in mind.[7]

Cora Hamman, a veteran of the 1982 rebellion, was another late addition to our cause. Actually, Cora had wanted to enlist much earlier, but none of us—neither Hevener, Webb, Coplen, nor I—wanted her involved during the planning phase of our campaign. For one thing, she couldn't keep a secret. If we told Cora anything, even stressing its confidentiality, we could not be sure she would keep it to herself. More than likely she'd say something to one of her friends, who'd tell someone else, and eventually the information would tunnel its way to Charlie Hauenstein.

Also, Cora was given to dreaming up bizarre schemes to undermine people who had offended her. A story about Cora's "loose cannon" bent began circulating among party activists following the 1982 election. Dick Celeste and the Democrats were firmly in control of state government, but Cora began to feel slighted—snubbed and ignored by local party leaders who were delivering jobs to Democrats who, in Cora's eyes, were less deserving than she was. Consequently, she established a friendship with a local FBI agent and began sending him tips that Charlie Hauenstein, Todd Hey, and Otha Harris were selling patronage appointments. According to one seemingly apocryphal part of this legend, Cora even tried to help the investigation along, stuffing a tape recorder in her purse and asking Otha Harris to help her get a job in return for money. As she shoved the purse in Harris's face, the story went, he backed away, proclaiming loudly that he didn't have any jobs to give.[8]

So, early on we decided that for our own sanity and for the integrity of our movement, we would keep Cora Hamman at a distance. Cora was persistent, however, and played mind games to manipulate the situation. In late summer 1985, with her husband Tim in tow, she confronted me at the Allen County Fair, pumping me for information about our effort to oust Charlie Hauenstein. When I admitted that several of us had been meeting over the summer, she became indignant that she had not been asked to participate. "Don't you trust us?" she demanded, linking Tim to the dispute. Tim was okay, but Cora was a different matter. I ignored her jibe and tried to reassure her that our movement was simply in an organizational phase and that she would be invited to join later.

It didn't work. She remained angry and called John Hevener about the DEP project. John, in turn, urged me to contact Cora and attempt, once again, to placate her. When I did, Cora hit me with a "guilt trip," telling me how sad and upset she had been because we had not included her in our meetings. She reminded me how much she hated Charlie Hauenstein and pressed me to let her join the cause. I responded with a line that Hevener and I had concocted: "The reason you have not been invited is because we are not including anyone who was directly involved in that 1982 overthrow attempt. Why, even Mary Hevener doesn't come to our meetings." This seemed to mollify Cora somewhat.[9]

If we could have managed without Cora Hamman, we would have, but by February 1986 we needed her help. Despite her temperament, Cora had at least two important virtues: She had a reputation for working hard, and she knew a lot of people on Allen County's political front. Steve Webb invited her to run in her American Township precinct, immediately northwest of Lima. Cora refused to become a candidate, however, unless she was brought into DEP's planning sessions, and so Webb invited her to a meeting. She immediately grabbed some voter lists for precincts that remained empty, suggested some names, and eventually recruited at least fifteen candidates by herself.[10]

A week before the filing deadline, we had recruited 130 candidates, and attendance at DEP meetings had begun to climb. In truth, the line between inner and outer circles was never sharply defined. Anyone could attend a DEP session and become as involved as he or she cared. Many, of course, chose to stay on the fringe, but others wanted to become more engaged. As news of our movement spread and excitement intensified, we finally had to move our meetings from the Alpine's conference room to the large meeting hall downstairs. We were building a democratic structure, one with a clearly defined leadership at the center but without the autocratic cliquishness of Hauenstein's organization.

Despite this renewed excitement, fresh challenges confronted us, foreshadowing a tough campaign. First, the city of Delphos had become a problem. The residents of Delphos have traditionally remained aloof from the rest of the county. Perhaps it has to do with geography. On a map, Delphos looks as if it had been shoved into the northwestern border of Allen County, spilling against and into two adjacent counties—Van Wert and Putnam—thus forming the "Tri-County Area." Its residents don't like outsiders meddling in their affairs, and they particularly distrust people from Lima. It's an old urban rivalry, dating back to the time when Lima was a rail hub while Delphos's commercial success depended on the Miami-Erie Canal. As Ohio's canal traffic dwindled in the late-nineteenth century, Lima grew at Delphos's expense, and the citizens there have looked on Lima with suspicion ever since.

Steve Webb and Bryan Hefner paid a visit to Joe Youngpeter and asked him to run for committeeman in Marion Township, right outside Delphos. Youngpeter not only agreed but promised to line up support from the incumbent precinct representatives in Delphos. However, Youngpeter pointedly crossed two representatives off his list—John Sheeter and Bob Wegesin. Webb and Hefner were so relieved that somebody from Delphos was helping us that they didn't ask what Youngpeter's specific objections were to the two men.

Someone from our group should have talked to John Sheeter, who was a Delphos city councilman (he would later become mayor) and operated the local license bureau. When Youngpeter began talking to Delphos's other incumbent committee representatives, Sheeter got wind of it and grew suspicious. When he discovered that Youngpeter hadn't talked to Wegesin either, Sheeter asked Todd Hey what was going on.

Although Charlie and Todd had long known about our rebellion, Sheeter's query alerted them to DEP's precise tactics, and it allowed Todd to sow some dissension.[11] He told Sheeter that Steve Webb and I had placed him and Wegesin on a "hit list," that we were trying to find candidates to run against each of them, and that if we won we were going to take Sheeter's license bureau and give it to someone loyal to our faction. Sheeter called me, furious, and accused me of stabbing him in the back and trying to take his money away. Struggling for words and trying to understand what Sheeter was barking about, I finally coaxed him into disclosing his little talk with Todd Hey. "Look," I declared, "Nobody in our group has ever discussed you or your license bureau, and as far as I'm concerned you should keep it. Yeah, we screwed up. We talked to Youngpeter first and should have talked to you and Wegesin. I'm sorry. I hope we can square matters somehow."

Sheeter did not respond to my offer of reconciliation, remaining noncommittal until I called him the next day. Once again, I apologized, emphasizing that we regretted what had happened, that there was no "hit list," and that the Delphos license bureau was a local matter, something for Democrats in Delphos to decide. "Well, Bill, you're my friend. As far as I'm concerned this thing's straightened out," Sheeter replied, seemingly placated.

"Are you with us, John?"

"Yeah, I'm with you. You're my friend. I'm with you."

I also phoned Wegesin, explained to him DEP's side of the controversy, and apologized, just as I had to Sheeter. He was considerably more distant than Sheeter, hard to reach and hard to read. "Well, thanks for clearin' the air," he remarked.[12]

I thought that I had put out the fire, but I was wrong. Too much suspicion lingered, blocking Webb and me from winning any support in Delphos.[13] As for Youngpeter, who had contributed to our predicament, he decided not run.

Then there was the matter of Susan Ebescotte, one of our Central Committee candidates. She reportedly had made disparaging comments about Steve Webb while collecting signatures for her petition, declaring that she hated Webb and that when she became a committeewoman she would support Todd Hey. This news surfaced shortly before filing day and threw our recruitment task force into a tizzy. How could we have enlisted a candidate who would not support Steve? More importantly, was it too late to correct our error? Webb, who did not recognize Ebescotte's name right away, eventually recalled that she was a disgruntled employee at the Allen County Home, that she had filed a grievance, and that she hadn't liked the way he had handled her complaint. Suddenly, a light bulb snapped on as he realized that she was a county employee working in a "classified" position and by law, she could not run for partisan office. "Why, she could get fired," I recall Webb saying. "I'll talk to Crit. He'll handle it."[14]

"Crit" was the county administrator, Crit Akers. He was a small, owlish-looking partisan who had a reputation as a hatchet man for Bob Holmes, the Republican chair. Crit talked to Susan Ebescotte all right, and then he talked to Holmes, who talked to Charlie Hauenstein.[15] Ebescotte was seen sobbing as she left work on the day Akers told her she could not run, and although she was not fired, she didn't file her petition either. We got the result we wanted.

The night after our petitions had been filed, Todd Hey phoned John Hevener to complain about how Steve Webb had pressured to get Susan Ebescotte fired. Decrying our attempt to "force a poor woman out into the snow without a job and with cryin' babies to feed," he admonished John for associating himself with such "dirty politics." Hevener immediately phoned me with the details of Hey's complaint. He was shaken up, swayed by Hey's stellar performance, and he was a little upset with Steve. I checked with Webb, who just shook his head. "Todd told John what? I didn't tell Akers to fire her. I told him that I didn't want her fired. Just wanted him to talk to her, that's all. A 'poor woman with cryin' babies to feed,' huh?"[16]

Hauenstein and Hey recounted the Ebescotte incident every chance they got. For them, it signified that we were a ruthless bunch of renegades who would do anything to win, to take the party from the loyalists who had commanded it for fourteen years. Along with Hey's maneuverings in Delphos, it also signaled something we should have known all along: Charlie Hauenstein and the party regulars would not take our challenge quietly. They would fight relentlessly to hold on to the party.

· 4 ·

Protest

4 p.m., February 27, 1986, Allen County Board of Elections
"C'mon, Charlie. Get on with it or we'll never get out of here," Bob Holmes muttered, as he lit another cigarette and tossed the empty pack into the waste can.

Unruffled by the interruption, Charlie Hauenstein looked up, stared blankly at Holmes, and returned to the task that was obsessing him—investigating the petitions filed by DEP. He knew who his Central Committee candidates were: their petitions passed easy inspections. But ours received careful and deliberate attention; Charlie scrutinized each one for flaws that would disqualify the candidate.

The board had been working since morning when it routinely approved candidates for countywide offices. They were on the ballot. But the meeting hit a layover as it began considering candidates for the Democratic Party's Central Committee. Over 250 petitions had been filed for these races, a record number, and Charlie meticulously read each DEP petition twice, sometimes three times, taking notes as he went and placing several on a "reject pile" directly in front of him.

At five o'clock Hauenstein began making his case for rejecting more than a dozen candidates sponsored by the DEP, some for legitimate reasons, others for reasons that were specious at best. Bev McCoy, for instance, was singled out because she had forgotten to place the exact date of the May primary in the appropriate space. Rick Siferd had signed and dated his petition on February 24, four days after the filing deadline, thereby disqualifying his candidacy, or so Charlie decided. Finally, shortly before 6 p.m., the board members—Hauenstein and Paul Prater for the Democrats and Bob Holmes and Charles Rossfeld for the Republicans—voted to reject the petitions of fifteen candidates for the Democratic Central Committee. All were sponsored by DEP.[1]

Democratic gubernatorial candidate Richard Celeste with John Hevener at an Allen County Celeste rally, April 1982. From the collection of Mary (Hevener) Kahal.

When we filed our petitions on February 20, we suspected we might lose a few candidates to disqualification, maybe five or six. We had worked in haste during the waning hours of our search for Central Committee candidates. On the morning of February 20, Pickle Felter, Steve Webb, Tom Doyle, Cora Hamman, and Bryan Hefner had all been in scattered precincts, collecting signatures for eleventh-hour recruits. In slapdash fashion, we had given their petition papers only a cursory inspection before submitting them to the Board of Elections.

Still, we surprised Charlie Hauenstein with the number of our petitions. At 2 P.M. on filing day, Webb and I walked into the Board of Elections and slapped ninety-one petitions onto the counter. Carol Falk, one of the Democratic clerks, time-stamped each one and rushed into the board's conference room, where Hauenstein was sitting. Whispering in a voice loud enough for us to hear, she informed him that we had turned in over ninety petitions. Hauenstein's face turned ashen.[2]

About three o'clock, Bryan Hefner and Pickle Felter showed up to file a few additional petitions, just in time to observe Charlie on the phone, chewing out Otha Harris. In a searing voice, Hauenstein emphasized the exact number of petitions Webb and I had deposited and wanted to know when Otha was going to deliver the ones he had promised. After concluding that conversation, seemingly unaware that political enemies were standing about, he called Todd Hey and berated him, just as he had Harris. Charlie was focused but a little shaken up.[3]

He became even more perturbed when I went public with DEP's challenge. It had always been a central part of our strategy to make the voters aware of the party's internal power struggle, and on February 21 in Webb's union office, I held a press conference and declared the party's need for vigorous, productive leadership. Furthermore, everyone had a stake in this battle, I said. One-party rule was not healthy for the county, but unfortunately, the current Democratic leaders had proven themselves incapable forging a viable challenge to the Republican colossus. I also outlined DEP's intent to campaign in the neighborhoods, where our candidates would go voter to voter and argue the need for fresh leadership. "It will be grassroots politics at the 'grassiest,'" I emphasized, in perfect sound-bite form.[4]

But in my enthusiasm to be open and genuine with the media, I committed a blunder that tarnished the moment. Trying both to highlight our group's inclusive character and to criticize Hauenstein for failing to broaden party support, I voiced an opinion that was open to misinterpretation. To this day, I am not sure exactly what I told Paul W. Smith, the *Lima News* reporter covering the event, but he reported me as saying, "The current party leadership has been a narrow group dominated by the interests of labor."[5] This caused even John Hevener's eyebrows to pop, and I had to explain that I had not intended to attack the unions; I had simply wanted to state categorically that a clique from the UAW was running the party.[6]

John P. Dornick almost left us when he read my comments. A retired international representative for the Oil, Chemical, and Atomic Energy Workers Union, Dornick was a florid-faced, cigar-smoking veteran of numerous labor struggles. Running in Lima's Seventh Ward, he threatened to resign his candidacy when he saw my "antilabor" statements in the newspaper. I did not know Dornick at the time but got word of his disenchantment from John Coplen, who, acting as an intermediary, talked to him and smoothed matters. When I finally met Dornick later that spring, I personally expressed my chagrin for allowing my words to be misinterpreted. "Well, I know whatya mean," John said, squinting at me through a puff of cigar smoke. "Those boneheads at the *Lima News* wouldn't know the truth if it bit 'em on their Aunt Fanny."

Charlie Hauenstein pounced on my gaffe. He huffed that DEP's members were Democrats who hadn't been "heard from since McGovern ran for president." He challenged my premise that the party had become a "narrow group dominated by the interests of labor." If there was such a problem, DEP-ers had fostered it, he explained, by "turning their back on the party." It wasn't his fault. In his eyes, DEP members had failed to take advantage of opportunities that he and other party leaders had offered them. "If they had put half the effort into electing Democrat candidates that they have put into this effort, then we would be more successful."[7]

In this blistering attack, Hauenstein sounded the theme he would play to defend his chairmanship. He would trumpet the idea that DEP was antilabor, castigate us as radicals who were out of step with the party's more conservative, blue-collar base. "They are single issue people who aren't active in the party unless there is something that they are interested in,"[8] Hauenstein warned sinisterly, an oblique reference to certain DEP-ers who wanted to rechannel patronage in their own directions. Hauenstein and Hey had already tried this ploy on John Sheeter, and they would continue to emphasize it throughout the coming campaign, claiming that we were going to get rid of poll workers, fire state employees, and appoint ourselves to the vacated positions.

From the very beginning, DEP feared shenanigans from the Board of Elections. In the 1982 "party fight," alleged irregularities had clouded the outcome. On election night, board officials had told the observers that ballots for the Central Committee races would be counted the next day. When the observers returned, they were told that the ballots had been counted the previous night after all. Also, a peculiar outcome clouded Howard Elstro's Central Committee race in Lima's Eighth Ward, which had officially been declared a tie. Board officials told Elstro that he would be called to observe the recount and that if the race still ended in a tie, a "coin flip" would determine the victor. Days passed, and Elstro never heard from any election official. Finally, he phoned the board office, only to discover that an "extra ballot" had been found and that there was no need for a recount. Troubled, Howard called his opponent, Jerry Pitts, to apprise him of this news, but Pitts was not sympathetic. The outcome might have been different, Pitts told Elstro, if Howard had been a bit "tighter" with Charlie.[9]

Worried about similar mischief in the 1986 Central Committee races, John Hevener and I requested a meeting with Donald Kindt and Dorothy Woldorf, both adjutants in the office of Ohio secretary of state Sherrod Brown. In a September 1985 session, we informed them of what we were trying to do, described our suspicions about voting irregularities in Allen County, and raised our fears of election fraud.[10] We wanted help to ensure a fair election.

To Sherrod Brown's staff, Hevener's and my suggestion that election officials would finagle ballots must have seemed outrageous. But our partners were in a suspicious mood in 1985–86, convinced that Charlie Hauenstein would never allow a fair fight, and Hevener and I had to lessen their anxiety.[11] Even so, our more suspicious comrades could not be placated, especially Bryan Hefner, who continuously grumbled, "We gotta watch them boys at the Board of Elections." Bryan knew. He was a veteran of the 1982 party fight, and as events unfolded, his apprehensions proved well founded.

One week after we filed our petitions, the board tripped up our effort with the disqualification of fifteen candidates. Infuriated by this power play, Pickle Felter took the first step in our planned counterattack, acquiring copies of all petitions filed for the central committees of both parties—we had no real interest in the Republicans but simply wanted to confuse election officials. Then, on Saturday, March 1, Steve Webb, Rick Siferd, Pickle Felter, and I met in Siferd's law office, combing over the Democratic petitions and plotting our next move. We noticed a number of irregularities in the papers for Hauenstein's candidates. James McClendon, for instance, had filed for a Central Committee spot in Shawnee Township but had listed his residence in Lima's Sixth Ward. Other petitions had what appeared to be forged signatures. That is, spouses had signed their own names along with those of their partners—a common practice, albeit illegal.

Searching through Ohio's Revised Code governing elections, Siferd found rule 3501.38, stating that an entire petition would be invalid if the circulator "knowingly [permitted] . . . a person to write a name other than his own on a petition paper."[12] Looking at several petitions, we noticed that clerks had written "NG" (for "no good") next to the names of the suspect signatures, yet the petitions had been ruled valid anyway. We protested all of these. Also, we noticed that Todd Hey's petition had signatures that looked as if they had been written by the same person, but they had been checked as "good." These were forged signatures too, we reasoned, and we decided to protest his petition. (This challenge was a stretch, but we were in no mood to be merciful to Todd.)

All together, DEP filed eleven protests against candidates from Hauenstein's faction[13] and three appeals asking for reconsideration of candidates from our side—Bev McCoy, Donna Moore, and Rick Siferd. On March 3, Pickle turned in the required papers—letters from DEP candidates filing protests against specific board decisions—and handed them to Carol Falk. "Carol's eyes opened wider than Eisenhower silver dollars," Pickle later told us, chortling. "And Charlie was there too. Man, you could just see the steam rising from the folds in his neck."[14]

Filing protests was a controversial move, but we had to do it. The election board's action had confirmed our suspicion that it represented an obstacle that had to be challenged. Not only had Charlie Hauenstein and his allies been handed an unfair advantage, but there was real concern that unless we took a stand, mischief at the board would continue, placing the fairness of the primary in jeopardy.

DEP hired a court recorder for the protest hearing, just to provide a written record of the proceedings and to force the board to justify the action it would take that day. Board meetings in Allen County had always been loose and informal, and although minutes were always taken, they recorded only the basic decisions the board made, never the deliberations. We wanted to put the board "on record" and to force the county's elections officials to take our protests seriously.

Siferd played "point man." At perhaps five feet seven inches and weighing no more than 150 pounds, his slight frame held the feistiness of a man who had once had played varsity ice hockey for Ohio State. He would fight for us as if he were digging for a puck deep in the corner. However, Tony Geiger, a partner in the Siferd law firm, took the first shift, as Rick was delayed in court on the morning of March 13, when the protest hearing opened. The board quickly dispatched two protests, upholding the one against James McClendon and dismissing that against Todd Hey; according to Charlie Hauenstein, it "had no merit."[15]

The board next turned to the protest filed by Beverly McCoy. In her affidavit McCoy brought evidence to support her case for reconsideration, citing a petition filed by Dorothy Loggi. Like McCoy, Loggi had omitted the date of the May primary, but the board had approved her candidacy anyway. Loggi, as it turned out, was running in a three-way race in a precinct from Lima's Fourth Ward, the only three-way contest in the entire county.

The board perversely decided that McCoy was filing a protest against Loggi, when she was doing nothing of the kind. Hauenstein, who loved the game of bridge, began the play. In this circumstance, he was willing to sacrifice Loggi—who was simply the third candidate in her race—if it meant keeping McCoy off the ballot. So he quickly moved that the so-called protest against Loggi be sustained, Rossfeld seconding. Before Tony Geiger realized what had happened, the board approved the motion, and Dorothy Loggi was off the ballot, even though no one—not Beverly McCoy or any other member of DEP—had lodged a protest against her.[16] Tony Geiger tried to make things clear, but it was too late. "I guess the way I read McCoy's letter is that she wasn't asking for Loggi's to be thrown out," he said, "but just using that as an example, saying that if you accept Loggi's, you should accept hers because it's the same."

Holmes: "All right. It's a protest."

Geiger: "Not on hers. She's not protesting Loggi's. . . . She is protesting her own, not Loggi's."

Hauenstein: "As part of her protest, she brought it to our attention. All we are trying to do is be consistent."[17]

The board followed this exchange with a quick vote to disallow McCoy's protest, not even considering the merits of her case. Hauenstein's shrewd finesse—moving Loggi aside—had made Geiger's argument moot. McCoy was still off the ballot. Furthermore, the board's action on Loggi's petition was highly questionable. Ohio Revised Code does not allow the board to invalidate a petition it has already approved unless a formal protest has been filed against it.[18] Legal technicalities did not matter that day, though. Loggi was off the ballot.

The board sustained none of our protests based on the "forged signature" claim. Here again, the Bob Holmes, Charlie Hauenstein, Charles Rossfeld, and Paul Prater cooperated to deny our protests against the old guard candidates. The first of these protests involved Willie Denson. When Holmes admitted that Denson's petition contained two signatures, those of John and Janet Upshaw, both of which were signed by Janet, Geiger responded, "I believe the law on that says the entire petition has to be thrown out."

"I don't know," Holmes replied, feigning ignorance. He understood perfectly well the point Geiger was trying to make. DEP had cited the appropriate section from the Ohio Revised Code, 3501.38 (f), in the letters of protest against Denson's petition and against six others that had problems similar to his. "You know, it's amazing," Holmes continued, trying to make light of the matter, "When you look at the signatures on the registration card, how many husbands and wives do write similar. . . . I guess they go together, become one."

"They start to look alike, too," Rossfeld joked.[19]

"There is something wrong," Geiger asserted, "because it seems to me that the board agrees that those signatures [on Denson's petition] are the same. So, if this person is saying that he witnessed every signature, he witnessed one person signing both names, and I don't hear anybody saying that the Upshaws' signatures were not signed by the same person."[20] At this point, Charlie Hauenstein jumped in to defend the board and its "forged signature" policy. "There are many, many petitions that are marked that way," he insisted. "To be consistent this board has not thrown out the whole petition. They have thrown out the signatures only . . ."[21]

By this time, Siferd had arrived. "If you disqualify the signatures, you got to disqualify the petition by law," he responded calmly, staring at board chair, Bob Holmes.

"Then, we are talking election falsification," Holmes replied, matching Siferd's stare.[22] Things had become serious now, and Siferd would not allow Holmes to bluff him down. "That is a separate issue, whether somebody is going to file charges. That is not the standard here."

"As far as I'm concerned, it is!" piped in Hauenstein, launching a monologue, his arms flailing and his face turning beet red with each phrase: "[If] we are going to charge somebody with enough to throw out a petition, then that person should be charged with falsification. Turn the case over to the county prosecutor for whatever action he sees fit. No, we want to load the system up and have it so nobody wants to run for office."

"The issue is this petition," responded Siferd, unruffled by Charlie's harangue.

"Fine," huffed Hauenstein.

"I don't think you can change the law. Now that it's our [protest] the law may be too strict," continued Siferd, jabbing Hauenstein and Holmes one more time.[23]

The subject turned to the issue of election falsification, as county prosecutor David Bowers, Paul Prater, Holmes, and Siferd debated whether or not criminal charges would be filed against candidates whose petitions DEP was now protesting.

Hauenstein picked up the monologue he had left moments earlier, articulating the board's thinking on the DEP protest, proclaiming the need for "fairness and consistency," and lamenting the prospect of charging fellow citizens with election fraud. "I would imagine that there are probably a hundred petitions in there," he declared, waving at the stack of petitions on the table, "where we threw out a signature because it didn't match what was on the petition. . . . Now, if you want to go back and throw out all of those petitions, call those people in and charge them with election falsification, the next time we turn around we are not going to have anybody that is willing to take a chance and run for office if they are going to have to go through this kind of procedure."[24]

It was "slippery slope" logic, but Charlie's jeremiad raised the specter of "election falsification." In filing a protest on the forged-signature claim, DEP had separated the objective of our protest from its consequences. As Siferd had said, we simply wanted the board to eliminate the targeted candidate; the matter of election fraud, we believed, was a separate issue. In counterpoint, Hauenstein cleverly linked our objectives with their consequences. By declaring hyperbolically that we were charging fellow Democrats with election fraud, Hauenstein could claim political high ground. The people—Charlie's people— who circulated the challenged petitions would have to face criminal charges, he reasoned. Charlie Hauenstein was a loyal man. By collecting signatures and filing their petitions on his behalf, Charlie's Central Committee candidates were proving their loyalty to him, and he was not going to allow them to face criminal charges. As it turned out, none of them would.

"Set for the motion," Holmes finally announced.

"I will make a motion that the request be denied, protest be denied, whatever language we are using," Charlie responded, still fuming.[25]

The motion passed unanimously, and Willie Denson maintained his candidacy, even though his petition contained the forged signature of John Upshaw. The board followed this precedent in rejecting each protest where the circulator had witnessed an improper signature. It acted quickly and unanimously, claiming, "We are just being consistent with what we have done." Consistency was a virtue that day. If the candidate had enough true signatures, his or her petition would pass. That's the way the board had customarily handled the problem, and it wasn't about to change, not even in the face of a clearly worded election code.

The board did sustain three of our protests—the one against James McClendon and two on behalf of Rick Siferd and Donna Moore, whose petitions had been mistakenly invalidated.[26] "We are pleased with the protests we won," Siferd declared to the press after the meeting, "not the ones we lost." What about the ones that were lost? "We're considering our options," replied Siferd tersely.[27]

Actually, we had few options. We briefly considered filing a lawsuit against the Board of Elections but quickly dropped the notion. With less than eight weeks before election day, it would have made little sense to waste energy and money in the courts, where we might end up losing anyway. Our mission was to win enough precinct races to take over the Central Committee. Although the Board of Elections had handed us a setback, we had to recognize that this particular battle had ended; it was time to fight in another venue, the May 6 primary.

Also, our protest had garnered bad publicity. Soon after the hearing, Charlie and his cohorts began spreading the word that DEP had wanted to charge good Democrats with "election fraud." Why, "they even filed criminal charges against Todd Hey," went the line, turning Todd into a poster boy for the cause. Suddenly, media coverage, which had been favorable in February, turned sour. Although our protests filed with the Board of Elections and our public tantrum at the outcome created good copy, we now found ourselves cast as "a group of rebel Democrats," whining that the election board's action was "'inappropriate and unfair.'"[28] Pursuing our case through the courts would only have hardened DEP's rebel image, confirmed Charlie's denunciations, and created more negative publicity.

So we moved on. But in losing, we had won something—the attention of Sherrod Brown. We now had proven that the Board of Elections in Allen County needed watching. Linda Coplen, John Coplen's wife, had been helping us with the secretary of state's office, keeping Sherrod Brown closely apprised of our effort. Linda was Brown's field representative for Allen County and surrounding counties, a job that meant working a circuit of boards of election and informing the office of important issues facing the outlying areas. Her duties in Allen County had been temporarily assigned to another field representative, because she was on the local ballot, running for Central Committeewoman under the DEP banner. This was a commitment that endangered her employment, but still, she remained steadfast to our effort.

At Coplen's urging, I wrote Brown a forceful letter warning him of the board's disregard for the law and arguing that the matter was larger than a dispute between contending factions in the Democratic Party. The statute in question, ORC 3501.38, was specific and clear, but the board had chosen to ignore it. This action, I wrote, "reflects a general attitude of contempt for Ohio's election codes, an attitude that renders those codes meaningless in Allen County. All candidates and citizens have cause to be concerned if such an attitude persists."[29]

Sherrod Brown conducted a brief investigation into the matter of the March 13 protest hearing, and in early April his elections counsel, Jonathan Marshall, chided the board for its disregard of procedure as outlined in Ohio's election law. In a sternly worded letter, he cited the Ohio Supreme Court Case *Carson v. Jones* (1970), which declared that if a petition circulator witnessed an invalid signature, the whole petition, not just the signature in question, was to be invalidated. Specifically, the board had to determine not only whether there were false signatures but whether the circulator had "knowingly allowed" those signatures to be placed on the paper. Thus, Marshall emphasized, in conducting a protest hearing, board members needed to do more than decide a case solely on their own interpretation of the facts. "The board needs to hear evidence and testimony under oath from the challenged signers . . . as well as the circulator," he wrote. "Only then can the Board arrive at a decision which conforms to requirements of the code."[30] The overall message was clear and helpful: In conducting hearings and reviews, the Allen County Board of Elections would have to pay less attention to customary practice and more attention to codified statutes. More importantly, the secretary of state promised to send additional field representatives into Allen County on primary day to monitor both the casting and counting of ballots. We wanted a fair election, and finally it looked as if we were going to get one.

Shortly after DEP's petitions were handed over to the Board of Elections, John Hevener and I were sitting in his office, drinking coffee and handicapping the Central Committee races. "We've already won something, just by filing those petitions," I said. "We've said something about the state of leadership in the party, and no matter what happens in the primary, the party will never be the same." Hevener rubbed his chin, rocked back in his chair, and chuckled, "Yeah, but it sure would be nice to win."

The fight with the Board of Elections, however, had transformed the whole campaign into something resembling a morality play. We DEP-ers soon began referring to ourselves as "The Jedi Council," after the warrior knights of the *Star Wars* trilogy, fighting the forces of "the dark side." We began to vilify and demonize Charlie Hauenstein. For a long time we had jokingly referred to him as "Jabba"—after "Jabba the Hut," the grotesquely obese and corrupt character who tortured Han Solo in *Return of the Jedi*—but in the wake of the Board of Elections hearing, the nickname became more ominous. Charlie Hauenstein was more than just an enemy. In our eyes, he was a wicked public official who had little respect for legal procedure and would do anything to hold on to his power.

Many of our foot soldiers stood to lose more than an election. Tim Hamman was an assistant attorney general, an appointed position in the Ohio attorney general's office. The proceeds of casework for the state of Ohio supplemented his income from his law practice. But Hamman's wife (Cora) and father (Ray) were both running on the DEP ticket. In fact, Ray Hamman was challenging Charlie Hauenstein in the Bluffton precinct, where they both lived, practically next door to one another. Hauenstein lobbied Ohio's attorney general, Anthony Celebreeze, to discharge Hamman from his post. He did the same regarding Mike Bender, another assistant attorney general and a DEP candidate. Also, Hauenstein put relentless pressure on Sherrod Brown to fire Linda Coplen, and on state auditor Tom Ferguson to dismiss John Coplen, who held a part-time billet in Ferguson's office. He even harangued Steve Webb's supervisor, complaining that Steve was so involved in politics that he was neglecting his union duties.[31]

None of these officials paid attention to Charlie's machinations; our Jedis' jobs were safe, at least until after the primary. Nonetheless, Hevener and I had recruited a number of good people into our cause, and now their livelihoods were on the line. It wasn't college any more. It was the real world.

· 5 ·

LaRouchies

April 2, 1986

Bob Mihlbaugh should have been a congressman.[1] He certainly looked the part, with long gray hair brushed straight back over his head, the strands trellised over the collar of an expensive, tailored suit. His hair streamed behind him when he walked down the sidewalk or drove around Lima in his green Rolls Royce, waving at people as he made his way to the courthouse or to his law office on South Main Street.

Bob was a hands-on politician. If he stopped to share a few words with a client or colleague, he'd grab an arm, slap a back, or, if he wanted to get really intimate, throw his arm across a shoulder and press his face close to the captive listener. His blue eyes could dance and sparkle like the ocean—especially if Bob was sharing a story about a personal triumph, in which case his feet would dance too, in rhythm with the music in the eyes. But if he felt pressured, which didn't happen often—Bob was usually the aggressor—or if he wanted to put someone on the defensive, the eyes would glare hot enough to strip paint off a clapboard farmhouse.

I received both looks this day. I was on a mission, seeking money, a contribution from Bob Mihlbaugh to Democrats for an Effective Party. The amount was less important than the act of contributing, for the donation itself would signal to Lima's Catholic Democrats—Bob was Irish Catholic to the core— that DEP was okay, that they could feel comfortable giving their votes to DEP-backed candidates.

The reception area of Mihlbaugh's richly paneled office was empty when I arrived. On the walls photos of John F. Kennedy and Lyndon Johnson greeted me, telling me that Bob Mihlbaugh was an important guy. An eye-level photograph showed Bob in fatigue uniform on a mission to Vietnam. It was a group picture with President Johnson and others, and LBJ's thanks were scrawled in the corner, lower right. When Bob ushered me into his office, another picture, hanging on the wall behind an ornate, Victorian-era desk, caught my eye—a color photo of President Jimmy Carter, Rosalyn Carter, and Pope John Paul II waving from the balcony of the White House. As I sat in a wing-back chair directly across from Bob Mihlbaugh, I could see this political trinity blessing him—or so it seemed—as he spun political stories, his eyes twinkling, his feet tapping.

He gave me a palm card from his 1964 run for Congress, which he had lost. He once told me that losing that race was the best thing that ever happened to him. On the day after the election, Bob claimed, people had lined up outside this office, all the way down the block—folks he'd met during the campaign—who now swore they had voted for him and wanted him to be their attorney. If so, Bob Mihlbaugh wasn't the first lawyer to build a practice out of lost campaign.

The discussion turned to DEP's effort, and I made my request for a hundred-dollar donation. Mihlbaugh's eyes began to glare as he asked a series of rapid-fire questions.

"Who is helping you?

"Anybody with a state job?

"What are you going to spend your money on?

"What are your chances?

"How many candidates do you have?

"What are the folks in Columbus doing for you?"

I answered the questions candidly, maybe a bit too honestly, especially the one about "folks in Columbus."

"Those assholes are being pretty cool to us," I snorted. "All John Hevener and I have ever heard from people in the governor's office is 'When are you guys gonna do something about Charlie Hauenstein?' Well, now we're doing something about him, and they act as if we have the plague." Bob feigned perplexity, scrunching his eyebrows and hunching forward on his desk as he asked why the "pols" downstate were acting that way. "Oh, they probably don't want to offend a party chairmen in an election year."

"That's bullshit, Bill!" he declared, popping straight up, then sagging back into his chair, waving his hand derisively. "You know that! What can party chairmen do to the governor? He's the only horse they have. No, I'd say they view your challenge to Charlie as a toss-up."

We kicked this idea around as I described critical moments in our campaign, including the protest hearing at the Board of Elections and my confrontation with Charlie at the Executive Committee meeting of March 12, the one when Charlie warned me about "the real world." Bob was letting me talk—finally—and I cut loose, hoping candor would cause him to open his checkbook.

It didn't. Suddenly Mihlbaugh cleared his throat and began his summary:

"You know, Bill, I think Charlie has sold the folks in Columbus on the message that you guys are splitting the party and that you will hurt the statewide candidates. Isn't that what Charlie said in that meeting?" This was more than a lawyer's hypothesis. Before I had a chance to reply, Bob leaned forward and whispered, even though we were the only ones in the office. "In fact, I got word the other day from three state candidates not to get involved with you," he said, shaking his finger at me.

"Who?" I asked, looking him directly in the eye. Unblinking, Mihlbaugh asserted that he was unable to say, then stood up, signaling an end to our meeting. "I'll think this thing over and get back to you," he said, slinging his arm over my shoulder and squiring me out of the office.[2]

DEP would never see any money from Bob Mihlbaugh. He liked to back winners, and in early April the DEP campaign seemed far from a sure thing. Although it was no surprise that Mihlbaugh expressed doubts about our ability to win, his excuse caused concern—that Democrats at the state level had warned him off our challenge to Charlie Hauenstein. I could not judge how pervasive this attitude was, but we had begun to receive other signals that our effort was viewed with mixed feelings by Democrats at the state level. For instance, John Hevener had suddenly begun to have trouble getting Kathy Tefft-Keller to return his phone calls. He and Mary were still the Celeste coordinators, but suddenly a chill had set in between the "Celestials" and the Heveners. Two weeks after I had paid my visit to Bob Mihlbaugh, Celeste visited Lima to speak before a regional meeting of the UAW. Normally, the governor's staff would have notified the Heveners, but not this time. Janet Quinn, a UAW retiree herself, went to the meeting and managed to pull Celeste aside and tell him, "John and Mary Hevener would have come, but your staff never notified them."

"I know. I know," the governor replied. "It's okay."[3]

But it wasn't "okay." Word got back to me that Jean Hatcher, Democratic committeewoman for the Fourth District, had begun deriding our effort. She reportedly had told members of the governor's staff that although I was book-smart, Charlie Hauenstein was street-smart. According to Hatcher, we didn't have a chance of defeating him. In the 1984 campaign she had been one of Hauenstein's sharpest critics, criticizing him and the Allen County Party whenever John Hevener or I ran into her, but now she was coming to Charlie's defense.

There were other snubs. Sherrod Brown stopped calling Steve Webb, his local coordinator, when he visited Allen County. This was unusual behavior for Brown, who was normally conscientious about touching bases with supporters when making even brief local appearances. Similarly, state treasurer Mary Ellen Withrow was freezing us out. Six months earlier she had asked me to coordinate her reelection campaign in Allen County, but once I had publicly announced the existence of DEP she withdrew her support, pleading lamely that decisions like naming coordinators would be firmed up after the primary. At the Ohio Democratic Party's state dinner in late April, I bumped into Greg Haas, Withrow's statewide coordinator. I had picked up a rumor that Withrow was holding a fund-raiser in Allen County and asked him if it was true. "Yeah, but we weren't happy with the way things were going and canceled out. Charlie just offered to put something on, and we gave him a shot," he replied, and then he turned his back on me.

I didn't let him escape. Before he had spun completely away, I pulled myself next to him and whispered clearly and defiantly, "Things are going well with us, Greg. We're going to win. You need to know that."

"Good," Haas responded, not even bothering to look at me as he slipped completely into the crowd.[4]

In Columbus we had become pariahs, just as Bob Mihlbaugh had said.

We lacked honor in our own county, too. Charlie and Todd had initiated a whispering campaign, laced with caustic innuendos about our sexual and moral characters. It was bruited about that DEP members were a "bunch of homosexuals" and that I had left my wife to "live with a black girl."[5] Although the inconsistency of these rumors made them laughable, events elsewhere handed the Hauenstein group more threatening charges to exploit.

In Illinois's Democratic primary that March, two followers of Lyndon LaRouche won races for lieutenant governor and secretary of state, defeating the party's mainstream candidates.[6] Facing the awkward prospect of running on the same ticket with a pair of LaRouche Democrats, Adlai Stevenson III, the Democrats' gubernatorial candidate, refused the party's nomination and ran instead as an independent against incumbent Governor James Thompson, who overwhelmingly defeated Stevenson that November. The LaRouche coup in Illinois sent shock waves throughout the Midwest and especially in Ohio, where fears of infiltration of the Democratic primary reached almost hysterical proportions. Ohio's Democratic chief, Jim Ruvulo, for one, alerted county chairs to the LaRouche problem, particularly in congressional races, where several "LaRouchies" had filed.

LaRouche-mania charged the political atmosphere, and Bryan Hefner inadvertently struck a match. On April 3, he and I attended the meeting of the Women's Democratic Club, where the subject of Lyndon LaRouche came up.[7] "Who are these LaRouchies?" the women wanted to know.

"What do they believe?"

"Are any LaRouche Democrats running locally?"

"What are we going to do?"

Though not particularly alarmed, the women were concerned. I emphasized that Lyndon LaRouche's philosophy took a conspiratorial anti-Semitic view of world events, that his ideas were out of the mainstream and inconsistent with those espoused by the Democratic Party. Besides, I cautioned, only one LaRouche Democrat was on the ballot, a farmer from Auglaize County named Clem Cratty, running for Congress in the Fourth Congressional District, where Mike Oxley was the Republican incumbent. I encouraged the women not to vote for him. A few responded with unkind remarks about Cratty, mocking the alliterative quality of his name and wondering "what kind of nut" he was.

As discussion was about to end, Hefner lifted his five-foot-five frame out of his chair, rubbed his hand across the silver stubble of his closely cropped hair, and pursed his lips like he wanted to spit, before thinking better of it. The fact that he was standing told us he was agitated. These meetings were highly informal, like groups of friends gathered around the dinner table to swap stories and advice. No one stood unless he was mad or wanted to leave. Bryan did not want to leave.

"I've known Clem Cratty since he was a boy," Bryan proclaimed. He cocked his head sharply to one side, then stared directly at the women. "He's a farmer. Been through some tough times. I won't believe Clem Cratty's one of them LaRouchies 'till I hear from his own mouth. And I tell you if it comes down to votin' for Mike Oxley or Clem Cratty, I'm votin' for Cratty!"[8]

Word of Hefner's off-the-cuff speech got back to Charlie Hauenstein. His wife Elizabeth was attending that meeting, along with their daughter, Ramona. As I recall, Elizabeth had been looking straight ahead during most of the discussion, listening but not taking part, but when Bryan issued his "endorsement" of Clem Cratty, her glance jerked toward him then quickly away. The statement had registered.

Charlie wasted little time in reacting. Two weeks later, at the April meeting of the Executive Committee, Hauenstein called for a resolution endorsing all of his faction's Central Committee candidates and for a corollary resolution authorizing the expenditure of money to prepare and mail literature on their behalf.[9] When Mary Hevener, Pickle Felter, and I protested this action, Charlie barked, "We gotta do this because there are a bunch of LaRouche Democrats running, trying to overthrow the party, and we want to make sure that voters don't vote for any of 'em."

Todd Hey cleared his throat and added, "Yeah, we have to do this because there are supporters of Lyndon LaRouche who are members of DEP."

"Who?" Mary responded briskly. "Who's a LaRouche Democrat? What's your rationale for doing this?"

"Don't you come down here calling us names!" shouted Hauenstein, shaking his finger at her, apparently misunderstanding the word "rationale."

Rising to my feet, totally perplexed by Charlie's outburst, I tried to steer discussion away from Lyndon LaRouche. "Look," I declared, "Mary's concerned. You want to endorse people who have done nothing for this party, such as Mary Hevener's opponent, while failing to endorse good Democrats who have been longstanding Central Committee representatives."

"Whadya think you're doin', Bill?" Hauenstein sneered. "I've been a Central Committeeman in Bluffton for twenty years, and your group is runnin' someone against me!"

"That's politics," I replied.

"That's right, and this is politics, too." Hauenstein shot back.

"Tell 'em, Charlie," several backbenchers chimed in.[10]

Both resolutions passed, and soon after this meeting gossip intensified about DEP's supposed affiliation with Lyndon LaRouche. At first we paid little attention, smugly certain that no one would fall for such rumors, lumping them with those "Bill Angel is living with a black girl" stories. But in late April, Todd Hey severely jarred our confidence. During an interview with WLIO TV, he offered this LaRouche connection: "There are known LaRouche Democrats in Allen County, members of LaRouche's DPC. DEP and DPC are splinter groups, not mainstream Democrats, and we're advising our voters not to vote for their candidates."[11]

With that statement, Hauenstein's faction made its first effective use of the media. Ordinarily, Charlie hated reporters, and he was especially wary of televised news coverage. The camera was not kind to him; his jowly face filled the screen, and when the lights hit Charlie's photosensitive glasses, the lenses darkened, making him appear hideously sinister. So he left this errand to Todd Hey.

It was a deft performance. While Todd's unsteady glance created an air of discomfort, his unpretentious manner—he wore no suit and tie—made him look disarmingly sincere. As for substance, Hey did not explicitly say that DEP members were LaRouche Democrats, but he led viewers to that conclusion. By mentioning the acronym DCP (for Democratic Policy Council, LaRouche's organization) in the same breath with DEP, he linked the two groups. To underscore the connection, Hey declared DEP a splinter group, like LaRouche's faction, not part of the mainstream.

Jeff Fitzgerald, the WLIO reporter who conducted the interview with Hey, called me for a reaction. He summarized Hey's comments, telling me that Hey had charged that LaRouche Democrats were running as DEP candidates. "Is this true?" Fitzgerald asked.

"Absolutely not!" I asserted.

When I asked for an on-air response, Fitzgerald said, "No, this is Todd's show, and we've given you lots of air time anyway. But I'll report your denial."[12] But this denial, which ran at the end of the Hey piece, did little to deflect the interview's effect. Todd had fashioned his remarks to manipulate an unsuspecting electorate, sowing confusion and doubt by exploiting the voters' inattentiveness to political fine print.

The party's literature proclaimed this strategy. During the week before the primary, sample ballots arrived in the homes of Democratic voters, along with letters from party-endorsed Central Committee candidates. The sample ballot, however, was the critical enclosure. Its front contained two quotations that looked official. The first was from an editorial in the *Lima News*, dated April 21, 1986. It read, "One [LaRouchie] is running as a Republican and the rest as Democrats, and unless voters have done their homework, they will not know these are not mainstream party candidates." The second quote was not really a quote at all but a loose paraphrase of a statement attributed to Jim Ruvulo: "Ohio Democrat Party Chairman Jim Ruvulo has requested that the Allen County Democrat Party make a 'strong endorsement' of our candidates while denying LaRouchie people even negative media exposure."[13] It looked like an authentic quote, and its placement alongside the *Lima News* excerpt, over Ruvulo's name, gave it an air of authority.

It was a crafty scheme: Send a sample ballot, raise the specter of the "LaRouche Menace," and dispatch Democrats to the polls to vote against Lyndon LaRouche and DEP. Complemented by Todd Hey's television interview, broadcast the same week, the direct-mail campaign told voters that if they really wanted to avoid LaRouche Democrats, they should vote only for the party-endorsed candidates, especially those running for Central Committee. The choice had been framed for the voters, and Hauenstein and Hey were betting that the Democratic rank and file would select the party-endorsed Central Committee candidates—the ones backed by the old guard—in landslide proportions.

The strategy had impact. On Wednesday, April 30, at DEP's last meeting before the primary, we were in a near panic at report after report from candidates who had delivered their personalized brochures to voters' doors, only to be accosted with the question, "Are you one of them LaRouchies?" We had to do something, but a grand denial was out of the question. To hold a press conference and make a production of denying the party's charges would only have given the charges credibility. Instead, Steve Webb proposed the idea of an endorsement from the Allen County Democratic Women's Club, arguing that it would send the message that DEP candidates were safe. "Them women wouldn't go for no LaRouchies," went the reasoning. At the very least, the approval of this traditional, staid organization would reassure voters that our candidates were part of the mainstream, thus diluting the charge that DEP was a splinter group.

Linda Coplen, who also happened to be president of the Women's Club, readily agreed to let Webb and me speak to the club at its meeting the next night. The women welcomed us warmly, which was no surprise, considering the backhanded treatment the group had long received from the Democratic Party leadership. During the previous year, Hey and Hauenstein had needlessly harassed Coplen and her officers about alleged slights to the party leaders, demanded copies of the organization's financial reports, and publicly criticized the club's unwillingness to cooperate with the party.[14] Steve and I both explained DEP's purpose and objectives, which included establishing an active partnership between the party and the Allen County Democratic Women's Club, and we requested the group's backing. Hauenstein's mother and daughter were present at this meeting, but neither one dissented when the club voted to endorse DEP.[15]

Still, the women's support would prove meaningless—a tree falling in the forest, with no one to listen—unless we could get some publicity out of the event. But it was Thursday night, with the primary only five days away. News organizations in Lima were typically reluctant to supply political coverage on the Monday before an election, and Saturday and Sunday were "dead" as far as real news went. If we wanted publicity, we would have to move fast. Linda Coplen quickly arranged for a press conference, to be held the next day outside party headquarters. Not wanting to jeopardize her job with Sherrod Brown any more than she already had, Coplen did not attend the press conference but assigned Evelyn Vanek, secretary of the Women's Club (and a DEP candidate herself), to serve as the spokeswoman.

Noon on Friday, May 2, was breezy, sunny, and moderately cool. Vanek read her statement endorsing DEP, and several of her fellow club members stood by and applauded. "I just feel the present Democratic leadership has been ineffective," she stated. "There hasn't been a Democratic candidate elected to any county office in ten years. I also feel we ought to have two-party system in Allen County."[16] It was an engaging presentation. Vanek was a retired schoolteacher, in her middle fifties, hardly the kind of person who would support wild-eyed LaRouchies. She looked at the camera squarely, speaking evenly and convincingly about the club's and her own endorsement. Webb and I were there, too, beaming as brightly as the May sunshine.

Charlie Hauenstein and Todd Hey were furious, not only at the club's action but at the extensive radio, television, and newspaper coverage the endorsement received. On Saturday morning Hey hustled to WLIO TV to tape a reaction, claiming that the Women's Club didn't speak for all Democrats in the county. He tried one last time to raise the LaRouche connection, but by that time the television station had had enough of that line. The LaRouche charges never made it into Todd's broadcast response.[17]

In three days, thanks in large part to the endorsement by the Women's Club, we had stanched the hemorrhage in voter support for DEP. Over the weekend, as our candidates made one last push, contacting voters either by phone or in person, they noticed considerably less interest in the LaRouche issue. Our panic of a few days earlier diminished; the Women's Club had helped deflect the LaRouche issue, but would it be enough?

The primary was three days away.

· 6 ·

Taking Over

May 7, 1986

Locals sometimes called him "Doggie." A derisive nickname, never offered to his face, it implied the bulldog spirit of someone who would not back down from an opponent. That spirit was particularly evident on the day after the primary. Trounced seventy-nine to thirty in his own Central Committee race against Bluffton College professor Ray Hamman, Charlie Hauenstein was defiant. "I was defeated," he insisted, "because I live in a precinct where there are predominantly college professors, and I was running against a college professor."[1] In Charlie's eyes, it was a symbolic defeat only—not a loss of power. Citing support from over a hundred newly elected Central Committee reps, he declared, "We'd still be about 40 precincts ahead . . . if the [reorganization] election was held today."

I saw things differently. "We did real well," I told the *Lima News*. "We took half of the precinct races that were contested, and I expect another twenty or so uncommitted committee members to join DEP. It's real close only if you count those [uncommitted] others as being against us." I underscored Hauenstein's defeat: "The voters in his neighborhood say, 'It's time to get him out. It's time for a change.' I expect Hauenstein's defeat will influence other party members to vote against reinstating him as chairman."[2]

That's what I was hoping. In truth, the outcome of the primary gave neither side an advantage. Although Steve Webb and I had both won our races and so kept our leadership team intact, and although DEP had established a good base from which to build additional support, victory was most uncertain. Party regulars had defeated our candidates forty-two to forty in head-to-head contests,[3] and when our Operations Committee met the night after the primary to analyze the results, the mood was somber. With John Hevener painstakingly guiding us through the precinct list, we classified each winning representative as "for Steve Webb" [and DEP], "leaning for," "leaning against," or "against."

Our worst-case scenario counted sixty-seven votes with Webb; when we added the "leaning for" votes, Webb had only eighty-seven votes, a slim majority if all 169 Central Committee members attended the reorganization meeting.

The campaign had moved to a different plane. Steve Webb, John Hevener, Pickle Felter, Rick Siferd, Cora Hamman, and I all knew how to command election campaigns, but none of us had experience in anything like the parliamentary tactics we had to exercise now. Success depended on personal persuasion, one-on-one lobbying of freshly elected Central Committee delegates. Our hens-and-chicks strategy would come into full play; we DEP hens would keep in touch with our freshly hatched Central Committee representatives and pilot them through the process.

The outcome was so uncertain that one slipup could send votes cascading one way or the other. Although we had made effective use of the media during the primary, when we were trying to persuade a mass following, the current phase required a more subtle approach, as I painfully discovered. Speaking to Lima's Breakfast Optimist Club on the morning after the primary, I handed Hauenstein ammunition that he would later use against us. The press report of that presentation was generally positive, carrying the headline "Angel Predicts Brighter Future for Allen Democratic Party," but the lead portrayed me as arrogantly optimistic: "William Angel believes the success of Democrats for an Effective Party should indicate to Allen County that 'the Democrats are more acceptable to the voters.'"[4] That offended the party's blue-collar core, implying that the old regime offered an unsavory image, and asserting a class-based charge that the wrong people—blue-collar workers—were leading the party.

My speech to the Optimists had emphasized positive themes, stressing that the county's demographics—with a large black population and a strong blue-collar element—should have allowed the Democrats greater success than it had achieved, and that as party chairman I would work to unify all Democratic factions. But these ideas disappeared when I dove into matters of local political economy. Emphasizing the departure of "smokestack industry" and the pending arrival of high-tech businesses, I speculated that "Yuppie influence" would grow in the area. I even went so far as to cast myself as a representative of the leading edge, part of the "so-called Yuppie segment of the population."[5] By liberally sprinkling my presentation with the "Y-word"[6] and by stupidly offering an assessment of Lima's business climate better suited to a college lecture hall, I had dragged the issue of class into our confrontation with the old guard. I had allowed Hauenstein the chance to disparage DEP as a coven of smart-aleck Yuppies, out of touch with the needs of blue-collar Democrats.

That night at the Alpine, Steve Webb needled me about "all this 'Yuppie' stuff," a thin smile creasing his face. Embarrassed and suitably chastised, I could only shrug: "Yeah, that story didn't come out the way I wanted."

Still, there was truth behind my words. Although labor was a crucial partner in DEP's coalition, we were all offended by a party leadership that brazenly displayed "elitism in reverse," a fierce contempt for people, myself included, who fit the so-called Yuppie label—college trained, professionally minded, and intellectually sophisticated. Charlie Hauenstein had long dismissed our efforts as inconsequential, deriding us and our viewpoints whenever the opportunity arose. Still, my impolitic assessment of party affairs had jeopardized our chances of victory. My mistake lay in placing my ideas in the public realm, where Charlie could misrepresent and exploit them.

Outwitting Charlie Hauenstein would prove difficult. The Board of Elections hearing had taught us that. He could squeeze advantage out of any statute, and the more obscure the interpretation, the better. It was jokingly alleged that he kept a copy of Ohio's election code in his bathroom. Also, he was a master of the backroom maneuver; working with Todd Hey, who had eked out a victory in his own Central Committee race, Charlie could charm, cajole, and threaten wavering representatives into seeing things his way.

Consider what happened to Rochelle Twining. She was a candidate for the Ohio General Assembly, contesting a seat left open when the longtime Republican incumbent, Ben Rose, opted to run for state auditor. It was her first foray into electoral politics. Previously she had been president of the Ohio Abortion Rights Action League and had founded Crossroads Crisis Center, a shelter for battered women, where she served as executive director.

In addition to her candidacy for state representative, Rochelle was also running for Central Committeewoman on the DEP slate. Twining's unequivocal commitment to DEP made her a dangerous obstacle in Hauenstein's path, and he tried to bulldoze her aside. At the April 16 meeting of the Executive Committee—the one that endorsed a slate of Central Committee candidates and where Charlie and Todd raised the specter of Lyndon LaRouche—Hauenstein tried to push through an endorsement of Jeff Williams, who also was seeking the Democratic nomination for state representative. Hauenstein had no particular affection for Jeff Williams, but an endorsement of Williams alone, especially when issued on a sample ballot proclaiming a "LaRouche warning," would imply that Twining was a "LaRouchie." That, Charlie believed, would cinch her defeat.

However, Charlie's explanation for endorsing Williams was that Jeff had asked for the party's blessing and Rochelle had not. Hearing that, I rushed to a phone, contacted Rochelle at a meeting in the YWCA, explained what was about to happen, and secured her request for an endorsement. I then hustled back to the meeting, where Pickle Felter, Mary Hevener, and Bev McCoy were valiantly stalling the question, and declared that Rochelle also wanted the party's imprimatur. After additional procedural wrangling, in which Charlie tried to block Twining's request, he saw it was no use—a number of his own supporters were backing Rochelle for the state representative post—and allowed a vote endorsing both Williams and Twining.[7] They both appeared on the party's sample ballot; Twining would defeat Williams and capture the nomination, much to Charlie's chagrin.

Rochelle faced similar challenges in her contest for precinct committeewoman. That race ended in a tie, a circumstance that forced her to wait until May 17, when the final canvass of the votes would occur. If the tie held, a coin flip would decide the outcome. When Twining arrived at the board on the 17th, the clerks had already counted the votes in her precinct, and she was one vote short of her opponent. There would be no coin flip. She had lost—apparently.

But Bryan Hefner, who had been charged by DEP to observe the canvass, noticed a stack of ballots that didn't appear to be assigned to any precinct. "What about them ballots?" Bryan inquired, pointing to the strays. "Maybe there's a vote in there for Rochelle." Sure enough. Somehow a Central Committee ballot cast for Rochelle Dennis Twining had migrated to this orphan stack. No one inquired how it had happened. The vote was simply recorded for Twining, and her race was tied once again. She won the coin flip, and three days later the Board of Elections certified her as the new Central Committeewoman for her precinct.[8]

Shortly after this incident, Charlie Hauenstein summoned Twining's team—Twining herself, campaign manager Roger Rankin, and treasurer Tony Geiger—to a tête-à-tête at party headquarters. Todd Hey was there, as was Paul Prater. But Charlie, bellicose and bitter, did most of the talking. He made a point of disparaging Steve Webb and me personally, declaring Webb "incompetent" and calling me a "liar." We had no chance to unseat him, he boasted, telling Rochelle and her band that Hey had enough Central Committee votes to win handily and reminding Rochelle that she would need him in fall. "So, I wouldn't show up at that meeting if I were you."

Twining started to object, but Hauenstein interrupted, accusing her of being a friend of Bill Angel's. Her Central Committee petition had been in the pile that DEP had filed, he noted—that had been a mistake, and it would be a bigger mistake if she attended the reorganization meeting. Then came the threat. He and his allies had been too nice in 1982, when they hadn't punished those who had

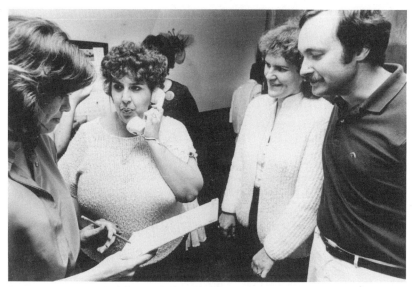

State representative candidate Rochelle Twining on the phone, receiving results from the May 1986 primary. Campaign volunteers Shelby Golden (with pad and pencil), Kathy Reeves, and Randy Reeves are listening in. *Lima News* photo from the collection of the Allen County Historical Society.

challenged their hold on the party; this time, he warned, it would be different: "Heads will roll, and any friend of Bill Angel's will be a dead Democrat."[9]

Twining and her pals flinched but didn't take fright. "Look, Charlie," one of her friends said, "All we want to do is run the campaign and win the election. We're not necessarily friends of Bill Angel."[10] Charlie didn't accept their protests. He wanted Twining to back down completely, and he persisted in trying to browbeat her into deserting us. No simple skirmish, this was a high-stakes confrontation between two strong-willed politicians.

Hauenstein wanted to dispirit the opposition, divide his enemies, and intimidate an important foe. But in Rochelle Twining he picked the wrong person. That spring, Twining was perhaps the most visible Democratic candidate in Allen County. She had won a hotly contested primary and had an excellent opportunity to win in November. Among local Democrats she had charisma; her voice mattered. It mattered a lot that without hesitation she had thrown her support to DEP. If Rochelle Twining believed a change in leadership was necessary, then it must be so, reasoned the Democratic rank and file. Wherever Central Committee representatives wavered in this battle for power in the Allen County Democratic Party, they would waver in DEP's direction as long as Rochelle stuck with us.

In the end, Twining's grit overwhelmed the Hauenstein bunch. After almost an hour of relentless badgering, in which Charlie and the others hurled invectives about me and Steve Webb, trying their best to intimidate Rochelle and her comrades, Twining remained undaunted. "I hear what you guys are saying," she announced before leaving, "but I still plan to go to that meeting."[11] When Rochelle Twining strode out of party headquarters that day, she left Charlie and his team to defend a losing cause, though no one, except perhaps Charlie Hauenstein himself, realized it.

In the days following Charlie's rhetorical brawl with Rochelle Twining, the hollowness of his chairmanship began to show. He still managed the calendar, however, and while none of us expected him to be forthcoming as to when exactly the reorganization meeting would occur, we grew anxious as the end of May approached without an announcement. In truth, he didn't have the votes—so much for the easy victory he had proclaimed in the showdown with Rochelle—and he needed more time to squeeze support from the Central Committee. He finally scheduled the meeting for the UAW hall on June 9, a date beyond the legally prescribed window for reorganization. We briefly considered calling our own session, within the legal time limit, but we quickly dropped that goofy idea and made ready for the June 9 encounter.[12]

Central Committee members soon found themselves caught in a crossfire of letters imploring them to support one side or the other. Hey and Webb began the exchange, listing their accomplishments and plans for the future of the party. Hey's letter was caustic; it accused Webb and me of spreading "outright lies" about party leaders, and it bragged about the most ordinary achievements, such as the circulating petitions for candidates, erecting yard signs, and maintaining a tent at the county fair. In contrast, Webb's message was positive and forward-looking; it stressed the intention to rebuild the grassroots base in the party and promised to maintain a party that would be open to all Democrats, even our opponents.[13]

But no other letter compared to the one Charlie Hauenstein wrote. "We have tried to keep the party 'out of' and 'above the dissent' created for the evening news, by a small group bent on recreating the Allen County Democrat Party in the 'YUPPIE' image," he declared in his opening, casting the entire message as a matter of "us against them." Besieged were the faithful, blue-collar Democrats who in the 1970s had seized the party from a cohort of lawyers and had put Charlie and Todd in charge. The party was threatened by a band of young upstarts—intellectual elitists, scions of the lawyers, and self-absorbed Yuppies—who were trying to take it away from its rightful owners.[14]

"Where were these people," Hauenstein bristled, "during the Rhoades [*sic*] years. . . ?" In his view, his opponents were a selfish bunch who only wanted to take over the party now that Ohio had a Democratic governor. These challengers had been miserly in their support of the party, whereas he had donated "$50,000 out of [his] own pocket" and Todd Hey another "$46,000" in 1984 alone.

Furthermore, the upstarts had orchestrated "Dirty Tricks" against fellow Democrats and party leaders, including "an attempt to get one committeewoman [Ebescotte] fired from her job, stories leaked to the F.B.I. that the Party was selling jobs, [and] a bribe offer made by a member of the DEP to two Executive Committee Members." He also brought up the protest hearing: "THE DEP filed charges with the Allen County Board of Elections against seven loyal Democrats (including Todd Hey) that could have brought them a fine and six months in jail." Hauenstein went on the warn, "These people have done little or nothing to ever help the Allen County Democrat Party, but they need YOU and YOUR VOTE to get control."[15]

On it went. Hauenstein singled out DEP activists for personal attacks like this one: "Sometimes we do get some thanks, as in this letter I received after the '84 election. It said in part, 'I am grateful for your help. . . . [W]e fought the good fight, but events—namely, the magnitude of the tax issue, the Republican media blitz, and the impact of the Reagan landslide—simply overwhelmed us. Again, I am grateful for your help and take pleasure in having . . . worked with you over the past few weeks.' And that letter is signed 'Best Regards' and 'Many Thanks! *Bill Angel*.'"[16] Indeed, I had sent this letter to Charlie, as a simple matter of courtesy following the Maurer campaign. Little did I know that he would throw the letter in my face with the caustic observation, "Seems that now Mr. Angel has forgotten about the 'HELP,' the 'GOOD FIGHT' and why our candidates lost. Now he wants to blame his losses on the Democrat Executive Committee."

Despite Hauenstein's bravado and sarcasm, though, he was in trouble, and he knew it. A bunker mentality reveals itself in the letter's conclusion: "THE PARTY HAS TRIED TO WORK WITH THEM [DEP], BUT THEY WANT TO CONTROL THE PARTY AND WILL SETTLE FOR NOTHING LESS. PLEASE DON'T GIVE AWAY THE PARTY THAT SO MANY HAVE WORKED SO HARD TO PROTECT. SUPPORT TODD HEY FOR CENTRAL COMMITTEE CHAIRMAN."[17] Charlie Hauenstein was afraid. Power was slipping away, and he could not understand why. In this remarkable letter, we find a man who truly believes he has done a noble job commanding the party. Feeling betrayed by rivals and ambitious adversaries, Charlie Hauenstein postures as "a man more sin'd against than sinning." In his eyes, he had sustained the party through hard times, managed elections effectively during two Reagan landslides, helped elect a Democratic governor, and had been generous in his financial support. But those achievements were not enough to satisfy malcontents who had done nothing except deny him the respect he thought he deserved.

Charlie Hauenstein had simply misunderstood the function of party leadership. Leadership meant more than filling patronage jobs, donating money to flagging campaigns, and "fighting the good fight." It was about making people feel involved and welcome in party circles. Hauenstein's cliquish style, in which only he and a few trusted lieutenants made decisions, was the real problem, a fact that he could neither accept nor understand.[18] Like Lear, Hauenstein was blind to the source of the fury that he had brought on himself.

However, Charlie's letter did rattle DEP's ranks, causing Linda Coplen and Steve Webb to piece together a response endorsing Webb and me for leadership of the party. It would be signed by Tim Hamman, Paul Rizor, John Coplen, and Mel Woodard—all former Democratic candidates.[19] It scathingly proclaimed, "It is shameful that the current leadership is unable to recognize the efforts and loyalty of *STEVE WEBB* and *BILL ANGEL* and feel that it is necessary to resort to excuses and 'pointing the finger' at someone else." The candidates further stressed the need for "*aggressive* and *effective* leadership" to "lead Democrats to success in the future."[20] But symbolism was more important than substance: The simple fact that the letter was signed by former Democratic candidates sent the unmistakable message that it was time to for the party to select new leaders.

Todd Hey fired off a last-minute rebuttal, accusing DEP of "pointing the finger" at him and Hauenstein; we let him have the last word.[21] We had a meeting to prepare for, and thanks to Pickle Felter, we knew exactly what to expect.

Two years earlier, June 1984

Lima's UAW hall was nearly empty. Most of the party's Central Committee members had filed out, having fulfilled their only official function—and obligation—that is, returning Charlie Hauenstein and Todd Hey to another term at the helm of the Allen County Democratic Party. Todd and Charlie were hanging around, accepting congratulations from their cronies, hearing pleas for appointment to jobs on the state highway crew, handicapping Fritz Mondale's presidential bid, and assessing the impact that campaign would have on local races. They were busy men, too busy to notice Pickle Felter sauntering toward the front of the meeting hall, where only a half-hour earlier Todd Hey had called this biannual ritual to order. At that time, Pickle had observed Todd shuffling through some documents before turning the gavel over to Paul Prater, the meeting's temporary chair. Hey had left the papers on the podium, never bothering to retrieve them, and Pickle was curious, wanting to know what was in them.

Now Pickle was at the podium. He looked up and saw a crowd of men talking intensely, Todd and Charlie at their center. Glancing down at the documents, Pickle saw Todd's scrawl—the order of business for the upcoming reorganization meeting, and important reminders on how to conduct it. He looked up again. Todd, Charlie, and others still hadn't seen him. He snatched the papers and casually stuffed them into his hip pocket. He ambled toward the exit, waving at the circle of men as he passed. They barely noticed. By the time he hit the parking lot, Pickle Felter was grinning broadly.[22]

June 8, 1986, American Federation of State County and Municipal Employees office, Lima

"If I have to, I'll march up to that sum bitch and rip that gavel right out of his hands," one of DEP's "Jedis" announced. A chorus of yells encouraged more bravado. Final tactics were being set. We had convinced ourselves that Charlie Hauenstein and Todd Hey would never conduct a fair meeting, that they would bend the rules to make sure the party's leadership would stay in their hands. We carried the wounds they had inflicted in their effort to smear us as followers of Lyndon LaRouche, and the scars left by their letters, with their corrosive allegations, were still raw. Our blood was up.

Furthermore, we now had Todd Hey's notes; for all we knew, he never missed them. After Todd called the meeting to order, he would appoint Paul Prater as temporary chair. Nominations and voting would follow. We decided to launch a "sneak attack" at the moment Todd attempted to appoint Prater, showing our mettle early in the proceedings. By challenging Todd's right to appoint a temporary chair, we reasoned, we would unsettle him and seize the gavel (and control of the meeting) before he knew what happened.[23] The plan would unfold as follows:

- Rick Siferd would start the play, jumping to his feet and shouting, "Point of order! Point of order!"
- Siferd would then move that the committee—not Todd—choose the temporary chair, John Dornick seconding.
- If Todd ruled against this motion (which was likely), Dornick would offer a motion challenging the ruling of the chair.

We agreed that Dornick's motion would have to be decided by secret ballot. If we lost this vote, we would probably lose the critical vote for Central Committee chair.

All of this was terribly complicated, of course, and it was made even more complex by the fact that the strategy was being set by a coterie of DEP insiders. The rest of DEP's followers would come to the meeting not knowing what to expect; we risked baffling them by excessive wrestling over procedure. When we challenged Todd on the question of the temporary chairman, would they know how to vote? How would they respond to other protests that might occur?

"Ping pong paddles," someone suggested. "We'll bring ping pong paddles labeled 'YES' and 'NO.' Then when the time comes, those of us who know what's goin' on will hold up the correct paddle, instructing our folks how to vote." While some of us obsessed over additional scenarios and responses, others set to work locating and labeling ping pong paddles. We were overprepared. Having exercised ourselves into a lather, we had readied ourselves for a "railroaded" meeting—and when the train did not arrive, we stuck to our plan anyway.

On June 9, Charlie and several of the old guard met us in the lobby of the UAW hall, checking identification cards and handing out credentials. At promptly 7 P.M., Hey ordered the doors to the cavernous hall shut. The meeting began first with the Pledge of Allegiance and then with Todd's scripted attempt to appoint Prater as temporary chairman. Rick Siferd duly sprang to his feet; "Point of order, Mr. Chairman! How will this meeting be conducted?"[24] A bewildered Hey replied, "Mr. Siferd, we will have a secret ballot, and I will appoint a temporary secretary and a temporary chairman. We will get on with the business of this meeting, which is to elect a permanent chairman."

"Point of order!" Siferd cried. "The Constitution and By-Laws state the Central Committee will elect . . ."

Hey wouldn't let him finish: "Out of order! Please sit down so we can get on with the meeting. At this time, I appoint Carol Falk temporary secretary."

But Siferd was relentless: "Point of order! Don't we already have a secretary? Why do you have to appoint one?"

"Yes, we do. Mary Finn," retorted Hey, innocently. "Mary, will you please come forward?"

Mary Finn was an elderly, well-respected Democrat, a former clerk at the Board of Elections and the *grande dame* of the Allen County Democratic Party. She was also hard of hearing and could not understand Todd's question or what was expected of her. She was totally confused as Carol Falk and Bill Johns escorted her to the podium. Bent and looking extremely frail, she drew sympathy for the regulars as she took her place beside Todd Hey; Siferd looked like a mean whippersnapper picking on an old lady.

But even as Finn made her way to the stage, Rick remained on his feet, proclaiming, "At this time, I move we have secret ballot." John Dornick pounced on his cue: "I second the motion!"

"Out of order!" Hey ruled.

A boiling Siferd shouted, "Listen, I made a motion, and it's been seconded. So, let's vote on it! If you don't call for a vote and run this meeting according to Roberts Rules, we'll ask you to step down. And if you don't do so, we'll remove you *by force* if we have to." At this, Hey's supporters leaped to their feet, shouting, "Boo! Boo! Shaddup! Make 'em sit down, Todd! Git on with the meetin'! Make 'em sit down!"

Hey tried to shout above the din, "Your motion is out of order! This meeting is going to be fair. We are going to have a secret ballot. We're going to do this the democratic way. I'm going to appoint Paul Prater temporary chairman and Carol Falk temporary secretary."

With this, the small-framed Siferd embarked on a course that none of us had forecast. He marched toward the stage and bounded onto the platform like a welterweight fighter entering the ring, shouting as he made his way: "Since you won't run this meeting according to Roberts Rules, I have no choice but to take over." He was clearly freelancing. Then with one athletic move he elbowed the much taller Hey aside, grabbed the podium with both hands, and addressed the meeting: "All in favor of the motion, please stand." Half the house stood, a few waving ping-pong paddles marked "YES," most looking dazed and confused; the rest shouted epithets at Siferd.

By this time, Paul Prater and Otha Harris, two thick-bodied men who had followed Siferd to the stand, had jerked Rick from the microphone as if he were a turkey wishbone at Thanksgiving. Todd, having regained the microphone and a bit of composure, proclaimed, "I have been threatened by force! Will somebody please get the deputy sheriff standing outside? We're going to run an orderly meeting, and I'll not put up with these threats."

A *Three Stooges* farce was unreeling. Steve Webb leaped to the stage in an attempt to rescue Siferd, tugging at Rick and simultaneously trying to cajole Harris and Prater into releasing him. Then the deputy arrived. He called the men over, and they all sheepishly assured him that Todd was in no danger, that the meeting would continue. Assessing the chaos, which had begun to simmer down, the officer shrugged, then muttered, "Damned Democrats," before returning to his post outside the door.

Hey continued the meeting, once again declaring, "I appoint Paul Prater temporary chairman, and Carol Falk temporary secretary." Prater took his place at the podium and Falk at the table beside him. Mary Finn had somehow escaped in the confusion. I moved to the stage, beckoned Siferd and Webb to the apron, and said, "Let's sit down."

"You're going to roll over?" Siferd asked.

"Let's say, I think it's better we let them run the meeting."

Siferd, Webb, and I returned to our seats while Paul Prater began conducting the meeting. Once Hey and Webb had been nominated, Prater asked the nominees to appoint one teller each, and he selected one himself.

"Do you want me to fight this?" Siferd appealed, seeing that their tellers outnumbered ours two to one, wanting to climb back into the ring for one more round.

"No. Let's get on with it," I replied.

Within thirty minutes, all 146 electors attending the meeting had voted, but not without one final incident involving Rick Siferd. As Rick received his ballot and walked past the platform, he grabbed some papers he had left on the secretary's table moments before. Paul Prater challenged him, "What do you think you're doing? Stealing them notes?"

"Them's *my* notes," Siferd shouted, brashly, defiantly.

"Todd, did you have any notes here?" Prater asked.

"No," Hey said, "They're probably his." With that Siferd stalked to the voting booth, notes and ballot in hand.

Once the ballots were cast, committee members and hangers-on mingled in the parking lot, smoking, talking quietly, waiting. When they were called back inside, the normally swarthy Paul Prater was ashen as he read the tally: sixty-seven votes for Todd Hey, seventy-nine for Steve Webb. Whoops and curses followed. Hey quickly abandoned the hall, accepting condolences from the party faithful who had stuck with him. Charlie disappeared, too, leaving only a few of the old guard to observe the final stages of the reorganization. The last act took only ten minutes. Webb, now the freshly elected Central Committee chairman, appointed a preselected panel, which caucused briefly to appoint a similarly preselected Executive Committee. When the names were announced and this new group assembled, Webb opened the floor to nominations for party chairman. Cora Hamman, rose to her feet, a smile brimming her face: "I nominate Bill Angel." There were no other nominations. By acclamation, I was elected the new chairman of the Allen County Democratic Party.

We had done it.

It had been a collective decision. Individual contributions had been significant, to be sure, but in the end the party, working through a democratically elected

Central Committee, had determined that it was time for new leadership. Charlie Hauenstein and the old guard had lost.

The price of democracy is knowing failure. Politicians who hold power are stewards over their communities, and when the time comes, through elections and other legal processes, their grip can be removed, their stewardship entrusted to others. Losing is as an important part of democracy as is winning.

Even more important is the tension between democracy's winners and losers. It drives our politics. A sincere democracy has no guillotine, no gulag. Losers can regroup. Winners can never be secure in victory. I learned this lesson within twelve hours of our victory celebration. On June 10, I phoned Jim Ruvulo to report the news, but he had already heard. Todd Hey and his wife had appeared in Ruvulo's office at eight that morning, begging to retain Hey's license bureau.

"What'd you tell him?" I asked, incredulous that Hey would make a two-hour, early morning drive to Columbus. Ruvulo had assured Todd that he was not making any changes in any license bureaus. Ruvulo was the middleman, the link to the governor's office on matters of patronage, and citing the governor's reelection fight, he stated that he was not about to put the election at risk because of Allen County's intraparty feud. Todd would keep his agency.

I tried to object, "I was hoping we'd have some say in this mat . . ." Ruvulo interrupted with the promise that he would consider a change in Todd's license bureau in 1987, "after the election." He pledged to support such a move at that time if we wanted to give the agency to someone else.[25] With that, he concluded the conversation and extended congratulations for our "well-deserved" victory.

Yes, we deserved to win, but apparently some still needed convincing, including folks closer to home. On the night of our victory, I had noticed Carol Falk lingering to watch the transition to new leadership. A pretty and gentle woman, Carol had loyally served as party secretary under Charlie. I liked her, as did most of my fellow DEP-ers, and so, swelled with pride and feeling magnanimous, I approached her as she turned to leave. "Carol, I'd like to appoint you to the Executive Committee. Will you join us?" I asked.

"No," she responded, somewhat angry, her eyes welling with tears. "I have some grieving to do first." Many of the regulars—Paul Prater, Bill Johns, Otha Harris, among others—felt the same way, but their male egos would not let them display Falk's emotion. They offered polite handshakes to Webb and me, but their eyes conveyed resentment and a touch of arrogance. It would not be an easy transition.

The coming weeks underlined the rancor that would cloud our party's future.

In midsummer, for example, Sherrod Brown passed through Lima, scheduling a stop at the Allen County Board of Elections to meet with the media and tout voter registration. Webb and I both attended this event, which turned out to be our first encounter with Charlie Hauenstein and Paul Prater since the takeover of June 9. Before Brown arrived, we stood on one side of the lobby in the board's office, while Hauenstein, Prater, and the Democratic clerks, fidgeted on the other side. Webb unsuccessfully tried to banter with Prater while Bob Holmes, Charles Rossfeld, and the Republican clerks hung in the background, watching this "dance of the enemies." Everybody wanted the event to pass quickly.

Brown, arriving a few, painful minutes late for the 1 P.M. news conference, greeted me warmly. "Mr. Chairman," he said. As he turned to Hauenstein's group, Paul Prater grasped him around the shoulder and muttered, loud enough for me to hear, "Don't pay no attention to them guys. They won't be around long."

But on the evening of June 9, 1986, we were unconcerned about resentments and hurt feelings. We had won. There was celebrating to be done . . . and a present to open, neatly wrapped and handed to me by Janet Quinn, who over two years before had kindly informed me about "the power of the chair." It was a slim package but hefty, and as I removed the ribbon and foil, I found a gavel, its brass band inscribed: "Bill Angel, Chairman."

Part Two

Dead Rabbits

· 7 ·

Not Like the Old Bunch

June 11, 1986, The Alpine Village Restaurant
The meeting had turned ugly. I had already unbuttoned my collar, loosened my tie, and removed my jacket. Dick Hullinger, one of DEP's stalwarts, got up suddenly and lumbered toward the stairs leading to the Alpine's main floor. I followed, leaving Steve Webb temporarily in charge of the first session of our newly formed Executive Committee.

Hullinger looked disgusted, and though he had leg problems and walked with a cane, he seemed to have little trouble negotiating the stairs. As I neared him, I could hear him mutter, "No better than the old bunch."

"Hey, Dick, thanks for coming," I said, hoping he'd reveal the reason for his abrupt departure. He looked at me coldly, turned away, and continued his trek upstairs, grumbling, "Yeah, just like the old bunch."

Hullinger's exit signaled trouble. The previous evening, DEP's coordinating committee—Linda and John Coplen, Bryan Hefner, Pickle Felter, John Hevener, Janet Quinn, Tom Doyle, Steve Webb, and I—had met at Webb's house and laid plans for the upcoming campaign. Naively thinking we could roll the DEP structure into the party organization, we had selected a slate of members to supplement the Executive Committee.

The revelation tonight of this slate set off a firestorm. Several DEP members were upset that they had been left off. Others took exception to the seemingly secretive, high-handed nature of the meeting that had produced the list. "Who decided on this?" someone demanded.

Once I had finished naming the individuals who had produced the slate, everyone, it seemed, began talking at once, quietly at first and then louder, until I had to use my gavel to restore the meeting to some semblance of order. Of the nine members of the DEP coordinating committee, only five—Linda Coplen, Tom Doyle, Steve Webb, Bryan Hefner, and I—were Central Committee representatives who had been elected members of the Executive Committee. This

Governor Richard Celeste at Allen County Democratic fund-raiser, July 1985. *Lima News* photo from the collection of the Allen County Historical Society.

realization of this set off Rochelle Twining, who exclaimed, "I find it quite surprising that several people who are not even members of the Executive Committee have presented a list proposing new members to the Executive Committee."

The commotion got more tumultuous when I tried to defend the procedure. I argued that because this group had coordinated operations for DEP, it now should be trusted to serve in a similar capacity for the party. "No," was the emphatic response. "The party's officers ought to make these decisions, not a handpicked group of favorites," said one person. It was then, as these sentiments banjoed across the room, that Dick Hullinger quit the meeting in protest.

"I'm concerned about process," Twining stated, regaining the floor. She issued a stirring denunciation of the manner in which the slate had been constructed. "If we are to build a party that is better than the one Charlie Hauenstein led, then we must stick to process. Otherwise the effort of the past year will have meant nothing."

I beat a quick retreat and suggested that the current slate be replaced by a new one chosen by an Operations Committee consisting of current party officers and other officers the Executive Committee would elect. My suggestion was moved, seconded, and approved unanimously. Before adjourning we elected six vice chairs and scheduled for June 25 a meeting at which the additional members would be appointed and a committee structure established.[1]

A considerable portion of the anger that night arose more from jealousy than from dismay at questionable procedure. "Why were the Coplens involved?" grumbled one party activist, chagrined at not being made part of the "inner circle" that had shaped the list of new members. After the meeting, I heard similar protests about who had been included on the slate and who had been omitted—"too many labor representatives," "too many blacks," "not enough women."

But this bickering foreshadowed deeper and more fundamental challenges. Circumstances had changed. What had been the DEP coalition had shifted focus. I was no longer leading an alliance of Democrats committed to a single cause—the overthrow of Charlie Hauenstein—but leading an organization with a considerably more complex purpose, which included mobilizing activists whose motives and expectations were agonizingly diverse. I had won my chairmanship by dividing the party, and now I had to heal the split, create consensus, and mold an organization that could challenge Republican hegemony in the county. A tough road lay ahead.

An important lesson emerged from that chaotic meeting of June 11: Process was vital, especially if we were to live up to DEP's promise of becoming a more effective party. None of us who had met at Steve Webb's house the previous night had been driven by venal motives, but our decision—to assume the power to nominate members to the Executive Committee—had been nonetheless arbitrary, autocratic, and arrogant. Rochelle Twining provided a strong reminder of who we were and why the "New Allen County Democratic Party" was different from the one "the old bunch" had administered.

Steve Webb was not happy when I broke the news about Todd Hey's meeting with Jim Ruvulo. "The one thing I wanted out of all this was that license bureau. That damn Todd! Sneakin' behind our backs like that," he responded. I tried to assuage Steve with Ruvulo's commitment to support a change in the agency in 1987. "He'd better," Webb replied tersely.[2]

I had expected Webb to be disappointed with Ruvulo's decision, but I was taken aback by Steve's admission that his motive for contributing to the takeover had been the crass desire for Todd's license bureau. But then, it was no accident that Webb's best friend in the party was John Coplen, who had an advisory relationship with him, not unlike John Hevener's with me. For both Webb and Coplen, politics was a process driven by self-interest, and while they may have humored my ideals of good government and a better community, these were clearly secondary concerns.

During the DEP campaign, I had promoted the idea that Webb and I would become a leadership team, joint managers of the party. I recall Janet Quinn saying to me shortly after our takeover, "It's a nice idea but it won't work. You're too different, you and Steve. And if you don't watch it, he'll take over completely."[3] Now, I began to understand the truth in Quinn's assessment. Webb's attitude toward party politics was not much different from Charlie Hauenstein's or Todd Hey's. Consequently, the leadership-team idea, while a noble concept, simply would not function. Webb and I held different visions of the party's future, spoke with different voices, echoed different ideals. There would be a split message unless one of us took charge.

In the coming weeks, I would confront petty challenges to my status; apparently some Democrats believed they could jostle me aside. For instance, John and Linda Coplen tried to minimize my role in the "ox roast," the party's fall fund-raiser and campaign rally, which had been scheduled for October, with Senator John Glenn as our guest speaker. The Coplens, who were jointly coordinating the event, wanted an emcee, someone like attorney Mike Bender, to host it, which would relegate me to a minor role—introducing Sherrod Brown, who would in turn introduce Senator Glenn.[4] I brusquely rejected this suggestion; I was the party chairman, and I would serve as emcee. Jan Quinn, Mary Hevener, Elsie Crowe, and other members of the Democratic Women's Club (which was cosponsoring the event) got wind of the Coplens' scheme and raised hell with Linda, forcing her to relent.[5] I hosted the ox roast, but the relationship between the Coplens and me would never be the same. When it came to the question of who would exert power in the party, they did not exactly share my interests.

My relationship with Steve Webb was more important, however, and I did my best to placate him on the matter of Todd Hey's license bureau. Webb and I together visited Jim Ruvulo to try to talk him into awarding the agency to Steve, but Ruvulo was adamant. He had to be. To support a change in Allen County would force him to make changes in bureaus throughout the state, something he simply did not want to do—not then, not in a campaign year. After the election he would support such a move, and Steve Webb heard him say so.

Webb and I also had a tête-à-tête with Todd Hey. It occurred in a dark corner of the Alpine during the first week after the takeover. Hey was accompanied by his wife, Judy, and John Hevener sat in, at my request. I admonished Hey for beating a path to Ruvulo's doorstep on the morning after the reorganization meeting and for interfering with a decision that belonged to me. Hey responded simply that he had done what he had had to do, and he pledged to continue his financial support for the party and its candidates. He also made the somewhat amazing announcement that he was through with politics. "I'm glad the job is yours now," he said, stirring his drink, his eyes darting to Judy Hey, who sat impassively, her eyes flat, betraying neither emotion nor surprise at this assertion. I asked Todd to write a letter to all Central Committee members, expressing his support for the party's new leaders and urging Democrats to get behind the party's candidates for the fall campaign. He agreed—although the letter, when it was finally sent, was a lukewarm endorsement at best.[6]

It was an unnerving scene—Webb, Hevener, and I sitting in a restaurant with Todd and Judy Hey. We didn't trust them; they didn't trust us. Hey was trying to strike a bargain: Allow him to keep the license bureau, and he would not challenge my leadership in 1988. In the meantime, he would continue to send money to the party, to show good faith. This was not a deal I was willing to consider.[7]

As it turned out, Jim Ruvulo saved me a few headaches by allowing Hey to keep his license bureau. For one thing, as long as Hey felt he had a chance to retain the agency, he would continue to send his monthly allotment, and the party desperately needed the revenue. The treasury was nearly empty, and the party was over five thousand dollars in arrears in its monthly assessment to the Ohio Democratic Party.[8] The thousand-dollar check that came regularly from Todd Hey was essential to restoring the party's finances and to paying down that debt.

Furthermore, any change in Hey's license bureau would have been messy business. During the first week of my chairmanship, I received a half-dozen requests for Todd's agency, most from DEP activists, all of whom felt they deserved this patronage plum more than anybody else did.[9] In addition, I still had hope of reconciling Hey's supporters. They would have been offended by an immediate decision to give his bureau to Steve Webb. Todd would have been martyred, and his allies would have said, "See, told ya" and turned away from partisan activity during the fall campaign, at a time when we needed all the help we could muster.

Finally, with Ruvulo's commitment to support a change in bureau ownership, Steve Webb had every incentive to work hard for the party and its candidates. Further, he would be unlikely to try to shove me aside as long as he knew my word was necessary to pass Todd's bureau to him. My relationship with Webb would become strained over the next few months, even adversarial at times, but I now had the leverage to keep command of the party. The awarding of Hey's license bureau was one patronage decision I would protect judiciously.

Other patronage choices were more aggravating and time consuming. Early on the morning of June 16, one week to the day after I had assumed the chairmanship, I received a call from Jim Ruen, associate administrator of District One of the Ohio Department of Transportation (ODOT). Ruen's responsibilities included patronage appointments in the district, and he wanted an afternoon appointment—though, curiously, he insisted on meeting me at my office on the OSU/Lima Campus. "Feelings are still running pretty strong here about your beating Charlie," he said.

Ruen wanted to discuss a full-time position that two of ODOT's summer workers were trying to secure. One was Susan Ward, whose mother, Pearl Ward, was an old guard Central Committeewoman who had lost her seat in the May primary. Susan's father, Dick, was a UAW friend of Charlie Hauenstein (and would later become president of the Ford local). The other candidate was Chris Burden, a student of John Hevener's who had earned her summer job with John's and Mary's recommendation. According to George Fetter, one of my supporters who worked in the State Highway Garage, "Chrissie" was the better choice, a harder worker and more deserving of the appointment. Even so, I'd already made up my mind to select Susan Ward. It seemed an appropriate way to improve my relationship with the UAW and repair the breach that DEP's takeover had created with organized labor. But I did not want to let either woman know of my decision until I'd conferred with Jim Ruen.

As it turned out, the decision had been removed from my hands. According to Ruen, Dick Ward had "called Columbus" and insisted on his daughter's appointment. "So," Ruen said, "it looks like we have to go with Sue Ward as a 'Columbus appointment.'" I asked Ruen what "calling Columbus" meant; he was evasive, but then, Jim Ruen always talked around issues, in a way that made him appear deliberately inarticulate. When I pressed him further, he speculated that perhaps Dick Ward had called ODOT's headquarters directly or had contacted someone in the Ohio Democratic Party. "But it's a Columbus hire," he shrugged, washing his hands of the matter, "and there's not much I or you can do about it. If they say they want someone hired, that's it."

This was my first patronage decision, and someone had interfered with it. I was furious and immediately called Dannette Palmore, who handled patronage hires for the Ohio Democratic Party. She knew nothing about a call from Dick Ward; she checked with ODOT's main office, and no one there had received a call from him either. More than likely, the appointment did not represent a "Columbus hire" at all; Ruen had apparently been hiding the fact that Charlie Hauenstein had pulled one last string and had wangled a patronage gift on behalf of Susan Ward's mother and father.[10]

I had allowed myself to get sucked into the patronage game, at which Charlie excelled and in which I had little interest. It was a contest I could not win. I thought briefly about fighting the Ward appointment, thus risking further alienation from the UAW, but I ultimately went along with it. More importantly, I decided to distance myself from patronage responsibilities by delegating them to a Patronage Committee, chaired by John Hevener, with Steve Webb, Rochelle Twining, and Leonard Boddie serving as members.[11] Under John's leadership, this committee established a procedure for announcing job listings and receiving resumes: Job openings would be regularly announced at our monthly meetings, and resumes would be collected, filed, and professionally maintained.

Hevener was the perfect choice to head the group, because everyone trusted him. Furthermore, he would work to protect my interests on routine issues, keeping me alert to patronage appointments that were important enough to demand my attention and involvement. But John never grew comfortable with presiding over patronage decisions. He always began his reports to the Executive Committee with an awkward, almost embarrassed smile, tugging an overstuffed folder from his briefcase. Once Pickle Felter observed this ritual and wisecracked, "There goes the 'Sleaze King.'" Those who heard Pickle's irreverent quip chortled at such a moniker being attached to John Hevener. The Heveners chuckled, too; Mary teasingly responded, "Sleaze King? Well . . . okay, just as long as no one expects me to be the Sleaze *Queen*."

August 22, 1986, the Show Barn, Allen County Fair
"You wanna buy the reserve champion rabbits?" The question jerked me sideways toward Bryan Hefner, who wanted an answer immediately. He was chewing on a plug of tobacco and wearing bib overalls; a green-and-yellow John Deere cap, tilted upward, exposed gray, crew-cut stubble. "Rabbits?" I asked, not certain what I was getting into.

I had just walked into the Junior Fair Auction, where 4-Hers were selling their animal projects at highly inflated prices to boosters of the agricultural community. The party had allocated Bryan $350 to buy 4-H stock,[12] and he wanted the "okay" to raise the bid on the reserve champion rabbits—that is, a pen that had come in second to the "grand champions." The bid stood at ten dollars, and Bryan was requesting permission to boost it to $12.50.

I squinted toward the far end of the wood-chip-covered floor of the arena, and saw a pen with three fluffy, white, nose-wriggling bunnies. "$12.50 a rabbit?"

"Naw," Bryan muttered, then spat as if to punctuate his disgust at having to answer such a dumb question. "$12.50 a pound." The auctioneer, who noticed Bryan giving me a tutorial on livestock auctions, figured a higher bid was in the offing and extended his rapid-fire cadence: *"Gotta ten gimme $12.50—who gimme $12.50—gotta ten needa bidder gimme $12.50!"* Bryan persisted, "Bill, them's the reserve champions. We buy 'em and you can git yer picture took. You wanna git yer picture took?"

"My picture took? With the rabbits?"

"Yeah, you and them rabbits."

"Gotta ten dollar once!"

I looked at the rabbits again, trying to figure their combined weight without any experience to guide my judgment.

"You wanna buy 'em or not?" Bryan demanded.

"Ten dollar twice!"

I nodded to the "bid buyer," standing bemused in front of us.

"$12.50!" he yelled, twisting his body toward the auctioneer and simultaneously thrusting a fist upward into the barn-scented air of the show arena.

"$12.50 gimme fifteen who gimme fifteen!"

A farmer, sitting in the bleachers ringing the arena, had noticed the earnest discussion between me and Bryan. He grinned and snapped his program into the air, signaling a bid of fifteen dollars. He knew he wouldn't end up paying. Bryan really wanted those rabbits. The bid buyer returned. "Bill, you can have 'em for sixteen." I looked at Bryan, who was pleading, "You'll git yer picture took." I stared once more at the rabbits and nodded. The bunnies were ours, all fourteen pounds of them. I got my picture "took," too, accepting the reserve champion ribbon. I also received a bill for $225.60, almost the entire amount we had allocated for livestock purchases.

But Bryan wasn't finished. The next morning when I strolled toward the show arena where the large animals—hogs and steers—were being auctioned, a somewhat agitated Bryan Hefner grabbed me and asked, "Where ya' been? I coulda bought the reserve champion hog, but couldn't because you weren't here." Sensing trouble, I asked. "Did you buy any hogs?" Bryan hesitated, turned away, spat, and admitted, "Yep. Bought some pigs."

"How many did you buy?"

"Don't know. Gave one of 'em to the El Karan Grotto for their pig roast, you know, for them cerebral palsy kids." Bryan was scratching his chin and avoiding eye contact. "How much did you spend?" Bryan shook his head. "Don't know. But it's good for the party. Them 4-H kids need our help," he said, expressing our rationale for entering the Junior Fair Auction. It was good for the party to buy 4-H and FFA livestock, the argument ran; these purchases would get the Democratic Party's name mentioned and publicized in the farming community. As for "kids needing our help," Bryan Hefner liked to help people, and he believed the Democratic Party should help people too, especially fellow farmers and their families.

We entered the show arena where a consortium of buyers was being photographed grouped around the reserve champion steer. Collectively, they had paid over five dollars a pound for a 1,600-pound animal. It was too expensive for me, and I hung around with Bryan, just to make sure no further damage was inflicted to the party's treasury.

I failed. As we watched the steer auction proceed, Bryan fidgeted; he really wanted to enter the bidding. After a dozen or so steers had clumped through the arena, selling at prices ranging from eighty-five cents to a dollar per pound, Bryan lost his restraint. His hand shot up in a bid of eighty cents on a Hereford steer owned by a 4-H'er from Lafayette, Bryan's home community, east of Lima.

I fired him an incredulous look. Bryan spat and shook his head apologetically. "That kid's been through rough times. Had a huntin' accident last year," he said in a voice that sounded like loose gravel rolling across a sidewalk. "Don't worry. I'm just tryin' to bump the price, git him some more money." Almost immediately eighty-five cents countered our bid, and before I could stop him, Bryan thrust out his hand and pushed the price to ninety cents—and the bidding stopped. The Allen County Democratic Party had purchased a 1,500-pound steer for ninety cents per pound, and I had watched it happen.[13]

Total damage to the party for one steer, three rabbits, and—as it turned out—eight pigs was $1,745.40.[14] I was dismayed, but when I reported the amount to Steve Webb and Linda Coplen, they tried to put a positive face on the debacle, remarking on the beneficial publicity the party would receive among farmers. Several 4-H families did in fact commend the party for its largesse and even vowed to "vote Democrat" in November, but I knew the full value of commitments and commendations received in August, and they seldom added up to $1,700.

My tenure as county chair could be encapsulated in that morning I spent in the show arena, watching Bryan Hefner whip his hand into the air, offering money the party didn't have. I was physically present, but at times I felt more at the mercy of events than in charge of them. Outside forces seemed in charge; artifice and intrigue ruled. My chairmanship was less than three months old.

Still, our efforts at the Junior Fair had earned the party free passes to the carcass show, where the dressed-out flesh of all grand champion and reserve champion livestock was on display.[15] I urged all the party's candidates to attend and take advantage of the publicity our free-spending ways had won us. Rochelle Twining went and paid her "last respects" to our reserve champion rabbits. "They looked lovely in death," Twining quipped.

· 8 ·

Ice Skating in Hell

June 24, 1986

The phone rang. It was Cora Hamman, wanting to know if I had decided who would be Tony Celebreeze's local campaign chief. Running against light opposition for a second term as Ohio attorney general, Celebreeze was a shoo-in, and Cora very much wanted to coordinate his campaign in Allen County. Unfortunately for Cora, the Celebreeze committee did not want her—Pat Garrity, one of the attorney general's aides, had already told me as much—and I had already settled on Mike Bender to head up the county's Celebreeze effort. Cora had been pressing the issue for over a week, and now it was time for me to break the news.[1]

I did. As quickly as if she had already known my answer, Hamman launched into a diatribe:

"You've stabbed me in the back. . . .

"Mike Bender won't do the job. . . .

"I did all that work for you and this is the thanks I get. . . .

"The trouble with you, Bill, is you only like lawyers and college professors. . . .

"I know you want to get rid of me, and you just may. . . . I'm going to resign!"[2]

Click. She hung up.

We did not talk for two days. Cora even stayed away from an Executive Committee meeting, which was highly unusual for her; when I finally phoned just to see how she felt, she offered a backhanded apology for missing the meeting. "I just thought I might lose my temper and say something awful. That was the first time I hung up on anybody since I hung up on my first husband."[3]

I invited Cora to chair the Candidate Recruitment Committee. "You know, I'd be good at that," Cora replied cheerfully, accepting the appointment and suspending any talk of resignation. She was back in the fold.[4] This experience heralded a pattern in my relationship with Cora Hamman. I'd offend Cora; she'd blow up, threaten to resign, and hold out until she won recognition.

This time she won. Cora was now head of candidate recruitment—but few Democrats wanted to serve on her committee. I had to twist arms to get Leonard Boddie, Babette Mack, Steve Webb, Cathy DeLuca (one of Cora's DEP recruits), and Mike Bender to join up. Most folks in the party—women more than men, it seemed—were wary of Cora and her irascible temperament. Rochelle Twining and Janet Quinn, in particular, asked me point-blank if I had taken leave of my senses and warned me that I would regret putting Cora Hamman in charge of candidate recruitment. They were right, on both counts.

Recruiting candidates is normally not a top priority in the midsummer of a campaign, which is why I had given Cora this responsibility. But this was not a normal election year, and Cora Hamman threw herself into her seemingly benign new assignment with undisciplined verve.

She began by recruiting Leonard Pollack to run for state school board against Virginia Jacobs, the incumbent member from our district. It was a highly unusual move—local parties did not usually intervene in the nonpartisan elections for state school board. In addition, not only was Virginia Jacobs highly responsive to the needs of education and well respected by teachers, administrators, and board members, but she was a Democrat. At least, she had been until the May primary, when, according to Cora, she crossed party lines to vote in the Republican gubernatorial contest. This flip in partisan affiliation had offended Cora, who for that reason talked Pollack into mounting a futile campaign. He lost by over fifty thousand votes.[5]

More significant recruitment opportunities emerged, however. That spring, the Ohio General Assembly had created a new judgeship for the Third District Court of Appeals. There was no time for a partisan primary, the usual procedure for securing nominees.[6] Instead, all comers—Democrats and Republicans—were invited to run in an open race for the newly created seat, the winner being the candidate with the plurality of votes. Steve Shaw and Richard Rogers, who had both recently lost in the Republican primary for an established seat on the Court of Appeals, were in the race, as was Joe DaPore, a Republican attorney from Lima. With the Republican vote split three ways, I reasoned, a Democrat might be able to take the office. I did not entrust this recruitment task to Cora. It was too sensitive, and with the filing deadline only days away, I needed to move fast.

Eventually, Lima attorney Richard Meredith agreed to run. Meredith had solid roots in the Democratic Party; his father, Harry, had chaired the Central

Committee in the era before Charlie Hauenstein and Todd Hey. Meredith, who specialized in estate and tax law, was intrigued by the opportunity to serve on the appellate bench, which he regarded as more cerebral than the gritty work at the common pleas level. Also, he sensed as I did that he had a legitimate chance—a one-time shot—at taking the seat on the Court of Appeals.[7]

Recruiting a nominee for Court of Appeals was a mere preliminary, a sideshow, compared to the attempt to enlist yet another candidate. On August 11, Republican clerk of courts Herb Dunlap died, creating a vacancy that would be filled in the November election. We needed to find a nominee, but the county fair had just opened, and I was tied down with responsibilities there. I delegated the job to Cora and her committee, asking Steve Webb, who had a better working relationship with Cora than I did, to oversee the process.

Confusion set in immediately. On Monday, August 18, Webb mailed letters to Central Committee representatives, notifying them that the committee would gather at the Alpine on Thursday evening to nominate a clerk candidate. On Tuesday I phoned George Dunster, news director of WLIO TV, to apprise him of party activities at the fair, but Dunster was not interested in the fair. He wanted to know when we'd have a candidate for clerk of courts. I told him Thursday evening; he responded, "No, I don't think so. You have to have the nomination in before then."[8]

Dunster was right. We had until 4 P.M. on Thursday the 21st to file the name of our candidate, and unless we rescheduled that meeting Webb had called, the party would be unable to field a nominee at all. Temporarily stunned, I called Cora Hamman, who formed a telephone committee that contacted every Central Committee member, notifying them of the change of schedule for the meeting. In the meantime, I arranged with Joe Guagenti, owner of the Alpine, to have the room reservation shifted to Wednesday, the 20th. The scheduling crisis passed.

But how had we gotten so mixed up on the timing? Steve Webb, who originally checked with a clerk at the Board of Elections, had thought that the party had fifteen days, not ten, to report the name to the Board of Elections. He had either misunderstood the clerk, or the clerk had misspoken about deadlines. In any case, Steve had never bothered to check Ohio's Revised Code, nor did he seek advice from any of the party's lawyers. For that matter, neither had I.[9]

I had absorbed yet another lesson: As chairman, I could delegate the authority to accomplish an important task, but I could never distance myself totally from the effort; I would have to stay connected.

In the meantime, a new crisis unfolded as the party began recruiting a candidate for the clerk race. Cora had begun the process well enough, finding

Roger Brown—a local minister and career counselor who had won his Central Committee race as one of Cora's "Jedi" recruits—to carry the party banner. But then she focused on Brown as if he were only Democrat interested in running for clerk. Leonard Boddie had other ideas. He was associate pastor at Shiloh Missionary Baptist Church and director of Salvation Army's Community Center in Lima's south end, and like Cora, he had paid his dues. Not only had he convincingly won his own Central Committee seat, but he also had recruited several victorious DEP candidates, thus chipping into Otha Harris's strength in the minority neighborhoods. Now in a bid to flex his muscles in the African American community, he wanted the party to field a black candidate.

He floated two names. One was Mel Woodard, owner of an insurance agency and pastor of Lima's Second Baptist Church. He had run for county commissioner in 1984, recruited by Hauenstein and Hey in an effort to attract minority voters to the polls that fall. But 1984 had not been a Democratic year, and like the rest of the party's candidates, Mel had lost overwhelmingly, pulling only 31 percent of the vote.[10] However, I knew Woodard had aspirations of running again, and when I bumped into him at the county fair, I inquired about his interest in the clerk's spot. "I'd consider running," he said, "but only if the party could not find a respectable candidate."[11] It was a tepid commitment at best.

Boddie's other candidate was Jerry Pitts, a black attorney and an associate director of Allen County's Community Action Commission. I had my own history with Pitts. During the Steve Maurer campaign of 1984, he and I had become embroiled in a turf battle over who would head Maurer's effort in the minority wards. But that was old business. Besides, Jerry had been cordial to me during the early days of my chairmanship, facilitating a meeting between me and State Representative C. J. McLin when McLin's organization, the Black Elected Democrats of Ohio (BEDO), held a summer conference in Lima.[12] Though wary, I was not bothered by the prospect of a Pitts candidacy.

But Cora Hamman hated Jerry Pitts. The source of this animosity was never clear, although legend placed its origins in the 1982 gubernatorial primary, when both were working on behalf of Bill Brown's candidacy; Jerry, in Cora's view, had not pulled his weight in working the black precincts. Cora's feelings toward Pitts were so strong that when she heard he might want the nomination, she snarled, "We'll ice skate in Hell first."[13]

As Cora continued to badmouth Jerry, I grew concerned about how she would handle the screening process, especially if he materialized as a serious contender. My apprehension mounted when I entered the candidate-screening session, which Cora had scheduled for August 18. The first person I saw was

Edith Woodard, Mel's wife, sorting a batch of her husband's resumes. "I don't really know what's going on," she sighed. "Somebody called and told me to bring some of Mel's resumes to this meeting. Mel didn't say anything to me about running."

Roger Brown was there, too, ready to be interviewed, but Jerry Pitts was missing. Where was he? Cora had not bothered to invite him. "I thought Leonard would do that," Cora growled. "Why should I call?" Leonard snapped. "You're the chair of the committee. Are you saying I should call just because I'm black? That's bullshit!"[14]

The very first session of the Candidate Recruitment Committee had begun with Cora Hamman and Leonard Boddie bickering over who should have invited Jerry Pitts. They fussed for a few more minutes, then ceased their argument long enough for the committee to interview Roger Brown, who was fed a series of "softball" questions by Cora Hamman and Steve Webb. He would be a "respectable candidate," though he had little understanding of the responsibilities of a clerk of courts.

Then the focus returned to Pitts. Leonard objected that it was unfair for the committee to issue an endorsement without interviewing all the candidates. After some additional skirmishing, the committee agreed to interview Pitts on Wednesday evening, the same night the Central Committee would select the final candidate. At this point I relayed the news of my conversation with Mel Woodard, which the committee accepted on face value. That left Edith even more confused; if her husband wasn't interested in the nomination, why had she been invited to the meeting? Most of us were confused too.

After Woodard and Brown had departed, Hamman and Boddie resumed their quarrel. This time the argument centered on whether the committee had the authority to recommend a candidate to the Central Committee. Of course it did, Cora contended: The committee's mission was to recruit candidates, and that meant screening them and producing a recommendation for the party. Boddie took the opposite position: If two or three candidates wanted the nomination, the Candidate Recruitment Committee should confine its task to screening them and reporting the qualified names to the Central Committee, which would then make its own selection. "It would be unfair for this committee to make a recommendation," he insisted, "because the process had not been well organized." After a protracted and bitter argument in which Hamman and Boddie fired insults at one another, the committee postponed further deliberation until after the interview with Pitts. The session had ended in disarray two hours after it began.

It had been a disaster. The meeting had lacked direction and had been inattentive to procedural matters. Furthermore, it had been tainted by Cora's obvious favoritism toward Roger Brown and by her failure to invite Jerry Pitts—not to mention her openly expressed contempt for him. The nomination process appeared rigged, leaving the party open to charges of racial bias. I was distressed, as was Babette Mack of Spencerville, who left the meeting, muttering "Incompetent"—an apparent reference to Cora. Cora overheard this remark and was steamed, but not at Babette Mack. Instead, she vented her ire toward Leonard Boddie and Jerry Pitts, who together, in her view, had forced this embarrassing spectacle on her.[15]

I notified Jerry Pitts of the committee's desire to interview him. His response baffled me, adding more confusion to an already bewildering situation. "I told Leonard I would consider running, but only if the party could not find a qualified candidate," he said, taking a stance parallel to Mel Woodard's. Then striking a diplomatic pose, he continued, "I'll step aside—in the interest of harmony—since it appears that Mr. Brown will be a good candidate."[16]

On Wednesday night Pitts repeated this position to the Candidate Recruitment Committee in the Alpine's upstairs conference room. "I am not a candidate," he said, and he pledged to support Roger Brown. As he got up to leave, Cora Hamman reached across the table and offered her hand. Pitts paused before accepting it, as amazed at the gesture as the rest of us.

After Pitts' departure, Leonard Boddie took up the battle of two nights earlier. "I am grieved that process had not been handled properly," he said in a high-pitched yet superior-sounding voice. He asserted that race had divided the committee and that it would continue to be divisive force unless "we committed ourselves to treating each other fairly."

The recruitment committee had resolved two immediate concerns. It had recruited a candidate, Roger Brown, and it no longer had to worry about the procedural issue of whether it had the right to issue a recommendation in this case; Brown's lone candidacy made that question moot. But the group now found itself tangled in a philosophical debate over racial equity. With Central Committee members now filing into the Alpine, I tried to refocus discussion. I thanked Leonard for his comments, stressing that his concern about fairness was justified and stating that the committee would need to create procedures that would ensure evenhanded treatment of potential candidates.

But Boddie was not finished. Still smoldering, he steered discussion to Cora Hamman's conduct as committee's chair. "I had to raise these issues and speak out," he asserted. "Things were said about me and Mr. Pitts which I believe were unfortunate and ill tempered. I just believe we need to get these things settled."[17] Before Cora had a chance to respond, I stepped in, commending Boddie's forthrightness. "I want to build a coalition of white Democrats and black Democrats," I emphasized, "and we can't do that unless we speak freely and openly about problems we have with each other."

Cora, who had been relatively subdued, now apologized for having become so visibly angry about Jerry Pitts. "My Irish temper got the best of me. I tend to carry a grudge," she stated contritely. Others praised both Leonard and Cora, and before the meeting adjourned, I let Cora off the hook, reminding everyone that all committees make mistakes. I congratulated her for "shouldering the blame" for errors made in this situation and then extended a bit of praise: "When I discovered that we had to move the Central Committee meeting ahead twenty-four hours, the first person I called was Cora Hamman. She put together a phone committee and helped put this meeting together. I think we all owe her our thanks."[18]

Everyone applauded, relieved that important matters had been resolved, and then filed downstairs, where the Central Committee was waiting to nominate the Democratic candidate for clerk of courts. Roger Brown won by acclamation.

After Roger Brown was awarded the party's nomination, Boddie sought me out and thanked me for supporting him earlier that night. Cora Hamman was pleased too. As I issued my meeting-ending statement, complimenting her virtues, I had noticed Cora straighten in her chair, a smile crease her face, and her eyes brighten. She had won public affirmation of her work.

But Cora's and Leonard's battle said more about their similarities than their differences. Politics is about getting what you want, and Boddie and Hamman both wanted the same things—influence and status—and in this respect they each represented two disturbingly parallel but disparate strains within our party. Blending their energy into a positive force would be hard task.

Cora represented the party's hardscrabble side, and her approach to politics was much closer to Steve Webb's or John Coplen's than it was to mine. Consider another incident. Shortly after I had talked to Dick Meredith about becoming a candidate for the Court of Appeals, Cora pointedly let me know that she was circulating a petition for Joe DaPore. When I questioned her wisdom in doing that, she responded, "He gave me a lot of money for my husband's race and he's given money for Steve Maurer and Gary Hart."[19]

My mind was reeling. Here was Cora willfully passing a petition for a Republican shortly after she had worked like a dervish to find a Democrat to run against "Ginny" Jacobs for the state school board. But Cora saw no incongruity.

It was matter of pragmatism: DaPore had once helped her, and now she was doing a favor for him. When I continued to challenge Cora, reminding her that it was unseemly for someone of her status in the party hierarchy—she was a vice chair—to gather signatures for a Republican, she was nonplussed. It would be okay, she said; she would simply find someone else to sign the petition as its circulator.[20] Simple. An end-justifies-the-means solution.

At the Webb-Coplen-Hamman nexus, politics was a matter of confronting practicalities: When faced with a task, accomplish it, and don't concern yourself with long-term consequences or large, philosophical questions. People might be offended, but "they'll get over it," as a favorite expression of Steve Webb's went.

In the Roger Brown/Jerry Pitts episode, the controversy was not as much about race as about power and who would exercise it. Cora Hamman was no bigot, as Boddie had insinuated. She was simply indignant at Boddie's attempt to usurp her power. In this respect, Leonard's personality would prove as irksome as Cora's. He wanted to be the party's broker among black voters; he tried to play that role in the fight over the clerk-of-courts nomination. Although neither Mel Woodard nor Jerry Pitts was seriously interested in becoming a candidate, Leonard wanted to manipulate the party into accepting one of them. When Cora's quick recruitment of Roger Brown preempted that possibility, he stirred up racial animosities, playing on guilt among the party's white liberals, just to let us know that he was a politician to be treated seriously.

In this instance, Boddie made us dance to his tune, and brought racial tensions into his clash with Cora Hamman. Peeved by Cora's newly acquired status, he sought to undermine her authority by playing race like a poker chip, and in doing so he trivialized serious questions about racism. Like Cora, he was maneuvering for a higher spot in the party hierarchy, and he would manipulate and scheme until he got what he wanted. Only much later would I realize that there was nothing I could do to accommodate him.

The party worked hard in the minority precincts on election day, turning out over 70 percent of the registered voters in some southside neighborhoods.[21] Even so, our organization still displayed vestiges of its old-style, paternalistic relationship with Lima's African American voters. Witness, for instance, the postelection financial statement, which specified that a total of nine hundred dollars had been given to the "minority caucus" in three separate installments, each listed as "Get Out the Vote Expenses."[22]

The caucus, which consisted of all minority members of the party's Central and Executive Committees, was under the chairmanship of Leonard Boddie, who supervised the spending of funds. Under his direction, the organization registered new voters, canvassed black precincts, and secured workers to distribute ballots at targeted polling places. In September, however, I began picking up rumors that Boddie was discouraging minority volunteers from registering voters, reminding them that the party was paying workers to sign up new voters. But if paying registrars facilitated the enrollment of black voters, it did so at the cost of discouraging the party's own volunteers. Tommie Skipworth, a hardworking committeewoman from the Fifth Ward, candidly pointed out this problem. "Leonard said the party was going to pay people to do registration," she told me, "and I only wondered why I should be doing it for free when the party was going to pay people." As for herself, Skipworth continued to register voters, never once asking for compensation.[23]

The party's curious payments to the minority caucus looked, especially in the context of Skipworth's story, like street money. So be it. However, this was the last time during my tenure as party chairman that such an expenditure would occur. The whole idea of street money was tainted; it implied that somehow campaigns in black neighborhoods were different from those in white neighborhoods. It was one thing to provide food for volunteers and to reimburse them for actual campaign expenses, but it was quite another thing to pay "volunteers" to contribute their time. Such a practice opened the window for corruption and encouraged the condescending attitude that African Americans would work for their communities only if paid.

In a very short time, I had learned much about black politics in Lima, or at least I knew better now than to entrust the party's connection with the African American community to self-appointed and self-interested politicians. The controversy over the clerk-of-courts nomination had moved me toward a fuller appreciation of African American politics, but I still had a long way to travel. The party and black Democrats themselves would have to take responsibility for building their relationship.

· 9 ·

Not One of the Boys

August 16, 1986
The Allen County Fair parade launched the campaign, just as it always had, serving up an opportunity for candidates to meet voters and extract free publicity. Most office seekers were riding comfortably in convertibles plastered with campaign signs. But not Rochelle Twining. She rumbled down the parade route on a mule-drawn Conestoga, its canvas top trimmed with a "Twining for State Representative" banner. Unorthodox, yes, but the wagon drew attention to Twining's candidacy and separated her from the rest of the boys running for public office that fall, including her opponent, Bill Thompson.

Thompson's method of travel was equally distinctive. Hand in hand with his wife Kay, he walked the entire parade route, pulling their children in a red wagon bearing a hand-painted sign proclaiming, "Vote for our Dad." The conveyance might have been unconventional, but the image was straightforward— a nice family man taking a stroll through his community with his wife and kids. It starkly contrasted with the opinion many voters had begun to form of Rochelle Twining, a conviction represented by a "good ol' boy" who stared as her mules clopped by and muttered, "Not a chance, lady. Stay home and take care of your kids."[1]

In July, a delegation from Rochelle's committee, headed by David Berger and including Roger Rankin, Tony Geiger, and Rick Siferd, called on Steve Webb and me. With Berger and Siferd doing much of the talking, they argued that Rochelle's was the best organized, the most effectively financed, and the most articulate of the local Democratic campaigns. Then, declaring that Rochelle had the best chance of winning, they pitched a bold request—an eight-thousand-dollar contribution from the party to her campaign alone.[2]

Webb and I protested that the party could not afford a financial donation of that size. Considering the poor state of the party's treasury, we knew we would

Allen County commissioner candidates at the League of Women Voters' forum for candidates, October 1986. *From left:* Ed Schwieterman (D), Bob Townsend (R), Dale Leppla (D), Joan Petty (I), and Don Reese (R). *Lima News* photo from the collection of the Allen County Historical Society.

have our hands full subsidizing the sample ballots that the Ohio Democratic Party would mail into the county.[3] Also, we questioned the wisdom of giving money solely to one candidate. Such a move would create unnecessary enmity and friction within party circles, and with the party fight less than six weeks behind us, Webb and I were reluctant to open ourselves to further attacks from fellow Democrats.

Twining's allies persisted, however, reminding us that Twining had backed DEP at a time when other Democrats in the field—Dale Leppla and Ed Schwieterman, both running for county commissioner—had carefully steered clear of our challenge to Charlie Hauenstein. Rochelle had stood up for us, and now they were asking the party to stand up for her. I realized that I owed Twining a considerable debt, and I also understood that of all our candidates, she was the most committed to inclusiveness, an ideal that had been central to DEP's fight against Charlie Hauenstein. I gave her committee the go-ahead to search out a loan.[4]

They had little luck. Banks were reluctant to lend money to a political campaign, especially a Democratic one. But Smokey Hower, a member of the Executive Committee, generously offered the party twelve thousand dollars from his personal savings.[5] The Executive Committee accepted Hower's offer (which it paid back within a year at 10 percent interest). Twining would end up with half of this amount; the rest would be split among the remaining candidates.[6]

The decision to focus on Rochelle's campaign contained obvious risks. She would find it tough going in Allen County, where voters had elected female candidates but only those they considered "safe" women. Rochelle Twining was not a safe woman. Flamboyant in her wide-brimmed hats, which she occasionally wore with suffragist white, she was proudly articulate in her opinions and willfully shared them with anyone who would listen. In fact, Rochelle evoked the image of a young Bella Abzug, the colorful feminist politician and late congresswoman from New York City. It was a comparison that did not work in Twining's favor, not in Allen County, where voters preferred their politicians, even the male ones, modest and unassuming.

In addition, Twining could not avoid voter scrutiny of her domestic life. In 1986, Rochelle Twining was in her thirties and had three children, all living at home. Although she was happily married to her husband Rick, who worked at the General Dynamics Tank Plant, she constantly had to fend off remarks regarding her marital status and her sexuality. "What does your husband think about this?" and "Who's taking care of your kids?" were two of the more polite questions Twining received along the campaign trail. Other, truly vexing comments implied that she was an uppity man hater—a view apparently accepted by the "bubba" along the parade route.

While some voters may have liked Twining's forthright, articulate expression of issues, many were apprehensive about her, disconcerted by her outspoken advocacy of women's rights and her well-documented career confronting male-dominated institutions. In 1976 she had established a rape hotline, which later evolved into Crossroads Crisis Center, a shelter for battered women. As director of the shelter, Twining continually had to challenge the police, the county prosecutor's office, and local judges, to cajole them into granting protection and assistance to battered women and abused children. As a former president of the Ohio Chapter of the National Abortion and Reproductive Rights Action League, she held strong pro-choice views, much to the distaste of Allen County's substantially pro-life electorate.[7] Twining's assertive style meant that she would not back away from the district's conservative nature; she would not pander to voters' opposition to taxes and the welfare state.[8]

Most voters simply felt more at ease with the affable Bill Thompson, who was a known commodity, a safe choice. Thompson's father had served as county commissioner until losing to John Coplen in 1976, and for many years his family had owned a seed business in Delphos. Farmers knew the Thompson name well—and, for that matter, so did the rest of the electorate.

Bill Thompson's campaign portrayed him as the nice, successful family man. The family walk in the fair parade signaled as much. However, no amount of image-creating gimmickry could top the letter that Kay Thompson sent to all female voters in the First District. Written in Kay's own handwriting and personally signed, the note began, "Dear Friend" and declared how proud she was that her husband Bill was running for state representative. Bill was such a good husband and father, she proclaimed, he would surely do a good job for the people from his district. As a finishing touch, she enclosed a picture of her, Bill, and their children, and signed the letter "Best Wishes, Kay Thompson."[9]

Though aware that Republican candidates had used similar mailings before, I knew this one packed a stunning wallop. Several of us joked that perhaps we could get Rick Twining to write a "Dear Bubba" letter, but we knew that no mailing could counteract this one. As for Rochelle, she glumly stared at Kay Thompson's letter and murmured, "Right, and Rick can say what a good gal I am and how I cook a really mean pot roast."[10]

At the Junior League Style Show, about two weeks before election day, Twining endured yet another display of the Thompson theme. Though far from being a Junior Leaguer, Rochelle had long embraced this event, because the proceeds went to help a number of women's causes, including the Crossroads Crisis Center. For her, the Junior League Style Show sent a "women helping women" message. But not that night. The show's organizers had enlisted Bill Thompson to model clothing and had prepared a script that promoted Thompson's candidacy. As Thompson made his entrance, looking dapper, his dark hair smoothed back and moustache neatly trimmed, the announcer gushed, "We'll all vote for Bill in that suit!" At the candidate's encore, the emcee crooned effusively, "And here's Bill in a cashmere coat running for reelection!"[11] Those who watched the style show, whether in person or on cable-cast the following week, could not miss the point that women liked Bill Thompson, especially in elegant attire that enhanced his masculinity. Twining simply could not compete against that sort of image making.

Thompson's image, however, was more than just a positive presentation of self; it was designed to raise and reinforce doubts about his opponent. For instance, at a fund-raiser in early September, he proclaimed, "I'm not running for seat in Columbus to change things. I'm not the candidate with a particular cause."[12] Though uninspiring, the message was clear: Rochelle Dennis Twining was the candidate "with a particular cause" (feminism), and she was the one who wanted "to change things." Bill Thompson was simply a nice guy who wanted to go to the state legislature and do the people's will.

It was an image Twining wanted to challenge. Her only chance was to force Thompson into open debate, where she could apply her rhetorical skills and present herself as a substantial alternative, but Thompson cleverly dodged this ploy. At candidates' forums, when Twining would outline strong positions on health care, public education, and agricultural policy, Thompson would respond blandly, "I agree with Rochelle," and then analyze the issues in a way not much different from hers. After one such encounter, Twining stormed into a Campaign Committee meeting and kicked at the shins of PC Wrencher, a massive Central Committeeman, who was scurrying to get out of her way. She slammed her attaché case on the table, plopped into a chair, and roared, "Bill Thompson's got M&Ms for balls!"

"Plain or peanut?" I asked, straight-faced.[13]

The wisecrack snapped Rochelle out of her sour mood, but the reality was that unless she could draw Thompson into a substantive debate, she would lose the election. Accordingly, Twining publicly laid down the challenge. She lambasted Thompson for his failure to take "definite stands on the issues." She skewered him as a "political candidate," a man who lacked the capacity to tend to "the needs and wants of county voters." Furthermore, she proclaimed dismissively, "He is a candidate without a cause, and a candidate without a cause should not be a candidate." She ended her manifesto by daring Thompson to come into the open: "We challenge him to a series of debates in every corner of Allen County. We will meet him any time, any place."[14]

Thompson immediately rebuffed Twining's challenge. Dismissing the need for debates, he labeled Twining's statement as a desperate ploy "usually done by a person who feels they are behind and trying to catch up." He shrugged off the charge that he had failed to differentiate himself from her: "I'm not going to get into an argumentative campaign. If we agree with each other, so be it."[15]

But Thompson never directly rejected Twining's call for debate; he issued his reaction only through the media. Rochelle should have let the controversy fall away, but two weeks later she once again stirred the "debate over debates" with a sharp-tongued challenge to Thompson's manhood. "He is afraid to debate," she pronounced, "[but] I never expected him to accept my challenge because he doesn't have an in-depth grasp of the issues. He thinks that if he sits back and doesn't rock the boat, the people of Allen County will do what they've always done, and that is vote for a male Republican."[16]

Thompson had drawn Twining into a trap. Rochelle's assault, mounted in frustration, only reinforced the Republican candidate's good-guy image and emphasized hers as a shrill feminist. "She intends to engage in a negative campaign,"

Thompson stated in response to Twining's second call for debate, "and I refuse to go down to that level. . . . She has yet to come out with positive proposals on the issues, and I don't think the people of Allen County want a negative campaign."[17]

Rochelle Twining's combative attacks persisted throughout the campaign. She tried aggressively to paint a picture of Thompson as "one of the boys." She even produced a campaign brochure, triple-folded, with a cartoon caricature of a smiling male candidate on each fold. The captions read, "Tired of the same old Mr. Perfect Smile, and the same old Mr. Perfect Hair, and more of the same old Mr. Perfect Line?" The final fold in the brochure bore a caricature of Rochelle Twining herself and the caption, "Not just one of the same old boys."[18]

In the meantime, a Republican-mounted whispering campaign was bolstering Thompson. When Twining blasted him for turning down her challenge to debate, all sorts of rumors about Rochelle began to accumulate. Some were highly personal. "What's that little butterball doing here?" one prominent businessman remarked, a sneering observation on Twining's weight, on seeing her at a Chamber of Commerce event. Others attacked her femininity: She hated men; she was going to leave her husband; she had preached lesbianism to the women at Crossroads Crisis Center. Even high-ranking Republicans got into the act. On election night, according to one reporter, a GOP insider spat an expletitive-filled rant that crudely berated Rochelle, her physique, and her feminist views.[19]

Voters in Allen County weren't the only ones harboring reservations about Twining's candidacy. House Speaker Vern Riffe, whose office had encouraged Twining to run, was now giving her only token financing—a thousand dollars. Riffe, who died in 1997, served in the General Assembly from 1959 to 1995, the last twenty years as speaker. A leviathan among Ohio politicians, his titanic reputation impressed even Ralph Nader, who once called him "the most powerful floor leader in any legislative body, including Congress."[20] Through a series of annual fund-raisers, Riffe controlled campaign committees which could raise and spend as much four million dollars in an election year. Ambitious politicians and lobbyists, irrespective of age, experience, or party affiliation, attended Riffe's summer birthday bash, which routinely raised one million dollars by itself.[21] By amassing prodigious amounts of campaign money, Riffe followed this quintessential principle: "To control the legislature, you have to elect it."[22] He commanded legislative votes by dolling out war-chest monies to favored Democrats: those who might assist his bill-passing exploits received a portion of the largesse; prospective losers and enemies were ignored.

Twining fit the "prospective loser" category. Leastwise, that was the message

I received the day I visited the State House to lobby Tom Winters and Ty Marsh, a pair of Riffe's adjutants. Winters, a tall, bespectacled man with a boyish face, firm handshake, and a politician's banter, greeted me at the door: "Bill, I hear you're doing a helluva job, filling the slate and working the campaign. We sure would like to turn Allen County around." Then, he introduced me to Marsh, a quiet man with dark hair, gray skin, and a handshake as limp as Winters's was strong.[23]

After the introductions, I launched a pitch for a four-thousand-dollar boost to Twining's candidacy. "Rochelle has been running a well-organized, aggressive campaign," I said. "She's confronted her opponent on the issues, worked the precincts, and raised money. . . . I think she'll win, and I'd like the Speaker to give her more support." Winters's response puzzled me. "Bill, you have to consider that's a strong Republican district, and with Ben Rose on the ticket [the district's longtime representative, now running for auditor of state], we really aren't counting on that race."

"What does Ben Rose have to do with it?" I countered.

"Ben's a hometown boy, and hometown boys traditionally draw a big vote for their party—like Sherrod Brown in Richland County and Mary Ellen Withrow in Marion County."

"Maybe so," I replied, momentarily bemused by the image of Mary Ellen Withrow as a hometown boy, "but I think you need to realize it's a new game in Allen County. We have a new party with new leadership, and voters are taking a fresh look at our ticket. Also, I can't see Ben Rose as a relevant factor in Twining's race. . . . In fact, I expect Ferguson [Tom Ferguson, the incumbent auditor and Rose's opponent] to carry Allen County."[24]

"You really think Ferguson will carry Allen County?" Winters responded. It was more of a statement than a question; it signaled that my spiel had not impressed him. Then he looked toward Marsh, who was sitting nearby, taking notes. Marsh looked up from his note taking and shrugged. Finally, Winters returned his gaze to me and said, "I'll take this up with the Speaker and get back to you. Rochelle may get a little more money but probably not much more than a thousand."[25]

Vern Riffe had written off Rochelle Twining, and along with her the Allen County Democratic Party. In a follow-up letter to Winters, I voiced my frustration at being expected to recruit a House candidate without the assurance that the Speaker would provide adequate financing. Concluding with a statement that could have been interpreted as a threat, I wrote, "If you expect first rate candidates to run for this seat—and you have one this year—you simply will have to give them more support."[26]

I received no reply. Two weeks later, Twining took matters into her own hands, making a journey to Glandorf in Putnam County, twenty miles north of Lima, where Randy Bachman was holding a fund-raiser. Bachman was the Democratic candidate in the Eightieth District; though he was mounting a futile challenge to an established incumbent, Lynn Wachtmann, he was receiving "fair-haired boy" treatment from Riffe's office. Bachman was a political neophyte who was centering his campaign on a "right to life" platform, despite the fact that his opponent had already locked up the endorsement of pro-life organizations. Still, Riffe found him worthy of a substantial contribution (I'd heard it was five thousand dollars), and that evening he would speak at Bachman's fund-raiser and hand his campaign an additional ten thousand.

Twining attended the event to confront Riffe directly. When she approached him during dinner to say "hello," he never even acknowledged her greeting but snapped testily, "I can't talk to you now. I'm eating." After the speeches, Twining followed Riffe to the bar, where she shouldered her way through the crowd until she found the Speaker, his feet propped on a table. She put her request directly to him: "My campaign needs more money than your office has given me." Riffe glowered at her over his drink: "Sorry, honey. The numbers aren't there." Twining persisted though. She approached Riffe en route to the parking lot in a bid to convince him that the numbers were wrong, but he fended her off. "Keep up the good work," he advised, planting a kiss on Rochelle's cheek before escaping into his car.[27]

A week later, Riffe admonished her—"Keep your campaign in your own district"—but he also sent word, via Ty Marsh, that a check for two thousand dollars was in the mail. Twining was not fazed by the rebuke. Joyful at receiving the extra contribution from the Speaker, she bust into the conference room at the Alpine, where a meeting of the Campaign Committee was in progress, and joyfully shared her news with everyone in the room, including a waitress on hand to take drink orders. She later handed me a gift, chortling gleefully, in appreciation for my mission to Winters's office. It was a sixteen-ounce bag of M&MS . . . peanut.

Dale Leppla didn't see anything funny about that bag of M&MS. In fact he was downright annoyed, scowling at me as if to say, "So, now Twining's getting more money."

Leppla, who was running for county commissioner against incumbent Don Reese, had become more and more hostile ever since the takeover of the party chairmanship. Back in July, during the very first meeting of our Campaign Committee, he had hurled a cascade of complaints about the party's new leaders:

"You're no better than the last bunch. They promised me they'd do this and that, and I knew then they'd never deliver. You guys don't seem to be doin' anything, either."

"Whaddya want, Dale?" I shot back.

"You know what I want. I want you to find me a coordinator and a bunch of volunteers, give me yard sign locations, and line up phone banks." In other words, he wanted the party to organize his campaign for him. Unlike the party's other candidates, Dale Leppla had not created even the semblance of an organization. He had no money, no coordinator, no staff, and no volunteers, except his own family and a circle of close friends.

But we couldn't do his work for him, I explained: The party would be busy, coordinating the statewide campaigns, planning the fall fund-raiser, and preparing the get-out-the-vote drive. He would have to build his own campaign organization himself. "Yeah, well, I'm gonna win this election, an' I don't want any of you guys takin' the credit," he rumbled in reply.[28]

After that outburst, Leppla mellowed, entered into the business of the meeting and shared his ideas on county government. In fact, Dale Leppla knew more about local politics than anyone else there that night. His political base was in Lima, where for many years he had lived on the north side, and where he had served as purchasing director in Mayor Harry Moyer's administration (1973–85). Dale's long affiliation with local government had educated him well in the nitty-gritty of county governance. Potential crises were looming: The area's only landfill was due to close; the county's fiscal situation was so unstable that a tax increase was likely; and the county desperately needed a new jail. Dale Leppla possessed a detailed and ready command of each one of these problems, which would soon demand the attention of the new county commission.

Nonetheless, relations between Leppla and the party worsened as the summer wore on. During a mid-August meeting, when I broke the news that the party was going to accept and repay a donation of twelve thousand dollars and concentrate most of it on Twining's campaign, he sneered, "Was this a popularity contest? I've heard the Republicans are targeting the commissioner's races. What makes you think they're targeting the state rep's race?" I responded that we hadn't checked with the Republicans before designing our strategy, but he wasn't listening. He smirked, then snuffed out his cigarette as if to emphasize his contempt.[29] Our other candidates quietly accepted the news, but Leppla left the session grousing, "Next time I'll run as a Republican."[30]

In mid-September, the feeble connection between Leppla and the party nearly broke entirely. With his campaign still needing a coordinator, I had tried to persuade his daughter, Pam Falke, to manage his candidacy. She had been a successful DEP candidate for Central Committee and had worked Lima's north end for Steve Maurer in 1984. I thought she would do a good job, but I should have talked the matter over with Dale first. He acidly rejected the idea.[31]

At this point, Steve Webb entered the quarrel. In early September, I picked up a rumor that Steve had assigned Bob Rowland, one of his pals from the labor movement, to coordinate the Leppla operation. In part, this was good news. As a representative of the Ohio Public Service Employees union (OPSE), Rowland could supply effective, reliable leadership for that troubled campaign. Still, I was perplexed by the Steve's freelancing on Leppla's behalf and curious about why he had not mentioned this move to me. I phoned him to inquire if what I'd heard about Bob Rowland was true. "Yeah, Dale came to me, asked me to find him a coordinator, and I asked Bob Rowland to do it. Bob's agreed," Webb breezily replied, making it sound as though the decision had materialized so suddenly that he had not had time to discuss it with me.[32] This was plausible, as I had been on a short backpacking trip when the maneuver occurred.

The Leppla problem was solved, I thought, until I called Roger Rankin, Twining's manager. Rankin, who taught in the Shawnee School District, was experiencing trouble trying to guide Rochelle's campaign while tending to classroom responsibilities. He needed help, and OPSE came to the rescue by assigning Bob Rowland to work full-time for Twining. He and Rochelle were "thrilled" by this move, he told me. "That's interesting," I responded, "Steve just told me Bob is going to coordinate Dale Leppla's campaign."

"Not if we can help it," Roger said, his voice going suddenly flat.[33]

I called Webb back and instructed him to get with Twining and settle the matter. In the end, Rochelle forced Steve to reverse his decision, and Bob Rowland returned to her campaign. All of this left Webb with egg on his face, Dale Leppla still without a coordinator, and me wondering what had possessed Steve to make a decision of this magnitude without checking with me.

Finally, Leppla corrected his problem himself. At a Campaign Committee meeting a week later, he declared in a matter-of-fact monotone that he had asked Todd Hey to direct his campaign. It was one jaw-dropping stunner of an announcement, but I should have seen it coming. Leppla himself had already indicated that Hey and Hauenstein had coaxed him into running with promises of assistance. Dale had bought their line, which left him with nothing but a belly full of resentment when I became party chairman.

Now he was shoving Todd Hey into my face and creating a dilemma. I could not abandon Leppla, or denounce his candidacy, or impart even the slightest hint that there was tension between him and me. But at the same time, a Leppla setback would not exactly sadden me, especially with Todd Hey in charge of it—Leppla's loss would be Todd's failure too.

The night that Dale lobbed his bombshell was also the night I distributed checks from the Hower loan—six thousand dollars for Twining, two thousand each to Meredith and Schwieterman, and one thousand apiece to Leppla and Brown. Leppla, who had always hated the Twining-first strategy, was especially stung to receive no more than Roger Brown, the party's recently nominated candidate for clerk of courts.[34] Afterward, he waved his thousand-dollar check menacingly in my face: "I consider this an insult."

"Well, we won't insult you anymore," I thought to myself, holding my tongue as he stalked away.[35]

Two nights later, John Hevener expressed that thought out loud to Pam Falke, who had cornered him after a meeting of the Executive Committee. She wanted to voice her concern about the way the party was treating her father and to enlist John's help in prying loose more funding. Hevener was not sympathetic. There would be no more money, he said, emphasizing that the party had grown weary of her father's antics and that his latest move—appointing Todd Hey as his campaign manager—had been so odious that many Democrats were not in a mood even to vote for him, much less help his campaign.[36]

It was a stern lecture, and Hevener's words apparently got back to Dale. The next morning, at a special breakfast that Linda Coplen had scheduled for Sherrod Brown, Leppla approached me. "I just want to smooth the waters," he began. "I've noticed some tension between the party and my campaign since I asked Todd to be my coordinator." (It had been but three days.) Then he began to justify his decision. "You guys gave me no help when I asked for it. I needed a coordinator and had no choice but to ask Todd."

I accepted none of this. "Oh, you had a choice all right," I responded, my voice rising with each syllable. "You made unreasonable demands on the party. You wanted me to build your campaign, and frankly I didn't have time for that. You needed to organize your own campaign, just as the other candidates have done. And when I tried to help and asked Pam [Falke] to be your coordinator, you threw it back in my face." Pointing to Steve Webb, who was standing nearby, I continued—the volume lower but the words crackling—"We've created a new party, and what you've done is align yourself with the old. Todd is just exploiting your campaign to worm himself back inside."

This blistering invective said as much about the party's lack of unity as it did about Leppla and his campaign. Many of us, myself included, were still fighting Todd Hey and Charlie Hauenstein, and as long as we continued this struggle, we would never be able to move the party forward. Leppla seized upon this idea. "Bill, I think you need to have more confidence in yourself than that. I would like you to smooth the tensions that have occurred so the rest of the ticket doesn't get hurt by this situation."

He was trying to foist responsibility for Democratic losses onto my shoulders. "What an asshole!" I later declared privately. "He creates tension, then wants me to smooth things."[37]

Steve Webb had been observing our exchange and interjecting conciliatory, cloying comments to pacify Leppla. Finally, he suggested, "Dale, it might be better if you wouldn't bring Todd to our campaign meetings." Leppla reluctantly acceded to this proposal, which ended the spat, although neither Dale nor I had changed our views.

Within a few days the crisis relaxed, as did the strain between Leppla's campaign and the party. As for me, I heeded Leppla's advice and began to gather confidence in my own leadership, to focus my energies on the election ahead. Besides, there was not much I could do about Leppla and his choice of coordinators. I simply learned to live with the warts in that campaign.

Dale, for his part, began courting the party's cadre. He invited John Coplen to a brainstorming session with his campaign's core leadership, which included members from the party's old guard, including Bill Johns and Charlie Hauenstein. He tried to woo Leonard Boddie, to gain access to Lima's black community, and he even held a quiet thirty-minute chat with John Hevener—who told me afterward, a wry smile sliding across his face, "I feel better about Leppla now . . . but not much."[38]

The Leppla/Hey fracas marked a watershed in my relationship with Steve Webb. On September 16, the day after Leppla issued his surprise announcement about Todd Hey, I had lunch with Rochelle Twining to discuss the crisis. Twining was worried by Webb's involvement with Dale Leppla, specifically by his bid to side-rail Bob Rowland to the Leppla campaign. Steve's explanation to me had been disingenuous, Rochelle declared, insisting that he had known about Rowland's appointment to her organization and had acted on his own in ordering the reassignment. He had been both high-handed and secretive, in neither checking with me nor considering the implications for her candidacy. Furthermore, his machinations had unnecessarily fueled tension between Dale Leppla, her campaign, and the party leaders.[39] In Twining's view, Webb's action constituted a serious threat to my power.

Rochelle's words were on my mind the next morning at the Sherrod Brown breakfast, when Webb attempted to soften my reprimand to Leppla. At a time when we needed to present a united front, his mollifying interruptions sent the message that he and I were divided in our attitudes.

I decided to talk to Steve at the first opportunity and express my concern. I did not have to wait long. The next morning, September 19, he and I were meeting in Twining's headquarters, along with Bob Rowland and Rochelle, when the Leppla/Hey situation came up. As I expressed my frustration with having to associate with the Leppla campaign, Webb chided me—"Bill, you need to keep your temper under control"—which I interpreted as a criticism of the scolding I had given Leppla the previous morning. I looked Webb straight in the eye and responded sharply, "Steve, we need to keep in touch with each other about our contacts with the Leppla campaign. Since Dale is more likely to talk to you than to me, you need to let me know about anything going on in his campaign." I told him that I did not appreciate his freelancing decision to send Bob Rowland to Leppla's campaign, that he should have consulted me before he made such a move, and that any future decisions of similar magnitude had to be cleared with me. I had blindsided Steve with chewing-out in the presence of two political colleagues, just to see how he'd respond. Steve absorbed it fidgeting in his chair, staring the floor, responding only that he understood.

Until this moment I had believed that together Steve Webb and I could reconstruct our party and foment change in our community. But his maneuvers on Leppla's behalf testified that Steve did not share my vision. His efforts had been disquietingly subversive and counterproductive. Steve would work, and work hard, if there was some tangible benefit for him, such the license bureau at the Lima Mall, but he was not seriously interested in molding the party into an issue-oriented political force.

The dissimilarity of our natures and political styles had helped unify the DEP coalition, but now it prevented us from moving beyond "beating Todd and Charlie." Steve and I simply wanted and expected different things from our party, and our contrasting attitudes would continue to generate tension within party circles. Perhaps sensing this, Steve eased away from high-profile leadership activities, such as get-out-the-vote coordination, and threw himself instead into assisting specific campaigns, mainly those of Dale Leppla and Ed Schwieterman.

Schwieterman was our party's other candidate for commissioner—Ed "The Man" Schwieterman, as in Schwieter-*man*. Wordplay supplied the theme for his campaign. Its "I Love the Man" message bellowed from buttons, ads, and brochures, a garish red heart standing for the word "love," as it did in those bumper stickers proclaiming "I ♥ NY."

Ed's campaign was a continuous foray into political schlock. At the county fair, Ed carefully prepared a shrine to his candidacy, replete with music and visual effects. He mounted a poster-sized, framed photograph of himself on an easel, from where his smiling visage beamed onto the midway outside the Democratic Party's tent. Next to the easel Ed had carefully arranged various citations and commemorative letters, all individually framed and extolling the virtues of "The Man." A tape player continuously played Billy Ocean's "When the Going Gets Tough," which Ed had made the theme song for his campaign, making his the first campaign in the county—to my knowledge, at least—to have one.

Perhaps Schwieterman's fifteen years as superintendent of public service for the city of Delphos had encouraged this compulsive and fervent fixation on detail. It was a character flaw that swamped the campaign in a comedic morass, but Ed was oblivious to the problem. For example, when he helped plan a house party held by Margie Weidel, a longtime Democratic activist, he became obsessed with finding, of all things, a donkey head, to be used in a skit that Margie had prepared as a way of enlivening the event. Ed priced a number of donkey outfits, finally striking an excellent bargain for one, or so he insisted to Rochelle Twining, who irreverently interrupted his story: "How much for just the head?"

"Oh you can't purchase just half the donkey," Ed replied earnestly and went on to explain why, not realizing Rochelle was teasing.[40]

Then there was the "Yard Sign War." In mid-October Ed began erecting thirteen-foot obelisks throughout the county, each structure consisting of two poles anchored into the ground and plastered all the way to the top, front and back, with red, white, and blue "Schwieterman for Commissioner" yard signs, one sign on top of the other. Resembling giant phalluses, they were, frankly, comical. But Ed was proud of them, saying that he intended to erect one in each jurisdiction in the county, as a symbol that he would treat everyone equally.[41]

He placed one of his towers on Steve Webb's lawn at the heavily traveled intersection of Market Street and Cable Road in Lima. It turned out that Ed's sign was not on Steve's property but on a corner lot owned by a prominent Republican family. The owner inspected the site shortly after the structure had been assembled, ascertained that the sign encroached on his land, and had it unceremoniously torn down. An enraged Schwieterman truculently vowed that he would raise another.[42] He did—an even taller one—but this time on Webb's ground. Of course, the Republicans countered by installing a "Townsend for

Commissioner" billboard on their lot. (Robert Townsend was Ed's opponent.) Webb responded with more Democratic signs, and not to be shown up, Republican candidates retaliated with additional signs of their own. By election day the corner of Market and Cable was a sign-strewn mess.[43]

Ed took immense pride in this confrontation. "The Republicans are getting very worried," he later crowed to a rally of Democratic supporters. "Most of you know they took down my Lima tall yard sign and tore it up. . . . Well, ladies and gentlemen, the sign is back, and it is on Steve Webb's property, and they better not touch it again!"[44]

As October drifted to a close, Schwieterman still had not staged a press conference or voiced any substantive pronouncement on issues facing the county. Once, after a Campaign Committee meeting, Steve Webb and I were in the Alpine, commiserating about this circumstance as we watched Ed circulate through the restaurant, greeting patrons and distributing his stickers. Finally, I motioned him to our booth and suggested that he hold a press conference and take advantage of the free publicity. Ed sat down, leaned toward the center of the table as if inviting us to join him in a huddle, and in sotto voce promised that he was going to make "a *big* announcement" soon and that it would "really shake things up." When I asked him what he had in mind, Ed responded that he was not at liberty to say, beyond emphasizing again that it would cause a real stir.[45]

The "big announcement," however, was a first-class disappointment. It came on October 26, at a Schwieterman-staged press conference and steak fry. As was his custom, Ed had paid meticulous attention to every detail, but if this was to be a press conference and the objective was the generate serious coverage of the Schwieterman candidacy, Ed's plan was tactically flawed. For one thing, the announcement occurred on Sunday evening, generally a poor time to solicit news coverage. Additionally, the setting itself undercut the seriousness of Schwieterman's purpose. He wanted to express his views on significant issues facing the county, but the press conference occurred at a party, replete with food, flowers, balloons, a stage band, and dancing. Consequently, the media covered the event as a campaign rally, thus trivializing Schwieterman's objective.

More substantively, Schwieterman's prepared statement did little to "shake things up." Filled with flabby generalizations, it communicated little about Ed's approach to the coming landfill crisis, the pending need for a tax increase, or the immediate demand for a new jail. He filled his pronouncement with symbolic items—a "rotating agenda" allowing neighborhoods to address the commission on a rotating basis; or a suggestion that communities receive free use of the Veterans Memorial Civic and Convention Center. The only substantive proposal was an arcane one, advocating an annexation plan "for each county community," and although Ed contended this scheme would encourage "orderly and accelerated growth," it sparked little reaction and did nothing to boost his flagging candidacy.[46]

Had Schwieterman given the speech two months—or even two weeks—previously, he would have had time to refine his thinking and substantively clarify his ideas before the vote. But his attention to issues came too late: It was nine days until election day, and voters had already begun to decide. Ed was finally trying to define himself as a responsive public servant with a handle on issues, but I suspected that the voting public had developed a different impression, seeing Ed Schwieterman as a nice guy with a firm handshake, a pleasant smile, and relentless energy, but a limited understanding of Allen County and its problems. Furthermore, he was facing an electorate already prone to vote Republican, and Ed Schwieterman offered the voters no reason to reject his opponent, the affable incumbent Bob Townsend, also a man with a nice smile but also with a firm grasp of the county's problems.

In late August, my friend and colleague Donna Kauffman dropped me a note: "I find the Schwieterman campaign offensive. The Man? Vote for the Man? I should think his campaign will hurt Rochelle."[47]

Kauffman's perceptive observation underscored a dilemma. The party could not disavow Schwieterman's candidacy, even though his "I Love the Man" message helped Thompson and contradicted what the party was asking voters to do in the campaign for state representative: vote for a woman. Perversely, the Twining campaign didn't help either, fostering as it did the impression that Twining was pandering to the female vote. Her "not one of the same old boys" brochures struck some voters as strident, as did a television spot that showed Rochelle talking to an interracial group of women, ranging in age from fourteen to seventy. "As women, we weren't born Democrat, and we weren't born Republican, and we weren't born yesterday," Twining proclaimed. The spot went on to attack traditional politicians, who in her view had ignored the needs of the family. These messages baffled the reporters covering the Thompson-Twining race. "What's Twining trying to tell us?" one of them asked. "That we should vote for her because she's a woman?"

But as the campaign barreled to a finish, there was little the party could do to extract itself from this conundrum, one that was forced upon it in part by gender politics, in part by Schwieterman's superficial campaign, and in part by the party's own decision to focus on Twining in the first place. I went into denial, burying my own misgivings in the belief that the controversial Twining-first strategy would prove successful and wise. "Things have begun to look very good for Twining," I reflected on election day. "I sense—gut reaction—momentum going her way."[48]

Some evidence existed for this belief. For instance, Thompson threw a mild tantrum after a debate at Lima Senior High School, a contest broadcast by WCIT Radio a week before election day. Thompson complained to the event's organizers that he hadn't known it was going to be a debate—something he'd been steadfastly avoiding—and he vehemently objected to taking a straw poll of the students who watched the debate. He had reason to protest. The results, which also were broadcast, showed Twining a decisive winner, twenty-five to eleven. According to Twining, who witnessed Thompson's tirade, "his lower lip trembled like he was going to cry." Why would Thompson get so upset, we wondered, if he didn't believe he was in trouble?[49]

Aside from Thompson's "wigged-out" behavior, there were other signals that Rochelle might actually pull it off. Several Republican insiders had told Twining that GOP tracking polls showed her "doing well." Bill Thompson had even been seen walking "swing" precincts—a meaningful signal in Allen County, where Republican candidates normally canvass only a few safely partisan neighborhoods and rely on the party machinery to turn out the twenty thousand or so votes needed for victory.

I was confident, and so was Rochelle. When she popped into party headquarters on election eve, just as the phone banks shut down, she was ebullient, joyfully planning her new career, wondering how Vern Riffe and the boys in Columbus would take to her.[50]

· 10 ·

Down the Tubes

Rochelle Twining did not become a state representative. The GOP swept all the local races, and by 10 P.M. on election night, the Democrats' only chance was hanging with Dick Meredith and his campaign for the Court of Appeals. Meredith was holding a slight lead in Allen County over Steve Shaw, his closest competitor in the field, and returns from outlying counties had not been reported. Meredith would win, we hoped, if he could stay close elsewhere, but Millie Workman, the Republican deputy director of the Board of Elections, crushed that slim prospect. She waltzed to a photocopier in the county courthouse, where election results were being tabulated, cracking her gum with each step, and began copying a printout showing that Meredith was doomed. "Shaw's won," she remarked to no one in particular, although Steve Webb and I were the only ones in the room. The printout, which contained results from all outlying counties, showed Shaw leading districtwide by more than twenty thousand votes, too big a lead for Meredith to surmount, even if he won Allen County.[1]

In fact, no Democrat had come close. Schwieterman and Twining did best, each grabbing 44 percent of the votes in their contests. Leppla scored 38 percent in a three-way race. Meredith took 31 percent of the county votes, finishing second to Shaw, who tallied 36 percent in the multicandidate Court of Appeals election. Roger Brown, who had barely mounted a campaign for county clerk, tallied 41 percent.[2]

A week later, party leaders and candidates gathered at the Alpine to slog through a wrap-up campaign meeting and gripe session. Bob Gehr had never attended any of these councils during the campaign, but he was there that night, pronouncing judgment. "Rochelle, I like ya, but that one was down the tubes. You had no chance," he declared, scornfully wagging a finger toward her end of the table.[3]

Twining winced at Gehr's abrasive judgment but said nothing. Ed Schwieterman, however, jumped in, as if on cue, to criticize the party for not helping his campaign more. Twining had lost convincingly to Bill Thompson—19,191 to 14,869—and although she led our local slate, she had garnered only 109 votes more than Ed Schwieterman, a point that Schwieterman hammered.[4]

Schwieterman's resentment of the party's Twining-first strategy had initially surfaced in early October. Ed was galled by a throwaway quip I had made on WLIO TV's "Mid-Day," a local news program, to tout the upcoming ox roast and to talk up our party. Focusing most of my commentary on Rochelle Twining, I observed at one point, "She's running a strong campaign, and she can carry our other candidates on her coattails."

"Twining coattails?" replied an amused George Dunster, the program's host.

"That's right," I smiled, "Twining coattails."

Ed was furious. A few hours before the ox roast, I dropped by the fairgrounds site to check on preparations. Schwieterman, who was busy setting up chairs, grabbed me and began chewing me out. "You mentioned Rochelle's name twice and didn't mention any of the other candidates once. And what's this 'Twining Coattails?' Rochelle is pro-abortion, and that will hurt her in Delphos, where just about everybody is Catholic. She'll have no coattails there." I fended off the abortion issue, explaining it was not an important element in Twining's campaign, then promised that in future media appearance, I would give all candidates equal play. "Well, I still wish you'd mentioned the other candidates," he grumbled.[5]

Now, a month later, Ed was unloading his grievances, pounding on vote totals that, from his perspective, demonstrated the party's wrongheadedness. He conveniently overlooked the fact that he had not carried Lima's predominantly Democratic vote but instead emphasized other statistical truths: He had lagged behind his opponent by fewer votes than Twining had trailed Thompson; he had polled a higher percentage in his race than Rochelle had in hers; and Rochelle had garnered only a few more votes than he did, despite the special attention the party had showered on her campaign. In Ed's estimation, these numbers offered proof that if the party had given him the kind of commitment it had given Twining, he would have won.[6]

Nobody responded immediately to the criticisms raised by Gehr and Schwieterman that night. Dale Leppla, who been the point man in protesting the party's strategy, was silent, content to let Gehr and Schwieterman carry the battle. So, for that matter, were Rochelle Twining, John Hevener, and Steve Webb. And so was I. All of us were second-guessing ourselves.

Steve Webb was among the skeptics. He had grown disenchanted with the party's emphasis on Twining, and during the campaign's closing phase he had gone practically into seclusion, surfacing occasionally to attend a meeting or help Ed Schwieterman with his phallic sign towers.

On at least one occasion, Webb's "assistance" proved counterproductive. When Dale Leppla wanted yard-sign locations, Steve went to Tom Doyle, who was Rochelle Twining's yard-sign czar, and requested the list of her sign locations. Tom complied, thinking that Steve would call people on the list and ask permission to erect Leppla signs on their property. But no. Webb simply passed the names on to Leppla, who thought the addresses had been "pre-approved." As soon as the unsolicited "Leppla for Commissioner" signs began sprouting, angry phone calls descended on Democratic headquarters, on the Twining campaign, and on me. In the end, Dale cooperatively removed the unwelcome signs, all the while mumbling, I imagine, "Dirtywacklsasslfrass."[7]

Webb's casual approach to duty also nearly short-circuited our "get out the vote" (GOTV) drive. I had asked Steve to coordinate GOTV, but he demonstrated little interest in handling the assignment. When I inquired about GOTV plans, he told me that he had requested Linda Coplen to supply volunteers from the Democratic Women's Club and that she would take it from there. This was not what I had in mind. Linda procured the volunteers, but I took over GOTV, securing phones, instructing volunteers on their duties, and managing the phone bank every day and evening it was open.

Webb's lackluster effort would have been easier to bear had he been a little less chipper at our "victory party." It was not much of a celebration. The few Democrats there at the finish were downright somber—all except Steve Webb, who was busily explaining to anyone who would listen where our campaign had taken the wrong fork. He held court separately with Ed Schwieterman and Rochelle Twining, pointing out the flaws of their campaigns like a teacher counseling a pair of wayward students. Then he moved to a table of Twining volunteers, where he waxed philosophical on what it would take to run a winning campaign in Allen County. I sat on the fringe of this group, listening to Steve explain the nuances of local politics. I resented his puffery: He was talking a good game now that the campaign was done, but he had helped minimally when it had mattered most.[8]

Still, I needed Webb's support, as he needed mine to wrest that miserable license bureau from Todd Hey. Ed Finn, Bob Gehr, and other UAW bigwigs had not forgiven me for dumping Charlie Hauenstein. Even though they were not exactly pals of Charlie and from time to time had been critical of his stewardship over the party, Hauenstein was still a union brother, and that bond, along with the class loyalty it entailed, was strong. As long as the UAW leaders remained estranged, I would need help from other elements in the labor community, and Webb provided it. There was no way around it: He and I were hitched in an alliance of mutual necessity.

January 12, 1987, Inauguration Day, Reception for
Democratic State Office Holders, Columbus

Speaker of the House Vern Riffe grabbed my hand with both paws, turned to Senator Howard Metzenbaum, who was standing right next to him in the receiving line, and barked, "Senator, this is the hardest workin' chairman in Ohio."[9]

Metzenbaum was nonplussed. And so was I. I'd never met Speaker Riffe before—nor would I ever meet him again—and that momentary connection exemplified the relationship that most county chairs, myself among them, shared with politicians at the state level. The "statehouse gang" knew who we were, and they could flatter us, but they had little understanding of the politics and problems we confronted at the county level. Attitudinal distance prevailed, undermining the very grassroots strategies that local parties tried to mobilize.

Riffe's treatment of Rochelle Twining illustrates the pragmatic qualities of attitudinal distance. "The numbers aren't there," he had told her. He might as well have said this: "Look, honey, it's no use giving you any more money. Thompson's gonna win, and the day may come when I'll need that guy's vote. There's no point in riling him because of you."

Riffe's pragmatism, however, contradicted the long-term goals of us Democrats in Allen County. In our view, Twining had energized a vibrant and enthusiastic following of volunteers, many of whom had never participated in politics before, but the Speaker's office had showed scant regard for her when handing out campaign checks. Twining had lost, and she had lost without the support and sustenance of the one Democrat in the state who mattered most, Vern Riffe. The Speaker's snub made it difficult for Rochelle to consider even the possibility of running for office again. She would stay involved in party politics, but cynicism began to contaminate her plucky spirit. Had Riffe stood with her in defeat, prying loose a few thousand dollars more from his campaign war chest and paying attention to the effort she was mounting in Allen County, he would have sent a positive message to us local Democrats, connected us with his office, and emboldened us to work harder and perhaps more successfully in future elections.

Instead, the 1986 campaign left us all feeling like political orphans, alienated and undervalued by statehouse Democrats. Consider, for example, my own treatment at the hands of Frank Celebreeze, chief justice of the Ohio Supreme Court, who had been targeted by the Ohio Republican Party for replacement by Thomas Moyer. In July, I had arranged for Celebreeze to present the program at the

Lima Rotary Club, notifying his office of all the particulars, including the meeting time (noon) and location. Despite my advance work, Celebreeze still had not arrived by 12:30, and the club's president, Earl McGovern, who had been stretching out the program as long as he could, finally turned to me and said, "Bill, you're on." I tried to stall some more, telling political stories, until finally at 12:40, a full forty minutes after the meeting had begun, the chief justice and his entourage arrived. A staff member brushed off the snafu—"We did not leave Columbus until eleven, because we thought Lima was only an hour away."

Frank Celebreeze then droned through a scripted recitation of environmental law and brusquely refused to answer questions, despite the fact that a half-dozen Rotarians were affiliated with the Standard Oil Refining Plant in Lima and had concerns they wanted to raise. The chief justice left the distinct impression that this was just another trip to some no-account backwater. "Thanks for the invitation," he muttered over his shoulder as he crawled into his navy-blue Lincoln, taking few votes and a great deal of ill will with him.[10]

But Frank Celebreeze, who would eventually lose his race to Tom Moyer, could perhaps be forgiven: He was a judge, not a politician, and therefore was unappreciative of the intricacies of party politics. The same cannot be said for Governor Richard Celeste, who would turn on the very people who had helped him secure his biggest triumph.

Celeste was cruising that fall, thanks largely to the ineptitude of his opponent, former governor James Rhodes. The Rhodes campaign had floundered throughout the summer, never able to spark much excitement at the grass roots. As election day approached, Rhodes began a gay-bashing gambit, attacking Celeste over an AIDS-awareness program that, Rhodes insisted, endorsed a homosexual lifestyle.[11] This line of attack only signaled the wretched state of his campaign, embarrassed Republican heavyweights like Robert Taft III (the party's nominee for lieutenant governor), and did nothing to boost Rhodes in the polls. Eventually, Rhodes entered a debate, something he had avoided with every opponent he had faced. The skirmish was televised two days before the election, and Rhodes was the clear loser, looking haggard and befuddled alongside the confidently articulate Celeste, who appeared to be toying with him.[12]

The old warhorse was over the hill, but Celeste had taken no chances. Having lost a big lead in the 1978 gubernatorial contest, he had grown obsessed with raising a war chest sizeable enough to pulverize Rhodes. Consequently, the governor's minions sometimes sought donations overzealously, using strong-arm tactics. In July, a Franklin County grand jury indicted Pam Conrad and Larry McCartney, two Ohio Democratic Party operatives, for shaking down contributions from state contractors.[13]

Dick Celeste and the functionaries who surrounded him, the Celestials, simply shrugged off the allegations. They believed the governor could do no wrong, saw Rhodes and Republicans as manipulating grand jury indictments to embarrass the governor,[14] and rarely listened to advice, especially if it came from the counties. In August, Kathy Tefft-Keller (deputy of the Governor's Committee), her husband Ron Keller, and Janis Miller, the campaign's liaison to Allen County—Celestials all—visited Allen County to brief me and the Heveners on the governor's race. Treating us to dinner at the Alpine, they spent most of the meal sharing tidbits of statehouse gossip with each other, rarely looking up from their plates to solicit our views of the local political scene. The Heveners and I felt like bystanders.

After dinner, when we were joined by county chairs and Celeste coordinators from nearby counties, Tefft-Keller told us that the governor would be hard to beat. The campaign had already purchased a million dollars in television time and was prepared to sink another million into commercials if needed. She boasted that the campaign expected to spend between six and eight million dollars, most of which had already been raised. It was doubtful, she smugly concluded, that Rhodes could keep up with Celeste in campaign spending. Although it was nice to hear that the governor's campaign was in such good financial shape, it was clear from Teft-Keller's demeanor—she spoke practically the entire time and barely listened to comments from the gathering—that the county organizations were superfluous to the effort, mere appendages. The Celestials had the money in the can, and all they needed from us was a good voter turnout.[15]

We county chairs turned out the votes, all right—1,858,372 of them, to be precise, compared 1,207,264 for Rhodes[16]—but received a solid kick in the face for our efforts. One week after inauguration day, Jim Ruvulo called a "county chairs only" meeting of the Ohio Democratic County Chairmen's Association. The admonition against bringing "camp followers" into the meeting sent the chilling signal that something serious was up.

It was. The governor came to the podium after a quick introduction by Ruvulo and announced a significant proposed reform of Ohio's system of deputy registrars. He wanted to depoliticize the license bureaus by making it unlawful for deputy registrars to contribute to political parties or campaigns, although they could keep the proceeds as before. He went on to announce that he had convened a task force to investigate the issue and to come up with a plan for implementing the reform.[17]

The governor tried to make the idea more palatable by proposing a "check-off" system, by which taxpayers could designate a portion of the income taxes to a political party fund, a portion of which would be doled out to local parties.

But no one was interested in this sop. In fact, the chairs were downright enraged, but Celeste held his ground. "I'm responsible for hundreds of license bureaus, many of which have serious problems and thousands of transactions," insisted Celeste. "I have to bring this situation under control or it could blow up in our faces."

At that point, Tim Barnhart of Ross County (Chillicothe), who headed the association, bitingly challenged the governor's motives. "Why are DRs being singled out? You say you're responsible for thousands of transactions. You were also responsible for a million-dollar no-bid contract with David Milenthal. Why don't you get your own house in order?"

Raucous and approving applause greeted Barnhart's pointed reference to Milenthal, Celeste's media advisor in the 1982 campaign, to whom the governor had granted a no-bid state tourism and travel advertising contract.[18] Barnhart's rebuke reminded all present that Celeste's generosity to his cronies stood in marked contrast to this hypocritical call for reform, which would work to the disadvantage of the county parties. The governor was trying to burnish his scandal-pocked image, largely at the expense of the county parties. As Barnhart made clear, we didn't like it one bit.

The governor didn't flinch, however, and handled Barnhart's admonition with a reference to an ethics bill that, he said, "will prevent such things from happening. So, we do have our own house in order." Disbelieving grumbles followed this response, which did not address the central question Barnhart had raised: Why had the county parties been singled out?[19]

Here's the answer: we were irrelevant. The governor needed business political action committees (PACs) and the corporate leaders who commanded them—"sugar daddies" like Marvin Warner, the Cincinnati businessman who had bankrolled the governor's 1982 campaign and whom Celeste later rewarded with the chairmanship of the Ohio Building Authority, the most lucrative patronage-dispensing billet in state government. He needed labor tycoons like Warren Smith, who headed up the Ohio Department of Transportation, and Marty Hughes, who was to be indicted for illegally diverting union funds to the Celeste campaign as vice president of the Communication Workers of America.[20] He needed minority bosses, like Arnold Pinkney, C. J. McLin, and Louis Stokes, who could deliver the votes of African Americans.

But Celeste didn't need us. Sam Barrone of Knox County (Mount Vernon) hinted as much when he voiced his displeasure at the governor's proposal: "You know the newspapers aren't going to give the governor any credit for this reform. They'll say, 'Celeste has milked it dry and now's he's trying to screw the goose.'"[21] A strange barnyard indeed. Yet Barrone had hit upon the critical point: The deputy registrar system, which the governor had exploited fully to win reelection, was now being sacrificed to overhaul his reputation. At the same time, Celeste's reform would not disturb the cozy system of deals that had gotten him elected in the first place. His proposal would do nothing to weaken the influence that political action committees, special interests, and wealthy contributors held over Ohio's parties and political candidates.

By forbidding the DRS to make political contributions, Celeste's reform ultimately debilitated the county parties. The deputy registrar system did have a sleazy reputation, shearing off a donation every time an Ohio driver paid a fee to a local license bureau. Yet it was a system, however crude and one-sided, of publicly funding political parties. In Ohio in 1987, it signified that as long as the Democrats controlled the governor's office, contributions via the local deputy registrars would flow into Democratic coffers at the county level as well as the state. License bureau money had helped fuel the Twining-first strategy. Our party could not have borrowed twelve cents from Smokey Hower, not to mention twelve thousand dollars, without the assurance that he would be repaid out of license bureau revenue. Of course, the Democrats' advantage would disappear if the GOP were to win the 1990 gubernatorial campaign, thus giving the county Republican parties access to funding from their own, freshly appointed DRS. That possibility, however, simply meant that the stakes in 1990 and succeeding elections would be exceptionally high, inducing local parties—Republican and Democrat—to work energetically on behalf of their respective nominees. As flawed as it was, the state's license bureau system linked the county parties with the governor's office, with their party at the state level, and with each other.

All of this was lost on Dick Celeste and Jim Ruvulo that night. Our protests mattered little. Before he adjourned the special meeting, Jim Ruvulo flippantly issued a macabre reference to what would eventually happen to the DR system. "The grave is dug," he said. "The only thing missing is the corpse."[22] A grim metaphor. The decision had been made.

As I returned from this meeting, the postelection atmosphere in Allen County seemed even more troubling. I already knew that 1987 would not be an easy year, especially with Bob Gehr and others sharing doubts about my leadership and with tension mounting between me and Steve Webb. Also ahead were preparations for Lima city elections, along with a renewal of the party fight, this time with Todd Hey and Charlie Hauenstein leading a revolt against me.

Still, and though the party split had not mended—as my concern about a Hauenstein/Hey comeback attested—the party was in better condition than it had been a year earlier. An observable commitment to process had entered our organization, beginning with a functioning committee structure. The party was living within its means, thanks to John Dornick's Budget Committee, which had established a plan for monthly spending, building a campaign war chest, and repaying debts. Also, our treasurer, Evelyn Vanek, had boosted the party's financial credibility by reporting each month's expenditures precisely and in writing. There would be no more grumbling about "where the money was going."[23]

More important, the party had made a strong statement about its new identity. In the logic of Twining-First, one can discover the meaning of what was happening to the Allen County Democratic Party. We were not working from the paradigm of the skeptics—Gehr, Schwieterman, Riffe, and the others—who had evaluated Twining's candidacy only in terms of her ability to win. Rather, Twining-First was a consequence of DEP's effort to build a party that was different from the one Charlie Hauenstein had led—an organization that would fearlessly engage the community in dialogue, brandishing ideas that challenged Allen County's conservative culture. If we were to create a party that could become an instrument of change, we would have to sponsor and encourage candidates who were not timid about addressing issues that made our fellow citizens squirm. Twining fit this role. She did more than any other candidate on the county ballot to raise the voters' attention beyond the conventional and the bland.

At one candidates' forum, for instance, Rochelle Twining and Bill Thompson jousted over the issue of poverty. Thompson argued that economic development would help the poor, declaring, "Putting people to work is the best way to decrease the amount of poverty in the community." A safe, conventional assertion. Twining sharply took issue, deriding economic development as a wrongheaded and incomplete response to the poor. "Economic development too often means growing profit margins for companies while the living standards of employees remain the same," she proclaimed.[24] Throughout her campaign, Rochelle Dennis Twining had fearlessly employed such rhetoric, and although the voters ultimately rejected her candidacy, they were all challenged by her message.

The party held its own postelection conversation about Twining-First. In November, Gehr and Schwieterman had initiated the debate, and the discussion continued at December's year-ending meeting of the Executive Committee, where Dale Leppla tried to lead the onslaught. He was met head-on by Rochelle Twining herself, who responded, "This party gave me a chance and proved that it is not the party of rich, white businessmen. . . . It's a party that is open to women, to people of color, to working people, and to anybody who's been shortchanged by the good ol' boys who run this county."[25] Her remarks won warm applause, and while Leppla, Schwieterman and others would continue to gripe, it was clear that some Democrats had begun to embrace the conviction that a party had to do more than manipulate elections. It was a faith that would be severely tested in 1987.

Part Three

Off Year

· 11 ·

Gestapo Politics

December 12, 1986, 7 A.M.
Rick Siferd liked dawn meetings, preferably over breakfast, which is why I now found myself walking into a diner two blocks from Siferd's law office, snow-flakes and early morning gloom batting the door as I entered. The mood inside was cheerful, though, especially in the corner where Rick and other members of the Policy Studies Committee had gathered. Pickle Felter and John Dornick had already arrived and were kibitzing with Siferd, who was digging into a big bowl of cream of wheat and pronouncing judgment over President Ronald Reagan's mishandling of the Iran-Contra scandal.

Dornick's presence at this meeting was particularly welcome. A large, broad-shouldered man with a square jaw and a bowlegged gait, John was fond of smelly cigars, dirty jokes, and scotch on the rocks. But he also read history, wrote poetry, and composed long, expressive letters. Even the most simple com-munication from him bore the mark of a man who revered the written word. Personal crises had sidelined Dornick for most of the 1986 campaign. In July, his wife Jane had been diagnosed with cancer, and he had devotedly cared for her while she underwent chemotherapy. Then in September, John had suffered a mild stroke, which hospitalized him for short time and kept him out of the fall campaign, except for a shift at our get-out-the-vote phone banks. Now he was back, anxious to "saddle up."

The meeting started shortly after Rochelle Twining joined us. When she pulled up a chair, Dornick tapped on his wristwatch and lit his first stogie of the day, grinning broadly as Rochelle let loose a feigned yowl. Ignoring the raillery, Siferd opened, "We don't have any elected officials who can make noise for us. So we have to make our own noise." Rick was not one to waste time crying over a lost election. It was time to move on, and he figured that it was his job, as chair of the Policy Studies Committee, to help the party to get beyond its recent defeat. With Siferd's opening remarks, a strategy began to unfold: The party would

These men were enduring players in the Allen County GOP. From an Allen County
Republican Party luncheon, February 1992. *From left:* Ben Rose (at the podium),
Republican Party chairman Bob Holmes, and State Representative Bill Thompson. *Lima
News* photo from the collection of the Allen County Historical Society.

start publicizing different topics, one at a time, highlighting problems that were
vexing the county. The hope was that by drawing attention to controversy, the
party could build issues that our candidates could exploit in 1988.[1]

For over a month, word had been circulating that the county commissioners
would soon double the local "piggyback" sales tax, from 0.5 percent to 1 percent. In fact, the rumor of a tax increase had begun to swirl even during the
waning days of the 1986 campaign. Robert Townsend, running against Schwieterman, had admitted that a tax increase was needed to finance construction of
a new jail and that the taxpayers would have to be educated about the need for
new revenue—though he had held out the hope that a tax increase could be
avoided if the state legislature approved a local revenue-sharing plan.[2] Don Reese,
Dale Leppla's opponent, had been even more equivocal, stating on one occasion that he doubted the need for a tax increase, and on another that the construction of a new jail would require one.[3] Then, following his election victory,
Reese had declared that doubling the piggyback sales tax was a sensible solution
to the county's revenue problems, but he would not say whether the increase
should be simply imposed or put to a vote of the people.[4]

Of course, it did not bother us on Siferd's committee that our own candidates had been just as mealy-mouthed about county finances, ducking the prospect of a tax increase by pledging they would study the county budget and try to cut spending.[5] That didn't matter now. The Republicans had won the election, and the fire was in their corner. We aimed to stoke the coals, targeting the inability of the Republican commissioners to speak forthrightly on taxes as the first topic to bring to the voters' attention.

Wanting to pounce on the issue before the county commission acted, the Policy Studies Committee met several times in January to discuss our approach. With help from Steve Webb, who supplied insights from his own experience negotiating public workers' contracts, and Pickle Felter, who built a research file from back editions of the *Lima News*, we pieced together the seriousness of the county's financial condition. We discovered that the county had rolled its December payroll into January to overcome an end-of-year shortfall. Other reports showed that the commissioners had been shifting revenues from the capital improvements fund to the general fund to pay operating expenses. Furthermore, they had already slashed the budget of all county departments by 8 percent and now were poised to make another 5 percent across-the-board reduction.[6]

The overriding concern was county's desperate need for a new jail. According to federal courts, the existing 110-year-old facility was inadequate. The state of Ohio was willing to chip in $3.2 million for the new facility, providing that the county came up with a matching sum. The county would miss its chance, however, unless it could find funding for the project by June 30, the end of the state's fiscal year. The only way Allen County could hold up its end of the deal was to raise the piggyback sales tax—immediately.

For the Policy Studies Committee, however, the principle of trust was at stake. Siferd put it best when he reminded us of the election two years earlier when Republican commissioner candidates had insisted that "the county's financial condition was sound" and then tried to increase taxes after their victory. "Okay, so it's the same thing here. Basically, they lied. But what if we're asked whether we oppose the tax increase?" someone queried. Siferd replied, "Then our position is that the tax should be put to a vote of the people."[7]

At this point, Webb pulled back somewhat, realizing that his public-employees unions would probably favor the tax increase. The party's position, no matter how clearly expressed, could be perceived as a stand against the tax, and that stand would place Webb in a conflict of interest, torn between his obligations to the American Federation of State County and Municipal Employees (AFSCME) and his party duties.[8]

We offered little sympathy for his plight, failing to understand that Webb's quandary was also the party's. Instead, we pushed ahead with our plan and scheduled a press conference for January 29, 1987—at AFSCME headquarters, no less. Dornick suggested that I issue the statement on behalf of the party and handle questions from the media. "Just don't use any of those big words you 'poly sci' profs like to throw around," he advised with a wink.[9] He could hardly wait for the fun to start.

January 30, 1987

The lead in the *Lima News* story blared, "The Chairman of the Allen County Democratic Party lashed out Thursday at the County's Republican commissioners, charging them with dishonesty and poor management of county coffers."[10] Perfect. Exactly as planned, my salvo had disparaged the commissioners' integrity and had asserted the Allen County Democratic Party's claim to be a player in local politics. Even if our candidates had all lost in the November elections, we were still alive, offering aggressive opposition to Republican hegemony over county government.

A week earlier, the commission's president, Don Reese, had observed on WLIO TV that the county's financial problems were "five years in the making," that they had not "happened overnight." This was the same Don Reese who, while running for office, had doubted the need for a tax increase. Now he was not only building the case but making it sound as if the commissioners bore no responsibility for the pending tax. The commission's hand had been forced, he alleged, by cuts in revenue sharing, more costly liability insurance, and state-mandated expenditures.[11] I believed otherwise and said so, accusing the commissioners of "deliberately" deceiving the public. "When the Commissioners' election prospects are in jeopardy," I charged, "they assure the voters that the county is in solid financial shape. But as soon as the ink is dry on the election results, they begin groaning about the condition of county finances."[12]

That was from a three-page statement, which did not much interest the reporters attending the press conference. Following my declaration, a procession began. First, the radio reporters pushed around me, pulling out their tape recorders, punching "record" buttons, and bombarding me with questions. Once they had accumulated enough sound bites, they snapped off their recorders and moved on to the next assignment. There was no follow-up, or effort to tease out the complexities of a story. The shorter my answers, the better. In fact, one reporter once admonished me for speaking in complex sentences: "If it's longer than ten seconds, I can't use it."

Next in line was a television reporter and a camera technician from WLIO TV. After the technician focused the mini-cam and checked the sound, the reporter led off: "Why did you call this press conference?" Perplexed by the banality of the query, I gave a thumbnail summary of my statement, responded to a cursory follow-up, and watched the crew gather their equipment and speed to their next job.

Last in the queue was Paul W. Smith, who covered county politics for the *Lima News*. With mussed blond hair, a knit tie worn loose around his collar, and wire-rimmed glasses that never seemed to fit right, he bore the disarming look of a college undergraduate. Plopping into a folding chair, he pulled out a notepad and began firing questions. Although Smith let me hammer away at the commissioners' handling of county finances, he quietly began pressing me on whether the Democratic Party was against the tax.

I asserted that the party was not necessarily against the tax, that we simply thought the voters needed to be informed of the reasons the county found itself in a financial predicament and of the fact that the commissioners bore total responsibility for it. But Smith would not let go. "Will the party support a referendum to repeal the increase in the sales tax?" he asked. I tried to dodge a direct answer by saying that I thought the voters deserved a chance to vote on the issue. "But will the Democratic Party support a referendum?" Smith persisted. He really wanted to know. I relented. "It's my sense the Democratic Party's Executive Committee will support a referendum effort," I responded. "That doesn't mean we oppose the tax increase or support it. That means we think that the voters ought to have shot."[13] With that, Smith flipped shut his note pad. The interview was over.

February 4, 1987, Lima City Council Chambers
Don Reese was doing most of the talking at the first of two public meetings on the piggyback sales tax proposal. He was itemizing the uses that the increase would serve, devoting most of his time to the case for the new jail. "The $3.2 million needed to match the state jail grant is a large sum of money," he observed, "but the cost of not having that jail is a lot bigger."[14]

Reese's enthusiasm for the tax increase was echoed by other county officials, including Sheriff Charles Harrod, Judge Michael Rumer of the Common Pleas Court, and Judge David Kinworthy of the Juvenile and Probate Court. In addition, a couple of local businessmen, Alan Blattner and Wesley Runk, were on hand to add their flourish. "I'd like to think I live in a community that is as good as it can be," Runk said, bubbling like an evangelist. "We need the tax increase, we want it, and I would hope the rest of us would stand up and be counted!"[15]

Only one person voiced opposition—Bryan Hefner, who challenged the regressive character of the tax increase, claiming that it would hurt poor people.

Reese shrugged, observing that the tax would cost an average family of four only thirty-one dollars per year. "And thirty-one dollars a year isn't going to hurt anybody," he sermonized.[16]

The rhetoric that night was one of high-principled boosterism. "If you want the county to grow and become more economically progressive," went the argument, "then you must support the tax increase." To do otherwise would mean that you were against progress. That message, plus a combination of other factors—the risk of losing the jail grant, the prospect of draconian budget cuts, and the prediction of layoffs of county employees—created a forceful and convincing case for the tax.

After the hearing, Bob Townsend reminded me of a fundamental political consideration. Shaking my hand, he smiled grimly and said, "Bill, I hope that when you elect a Democrat commissioner, he'll have the revenues to do the job." I could only respond that he and Reese should have been more forthcoming during their campaigns. Townsend stared at me curiously to see if his point had registered, then flashed another smile and ambled toward his pals massed on the opposite side of the room.

February 12, 1987, the Alpine Village Restaurant
"What's the point?" I exclaimed. "Huh? What the hell is the goddamn point? Did we just take over the party to pander to the antitax sentiment in this county? Did we? If all you care about is winning and not trying to build a better community, then I'll just walk out that doorway, and you can find yourself a new chairman."

Dead silence. As I spoke, my gaze fell on each Democrat sitting around the table, lingering especially on Steve Webb, Mike Bender, John Dornick, and Cora Hamman. They shifted in their seats. Earlier, they had been vociferously advocating the idea that our party should head up a referendum on the piggyback sales tax.

I stared particularly hard at Steve Webb, who had been especially outspoken and cocksure, declaring, "The party should take a direct stand on this issue and lead a referendum. That's going to give our candidates the best chance to win." It was this pronouncement, especially the part about "giving our candidates the best chance to win," that had set me off. My expletive-laced statement had not fazed Webb, who responded condescendingly, "Bill, you have to look at this politically. Being against taxes is good politics."

"I am looking at it politically," I shot back. I had calmed down—somewhat. At least my voice was more subdued. "What makes us Democrats?" I continued. "Republicans can run on an antitax platform. It fits them. Not us. If we take an antitax stand, we might as well go out and join up with Reagan. That's his program. It's not mine. And it's not going to be this party's program, either," I insisted, thumping the table.[17]

A contentious spirit drifted around the table. Our political world had gone topsy-turvy: Republicans were gleefully promoting a tax increase, while Democrats were glowering and conspiring to stop them.

In fact, both sides were trapped. Two days earlier, the Allen County commissioners, all Republicans, had resolutely doubled the piggyback sales tax, but in doing so they had put themselves in a tight spot, or at least their party had. In election after election, the Republican Party had piled up national and statewide victories by pounding the antitax drum—my scars from the Maurer-Cupp race bore witness to this strategy. At the same time, the GOP had triumphed locally by praising their commissioners' sound, frugal management of county finances, never speaking frankly about the need for tax increases. This had happened two years previously, when a proposal to raise the sales tax was put to the electorate six months after a brutal Republican sweep of all county offices. The voters had rejected it, three to one. Now, the county still needed money, and the commissioners couldn't risk putting the question to the public, as they had then. The only way to increase the sales tax was to decree it, an autocratic move sure to anger the voters.

None of us gathered at the Alpine were of a mind to let the commissioners escape, but we also were in a muddle, entangled in a "catch-22" of my making. Was it good politics for us, leaders of the Democratic Party, to sabotage the county's treasury for the sake of partisan advantage? At my press conference, I had scourged the commissioners for their duplicity and had roused Democratic troops to action. Now, having told the *Lima News* that the party would back an attempt to put the tax increase to a referendum, I had set into motion the forces to do just that.

Cora Hamman, for one, was itching to move against the tax. Her attitude was not new to me. I had first met her at a Democratic dinner in May 1983 when I was promoting a park district levy. I stopped by a table where Cora was sitting. She took a brochure, glanced at it sullenly, and muttered that she wouldn't support the levy—that as a matter of principle, she didn't like taxes. In four years, her philosophy hadn't mellowed. Shortly after the commissioners imposed the tax increase, I met with her and Steve Webb. "I must have received fifty calls," Cora claimed, citing phone conversations that had been call-forwarded, at Cora's suggestion, from the party's number to her home telephone. "Everybody wants to know what the Democrats are going to do," she said. "I think we ought to referend that sucker."[18]

I avoided an immediate commitment to such a strategy. Leading a referendum campaign was not what I had had in mind when I had held that press conference in January. Furthermore, I knew it would be a monumental task to circulate petitions and gather enough valid signatures to place the matter on the November ballot. More importantly, Bob Townsend had gotten into my head with his observation that Democratic commissioners would need revenue, too.

I called John Dornick to air my misgivings. He had been in on the work of the Policy Studies Committee from the very beginning and understood the nuances of the tax issue. I figured that in him I might find someone who favored a more cautious approach. But no. Like Cora and Steve, he thought it would be a good idea for the party to take on the referendum directly.[19]

So did other Democrats, and now, at this meeting of party officers, most of whom were former DEP activists, we were wrangling over the party's role in a controversy that I had launched. In a mellow drawl that momentarily eased the tension in the room, John Hevener observed, "I really think the tax increase is needed, and I don't much like the idea of the party leading a referendum fight." With that, we quietly began discussing the dilemma facing us. The party—that is, its chairman—had raised the issue, went one line of argument, and now it had to live up to the commitment made during the press conference two weeks earlier. Also, Mike Bender reminded us, if commissioners produced the revenue needed to build the jail, improve the roads and bridges, and expand other county services, they would simply take credit for all the good things they had done.[20]

"Yes, but the tax increase is necessary," someone countered, which reminded the group that a decision to lead a referendum would almost certainly doom the jail project and lead to cuts in county services. "We can play politics with the issue and offer the citizens a chance to vote on the tax increase, but we cannot avoid responsibility for the outcome should the referendum repeal it."

"What responsibility?" someone replied. "All we're trying to do is give the people a chance to vote. Let the voters decide."

"We know that, but will people outside this room know it? The tax and the referendum can't be separated. To be for the referendum is to be against the tax and the purposes it would be used for."

And on it went, until, finally, I called for a vote of party officers, offering three alternatives—the party itself leading a referendum on the tax increase; the party indirectly assisting a referendum effort but not spearheading the drive; and the party taking no action on the tax increase. Interestingly, no one favored the "direct leadership" alternative, the position Webb had advocated moments earlier. The vote came down initially to a four-to-four split between "no action" and "indirect assistance," but at the last minute the party secretary, Elsie Crowe, switched her vote to the indirect-assistance side, the position ultimately favored by Webb and Hamman.[21] A week later, I was still ruminating about the party's decision to assist a tax repeal campaign, howsoever indirectly. "There's too much looseness and uncertainty built into that option," I wrote Susan Gibler, "and I fear that if the tax referendum goes to the voters, it may be signed with Democratic ink."[22]

February 19, 1987

Bob Routson was not a political activist. He was a good citizen—voting regularly, keeping track of current events, and occasionally attending political rallies—but nothing had prepared him for the day he marched into the Board of Elections and requested a set of referendum petitions. Declaring his plan to organize a fight against the piggyback sales tax, Routson stressed the Democratic Party line: "I'm not against the tax increase. I just think the people should be making that decision."[23]

Routson had arrived at this moment because he lived around the corner from Cora Hamman. The two had gotten to know each other over the years as Cora trooped through their precinct, on Lima's northern perimeter, circulating nomination petitions and canvassing for Democratic candidates. Routson had encouraged Cora's activism, and when the party authorized indirect assistance to a referendum drive, Cora naturally squeezed him into her sights as the potential front man for the effort. With Bryan Hefner and John Dornick in tow, she had paid Routson a visit, and together all three talked him into heading up a committee to "referend" the tax hike.[24]

A UAW retiree who had worked at the Ohio Steel Foundry (later Teledyne), Routson was understandably nervous about taking on this high-profile job. The Hamman-Dornick-Hefner contingent promised that he would not be left on his own. Democrats would be on hand to help, they said—though they cautioned that none of them, or any member of the party's Executive or Central Committee, could assist "out front." They could circulate petitions and provide informal guidance, but nothing more. "Bill wants us to keep the party out of this," the group emphasized.[25]

The job required Herculean effort. Referendum organizers had to circulate two sets of petitions—one for the sales tax increase as it applied to motor vehicles, and the second for goods other than motor vehicles. Furthermore, each set required 3,358 valid signatures to put the respective measure before the voters. Even more daunting was the narrow time-window Routson had to squeeze through. Once the commissioners had approved the tax ordinance, a referendum committee had only thirty days to circulate and file their petitions with the county auditor. Nine days had already passed, leaving Routson less than three weeks to get the job done.[26]

Despite the obstacles that stood in Routson's path, the county's Republican establishment did not feel secure. On hearing that Routson had picked up referendum petitions, commission president Reese wrung his hands like the father of a recalcitrant eighteen-year-old, fretting because plans for the new jail were now in jeopardy; "I'm disappointed that the people feel that way, but at the same time it's their privilege," he said. [27] The county administrator, Crit Akers, was more blunt. "If enough signatures are obtained," he lamented, "you can say 'goodbye' to the jail."[28]

But first Routson had to get his petitions past H. Dean French, the county auditor. Tall and athletic, with a gray thatch of hair and a wide handsome face that sometimes bore a puzzled look, French had been appointed to his post in 1979, when his predecessor Dick Ditto resigned to accept an appointment to the state senate. Although French was an elected official, he had never had to worry about serious electoral opposition. He had last faced a contested election in 1980, defeating Democratic challenger John Lewis by over thirteen thousand votes in the race to fill Ditto's unexpired term.[29]

Perhaps this dearth of battle experience explains why French normally shied away from confrontational politics, the kind election campaigns generate. Consider, for example, a dispute that embroiled the Republican Party in May 1986. When the county treasurer, Herb McElwain, died in office that spring, the Republican Central Committee was called upon to appoint a successor. Maxine Jones, McElwain's assistant and fixture in the treasurer's office, emerged as the candidate whom the party's grassroots members favored. However, GOP chairman Bob Holmes wanted the post to go to Dick Ditto, who had been politically unemployed since 1980, when he lost his senate seat to Steve Maurer. Holmes appointed a screening committee of allies, including French, expecting them to send Ditto's name to the Central Committee.

French felt uneasy at this assignment, but he did his duty and voted, along with the others, to recommend Ditto. The Central Committee rubber-stamped that decision in a raucous session in which a roll call forced each representative to vote publicly. Most didn't wish to challenge Holmes openly, and despite muttering and protest, Ditto won handily. French, who had business in Columbus that day, was not on hand to view the fireworks. He didn't mind, though; showdowns like that made him uncomfortable.[30]

But today events were dragging Dean French smack into the center of a public controversy, where political pressure would bear down on him. The law required him as county auditor to receive the referendum petitions, inspect them, and determine whether the issue should be presented to the voters. It was his call. Whether French liked it or not, his office would become the initial line of defense against the referendum.

There was some initial jousting over a requirement that petition organizers had to file a "verified" copy of each tax resolution with the auditor. It's a sensible regulation, designed to make certain that petitioners understand what they are signing. Routson thought he had met the requirement, securing copies of both tax resolutions from the commissioners' office, registering them with the county stamp, filing them with French, and attaching copies of the resolutions to the petitions. However, exactly one day before the deadline, Routson was told by French and the county prosecutor, David Bowers, that the copies filed with the auditor had been only "certified," not "verified."[31] In fact, the prosecutor went public with his concern. "Under current law there is a question as to what the word 'verify' means," Bowers remarked to the *Lima News*. "I told Dean that I hadn't researched it, but it may present a problem. So [he] should inform the referendum group that the resolutions might not be legally correct."[32]

Actually, there was no question that Routson had mishandled the procedure. French has since admitted as much, insisting that as far as he knew, no difference existed between a "verified" copy of the tax resolution and a "certified" one.[33] But Routson saw it as an issue. In fact, these eleventh-hour maneuvers tossed him and his committee into bewilderment. Routson immediately called the secretary of state, Sherrod Brown, whose legal staff confirmed that he had done nothing wrong. He then informed both French and Bowers, "The Secretary of State told me that those petitions are legal, and by golly, those are the ones I am going to turn in."[34]

Bowers and French, it would appear, were trying to make Routson nervous, spreading disinformation and confusion by advising him first that he had processed the paperwork properly and then warning him later of procedural problems. Perhaps they hoped that Routson would reinitiate his petition drive (and so miss the deadline) or that he would submit a sloppy mess of inconsistently prepared petition papers. Maybe they wanted him to get so baffled that he would give up altogether.[35]

More games were to come. Routson's committee had done good work in gathering signatures. Petition circulators, including nineteen members of the Democratic Party's Central and Executive Committees,[36] had collected over four thousand names for each set of petitions, and most of the signatures were ruled valid by the clerks at the Board of Elections.[37] But when the board returned the

Bob Routson watches county auditor Dean French check referendum petitions for piggyback sales tax, March 1987. *Lima News* photo from the collection of the Allen County Historical Society.

petitions to the auditor for his determination as to whether the tax issue would be placed on the November ballot, French cautioned, "We're going to go over them with a fine-toothed comb." He hinted that despite the scrutiny the petitions had received from clerks at the Board of Elections, a large number of signatures might not be valid. "There are other things that have to be checked," he observed cryptically. "There are other reasons they may be invalid signatures." When pressed further, he concluded, "That's all I'm going to say. They may be all right."[38] Dean French had something up his sleeve.

There was something fishy about the petition circulated by Dr. L. Y. Soo. A whole string of signatures showed addresses on Reservoir Road, on Lima's eastern border; Dr. Soo, a prominent local physician, lived in a posh suburban neighborhood west of the city, ten miles away from those signatures. It was weird—unless, of course, Dr. Soo hadn't been the one passing the petition. And if that was true, the doctor would find himself in serious trouble, facing a felony indictment and the possibility of a jail sentence and a heavy fine. Of more immediate importance, the entire petition—and the nearly ninety signatures it contained—would be ruled invalid.

A sheriff's deputy, Sam Crish, and several other Republican *apparatchiki* had assembled at Dean French's request to comb through Routson's petitions. The auditor had been alerted to examine the petitions closely—the alarm most likely having been sounded by Republicans at the Board of Elections—and sure enough, Crish and the others found the obvious discrepancy in Soo's petition.[39]

It fell to Crish, who handled lot of political work for his boss, Sheriff Charles Harrod, to follow up on these suspicions. Spotting one signer of Soo's petition who, as a good Republican, ought to have known better, Crish decided to pay the guy a visit and find out who had taken that paper to his door.[40]

April 2, 1986, Thursday
Cora Hamman called early, as usual. She had just talked to her friend Clementina DePalma, and Clem had told her that sheriff's deputies had been to see her, asking questions about who had been present when she signed a referendum petition. Cora suggested that I try to find out what was going on, because it didn't seem right for deputies to be harassing citizens exercising their constitutional rights.

I agreed and called Paul Smith at the *Lima News,* asking him if he knew anything about deputies shaking down citizens who had signed Routson's petitions. Smith replied that it was true—sort of. French had received complaints that official circulators had not been on hand when folks signed the petitions, and the newspaper was running a front-page story reporting that sheriff's deputies were checking out the allegations.[41]

I blew a gasket. "We are witnessing the effect of one-party government," I responded. "Sending the deputies out in Gestapo-type fashion is no way to run county government." Then I moved to what I saw as the real story: "The boys at the Courthouse are looking for ways to defeat the referendum effort. It's been painfully obvious from the beginning that the commissioners are afraid of the vote."[42] I issued similar statements to the television and radio media.

By using terms like "Gestapo" and "one-party government" and accusing the commissioners of being "afraid," I ratcheted up rhetorical pressure on the Republicans. When asked to respond, GOP chairman Bob Holmes glared into WLIO's television camera and dismissed my charges, muttering, "Bill Angel needs to know the law."[43] At a party luncheon later that week, he blustered, "Bill Angel is totally political on the referendum issue."[44] Don Reese followed Holmes's lead, declaring, "The petition drive was started on the advice of Bill Angel, although he's worked to stay at arm's length. I think the Democrats are doing everything they can to embarrass the three Republican Commissioners."[45] I had burrowed under some Republican hide, all right.

The whole investigation had started with Sam Crish's informal inquiry. On off-duty time, he visited his friend on Reservoir Road and then talked to others in the neighborhood who had signed Dr. Soo's petition. He discovered that a woman, possibly a nurse or receptionist for Dr. Soo—but not Dr. Soo himself—had circulated the petition. He secured statements confirming that fact, and in a similar fashion he began to investigate informally other petitions as well.[46]

Documents other than Dr. Soo's had fallen under scrutiny. John Dornick had submitted nine sets of petitions, each containing a relatively small number of signatures, anywhere from fifteen to thirty-eight. It was highly unusual for one person to circulate that many petitions at once; the usual procedure was for a circulator to pass one petition and fill it up completely with ninety signatures before starting a new one. Perhaps Dornick, speculation went, had simply dropped off his petitions at a various locations, picked them up later, and affixed his name to them as circulator. At any rate, Dornick's petitions became the target of an official inquiry by Sgt. Larry Van Horn of the sheriff's department, who discovered that Dornick indeed had left a petition at Lima Cadillac, the local Cadillac dealership, then stopped by later to retrieve it. John had handled the others the same way, further inquiry revealed.[47]

Then, as Dean French later reflected, "things snowballed."[48] Word leaked that deputies were conducting an investigation of Routson's petitions, gathering testimony from citizens who had signed them. Someone informed the *Lima News,* which publicized what had been a quiet probe. It was at that point that I gave the pot a stir by labeling the investigation "Gestapo-type."

But the events also now took on a disturbing character. French, Bowers, and other authorities began receiving calls from citizens who either had signed petitions or who had observed petitions being signed, all claiming that the official circulators had not been present. These calls, in turn, prompted sheriff's detectives to expand their probe, asking their contacts if the named circulator had been present when they signed their names. As French and others have since stated, deputies did not sweep through the county, randomly picking people who legitimately had signed petitions, but contacted only those who had called the authorities to point out possible discrepancies in the documents.[49]

Most likely, this is how Larry Miller, Routson's son-in-law, got caught. He had circulated his petition at the Teledyne steel foundry, where he worked the first shift, then left it for workers on the second and third shifts to sign. One of these late-shift signers later contacted the sheriff's office and confirmed that Miller had not watched him affix his signature to the document. Similarly, another member of Routson's committee had left his petition at a St. Gerard's Parish bingo night; according to signers who later called authorities, he hadn't stayed with the petition as people signed.[50]

"We were our own worst enemy," Routson admitted years later. "We had limited time and limited knowledge. We were overzealous and made mistakes."[51] Routson is too charitable.

For one thing, there was the matter of the Democrats' wimpy tactics. Instead of leading the effort and taking over a campaign my own words had inspired, the party found a surrogate in Bob Routson to do its dirty work. This, as it turned out, was a tragic choice, because Routson and his committee fell into traps that more experienced activists might have avoided. They also felt deserted by the Democratic Party, which had put them up to this endeavor, then failed to come through with the hands-on guidance that the Hamman-Dornick-Hefner contingent earlier had promised.[52]

But even more troubling was the sinister atmosphere that materialized once the sheriff's probe began. Sam Crish's off-duty investigation, conducted on his own and without any official sanction, was less frightening than the formal investigation that followed. That inquiry sent a "power message," demonstrating that Bowers and French were serious about gathering evidence and pushing the case into the criminal-justice process.

People had informed on fellow citizens who were legitimately petitioning their government. Some of the informants had signed petitions, while others had simply been left in charge of them until circulators like John Dornick could drop by and retrieve them. These witnesses surely knew what the referendum committee wanted to accomplish; Routson's group had been candid in advising prospective allies. Most likely, the callers were scared that they had done something wrong, and acting on their fear, contacted the authorities. This is not the kind of thing that should happen in a democracy—citizens going to the police to inform on each other—but it was unfolding in Allen County.

The day the "Gestapo politics" story broke, a Democratic Central Committeewoman called me. She had signed one of the questionable petitions, and now deputies were coming to her house to collect an affidavit. She was frightened and wanted me to be there when they arrived. I obliged. Unperturbed by my presence, two plainclothes detectives questioned her, ascertained that the circulator had not been present when she had signed the referendum petition, and took her statement. I thought nothing of this incident at the time, other than that the detectives, who were exceptionally polite, had probably been on their best behavior. But years later, knowing what I do now, I ask, "Why did the detectives question her, unless she or perhaps her husband, both fellow Democrats, had called the authorities?" It is a question I'm not sure I want answered.

April 3, 1987, Friday

The sheriff's investigation had turned up more than enough invalid petitions to allow French to rule the tax issue off the ballot. But he wanted to make things easy on himself, and so he called in Bob Routson. Prosecutor Bowers sat in on this meeting at which French and Bowers told Routson what the deputies' investigation had revealed.[53] Dr. L. Y. Soo, John P. Dornick, Larry Miller, and others had falsely circulated petitions, swearing that they had watched the petitions being signed when in fact they had not. Altogether, deputies had contacted eighteen petition signers and had collected fifteen affidavits providing evidence that circulators had violated election law.[54] In addition, two petitions had been signed by circulators whose signatures did not match those on file with the Board of Election.[55] Consequently, the matter would return to the Board of Elections for a hearing, at which witnesses would be called and testimony received. If the board ruled the petitions invalid, they would be thrown out, and the referendum would not be put on the ballot. Also, French and Bowers warned, Soo, Dornick, Miller, and the rest would be subject to indictment and criminal proceedings, from which they could face up to six months in jail, plus a thousand-dollar fine.[56]

The two officials offered Routson a way out, however. If he were to pull the petitions—submitting a written request that they be withdrawn—the authorities would forget the whole thing. No hearing would be held; there would be no indictments. Of course, neither would there be any vote on the tax issue. It was up to Routson.[57]

Though angry, Routson took French's offer back to his committee, which unequivocally instructed him to withdraw the petitions. French has since claimed that he never threatened Routson. But Routson felt threatened.[58] The county prosecutor's presence had strongly signaled that the authorities were serious about hearings and indictments, and French himself has admitted that if need be, they had been ready to carry matters that far.[59] Routson announced the decision tersely: "Rather than subject [the circulators and signers] to any more embarrassment and intimidation, we decided to ... pull the whole thing."[60]

Routson's partners felt pressure, too, especially John Dornick, who was shaken by the prospect of legal proceedings. "I've spent days on picket lines and nights in jail," he told Rick Siferd, Pickle Felter, and me at a meeting of the Policy Studies Committee. "But I'm too old for this shit." Rick tried to jolly him out of his funky mood, joking, "Come on, John, the party needs a martyr. You'd make a good one. You know, like them Buddhist monks in Vietnam who doused themselves with gasoline. We'd rally behind you. What do you say?" Dornick would have nothing to do with Siferd's raillery. "I'm too old to be a goddamned martyr," he muttered.[61]

Routson's and Dornick's struggle did not escape the notice of the *Lima News,* which editorialized on their behalf, castigating county officials for applying aggressive tactics. "The Commissioners, Prosecutor, and Auditor are elected to be public servants—to serve the public not be lord over it," the newspaper observed. "In this instance, our officials leave the impression that they are primarily interested in throwing up any possible roadblock in the way of the referendum."[62]

Such backing from the *Lima News,* which normally held fast to the Republican Party line, was welcome, but it came too late. The decision had been made. On Friday, April 10, Bob Routson submitted a one-sentence letter to Dean French requesting that his referendum petitions be withdrawn. The fight was over.[63]

As a politician, I had "stunk great." My bombast of April 2, designed to provide rhetorical cover for Bob Routson and his committee, only made their situation worse and, ironically, contributed to the Gestapo atmosphere I would decry. By drawing attention to the county's investigation of the petitions and stoking up the controversy, I added to the fear felt by some petition signers, who, thinking they might have done something illegal, snitched on Routson and his committee.

Additionally, my efforts exposed the weak hand that Democrats held—this despite my intention to promote our party as a dynamic contestant in local politics. In particular, my January press conference, with its pessimistic and skeptical portrayal of the commissioners, starkly contrasted with the Republicans' can-do optimism. When the party tried to manipulate support for the referendum, the move only confirmed an attitude shared by many county residents: We Democrats lacked imagination; we could oppose, but we could not come up with positive, workable alternatives; we could debunk, but we could not build.[64]

Finally, the effort exposed troubling divisions within our party. Democrats were deeply nettled by the question, "Is the tax needed?" Many of my core supporters—Cora Hamman, Steve Webb, and Bryan Hefner, to name a few—had voiced a desire not only to put the issue before the voters but to fight against the tax itself. Yet with Steve Webb's unions and other important Democratic constituencies lining up in favor of the tax increase, it would have been difficult for the party to oppose it. This circumstance became apparent shortly after the referendum drive went public, when Webb's AFSCME locals denied me the use of their headquarters as a venue for press conferences.[65] Had Bob Routson successfully placed the issue on the ballot, the Democrats almost assuredly would have become even more deeply split.

But ruminations about what the Democrats could have or should have done ignore the central lesson of this controversy: The battle over the referendum revealed the absolute power of Allen County's Republican establishment and its brash recklessness in wielding authority. The county commissioners, the auditor, the sheriff, and the county prosecutor never wanted the issue to go the voters, and the authorities—especially the auditor and the prosecutor—put one hurdle after another in Bob Routson's path, just as the *Lima News* charged.

Most notably, the use of deputies to question petitioners was a heavy-handed display of power and, frankly, an unnecessary one. French has insisted that his office had to follow up on complaints that petitions had been illegally circulated. Had his office not investigated, he would have been deluged with charges of incompetence from those who favored the tax increase.[66] Fair enough. But did authorities have to rush out a sheriff's deputy to investigate the allegations? French and Bowers could have called in Routson and told him that several petitions—Soo's and Dornick's—looked suspicious and outlined the risks of filing falsely circulated petitions. Or, even more appropriately, French and Bowers could have invited Soo and Dornick to their offices and explained the problems found in the petitions they had turned in. If Routson, Dornick, Soo, and the others had proven obdurate and refused to help the inquiry, the sheriff's office could have been called in. A less ham-fisted approach, in other words, could have supplied the evidence needed to disqualify the referendum from the ballot.

Instead, Bowers and French initiated the inquiry as if Routson and his followers were engaged in a conspiracy to topple the state. Dr. L. Y. Soo, John Dornick, and others had indeed cut legal corners in circulating their petitions, but they had not intended to; their motives had not been corrupt. They were, as Routson has observed, "overzealous" in their desire to place the tax issue on the ballot, and they committed serious errors in passing their petitions. Ordinarily such indiscretions would have escaped official eyes, but not this time. The stakes were too high and the authorities too willing to do anything to kill the referendum.[67]

In this sense, the investigation worked. It stopped Routson and his committee dead in their tracks. They withdrew their petitions. The commissioners and the county received their revenue.

The investigation also succeeded in an even more fundamental way. It showed that the power exercised by Allen County Republicans was collective in its effect, transcending the power individually exerted by Reese, Holmes, Bowers, French, or any of the other establishment figures. In fact, the raw, undignified display of sheriff's deputies conducting a political inquiry sent the most important message of all: that the Republican Party dominated this edge of the state.

· 12 ·

Steering a Course

June 20, 1987, 4 P.M., AFSCME Headquarters
Steve Webb and I sat on one side of the conference table in the American Federation of State County and Municipal Employees office; Todd and Judy Hey sat directly opposite. I swiftly broke the news that Hey's license bureau was to be awarded to Steve. I then urged the men to cooperate and arrange a smooth transfer, so that the agency would be in operation by July 1, the day Steve would formally become the new deputy registrar at the Lima Mall license bureau.

Todd took the news calmly. He said that for two weeks he had heard rumors about the change but was surprised we had awarded it to Steve, adding, "I'm glad you didn't give it to who I thought." Probably Cora Hamman, I mused, not suspecting that Steve and Cora together had arranged a surprise for me. After the Heys left, Webb began speaking gingerly about his new post: "You know, Bill, I'll need a manager to run the place, and I wanted to check with you to see if it's okay. . . . I'd like to hire Cora for the job."

My jaw must have dropped, because he began picking up the pace, trying to convince me that this was a good idea. "It would give her somethin' to do, and she deserves it. But I wanted to ask you and let you approve it."

"She'll drive those women nuts within two weeks," I observed, referring to Todd's employees, who would be kept on by Webb. "Yeah, I know, but it'll give her somethin' to do." I let Steve know that I had reservations about putting Cora in charge of the license bureau. "Give me some time to think about it," I said.

Actually, I could do nothing about the scheme that Cora and Steve had concocted. Of course, I went along with it, but I was rankled by the dilemma Steve had forced on me. To veto Cora as manager of the license bureau would have made her a permanent enemy, and that was not something I wanted to risk—not then, anyway. But to concede to Steve and Cora's design would mean approval of Cora's involvement in the operation, and if Cora caused a problem through some rude offense, the party and I would receive the blame. "Bill authorized me to hire Cora," Steve might say in the event of a foul-up.[1]

I especially resented the secretive manner in which their scheme had been devised; it contrasted markedly with the pains party leaders had taken to discuss our move on the license bureau. Everyone had known Steve wanted it, and everyone had known our decision entailed important risks. The Operations Committee had supplied a venue for several open discussions, during which we had aired the positive and negative aspects of any decision we might make. Most party officers had favored taking the bureau from Todd. If we left the operation in his hands, went the reasoning, he would use his money against us, buying support for his bid to retake the party.

John Hevener had held a different conviction. By deposing Todd, he had warned, we would make him a martyr, thus handing him a claim to sympathy and a reason to come after us. Jim Ruvulo had stated a similar idea, observing that the best way to make sure that Hey would not challenge my leadership would be to allow him to keep the license bureau. He advised me to use the agency as an incentive for good behavior; I could tell Todd, "Look, you can stay on as deputy registrar if you promise not to challenge the current party leadership." This position did not have many advocates, as most members of the Operations Committee, even Hevener, believed Todd could not be trusted under any circumstances. Once he knew he still had the license bureau, they countered, he would be free to do whatever he wanted.[2]

The overriding consideration, however, was the "Steve Webb issue." Steve had made it crystal clear to me that he wanted that bureau, most recently in late February. It was shortly after that contentious meeting at which he and I had clashed publicly over the tax referendum; I had invited him to lunch to explain to him that I wanted to avoid any appearance of a rift between us.[3] Part of the tiff that night had been caused by miscommunication, and we settled the matter by agreeing to keep in closer contact with each other. (Of course, he and I had had this conversation before.) As we turned to other business, Steve notified me once again, "I have my eye on Todd's license bureau." He had not raised this topic for a while, and I was somewhat surprised by the timing, particularly given the purpose of our meeting. Perhaps he was a bit anxious, especially in view of the tension that had developed in our relationship, and of the rumblings about Governor Celeste's then-pending license bureau reform.[4]

But I had not forgotten the bargain that connected us, and for his part, Steve had remained loyal. I wanted to avoid a renewal of the party fight of 1986, but not at the expense of allowing Hey to remain as a deputy registrar. Were I to endorse Todd, as politically astute as that might seem to an outsider like Jim Ruvulo, I would lose Webb's support, as well as that of my other allies who believed Steve deserved the position. The former DEP coalition would have been tragically split, making the party easy pickings for Todd Hey and Charlie Hauenstein. No, I would recommend Steve—it was a necessary alternative—although I was sure that it meant a challenge from Todd Hey.[5]

The change was implemented, however, according to protocol. Webb and I called on Ruvulo in May and formally requested the move. Ruvulo said he'd support us if we still wanted to take the bureau from Todd, although he cautioned, "It's the governor's decision, and Todd has been very generous with the governor."[6] Ruvulo said the same thing to me two weeks later when I again visited Ohio Democratic Party headquarters—this time by myself—and informed him that the party's Operations Committee had unanimously endorsed Steve Webb's bid for the Lima Mall license bureau. Even John Hevener had voted in Webb's favor, and as Allen County's Celeste-campaign coordinator, Hevener's endorsement was crucial. Ruvulo again indicated that it was Dick Celeste's decision, but he was more positive in his outlook this time and reiterated that he'd support us when he took our request to the governor.[7]

June 21, 1987

Hey's calm acceptance of the decision was a facade. The day after Webb and I broke the news, Todd phoned Ohio Democratic Party headquarters and demanded to talk to Jim Ruvulo. Ruvulo was out of the country at the time, so he ranted instead at the executive director, Lynne Plannick. "Todd was really hot," Plannick told me in a telephone call later that day. "He said that he was 'shocked and astounded' to lose the bureau."

"That's interesting," I replied, "He told us he'd heard rumors about it for two weeks."[8]

It would be a rough transition, moving the license agency from Hey's control to Webb's. Hey had put the bureau in a suite, in which he managed a knife shop and conducted lottery sales in addition to selling license tags. It was quite an operation, and he did not want to give up these other business. Also, Steve preferred to move directly into Todd's facility, all set up with computers online, and begin operations without having to orchestrate an elaborate shift to a different office. A cooperative arrangement made sense for both men, and negotiations ensued on an arrangement whereby Steve would keep the license bureau in Todd's suite, subletting space from him, while Todd continued his other enterprises. But Hey insisted on exorbitant terms that would have siphoned revenue from Steve's operation into Todd's pocket, and negotiations stopped. Webb began looking for another location in the mall.[9]

Of course, this flap raised the prospect that the Lima Mall bureau might be unable to transact business on July 1, creating anxiety among the auto dealers around the mall. Tom Cody, an official with the Ohio Bureau of Motor Vehicles (BMV), eventually called me, asking me to negotiate a solution. "I'm fearful," he warned, "that BMV will be embarrassed, that the governor will be embarrassed, and that you'll be embarrassed."

"Nope, Steve's perfectly within his rights," I replied, explaining that Hey wanted to profit indirectly off Webb's operation by operating as Steve's landlord and gouge his profits. "There's not much I can do or should do," I said. Cody persisted, saying that he'd like to see service begin by July 1 and that he hated to see the feuding continue. "You have to realize that both sides are in a negotiating posture right now," I observed. "Something will be resolved soon." I did not offer to step in.[10]

As it turned out, my intervention was not needed. Webb finally worked out a deal directly with the manager of the Lima Mall, who offered Steve a separate location. The bureau opened on July 1, and although Webb had to muddle along temporarily without computer hookups, the operation was firmly under his control.[11] Todd, now bereft of the customer "draw" that the license bureau had provided, eventually closed his ancillary enterprises and vacated his suite. He had seriously overplayed his hand.[12]

As this situation rumbled toward resolution, Cora Hamman carried on as if Steve was going to move the bureau to a different mall. This was the exact problem I had feared would develop from Cora's involvement in the license bureau, and I told Steve so. "I have no doubt of Cora's loyalty," I acknowledged. "My problem with her has always been that she does not know when to keep her mouth shut. This is a good example of that."

"I'll talk to her," Webb replied, "and hopefully she'll be more careful in the future." I was not confident that she would.[13]

July 16, 1987

Steve Webb could be relentless in getting the best deal for himself. His confrontation with Todd over the Lima Mall license bureau had proven that. Consequently, when I had the opportunity to fill a secretarial position at the Ohio Department of Transportation (ODOT), I should not have been surprised when Webb promoted his sister for the post. The Patronage Committee had numerous qualified applicants, but somehow Steve's sister rose to the top of the heap.

Not coincidentally, Steve sat on that committee. So did Rochelle Twining, Leonard Boddie, and John Hevener, who was still serving as chair.

Webb had been deputy registrar for just over two weeks, and I had already heard objections to his arrangement with Cora Hamman. Critics complained that Steve and Cora were using their clout in the party to help themselves, just as Charlie Hauenstein and his cronies had done. In May, the party had appointed Steve's daughter to a summer job at ODOT, and that was followed in June by the decision to award him the long-coveted license bureau. Also, unbeknownst to most party hands, I had been lobbying Ron Nabakowski, director of Ohio's Lottery Commission, to install a lotto machine in Webb's license bureau. Now Webb wanted the party to nominate his sister for a job in the highway department. The complaints had merit.

The Patronage Committee took up the ODOT appointment on the morning of July 16, and although I was not anxious to endorse Steve's sister, I hadn't let anyone, including Steve, know of my predisposition. When I arrived an hour after the session had begun, committee members were speaking in agitated voices, unable to decide between Steve's sister or a candidate favored by Leonard Boddie. Things were not going well.[14]

If the alternative applicant had been anyone other than a candidate sponsored by Boddie, the decision would have been much easier. Boddie was still embittered by the way Cora Hamman had managed the clerk-of-courts nomination a year earlier, and he was among those who were objecting loudly to Steve's arrangement with her. Furthermore, he had been whispering allegations that Webb was a racist, all while pressuring him to hire minority employees for the license bureau.[15] Leonard had done a good job at alienating Steve, and I was placed in the position of supporting either Steve Webb, my most important political ally in the party, or Leonard Boddie, who carried weight in the African American neighborhoods. It was not an enviable choice, and I suggested a third applicant, but the committee was not in a mood to compromise. It was Webb's sister or Boddie's candidate.

"How does it look," I asked, "if members of this committee appoint their own family to patronage jobs? It would seem we're no better than Charlie Hauenstein if we do that." That appeal failed to move either Steve or the committee, and the vote split—Hevener and Boddie on one side, Webb and Twining the other—leaving it up to me to settle the issue. I cast the deciding vote against Webb's sister, choosing Boddie's candidate instead.[16]

Webb was livid. He wanted his sister to have the job and was angry at me and Hevener for opposing her. He stormed out of the meeting. I tried to reach him later that afternoon, but he made himself unavailable and refused to return my calls. He was still fuming that evening at an Operations Committee meeting. When I approached him beforehand, he sulked, declaring that he thought his sister—who, incidentally, was working part-time at his license bureau—deserved the job much more than did Boddie's nominee.

Toward the end of the meeting, I raised the "family problem" in making patronage decisions, repeating the arguments I had voiced that morning. Cora Hamman objected strenuously, taking up the cudgel for Steve Webb, who remained mute throughout the discussion. "If a person works, they ought to get the job, no matter who they're related to," she claimed. "I'm not saying that we should never appoint family members," I responded. "I just think we need a policy to regulate the matter, such as putting a cap on the number of family hires."[17]

From there, we kicked around other solutions, including the use of "sanitized hiring," by which the Patronage Committee would issue recommendations based upon qualifications and voting record, not knowing the names of the applicants or their sponsors. Rotation of membership on the Patronage Committee was another alternative, as was proscribing members of the Patronage Committee from sponsoring relatives for political jobs.[18] In the end, we sent the issue back to Hevener and his committee, which eventually approved a rotation system, whereby two members would be replaced annually.[19] By letting the Patronage Committee decide the "family problem," we had ducked only the immediate hostility, but everyone knew my feelings. The issue was unlikely to come up again.

Webb fidgeted and paid little attention to those deliberations. His behavior bordered on insolence, and he was still angry as the session closed. Afterward, he and I held a short private conference that resolved nothing. Two hours later, however, Mr. Hyde suddenly became Dr. Jekyll. Webb called me about 11 P.M. His voice was cheerful: "I just want to make sure there are no hard feelings between us," he said. "Of course not," I responded, accepting what appeared to be an apology. "You need to know that personally I wanted to appoint your sister but could not. I had to do what I felt was good for the party. I hope you understand." Webb replied that he did, but his petulant behavior earlier that evening had left me questioning his sincerity.[20]

I would go to great lengths to keep Steve Webb at my right hand, but I was less accommodating toward Cora Hamman. She bedeviled me constantly.[21]

At the Ohio Democratic Party's annual dinner, in May, Cora was in rare form. She was delighted to be rubbing shoulders with eminent state politicians, and she wanted to impress Dr. Dixie Soo, wife of Dr. L. Y. Soo, whom she had brought along with her. A neurologist from Lima, "Dr. Dixie" would become an important financial backer of party activities. Although Cora had recruited her to run for Central Committee and sponsored her appointment to Executive Committee, Dixie Soo was the complete antithesis of Cora Hamman, bearing herself with a reserved dignity and holding aloof from party squabbles. However, like Cora, she was steadfast in her commitment to the Democratic Party.

During dinner, Cora pointed to the dais, where Governor Celeste, Senator John Glenn (D-Ohio), and all the Democratic state officials were sitting, along with their spouses, and asked, "Bill, could you take Dixie up to meet John Glenn? He's her favorite senator, and she'd just love to meet him."

"Uh, I don't know, Cora," I said, struggling to respond to this rather bold request. "I don't think the seating arrangements allow for that kind of thing."

"What do you mean?"

"Look at the head table. It's about six feet off the main floor. To get to John Glenn, I'd have to climb up there and crawl over people. Maybe after dinner."

"Oh, you can do it. She'd love to meet John Glenn. He's her favorite senator."

I wolfed down my dinner, excused myself, and spent a half hour roaming the hall—long enough, I hoped, for Cora to forget her request. When I returned, I grabbed a seat at the far end of our table, far away from Cora Hamman and directly across from Rochelle Twining and her parents.

But there was no escape. Twining leaned across the table, batted her eyes, and whispered, "Bill, won't you take my Mom and Dad up to meet John Glenn? Cora took Dixie up. If she can do it, you can, too. I mean, Bill, what kind of a party chairman are you?"

"What?" I responded. "She didn't."

"Yes, she did. She climbed up on the platform, towing Dixie Soo behind her. Introduced her to John Glenn, Dick Celeste, and practically everybody up there."

By this time my eyes were popping out, incredulous that security guards had not tackled the two women as they crossed the dais. "She didn't! Right up on the platform? In front of everybody?"

"That's right, Bill. Now, won't you do that for us? Ple-e-e-ase."

"Shit!"[22]

When I had first become chair, Cora Hamman was simply a vexation, one of the many nuisances I had to endure. But as my term wore on, she incessantly pushed excessive demands on me, seeking additional authority within the party. If I denied or put off a request, she would find ways to work around me, inserting herself where I did not want her help and creating the impression that she enjoyed my confidence when really she did not.

Because I did not welcome Hamman's persistent meddling in party operations, I distanced her when it came to decision making. When I needed advice, I looked to others—the Heveners, John Dornick, Rochelle Twining, Steve Webb—and not to her. As her isolation grew, so did her resentment at being shut out of "Bill's inner circle," as she called it.[23]

But Cora Hamman was "a hard worker." That observation was shared overwhelmingly by those who valued her role in the party. They were right, too. When assigned a task with very specific objectives, even a logistically strenuous one, Hamman performed magnificently. For example, in the spring, she had been in charge of organizing a dinner rally at which Jim Ruvulo was to speak. Cora found a location for the event, monitored ticket sales, selected the menu, and badgered the party faithful to attend. She even made sure that Todd Hey and his camp were seated far from the podium. Hamman had organized a similar event in February, and on each occasion I warmly and publicly praised her. She was good at the "scut work" that few others wanted, and for that reason I was unwilling to alienate her totally.

But when a job was more subjectively defined, when a task required subtle diplomacy and creative thinking, Cora was simply incapable of handling it. I had learned that much from the fiasco over Roger Brown's nomination for clerk of courts. Of course, Cora's ego did not allow her to see things this way.

Then there was Cora's mouth. She had the annoying habit of gossiping and spreading rumors, usually with the intent of building herself up by knocking others down. One evening in early September, Rochelle Twining, with her children in tow, showed up at party headquarters to help send out a mailing. Cora was there, spreading invective about prominent locals, including one politician whom she hyperbolically scourged as "the best excuse yet for retroactive abortion." Twining was outraged, especially when one of her children later asked, "Mom, what's a 'retroactive abortion?'"[24]

Twining was still stewing over this incident at a committee meeting several nights later. Fed up with Cora's behavior, Twining issued a general pronouncement against "people who talk about other people." Although not mentioning Cora Hamman by name, it was clear whom Twining had in mind. "You may think that what you say won't get back to people, but, believe me, it does," she declared. "And when it does, people's feelings get hurt!" All the time she was speaking, Rochelle was looking directly at Cora.[25]

Hamman, of course, took umbrage and told me afterward that she might not run for Central Committee in 1988. I had only begun to recognize such declarations as a tactic Cora often employed—threatening to resign as a means of drawing attention—and on this occasion, it worked. "Why?" I asked. She waved me off, saying "I'll talk to you about it later, Bill." When I pressed the matter, she muttered something about being concerned about the party's direction, and before I knew it I had said, "Let's have lunch."

We did, too. For two hours at a Mexican restaurant I listened to Cora grumble about alleged slights. She particularly singled out Rochelle Twining, harshly criticizing her work on the Phoenix Society, a donor's circle the party had recently organized under Rochelle's direction. As for me, "You don't pay attention to what I have to say," she declared—but I'd heard that one before. She even griped about her benefactor Steve Webb. According to Cora, he had been piling most of the license bureau work on her shoulders, not picking up his share of the load, and he had been shortchanging her share of the profit. Cora vented her frustrations on me, but I had asked for it. Because I paid attention to her and offered sympathy, she returned to the fold by the time lunch was finished. I asked for that, too.[26]

July 17, 1987

It was one day after those exasperating confrontations concerning the ODOT job and Steve Webb's sister, and I was mulling over the whole mess with John Hevener. Patronage was sapping my energy and opening fissures and hard feelings within the party as we scrapped among ourselves for whatever crumbs fell onto our path. Moreover, I had become increasingly irritated by the Webb-Hamman alliance.

Hevener understood completely. "It's always possible Steve and Cora could join forces against us," he observed, "but if the ship goes down, it's going to go down steering a straight course."[27] An apt metaphor, but I didn't particularly welcome the image of our ship sinking.

· 13 ·

Boddie/Horne

The Executive Committee meeting began routinely. Pledge of Allegiance. Acceptance of minutes. Treasurer's report. Reports from various committees. Sixth Ward councilman Henry Horne sat in the front row, along with two other candidates for city office—Lima auditor Harry Vorhees and Eighth Ward councilwoman Dorothy Riker. All were Democrats and among the few Democratic office holders in Allen County. Sitting alongside were Tom Sciranka and Keith Cunningham—two other Dems who hoped to join Horne and Riker on city council.[1]

Furl Williams, running for his third term as president of Lima City Council, headed the group. Although nearly eighty years old, Williams still cut an imposing figure. Tall and dapper, he sported a pencil-thin moustache, and his jaw jutted out slightly, creating the effect of a man who almost never smiled. When in conversation, Williams spoke quietly and listened intently, his gaze indicating a mind deeply considering the words of the speaker.

The first African American elected to citywide office, Williams had begun his public life as an activist in the UAW, organizing workers in the Ohio Steel Foundry and later serving terms as head of the Teledyne local, president of the Allied Labor Council, and UAW international representative. In 1969, at the age of sixty-two, he had won his first election, becoming councilman for the Sixth Ward. A fourteen-vote victory for the council presidency had followed in 1979, and reelection to a second term had come four years after that by a more substantial margin.[2] Through each succeeding election, Williams had assembled a coalition of blue-collar workers from north Lima, black voters from the south end, and reform-minded whites from the western precincts. Now, with two successive citywide victories under his belt and optimistically preparing for another, Furl Williams had won the respect of black and white voters alike.

Furl Williams at the Allen County Democratic Party's fall fund-raiser, October 1989.
From the collection of Malcolm and Beverly McCoy, photograph by Beverly McCoy.

Although city elections were technically nonpartisan, Williams never hid his feelings for the Democratic Party. Whenever a Democratic candidate asked for his endorsement, Williams gladly gave it, often appearing in television or radio advertisements. He had been quietly supportive of my challenge to Charlie Hauenstein, although he had never openly aligned himself with DEP. Our future had been too uncertain for him to risk whatever rapport he may have had with the old guard.

But now I was chair of the Allen County Democratic Party, and tonight Williams was attending our Executive Committee meeting, warmly praising my leadership. His compliments were so generous that I was moved to observe, "We have these fine Democrats and candidates for city office. Although I know Lima city elections are nonpartisan, it might be a good idea for us, as fellow Democrats, to give them our endorsement."

Looking toward the group in the front row, I asked, "Would an endorsement from the Allen County Democratic Party be all right with you?" They all nodded. But how could they refuse? Then, I asked a fateful question: "Is there a motion to endorse these candidates?" John Dornick moved the question, Frank Winegardner seconding, and motion passed unanimously.[3]

The next morning an irate Leonard Boddie, who had not attended the meeting, called me. Like Furl Williams, Boddie was tall and well dressed, but the comparison ended there. Boddie was much younger, in his late twenties, and where Williams was serene and steady, Boddie was volatile and erratic. Leonard also carried on incessantly about slights, mostly imagined, committed by me or my associates in the Democratic Party. That morning he was in a mood to complain about our endorsement of Henry Horne. "Why did you do that?" I recall him saying. "I told you a long time ago that I wanted to run against Henry."[4]

He had indeed told me, way back in July 1986, but six months and an election campaign had passed since then. I had forgotten. My lapse in memory did not mollify Boddie, who griped that I should have remembered, especially after *all* the work he had done for Steve Webb and me. He proceeded to scold me, simultaneously venting a sense of betrayal and stressing that he was not about to alter his course. He had already had begun circulating petitions for the Sixth Ward council seat, and he wasn't pulling out. He still expected the party's help, he said.[5]

Although I was disturbed that Boddie had begun circulating petitions without out informing me, I was also angry at myself. As I later discovered, he had taken out petitions and begun circulating them almost two weeks earlier, corralling Furl Williams for the very first signature. Obviously, there had been a breakdown in my intelligence operation, in that no one at the Board of Elections or on the street, or even Williams himself, had let me know that Boddie had become a candidate.[6]

Nevertheless, as Boddie continued I kept my irritation in check and guided the conversation to a resolution, suggesting an endorsement for Leonard to go along with the one we had just given Henry Horne. Boddie accepted this proposal, which I ran past both the Candidate Recruitment and Operations Committees. Each group agreed to back Boddie's candidacy, and at an February 18 dinner meeting, the Central and Executive Committees jointly endorsed Leonard Boddie for city councilman for the Sixth Ward. The deed was done. The Allen County Democratic Party had blessed the candidacies of two black Democrats, both running for city council in the Sixth Ward.[7]

This second endorsement gave the impression that the Democratic Party was betraying Henry Horne. He had been a loyal Democrat, carrying the party banner in 1982 in a futile county-commissioner race against Robert Townsend. More importantly, he was a good councilman. In 1979, Horne had succeeded Furl Williams as the Sixth Ward representative, and during his early political career his mentor had been Williams himself, who cultivated Henry as an ally in matters Furl wanted to accomplish as city council president. This may explain why Henry shared some of Furl's mannerisms—the firm handshake, the sincere gaze while listening, the ability to look a person straight in the eye. However, during his second term, Henry had begun to side with conservative members of city council, voting to stymie community-development projects that his mentor favored. All this only proved that he could be his own man, but Furl didn't like it much.

Although I liked Henry Horne, as did John Hevener, Steve Webb, Cora Hamman, and other members of the DEP coalition, I recognized that we owed little to him; he was close the old guard, having landed his job as a labor relations specialist at the Ohio Department of Transportation through Charlie Hauenstein's sponsorship. In politics "you dance with them what brung you,"[8] and in this sense, we owed more to Boddie, who "had brung" DEP a half-dozen Central Committee representatives during the party fight of 1986. But Leonard could be irksome, and in the background was the possibility that he might flip to the old guard, taking his Central Committee following with him and leaving the former DEP coalition bereft of support in the minority precincts. The "dual endorsement," therefore, boiled down to an attempt to placate Boddie.

Although the decision made sense to us, outsiders saw obvious flaws. In early April, Cora Hamman and I attended a campaign workshop sponsored by the Ohio Democratic Party. During a question-and-answer session, Cora explained the Boddie/Horne endorsement to Rick Pfeiffer, a state senator from Columbus and a facilitator for the workshop, and then asked him how we should handle the situation. Pfeiffer was flabbergasted, saying that it would have been better for us to stay out the campaign altogether. He observed that if our incumbent was doing a good job but a young Democrat like Boddie wanted to take a shot at him and deserved the chance, no endorsement would be smarter than two.[9] Pfeiffer had put his finger on a problem that I was only beginning to discover.

May 18, 1987, 11:45 P.M.

I had just drifted off to sleep when the phone rang. It was Leonard Boddie, and he had a bone in his craw. "People in the Sixth Ward just don't understand why the party endorsed both candidates," he said. He wanted the party to rescind its endorsement of Henry Horne, making him the preferred candidate in the Sixth Ward council race. This was not the first time I had heard this line. Still, and despite the late hour, he and I held an amicable conversation. I promised to take the issue before the Operations Committee, which was to meet a few nights later.

But the committee members had grown tired of Boddie's carping, and we all told him matter-of-factly that a dual endorsement was the most he could expect from the party. In fact, we emphasized to him, he was fortunate the party had gone along with the idea of backing two candidates for the Sixth Ward race, especially when he was challenging an incumbent who had been faithful to the Democratic Party. He could hardly expect the party to rescind its endorsement of Henry Horne.[10]

Boddie began playing factions against one another. At a party rally and dinner meeting in May, I interrupted a tête-à-tête between Todd Hey and Boddie and overheard Todd promising various forms of assistance to Leonard's campaign, including help in conducting a poll. I later pulled Boddie aside and advised, "I'd be careful about getting too close to Todd. Most likely, he's coming after us." Leonard shrugged me off. "Todd's been the only one from the party who's given me help—two hundred dollars. So, I don't care. If he offers help, I'll take it."[11]

Although these machinations were troubling, I grew even more concerned about tension Boddie was provoking among my immediate supporters, especially with complaints about Steve Webb. Dismayed by what he saw as Webb's generally unsympathetic attitude toward minorities and disgusted by delay in hiring a minority employee for the license bureau, Leonard let it be known that he'd have trouble backing Steve for Central Committee chair in 1988.[12]

Matters came to a head at a DEP gathering in mid-August. Although DEP had been dormant since the takeover, it still existed as a distinct organization, and now it was time to reactivate it. A month had passed since the party had taken away Todd Hey's license bureau. I knew that Hey was angry and that he and other old guard activists were likely to come after my chairmanship in 1988. Consequently, I called a DEP war council to initiate our preparations for the 1988 Central Committee elections; we began with an assessment of Central Committee, speculating about which members were for us and which were for the old guard.

Boddie interrupted our deliberations to raise the issue of what he considered the party's inattentiveness to minorities. "I received two calls in three days from Central Committeewomen complaining about the party," he declared, claiming that both women were about to jump ship to Todd Hey's side of the party. (I later checked out their grievances and found that he had grossly overstated them.) He went on at length about the party's supposed racial insensitivity, casting several pointed barbs in Steve Webb's direction.[13]

Boddie had distracted us and dominated the first hour of an important DEP meeting. Steve and Cora were particularly indignant at Boddie's manipulative performance, and the next morning, Cora called to tell me so. "Bill, you can try to hold Leonard but you're going to end up losing the rest of us. He's no good. We can't trust him."[14]

By early September, Steve Webb's and Cora Hamman's contentious relationship with Leonard Boddie, along with Boddie's persistent grousing about the dual endorsement, had forced me to examine the party's relationship with the African American community. Earlier that summer, Webb himself had created a stir with public comments regarding a plan of the mayor of Lima, Gene Joseph, to impose a residency requirement on city workers. Following a public hearing over the proposal, the city's personnel director and the mayor admitted that one function of the new policy would be to increase minority hiring.[15] At the time, Lima was ineligible for Urban Development Action Grants, because its proportion of minority city employees was so low.

The public-employees unions objected strenuously to the residency plan, and Webb had been among the leading critics, saying that he thought the requirement would "deter qualified people from coming to the city."[16] He reportedly described the mayor's plan as a contrivance, implying that minority applicants would have a better chance of securing city jobs if they didn't have to compete against out-of-town candidates.[17] Although Webb was simply representing his union members, who did not like being told where to live, he left an impression of intolerance by the way he stated his view.[18]

Consequently, I spent late August and early September conferring with a number of black Democrats—including Beverly McCoy, Jerry Pitts, the Reverend Earl Thompson of the St. Paul Zion African Methodist Episcopal Church, precinct committeeman Charlie Henderson (Third Ward), and Community Action Commission head Joe Clark—trying to mend the party's bridges to the black community. The activists I consulted all expressed the view that I was using Boddie in the same way Charlie Hauenstein had used Otha Harris—as a one-person liaison with the county's African American neighborhoods. Not all African Americans regarded Boddie highly, they cautioned. Pitts, interestingly, echoed Cora Hamman's mistrust of Boddie, warning, "He's dangerous and power hungry."[19] The universal message from these conferences was that I personally would have to reach out to Allen County's black precincts, not depending on Steve Webb and not relying on Leonard Boddie.[20]

Until those conversations, I had more or less allowed Boddie to manage the party's relationship with its minority constituents. That changed immediately. I started seeking advice more regularly from black Democratic activists other than Boddie—including Bev McCoy, Charlie Henderson, and PC Wrencher, among others. In later years, the party would encourage these and other black Democrats to energize the minority caucus, which Boddie had commanded as his personal fiefdom. By 1990, Doug Dobbins—an activist with the NAACP and a member of both the Central and Executive Committees—would take charge of the caucus and help form it into an active and independent committee, one reflecting the pluralistic makeup of our party's black constituency.[21]

I began making my own rounds in Lima's Fifth and Sixth Wards, attending church services, participating in monthly meetings of the NAACP, going to festivals and dinners, and staying afterward to shake hands and talk to people. I also squeezed as many Martin Luther King holiday observances into my calendar as I could, along with celebrations honoring Black History Month (February). In other words, I began operating as a real party chairman should have been—heeding the advice of George Washington Plunkitt of Tammany Hall fame, who once counseled, "Go among the people, see them and be seen."[22]

These initiatives would eventually strengthen the party's relationship with Lima's black community, but they would do nothing to solve immediate problem of the Horne/Boddie race, which was splitting Democrats in the Sixth Ward. Boddie brashly and relentlessly attacked Horne's attendance record at city council meetings, claiming that Henry had missed eleven meetings in 1986 alone, often came to council meeting unprepared, and was inattentive to residents' needs. "The people of the Sixth Ward have not had a representative for the past eight years," Boddie charged.[23]

Henry Horne bristled in response. He had missed meetings in 1986, he admitted in a mailing, but only to negotiate a labor contract for employees at ODOT. "I had to feed my family"; his attendance record had been nearly perfect both before and after that period. As for his alleged inattention to the community, Horne responded, "Residents can call me any time of the day or night." He went on to recite a list of street repairs, lighting improvements, and neighborhood development projects that had occurred during his watch on city council, taking credit for all of them.[24]

The sparring continued through October. Boddie and Horne quibbled about the number of meetings Horne had missed. They squabbled over Boddie's failure to visit council meetings until he became a candidate. They bickered over whether Henry should take credit for the neighborhood improvements he had cited in a campaign brochure. "Horne is deceiving voters," Boddie snarled. "Boddie is an outright liar," Horn snapped back.[25] So it went—Whap! Thud!—neither candidate hitting the canvas.

It was impossible to remain neutral in this struggle, and as the campaign moved toward the late rounds, the party tilted toward Boddie. Each candidate had initially received a two-hundred-dollar contribution from the Democratic treasury, but Boddie, who had submitted a request for $650, was not happy with that amount and pressed for more. In late October, John Dornick's Budget

Committee granted the Boddie campaign, but not Horne, an additional three hundred dollars. This action made Leonard the only city council candidate to receive supplemental funding; his total allocation was equivalent to what the party had given Furl Williams.[26]

The party's preelection financial report left an unmistakable imprint of its leanings in the Sixth Ward race, and I sent my own message as well. On October 5, I attended a press conference at which Leonard had strongly encouraged me to be present. He was an endorsed candidate, I rationalized, and no one could construe favoritism by my appearing at his event. Besides, I would have done the same for Henry Horne, and I told Henry so at the time.[27] When I arrived at the Salvation Army Community Center, the site of the press conference, I noticed a larger than usual number of media hands present. The lobby was festooned with balloons and bunting, and Furl Williams was there too. Something big was going to happen.

Upon my arrival, Boddie asked me to introduce him—"I really want you to do this for me, Bill," I recall him saying—and I obliged, though by now I had surmised what was going to occur. I introduced Leonard, with generalized praise, mostly, recognizing the courage it took for Leonard, or anyone, to run for public office. Leonard followed, reciting his campaign theme "to work for and with" the people of the Sixth Ward, and ripping Henry Horne for missing too many council meetings.

Then came Furl Williams. He endorsed Leonard's candidacy, but in words that did not so much praise Boddie as condemn Horne for being part of an uncooperative faction that had resisted downtown redevelopment.[28] Still, it was an endorsement, and coming from Williams, it was significant.

In 1987 Williams could have lived anywhere in Lima, but he chose to stay in the south end, in his house on Reese Avenue. The Sixth Ward was his home, and as a former councilman for the ward, he was central to its politics, its most esteemed politician. Now, Leonard Boddie had won him to his side.[29]

In being there, I was not just a witness to this pivotal moment in the campaign but part of it. When Williams blessed Boddie's candidacy, I did too, or so it appeared. In fact, WLIO TV went so far as to pronounce, "Leonard Boddie is running with the support of Democratic Party Chairman William Angel."[30] I had never issued anything like a formal endorsement, and I had never told anyone to vote for Boddie instead of Horne. It did not matter. My simple presence at Furl's "laying on of the hands" was enough, especially considering the nuances of black politics, where actions have always meant more than words.

Truthfully, I did not mind this perception. Intraparty intrigue had pervaded the Sixth Ward race. Todd Hey's springtime effort to woo Leonard Boddie had been a mere flirtation, and by late October, Hey's partnership with Henry Horne had come out into the open. Bumping into Henry at the anniversary celebration for the Reverend J. D. White of the Eleventh Street Missionary Baptist Church, I notified Horne that if he wanted to designate witnesses for election night, he should let me know who they would be, and I would add their names to a list the party had already filed. Horne paused a moment before responding, "Well, Bill, I'd like to appoint Todd Hey and his wife." I must have flinched, because Henry quickly explained, "I hope you don't take this the wrong way, but Todd is backing my candidacy, and he has donated money to my campaign."[31]

Horne was Hey's candidate, and Boddie was ours. With Hey laying plans to retake the Allen County Democratic Party, Henry Horne had become his stalking horse. A Boddie triumph, therefore, would mean a Hey defeat. Leonard Boddie might have been a pain in the neck, especially in view of his efforts to manipulate me and others in the party, but he was *our* pain in the neck. We wanted him to win.

October 27, 1987, Whittier Arts Magnet School
Whittier School stands in the middle of the Sixth Ward, a few blocks south of the Erie-Lackawanna Railroad tracks, which separate south Lima from the rest of the city. Locals still refer to this boundary as Lima's "Mason-Dixon Line." The ward is predominantly African American, although one precinct, which happens to lie north of the tracks, holds a white majority.

To the north and west, shadowing Whittier's neighborhood like a bad memory, stand abandoned factories, crumbling reminders that the Sixth Ward flanks Lima's former industrial center. The Clark Equipment Plant, only a few blocks away, had once manufactured steam locomotives, but even in 1987 it had been closed for years; Teledyne and Westinghouse, farther to the west, followed in the 1990s. Single-family frame houses—old but well maintained—line the streets surrounding Whittier School, and more residential housing sprawls southward and eastward from the school grounds.

On October 27, 1987, if you had driven southward on Reese Avenue, which runs past Whittier's playground, and crossed Fourth Street—the ward's main east-west thoroughfare—you would have come to Victory Village and the worst housing in Lima.[32] Victory Village—so called because during World War II it had housed African Americans who had come to Lima for foundry jobs—consisted of landlord-owned, ramshackle barracks that had been carved into apartments, many with dirt floors. Behind Victory Village, on Eighth Street, was the Salvation Army Community Center, where Leonard Boddie worked and maintained his campaign headquarters.

Sixth Ward city council candidates Leonard Boddie (seated) and Henry Horne (at podium) during their debate, October 1987. *Lima News* photo from the collection of the Allen County Historical Society.

Boddie and Horne had slugged it out all autumn, and now, one week before the election, they were going to confront each other one more time, a face to face debate in the gymnasium of Whittier School. The Allen County Democratic Party had sponsored the event, and in my comments introducing the contest I explained why: "These candidates are both Democrats, and the Democratic Party feels an obligation to give them an opportunity to put their views and their ideas before you."[33] An obligation indeed—the party had blundered into this situation, endorsing Horne and then Boddie, and it wanted to see its decision through, to provide an arena where each man could express his views and the voters of the Sixth Ward could check them out.

To this extent, the forum worked. Boddie was bold in both rhetoric and performance. Aside from his opening and closing statements, he spoke without notes, although occasionally he waved rolled-up papers at Horne, to convey derision. Boddie's left hand gripped a ballpoint pen between thumb and index finger; he swung it toward the audience as if sprinkling holy water on the faithful. He assumed the role of pastor, curling his lip into a sneer that would scare off demons, then using his voice like a musical instrument—raising and lowering its pitch, changing its cadence, and adjusting its volume—depending on the tone he wished to convey.

Despite his energetic style, Boddie's substantive message consisted mostly of slashing attacks and fluffy platitudes. "Today I have a dream," Boddie opened, unabashedly connecting himself with Martin Luther King, Jr. "I want to take your dreams . . . your hopes . . . your visions. . . your concerns . . . your ideals . . . your thoughts, and make them become reality." He trumpeted this theme constantly throughout the evening, sometimes linking it to his equally fuzzy campaign slogan, "Working for you and with you"—to wit, "I will work for you and with you to make your dreams come true."[34]

Boddie seldom addressed questions in a concrete way, choosing to deal with them only generally and then proceeding to lambast Henry Horne. For instance, panelist Regina Clark, coordinator of minority recruitment at Lima Technical College, asked the candidates to explain what they would do to secure day care for the Sixth Ward. Boddie gave a one-sentence response, that the ward's councilman had a responsibility to induce day-care providers to come to the community, and then launched into an attack on points Horne had raised previously, finishing with a statement on job training. He almost totally ignored Clark and her question. Boddie went on like that most of the evening. If he didn't want to answer a question, he'd avoid it and use his time to skewer Henry or sermonize on an unrelated issue.

Horne that night was Boddie's antithesis. He carefully listened to each question, paused a moment before answering, and spoke slowly and deliberately, almost to the point of pedantry. Wooden in presentation, Horne lacked Boddie's oratorical repertoire, speaking primarily in a quiet monotone. Each time it was his turn to answer, he lifted a huge three-ring binder to the podium. The binder's presence seemed to offer Henry a certain amount of comfort. It was there when he needed it.

Horne's responses took a predictable flow. First he would flip through his binder. Then he would quickly summarize the background of the question, before moving to issues it raised. Finally, he would conclude by praising his own accomplishments or promoting a relevant agenda item. In this fashion he substantively addressed a number of thorny issues, including minority hiring, day care, community development, small-business growth, and public housing. Presenting himself in clear, rational terms, Horne acted very much the college professor, in marked contrast to Boddie's flashy "preacher" style.

"Politics is about conflict," I had stated earlier in my introductory remarks.

"Oftentimes it's not comfortable for those in positions of authority who have to deal with the conflict, but that's what the political process is about. . . . It makes us all stronger as a community."[35] Ironically, the Democratic Party, a community of activists, would in fact become stronger for having generated conflict in its own ranks. It had faced the ire of Leonard Boddie and had navigated its way through the tension created by having endorsed two candidates for the same race. The dual endorsement, as much ill will as it had provoked, helped inspire the party to build its own relationship with the black community and not simply to entrust that connection to self-interested power brokers. In fact, sponsorship of this event—in the heart of the Sixth Ward—galvanized our involvement with Lima's African American neighborhoods. "We want to be part of your community," I declared before turning the debate over to the candidates. "We want to be part of your effort here."[36]

Election Night, November 3, 1987

Leonard Boddie was ecstatic in victory, continuing to campaign even while accepting his achievement. "The people of the Sixth Ward have spoken," he trumpeted. "They want adequate representation." He even praised Steve Webb, a man he had condemned weeks earlier as an irredeemable redneck. "Steve Webb is a jewel," Leonard effusively announced, "If anybody complains about Steve Webb, you send them to me." A pair of license bureau–infused contributions had shifted Leonard's perception—but then, politicians generally come to their senses when money is involved.[37]

More Sixth Ward residents voted in the 1987 race for city council than had voted for governor the year before, and Boddie's win was substantial—603 to 444, or 58 percent of the total.[38] He had really wanted to put Horne away, and he had spent $8,575.69 to do so. It was an extraordinarily high figure for a city council race. Leonard had spent over $1,300 on television advertising (both broadcast and cable), an unusual expense for a city council campaign, as well as seven hundred dollars for billboards, also an exceptional outlay. Altogether, Boddie attained victory at a cost of $14.22 per vote.[39]

However, Leonard Boddie's power in party circles would never be the same. Having attained his goal of becoming Sixth Ward city councilman, his new duties would leave him little time for Democratic politics, and it was a touch of irony that his maneuvers to undo the dual endorsement had prodded the party into reducing his role as liaison to black voters. He stayed involved in party activities, owing primarily to his now-proven following, but he would gradually find himself sharing power with other neighborhood and community activists. Leonard Boddie had been a pest, all right, but his cantankerous spirit had actually improved race relations in the party, thus demonstrating that gadflies serve a valuable function in any political organization.

In one last piece of election business, the party received an unexpected boost from J. Vane Shepherd, who had challenged Furl Williams for the city council presidency. It had been a nasty contest; Shepherd had unabashedly attempted to exploit local fear of "scattered site" public housing in residential neighborhoods. He expected to link the anxiety of white voters to Williams, who was president of the Allen Metropolitan Housing Authority (MHA) board of trustees, and thus increase his chances of upsetting him. Throughout the fall, Shepherd pounded on the issue, calling public-housing residents lazy, demanding that Lima cut its financial ties to MHA, and even referring to MHA as a "community cancer."[40] As if voters were incapable of discerning the drift of his outrageous pronouncements, Shepherd ran newspaper ads that bellowed, "WARNING . . . Protect your neighborhood! Vote J. Vane Shepherd for Council President."[41]

Williams saw this rhetoric as scurrilous race baiting and ignored it, centering his campaign on economic development and community progress.[42] He defeated Shepherd 7,200 votes to 2,837, taking 71 percent of the votes cast in the council president's race. It was a humiliating setback for "Shep." In a stroke of good fortune for me, Steve Webb, and the other leaders of the Allen County Democratic Party—since we saw it as to our credit—he blamed us, accusing the party of interfering in a nonpartisan race. "Democrats worked in every precinct and the Republicans did not. It was absolutely a party thing," huffed the Republican Shepherd.[43]

The party had mobilized the troops on Williams's behalf, to be sure, but not to the extent Shepherd suggested. In September, Steve Webb, John Hevener, Cora Hamman, and I had begun hearing rumors that Todd Hey was heavily involved in the Williams campaign, and although the rumors turned out to be exaggerated, we all figured the party needed a stronger presence in the race for city council president.[44] Accordingly, Steve Webb enlisted members of our Central Committee to canvass their precincts for Williams, and in October the party formed a political action committee—"Democrats for Furl Williams"— with Webb serving as treasurer. The PAC raised $425 for the Williams campaign, augmenting the five-hundred-dollar donation that came directly from the party.[45] The Democrats for Furl Williams Committee allowed the party to accomplish at least two important objectives. For one thing, we sweetened Williams's treasury with money collected by the Democratic Party. For another, Steve Webb's service as the PAC's treasurer helped burnish his image among the party's black Democrats.

Even with these activities taken into consideration, our influence in Williams's race was not nearly as great as Shepherd would make it sound. Still, his proclamation drew attention to an active and involved Democratic Party. If he wanted to accuse the Democrats of orchestrating his defeat, I did not mind.

But Todd Hey did mind—a lot. Two weeks after the election, he wrote a letter to the editor of the *Lima News* decrying Shepherd's charge as "inappropriate." Pointedly reminding readers that he had once chaired the Democratic Central Committee, Hey insisted that Shepherd should not blame the Democrats for his defeat, boldly asserting, "There was less done by the Democrat Party this year than in the past."[46] If there had been any hope that Todd Hey had retired from politics, this letter certainly ended it.

Part Four

1988

· 14 ·

Warm Bodies

December 31, 1987, 1:30 P.M.

I had just walked through the door, meaning to relax a while then head out for some New Year's Eve fun, when the phone rang. It was Cora Hamman—Cora always had a knack for bad timing. "Bill, can you come to the license bureau right away? Jack Wade is here, and maybe you can talk to him." I left immediately.

I'd been trying to contact Wade for over two weeks. His name had surfaced as a potential nominee for sheriff, and I did not want to lose this opportunity. So far, the Democrats had only one candidate—attorney Paul Rizor for judge of the Common Pleas Court—and our ticket looked terribly empty. The sheriff's race held possibilities, especially in light of the deputies' role in the tax referendum.

Although the nibble was worth my time, I was skeptical about landing Jack Wade. For one thing, he had failed to return the messages I had left at his home. He was never around, I had been told, but he would call me as soon as he returned. The return calls never came. In addition, Wade was currently a deputy in the Allen County Sheriff's Department. It seemed unlikely that he would take on his boss, Sheriff Charlie Harrod.

Still, Wade was a former owner of Sonitrol, an electronic surveillance and security business in Lima, which he had sold for a handsome profit. With alternate sources of income, I reasoned, he might risk a challenge to Harrod. At least, it was worth finding out. Now that Cora had cornered him down at the license bureau, my New Year's Eve plans would have to wait.

After Cora made introductions, Wade apologized for not returning my phone calls. "I thought you were selling aluminum siding," he said. Not interested in siding, I spent almost three hours on New Year's Eve drinking coffee and trying to sell Jack Wade on the future of the Allen County Democratic Party. When I asked him to run for sheriff, he gushed, "I'm honored that you asked me. I really want to help you out, because that sheriff's department is really messed up. I'll get back to you early next week."[1]

Heading for home, I felt good about seizing the opportunity to talk with Wade, yet I harbored doubts that my foray had accomplished anything. Wade had said that things were "really messed up" in the sheriff's office, but it still struck me as unlikely that he would turn against Sheriff Harrod, a three-term incumbent. Besides, that prattle about "being honored" rang hollow.

I shelved my plans for New Year's Eve, got up early the next morning, and headed to the YMCA, where I bumped into Mike Bender and told him about my conversation with Wade. "That's Jack Wade, all right," Bender replied tersely. "I've been a neighbor of his for years. Known him most of my life. Yeah, he'll sound interested in doing something, then back out. This could be more of the same."

"So, don't get my hopes up," I said.

"Right. *Definitely* don't get your hopes up."[2]

That warning was prophetic. I phoned Wade three times during the first week of 1988, and each time he assured me that he was still interested in running and "honored" that the party was even considering him. But with each phone call he would come up with new reasons why he should not take on the challenge. Finally, the inevitable turndown came. "I just can't do it," Wade declared, explaining that he'd have to resign his deputy's job and that he could not afford the loss of income. He did promise to help find a sheriff's candidate, but that was a face-saving gesture. Our search ultimately came up dry, and Sheriff Charlie Harrod walked through 1988 without opposition.[3]

January 12, 1988

I had to talk to Cora Hamman—she was in "panic mode." As chair of the Candidate Recruitment Committee, she had recently held edgy telephone conversations with Rick Siferd and then Rochelle Twining in which the subject of local campaigns had surfaced. Siferd had chastised her for not doing enough to enlist candidates, and Cora, in turn, had called Twining to launch her own complaints about me. "Don't you think Bill ought to be doing more to recruit candidates?" It was a statement, not a question. "I'm really worried we're not going to get anybody to run."[4]

I did not like Cora Hamman's anxious chatter about the party's recruitment drive. In part, I saw this as an attempt by Cora to distance herself from candidate recruitment, finding others—me in particular—to blame if our efforts fell short. But I was especially concerned that she was feeding people on the fringe of party circles the impression that we were having trouble fielding a slate. In early January, Bob Routson, Cora's pal from the referendum drive, had expressed precisely this worry to John Dornick. Cora's defeatism could achieve self-fulfillment unless I put a stop to her fussing.

I called Cora and told her that I'd heard from several people that the party was having trouble drafting candidates. "I know you've voiced these feelings to me privately," I said, "but we really need to talk positively about our candidate recruitment efforts and avoid negative talk. We'll line up candidates. Let's not panic."

"Bill," she replied, "I lay awake nights. My stomach is tied in knots because I'm worried we can't find candidates."

"It's too early for this, Cora. We need to pull together. Put out feelers and bring in some Democrats to run. I need help from a lot of folks, and we can't get burdened by negative thinking."[5]

There was no doubt that we faced an uphill struggle. For one thing, ten separate offices in Allen County alone were up for reelection (eleven, counting the multicounty state senate race), and finding a candidate for each of them was an intimidating task.[6] The race for treasurer proved a "no-go" when Stephanie Rhine, an executive with Bank One, turned down a request from Dick Meredith and me. It would be nearly impossible to find candidates to run for county engineer or coroner, given the limited pool of engineers and physicians who happened to be Democrats. That obstacle did not stop me from checking on the interest of a couple of Democratic physicians whose names had been suggested; they had no political aspirations. I tried to convince Jim Schmenk, superintendent of the Ohio Department of Transportation, District One, to consider taking a stab at the engineer's job, but understandably, he couldn't afford to relinquish his job at ODOT to run in a futile race.

All of these refusals—from Jack Wade's to Jim Schmenk's— pointed to the real problem: a pessimistic spirit pervaded the Allen County Democratic Party. Charlie Hauenstein and Todd Hey, to their credit, had done a good job in 1984 and had fielded a respectable slate, finding candidates to run for county treasurer, sheriff, state representative, and for the two commissioner seats that were now coming open, but these candidates had fallen well short of winning. Similarly, the Democratic Party under my leadership, the so-called "New Democratic Party," despite its enthusiasm, had failed to produce a winner in an election year in which Democrats had swept the statewide contests. It seemed that try as we might, we Allen County Democrats simply could not succeed.

Part of the problem lay in the numbers. In the 1980s, the Republican Party in Allen County had fifteen thousand registered voters compared to the Democrats' twelve thousand. Assuming that those voters were going to stick with each party's nominees—and in my experience, that was a reasonable assumption for local races—any Democratic nominee faced the awesome task of trying to close a three-thousand-vote deficit.[7]

In 1988, a significant complication was the continuing drumbeat of counterrevolution. On December 18, at the Ohio Democratic Party's annual Christmas gala, Todd Hey recklessly informed Jim Ruvulo that he was going to run for chairman (apparently with Charlie Hauenstein's blessing) of the Allen County Democratic Party—and I was standing in the same room, not twenty feet away. Jim Ruvulo later pulled me aside and passed along this manifesto. "What balls," I muttered. "And right under my nose!"[8] If Todd had issued this audacious proclamation while I was nearby, I could only imagine what he had been saying when I was not around. At the very least, such brazen proclamations had sparked concern about who would actually be leading the party in 1988. Any candidate would have to think twice before committing to run under these tumultuous conditions.

January 19, 1988

I stepped into the Pioneer Bar on Pearl Street, a few blocks east of downtown Lima, to ask Dale Leppla to run for county commissioner against Don Reese. Dale owned and managed the place, a somewhat dilapidated tavern catering to a blue-collar crowd. Beer, boiler makers, and cigarette smoke. Sliding onto a stool, I ordered a beer and put the question to him.

He expressed interest but also stated that he would not do it if Ed Schwieterman wanted to run. He had taken this line before, but I could not understand why he was deferring to Ed. In December 1987, the party had commissioned a poll of county voters, and it had showed that Dale had higher name recognition (79 percent) than either Don Reese or Bob Mayer (both 73 percent); Schwieterman (48 percent) was not even close to Leppla.[9] Still, Dale had somehow developed the theory that if he and Ed both ran, even for different seats, they would siphon votes from each other in the general election; in any case, he didn't want to face Ed in a primary battle.

I pointed to the poll results, trying to convince Dale that he was more electable than Ed, but I finally gave up. I drank another beer and left for a DEP meeting, still waiting for an answer.[10]

January 20, 1988, Alpine Village Restaurant

I met Jerry Pitts at 4 P.M. Two weeks earlier Cora had suggested that I ask him to run for prosecutor, but I wanted him to enter the race for state representative in the First District. Ty Marsh and other aides from Vern Riffe's office had been badgering us to find a Democrat to challenge Bill Thompson, who should have been fairly vulnerable, waging his first reelection campaign.

Pitts said he was "definitely interested" and boasted that with his ample experience in the Ohio senate (he had once worked for Steve Maurer), he could beat Thompson. I was not as confident of his chances, but by the time he left, I sensed that Jerry sincerely wanted to run.[11]

A Candidate Recruitment Committee meeting followed. Dale Leppla and Ed Schwieterman were there and gave an "Alphonse and Gaston" performance regarding their intentions for county commissioner.

"I won't run if Ed runs."

"I won't run if Dale runs."

"What do you want to do, Ed?"

"I don't know. What do you want to do?"

Maddening. But then, it was dumb to hold a meeting of the Candidate Recruitment Committee in the presence of two Democrats we were trying to recruit. Eventually, the ball settled in Leppla's court. He declared that he had to "talk to some people" before deciding. Rumor had it that he was working with Todd Hey, possibly even running with Todd, as a candidate for Central Committee chair.[12]

After the meeting broke up, Rochelle and Cora sat down with me. Neither was happy about the prospect of Leppla running for county commissioner, and both women pressed me to talk Ed Schwieterman into the race. "Dale can't win," Twining emphasized. "He's too lazy, and he'll just be a pain in the ass."[13]

If party leaders such as Twining and Hamman had little use for Dale Leppla, the contempt was mutual. Two months earlier, I had shared lunch with Dale shortly after a rancorous Candidate Recruitment Committee meeting at which Bob Routson's name had surfaced as a possible candidate for county commissioner. "The party let Bob Routson down," Leppla muttered at the time. "Routson worked his ass off, running those petitions, and where was the party? The party should have been doing it."

He went on to declare his theory that the party had held back from the referendum because of Steve Webb. The county commissioners had put pressure on Steve, he claimed, threatening his public employees. "You guys really let Routson down," Leppla insisted. Dale's interpretation—casting Routson as a cat's paw to protect Steve Webb—contained a germ of truth, but it was grossly exaggerated. Rochelle Twining, Cora Hamman, and I all tried to argue the point, but Dale's mind was made up.[14]

He was such a pill that night that I figured he and I needed to sit down and talk. Emphasizing concern about the rift with the old guard, he said that I needed to surround myself with guys from the old leadership, like Paul Prater and Bill Johns. "And I'll tell you something else," Leppla declared that day, "The UAW boys don't like Jerry Pitts, and they don't like Rochelle Twining because of her feminist ideas."

In other words, he wanted me to turn my back on "them what brung me." Leppla also disparaged Steve Webb, once again protesting the supposed conflict of interest between his job as a labor representative and his responsibilities in the party. Then, as if aware of the tension that had mounted between me and Steve, he dropped this bombshell of a question: "Are you and Steve still running as a team?"

He was obviously probing for information, but I let him know I thought that it was foolish for us to switch leadership at this time. Still, I was disturbed by the question, wondering what could have prompted it. In fact, I had had conversations with the Heveners and with Rochelle Twining about moving Steve aside, though we determined that it was not worth the risk. But the question also piqued my curiosity. "Did you have any other leadership team in mind?" I asked. "Perhaps the team could be you and Todd Hey," he said.

I dropped my fork, and our conversation turned to more mundane issues about county politics.[15] Truthfully, Leppla was simply more comfortable with the old guard, and the new party leaders were not particularly comfortable with him. Memories of his 1986 campaign still lingered, unsettling reminders that indeed he could be "a pain in the ass."

January 26, 1988

I had lunch with Ida Kay Keller and asked her to run for county commissioner. Keller lived on a family farm outside Spencerville, a village southwest of Lima, not far from the Auglaize County line. She was a salt-of-the-earth farm wife, who slopped hogs, assisted with the harvest, and advised the 4-H Club, all while raising two school-age children and serving on the Spencerville school board.[16]

A year earlier, I had heard Ida Kay's name mentioned in a meeting at the Amanda Township House. Trustees and Spencerville officials had gathered there to fret over the news that two local realtors, John Mongoluzzo and Duke Fink, had acquired options on a six-hundred-acre tract northeast of Spencerville and intended to sell the property to Waste Management, Inc., for a landfill. "Does Ida Kay know about this?" one of the locals had asked then. I had no idea who this Ida Kay was, but I would soon find out.

In early January 1987, Keller met with several friends—Royce Engle, Samantha Rahrig, Sharon Purdy, and Judy Abbot—and formed the "Dumpbusters," a grassroots movement aimed at fighting the landfill.[17] As the group's chair and spokesperson, Keller struggled to guide those early Dumpbuster rallies,

Ida Kay Keller campaigning at the Allen County Fair, August 1988; Lima Sixth Ward Councilman Leonard Boddie is to her right. From the collection of William Angel, photograph by William Angel.

which were panicky gatherings filled with wild-eyed statements about dioxin and nuclear waste. Residents cursed openly and laughed derisively whenever Jack Nichols, Waste Management's district manager, tried to assure them that the landfill would be absolutely safe, not harmful to the community's health. A NIMBY (not in my backyard) attitude permeated these assemblies.[18]

Ida Kay Keller always knew that her community would need help from outsiders and that NIMBY-ism would not help the Dumpbusters in their fight against Waste Management. For one thing, she recognized that it would do nobody any good to keep the landfill out of Spencerville, only to have it placed somewhere else in Allen County. No community wanted the landfill, and under Keller's leadership the group began to investigate alternatives, such as composting, recycling, and incineration. They also sought assistance from the county commissioners and other elected officials. "We want your support and help in finding alternatives to a landfill in the county," Keller declared to a meeting of the commissioners in late January.[19]

The group began to visit other landfills in Ohio, acquainting themselves with the most modern waste-disposal technology. These field trips taught Ida

Kay and the Dumpbusters about landfill ecology and enabled them to educate the wider public about the hazards of landfill operations. Importantly, they acquired the expertise needed to fend off the bland assurances of Jack Nichols that the new landfill would be absolutely safe. Knowledge gained from these trips also provided the group with a fallback position: If indeed Waste Management won a permit, the Dumpbusters were prepared to make sure that any landfill would be "state of the art" and as safe as technologically possible.[20]

In the meantime, Keller worked to bolster the spirits of her followers. At one Dumpbuster rally, held at a time when the Dumpbusters felt they had no allies outside their own community, I heard her challenge an auditorium filled with over five hundred anxious people. "Waste Management wants us to think there is nothing we can do to stop the landfill," she began softly, then paused and focused her gaze on the crowd. "Do you want a landfill?" she asked. "No!" came the fierce reply, echoing off the walls.[21]

Keller could be equally firm when dealing with politicians. She was not physically imposing, but her brown eyes could glare into the eyes of any bureaucrat or elected official who tried to subdue her with rhetorical pablum. The "Keller stare" usually evoked more precise responses from even the most hardened politicians.

Under Keller's guidance, the Dumpbusters evolved into a sophisticated and well-financed community movement. They raised over $125,000, an amazing sum for a community of under five thousand residents. Weekly meetings were regularly attended by sixty to eighty citizens, and the group formed an effective committee structure to monitor and fight Waste Management's every move to secure a permit from the Ohio Environmental Protection Agency. The Dumpbusters hired an environmental lawyer from Columbus to help them with legal issues, and they purchased the services of their own geologist, who gathered field data that brought into question the company's early claims that the Spencerville site was geologically perfect for a landfill.[22] They also built a political network that connected Spencerville with politicians all over the state. With help from state senator Bob Cupp, for instance, Keller and the Dumpbusters secured meetings with Ed Hopkins, an aide to Governor Celeste and the group's liaison with the governor's office, and they also cultivated relationships with elected officials, including the attorney general, Anthony Celebreeze.[23]

In late summer 1987, the Dumpbusters' perseverance paid off—they persuaded the Ohio EPA to authorize a "pump test" on the landfill site. The results showed that water from the property was leaching into Spencerville's own water wells, a finding that ultimately doomed the landfill. Faced with undeniable evidence that the landfill posed a threat to the local water supply, Ohio EPA had no choice but to deny a permit. Waste Management did not wait for EPA action, however; on November 17, news arrived that the company was withdrawing its application. Ida Kay Keller and the Dumpbusters had won.[24]

On the evening of November 18, I stood in the Spencerville High School Auditorium, taking in the rally celebrating the town's victory over Waste Management. In an atmosphere the *Lima News* described as "Christmas and Thanksgiving all wrapped up in one,"[25] I watched Ida Kay Keller accept well-deserved plaudits from neighbors, friends, and politicians. Charlie Haskins, who served with Keller on the Spencerville School Board and had befriended me at previous Dumpbuster rallies, was standing next to me. He nudged my arm and declared, "Bill, she'd be one helluva county commissioner." I looked at him and grinned.

Now, two months later, I was putting the question to her myself. Throughout the Dumpbusters' struggle, Keller had made numerous overtures to the Allen County Democratic Party, attending party events and fund-raisers. In part, she was responding to attention I had paid the Dumpbusters; in addition, she was pursuing a strategy to broaden the Dumpbusters' local base. But these gestures also arose from Keller's strong Democratic roots. Her father, Dale Harruff, had been a Democratic committeeman when Bob Kuhn chaired the Allen County Democratic Party back in the 1960s, and her mother, Katherine, had been president of the Democratic Women's Club. As a teenager, Ida Kay herself had worked on Bob Mihlbaugh's congressional campaigns. She had always been interested in politics, and her years on the Spencerville school board and her success in guiding the Dumpbusters had started her thinking that a run for higher office might be possible.[26]

On the day we had lunch together, I showed her a party poll in which 32 percent of the respondents had indicated that the two most important problems facing Allen County were the landfill issue and solid-waste disposal.[27] Although Keller did not have the name recognition that other politicians did, I assured her that the party would help her build on the reputation she had gained from the Dumpbuster crusade. I did not mention anything about the party fight brewing between me and Todd Hey.

It would not have made any difference if I had. Ida Kay Keller wanted to run. She was simply waiting for someone to ask her; the sincerity in her questions and the intensity in her conversation said so. A few days later, Rochelle Twining came away with the same perception after meeting with Keller in a brainstorming session. No Alphonse-Gaston act here. By the beginning of February, Keller was circulating petitions to run against Bob Mayer, the commissioner who, in her view, had been least helpful to the Dumpbusters and the most indifferent to their plight.[28]

January 28, 1988

I called Jerry Pitts to inquire if he had made up his mind on the state representative's race. He complained that someone in the party had let his law partner (and former county prosecutor) Jim King know that he was thinking about becoming a candidate. King had chewed him out, threatening to discharge him from the firm. Maybe. A more likely explanation was that Jerry had simply had second thoughts and was looking for a face-saving way to say "No."[29]

February 2, 1988

A groundhog lumbered into Democratic headquarters, wrapped one arm (leg?) around Dale Locker's shoulder, and announced, "Folks, I saw my shadow this morning, and that means there's gonna be only eleven more months of Bob Cupp in the state senate. Groundhogs in the Twelfth District are votin' for Locker!" Dale Locker grinned broadly, shook the critter's paw, and chuckled, "Why thank you, Mr. Groundhog. I'll do my best to live up to that fine endorsement."

Dale Locker knew how to play the moment. He had been announcing his intention to run for Bob Cupp's senate seat when Pickle Felter, in groundhog getup, provided this zany interruption. Locker loved it. He was a skilled politician, having served ten years in the Ohio House, representing a district that took in Shelby, Mercer, and Auglaize Counties, south of Lima. In 1981, Locker had narrowly lost to Mike Oxley in a special election for Congress in the Fourth District. He probably would have won had the House Democratic Campaign Committee helped fund his campaign—but he was on the pro-life side of the abortion issue, and that was the wrong side as far as the national Democratic Party was concerned. Two years later Locker had won appointment as Governor Celeste's director of agriculture, resigning that post in 1986 to run again in his former district, only to lose narrowly to the incumbent, Jim Davis.

Locker could be charismatic and charming on the stump. As a child he had contracted polio, which had left him disabled from the waist down. But he ably maneuvered himself on crutches, and he cut a Franklin Roosevelt–like figure with his unique combination of pluck and humor, which we saw him display the day of his announcement. He knew he would have a tough campaign, but Locker was optimistic. "I'm excited about winning a major race," he declared. "The Democrats in Allen County have done so many positive things. It gives me encouragement."[30]

Locker certainly did not have a free ride to the nomination. Johnnie Mae Fuqua, a custodian for the Lima city school system, was opposing him in the primary. Fuqua, who was vice president of the Ohio Welfare Rights Organization, stressed a "common folks" message in her announcement: "This is a year to elect candidates that are for the people."[31] Knowing that Locker was going to run for this seat, I had tried to persuade Fuqua to apply this message to a campaign for Bill Thompson's House seat, but she stubbornly insisted on running against Cupp.

At the same time, I did not want Locker to think that I was double-crossing him by recruiting opposition from Allen County. So I brought him and Fuqua together for a "unity dinner" at the Alpine, immediately prior to our February Executive Committee meeting. They shook hands and agreed to put on a positive campaign. Still, I wished Johnnie Mae Fuqua were running for that House seat.

February 8, 1988, Monday

The filing deadline was ten days away, and the party still had no candidate for state representative. I had already broached the matter with Roger Rankin, who had managed Rochelle Twining's candidacy in 1986, but he had turned me down, as had Twining herself, who briefly considered the idea of challenging Bill Thompson once again. A year earlier, she had been appointed to direct Allen County's Bureau of Child Support, a position that fell right in line with her feminist principles, and she did not want to resign from that job, especially having so recently assumed it.[32]

On February 8, House Speaker Vern Riffe's office passed me the name of Kevin Gerken, who managed a trucking firm in Lima and whose father was a friend of Riffe. I tracked down Gerken and talked with him, only to discover that he had resided in the county for less than two years and had not registered to vote. But Riffe's people pressed the point, and Gerken was the only prospect who was even mildly intrigued in a House race. For three days Rochelle Twining and I encouraged him to say yes, but he turned us down. In the meantime, Riffe's aides exhorted me to scour the county, looking for someone to challenge Bill Thompson.[33]

February 11, 1988, Thursday

Dale Leppla filed for county commissioner against Don Reese and then headed for New Orleans and the Mardi Gras. Rochelle Twining and others in the party had tried to convince Ed Schwieterman to take on Reese instead, but Ed procrastinated. After Leppla had announced his candidacy on February 2, Ed withdrew his name from consideration. Though not enthralled by Leppla's candidacy, I was not as troubled by it as were others in the party. We needed candidates, and with the exception of Ida Kay Keller, Dale was the only one so far who had come close to expressing interest in running for office.[34]

But Leppla's announced candidacy—and the simultaneous removal of Schwieterman from the lists—apparently inspired the anti-Leppla faction to work harder. On February 16, two days before the filing deadline, they found their man: Joe Engle announced his candidacy for Don Reese's commissioner's seat. Engle, who had been reeled in by John Coplen, taught elementary grades at St. Charles Catholic School and sold real estate part-time for Yocum Realty, where John and Linda Coplen worked. Knowing that Leppla had already filed for the same seat and knowing that he would howl at having to face a primary challenge, I tried to talk Engle into running for county recorder or state representative, but he had his heart set on running for commissioner.[35]

The next evening, Engle attended the February session of the Executive Committee and circulated his petition, collecting over fifty signatures. He also brought additional copies of his petition, which several volunteers snapped up. The "Anybody but Leppla" bandwagon was rolling out of the station.

It did not take long for the news to reach New Orleans and Dale Leppla. Within a thirty minutes after the adjournment of that meeting, I received a call at the Alpine from Pam Falke. "Dad is really mad," she said.[36] He was still seething when he returned from Mardi Gras the following week and accused me of betraying him. I insisted that I had known nothing about Engle's becoming a candidate until John Coplen presented him to me. Besides, I said, "If a guy wants to run, I can't stop him. I can try to talk him out of it. I can suggest alternatives, as I did with Engle. But I can't stop anybody whose heart is set on a running." Leppla did not buy any of this. "Well, you did what you had to do, and now it's my turn," he replied grimly and shuffled off.[37]

February 13 1988, Saturday

My trek started at 10:30 with a visit to Kitty Hammond, a Fourth Ward activist in Lima, and ended ten hours later at John and Mary Hevener's house. I spent the entire day trying to find someone to run for state representative, and I found no takers. Traveling from Lima to Bluffton to Elida and back to Lima, I talked to Kitty Hammond, Marty Glazier, Ray Hamman, and Stan Carder, testing their interest in a state House race. I also checked in with Joyce Badertscher, a committeewoman from Bluffton, asking her to consider a run for county recorder, but like the others, she said, "No, thanks."

In between these stops, I enlisted a Central Committee candidate in Richland Township, and just before dusk I quickly passed a petition for another Central Committee nominee in Elida. These were my only notable achievements of the day.

Although my pitch to each of the prospective candidates was sincere, we all understood the realities of the contest for state representative. Rochelle Twining had run a skillful, well-financed, and enthusiastic campaign for an open seat in a Democratic year, and she had lost convincingly. Now, with Bill Thompson running as an incumbent in what appeared to be another Republican presidential sweep (Michael Dukakis, the likely Democratic nominee, was inspiring neither enthusiasm nor hope), could a Democrat even come close?

In my efforts to enlist these Democrats, I underscored a "duty to party" theme. While acknowledging that it would be a difficult fight, I said that the party needed to field a respectable, articulate candidate, one who would make Thompson work hard on the campaign trail. Additionally, the candidate had to be someone who could quickly grasp the issues facing the state of Ohio and present positions to the voters in a clear, articulate fashion. (It was no accident that all my prospects were teachers, used to thinking on their feet.) Most importantly, I emphasized, I did not want to send just anybody against Thompson. The candidate had to be someone who could give the party a campaign to build on—a trailblazer who could create a path to be followed by other campaigns in the years ahead.

They all politely heard me out, sympathized with the argument I was making, and recognized the importance of finding a qualified nominee for the Ohio House, but none wanted to be the one to take on Bill Thompson. At the end of the day, the Allen County Democratic Party still was without a legislative candidate.

On my way home, I stopped to commiserate with John and Mary Hevener. We sat at the kitchen table, drinking coffee, and I reflected on my "terrible, horrible, no good," frustrating day.[38] "You realize it's going to be hard on us, having only a handful of candidates," I grumbled. "Somehow, Todd and Charlie always managed to talk people in to running, but we're going to end up with four, at most. Now Todd'll tell folks, 'See, Angel's not up to the job.'"

John momentarily pondered my brooding pronouncement, then rocked back in his chair and said, "Maybe. But maybe not. It's not that bad, having a lean slate. Just might be good for the party. With only a few candidates, we can save resources and put all our energy into those races."[39] Good ol' John. He always preferred lighting a candle to cursing the dark.

February 17, 1988, Wednesday Afternoon
I had accepted the fact that the Allen County Democratic Party would not field a candidate to challenge Bill Thompson. My last prospect had been Ramon Moritz, whom Cora Hamman had suggested as someone who might be interested in the task. I had my doubts. Moritz, a Central Committeeman from

Jackson Township, worked at Ford and was a UAW pal of Todd Hey. Not surprisingly, he turned me down. "Maybe in 1990," he said.

Now Ty Marsh called. Marsh, who had succeeded Tom Winters as Vern Riffe's chief aide, urged that I find a "warm body" to file for the office, run in the primary, and then resign, giving way to another candidate who would be nominated by our Central Committee. I insisted that this was a flaky scheme, and I refused to pursue it. If I had been unsuccessful in finding a qualified candidate by now, I argued, I could not imagine finding one within the next four months.[40]

February 17, 1988, Wednesday, 7 P.M.,
Alpine Village Restaurant

I had finished dinner with Dale Locker and Johnnie Mae Fuqua, and members of our Executive Committee were gathering in the Alpine's assembly room downstairs, when Ty Marsh called again. He had been in contact with Cora Hamman, and now he was telling me that Mike Evans, Cora's eighteen-year-old son, wanted to run for the House seat. Exasperated, I advised Marsh that we wanted a credible candidate, not some "warm body" pushed on us by Cora Hamman.

Moments later, I spotted Cora flitting about the Alpine, her son at her side, and I asked her about this business of Evans running for state representative. "Mike really wants to run, Bill," she insisted. "I'm shocked, but he really wants to run. We can't talk him out of it." Incredulous, I pulled aside Evans and asked him if he was serious. He left a considerably different impression. "I don't know why they asked me to run," he replied. "I can't understand it."

This was hardly the enthusiasm that Ty Marsh and Cora Hamman had described to me. I urged Mike not to run this year but work for the party and its candidates instead. He could acquire fundamental experience that would help him in his own campaign when he was more mature and would be taken more seriously.[41]

I took this whole matter to the Executive Committee that evening and presented the "warm body scenario" that Speaker Riffe and his office had encouraged. No one liked the idea, and Stan Carder went so far as to move, "If and when the Allen County Democratic Party runs a candidate for state representative, it will let the Speaker's Office know." The motion was seconded by Ray Hamman and passed unanimously.[42] The Allen County Democratic Party had told Vern Riffe, "Go to Hell!"

Riffe was enraged at our decision. He wanted a candidate to run in each of Ohio's eighty-eight House districts; his staff had even gone as far as to line up eighteen-year-old Mike Evans to run against Bill Thompson, and I had sabotaged the attempt. I understood Riffe's game, all right. The greater the number of contested races, the more money the Republicans had to spend to preserve districts they already owned, such as Thompson's. Every uncontested race represented funds that the Republicans could shift to more competitive districts. Riffe didn't care whether candidates in backwaters like Allen County were qualified. He just wanted a human sacrifice, someone to draw the Republicans' fire.

I had spent almost two years trying to enhance the image of the Allen County Democratic Party, and by many accounts, I had been doing a good job. Running a politically inexperienced teenager against Bill Thompson would have made the Democratic Party in Allen County a laughingstock, not to mention the damage it would have inflicted to the kid's psyche. Vern Riffe's political interests were not even remotely in line with ours.

Most perplexing of all was that Riffe never bothered to understand our situation. Several weeks after the warm-body episode, Rochelle Twining had an "angry conversation" with Ty Marsh, who let her know that the Speaker was still furious with me for rejecting Mike Evans's supposed candidacy. Furthermore, Marsh had emphasized, Twining had had an obligation to talk me into embracing Evans; she had owed it to the Speaker for helping her 1986 race.

Of course, Twining didn't think the Speaker had helped her much at all, but Marsh did. The Speaker had known, he said, that she did not have a chance in 1986, yet he had contributed three thousand dollars to her campaign anyway. She should have been grateful for the financing that came her way, but instead she had turned her back on him. Furthermore, the Speaker really knew "his counties," Marsh arrogantly insisted, and he knew what was good for us. Twining and I should have been smarter and acquiesced to his judgment.

In response, Twining reiterated the Carder-Hamman motion, telling Marsh that he and the Speaker did not know much about the Allen County Democratic Party and that in the future they should keep "their damn noses" out of our politics.[43]

Rochelle Twining was right, of course. Vern Riffe and Ty Marsh did not know as much as they thought they did. Perhaps they knew the players and the issues in the various counties, but they did not comprehend the internal struggles that local parties experienced. Like most statehouse politicos, they were attitudinally distant from us, failing to understand that politics that were good for the Speaker—for example, sending out a "warm body" to challenge an established incumbent—would not be good for the local Democratic Party. To them, we were pawns to be maneuvered and sacrificed for the power interests of the downstate professionals. "Not all politics is local" was the dictum that guided their conduct.

February 17, 1988, Wednesday, 7:30 P.M.,
Executive Committee Meeting

The recruiting season had been cruelly chaotic. At times, I felt as though I was strapped into the "Tilt-a-Whirl" at the county fair, spinning up and down, never certain of where I was in relation to the earth. Occasionally I caught glimpses of prospective candidates, but they would dissolve before my eyes, to be replaced by others as the wheel rotated. Here I was at the Alpine, having done all I could to recruit candidates, uncertain what I had accomplished. My feet were on the ground, but I was still groggy from the ride.

There was a "gathering of tribes" that night. Dale Locker and Johnnie Mae Fuqua were on hand. So was Kevin Gerken, just to check out this politics business. Joe Engle and Ida Kay Keller were busy shaking hands and enlisting volunteers. The candidates were given the floor, each taking a few minutes to explain their qualifications for the offices they were respectively seeking. Dale Leppla was not present, but I would hear from his camp soon enough. All together, we had ended up with candidates for four offices—the two county commissioners seats, state senator, and judge of Common Pleas Court (Paul Rizor, who had addressed the committee at a previous meeting).

After the candidates presented themselves, Rochelle Twining asked for the floor. "I am concerned about our party's leadership," she declared, in reference to the challenge that Todd Hey was fomenting. "We now have a party that can bring good government to the people of Allen County, but unless we work to retain Bill Angel and Steve Webb, we won't be able to do that." John Dornick followed. "We've come a long way under the current regime," he stressed. "We have increased voter turnout, and Bill has held monthly meetings with the media. The party is more visible. We just can't give that up. We just have to keep Steve and Bill at the helm."

Then Bob Rowland popped to his feet, waving a copy of the treasurer's report that had been distributed prior to our meeting. "You know what I like best about this party? It's this little piece of paper right here. It lets me know where our money is going. We didn't have that before." Cathy Kohli, successor to Linda Coplen as president of the Democratic Women's Club, was next: "Thanks to Bill and Steve, the Women's Club is accepted by the party and has a role in party functions." Charlie Henderson, a black committeeman from Lima's Third Ward, capped the night's oratory by proclaiming, "Bill and Steve listen to me. They really listen."

These minispeeches occurred spontaneously, the comments from one speaker seamlessly energizing others into expressing their own opinions. We were all a bit distressed that night, knowing that Todd Hey and members of the old guard were poised to file their own slate of Central Committee candidates in an effort to reacquire the leadership they had lost two years previously.

"But the former leaders won't return," I assured the group, "because of what we together have accomplished. I am grateful to everyone who has spoken tonight. We all will have to work hard during the next few months, but our purpose should not be simply to return Steve and me to our current positions. As an effective party, we must elect good, responsive officials. Together we can do this."[44]

The factionalism that had pestered me over the previous eighteen months seemed to have melted in the face of the fresh challenge from Todd Hey. The Executive Committee was unified, but for what purpose? For another battle against fellow Democrats.

· 15 ·

Lean Slate

February 19, 1988

Paul Smith of the *Lima News* called. "Why do the Democrats have so few candidates this year?" he asked.

It was starting. And frankly, I was distressed. I had come into my chairmanship leading a movement committed to "electing candidates," and now, nearly two years after assuming power, I had obtained challengers to only two Republican officeholders, not counting the judicial and state senate races. And here was Paul Smith, wanting to know, "Didn't this situation spell doom for the new Democratic leadership?"

I could have answered Smith's questions candidly. I could have said that even though I had tried hard to recruit candidates, no prospect was willing to risk a run for office. I could have blamed myself, saying that I should have spoken more optimistically about the party and about the chances for winning, just to get names on the line. I could have apologized, then blamed my failure on Charlie Hauenstein, hoping that fellow Democrats and the general public would understand.

But I could not say those things, not if I wanted to remain party chairman. Instead, I applied the rosy analysis John Hevener had suggested a few days earlier as I sat at his kitchen table, feeling sorry for myself. What had begun as an encouraging, offhand remark about a "lean slate" now transformed into a master plan, a premeditated strategy for party success. In my brief interview with Smith, I applied some "spin control," asserting that the Democrats' lean slate of candidates was a perfectly reasonable blueprint for paving the track to victory. "What you have is a Democratic Party that is acting responsibly and going about its job in an effective manner," I said.[1]

"But how can that be if the Democrats have so few candidates running this year?" Smith wanted to know. "Look, a lean slate of candidates does not signify a weak party," I responded. "Such an argument overlooks what I am trying to do with the party."

"So, what are you trying to do?"

"The party officials and I hope that a concentration of races and resources in 1988 will lead to success in 1990 and 1992. A successful push to win the two most prestigious county offices on this year's ballot—the two county commission seats—will provide the foundation to build future campaigns."

Yes, I admitted, we were letting Bill Thompson pass without opposition, and the Democrats had no one to run for any of the minor county offices. Then came my central idea: "It always was our strategy to concentrate on the commissioners' races at first. The party is in a building stage right now, a growing stage. We have a limited amount of resources. Candidates were not recruited for county offices such as sheriff, recorder, clerk of courts, because to spend time and money on those races would have sapped the resources needed to win the two commissioner posts."

I took a swipe at Charlie Hauenstein and Todd Hey—I could not afford to be gracious—declaring, "The party is still trying to overcome the effect of fourteen years of mismanagement and apathy." However, my purpose was not merely to kick at the former leaders but to inoculate myself against criticism that I knew would come. "The party I took over is really a new party," I explained, "still trying to build and renew itself."

The *Lima News* bought it, complete with a headline proclaiming, "Democratic Party Boss Not Worried about Lean Slate in '88."[2] By focusing attention on the "lean slate strategy" as if it were a real strategy and not some post hoc rationalization, I had deflected debate from the question, "Why don't the Democrats have more candidates?" I had reformulated the debate in terms that would allow us to prevail in the upcoming struggle for supremacy within the party. Rank-and-file Democrats could choose between two competing interpretations: They could curse me for not recruiting more candidates, or they could view the "lean slate" as well-designed game plan. I was counting on the optimistic side to prevail.[3]

As events developed, it was much easier to maneuver perceptions of the party's lean slate than it was to control my own followers. John Coplen's recruitment of Joe Engle illustrates one aspect of this problem, but I could live with the controversy created by Engle's candidacy. In the end, Engle would lose, and Leppla would become a better candidate by having spurred himself into action for a primary battle. Something positive came out of that irksome development.

Jean Hatcher, left, listening to Ida Kay Keller; Democratic Party picnic and rally, Lafayette, Ohio, June 1988. From the collection of William Angel, photograph by William Angel.

But the same could not be said about another piece of business left over from filing day—namely, Linda Coplen's decision to run against Jean Hatcher for state Central Committeewoman in the Fourth District. That gambit had to do more with office politics than party politics. Coplen and Hatcher both served as field representatives for Secretary of State Sherrod Brown, working adjoining territories. Over the years, a feud had developed between the two women, and Linda saw the election as her chance gain the upper hand.

As for Jean Hatcher, a native of nearby Hardin County, she packed a fierce loyalty to the Ohio Democratic Party, especially to Governor Celeste. However, her allegiance did not extend to local activists, most of whom she regarded with barely concealed contempt. She liked to meddle in the internal politics of county parties, peddling rumors and generally stirring up trouble. Even ODP chairman Ruvulo, one of Hatcher's big supporters, admitted that she was "a rumor carrier."[4]

Hatcher had had her run-ins with me, too. I had not forgotten her gossip against Democrats for an Effective Party two years earlier. Then in 1987, she and I had sparred over her efforts, without letting me know what was going on, to arrange an appointment for Bryan Hefner to see Governor Celeste. I had chastised Bryan at the time, saying that while I didn't mind his request or his enlisting Hatcher's help, I did expect him to keep me in the loop. Hatcher caught wind of this rebuke and admonished me, "Well, Bill, can you get an appointment with the governor?"

"No, but that's not the point, Jean, and you know it. I don't like surprises. It creates a bad impression on those outside our Executive Committee."[5] I could have filed that comment for future use.

Hatcher was prodigious at raising money for ODP, the governor, and other state officeholders. She took so much pride in her fund-raising prowess that she looked down her nose at fellow Democrats—me, for instance—who in her eyes were not pulling their weight financially. At the May 1987 ODP State Dinner, I bumped into her, and she asked how many tickets—at $150 a pop— Allen County had sold. "Seventeen," I responded, pleased. To me, that figure seemed like a lot. "Well, I sold sixteen by myself," Hatcher huffed, "and they're *all* here. My philosophy, Bill, is, if you can't buy a ticket, you shouldn't come. That's right. If you can't afford to pay, you shouldn't be here."[6]

It was a dig, a snippy jibe, skewering me for not buying my own ticket. I had heard this before, secondhand, when she hyperbolically complained that I was the only Democratic chair who had not joined the "Governor's Club," a donor's circle with annual dues of a thousand dollars. In Hatcher's view, I set a stingy example.[7]

Jean Hatcher was no friend of mine, but her battle with Linda Coplen was not one I wanted to be part of. In fact, I knew nothing about Coplen's plans until Linda herself called me after she had filed. I immediately phoned Steve Webb and became angrier still. It turned out that he had passed Linda's petition, easily gathering the five signatures it took for her to become a candidate for the Central Committee post. Barely concealing my indignation, I told him that it was a dumb idea for Linda to take on Jean Hatcher just then. When I asked him what he, our party's Central Committee chairman, had been thinking of, he could only reply, "I didn't see any problem."[8]

It created a huge problem. Hatcher's tentacles ran right to the governor's office and to the central operations of the Ohio Democratic Party. During her tenure as state Central Committeewoman, her tireless pursuit of campaign contributions had won her many friends in Columbus. In fact, Governor Celeste was so smitten with Hatcher's devoted loyalty and fund-raising skill that he himself had appointed her to the secretary of state's office. Thus, when Linda Coplen took on Jean Hatcher, she was also taking on the governor and creating an immense headache for her boss, Sherrod Brown. The controversy rapidly ballooned into something much larger than an intra-office spat between two employees who didn't like each other.[9]

Coplen's machinations also created a controversy that Charlie Hauenstein and Todd Hey gleefully exploited. I called Hatcher the night I heard the news to reassure her that I had had nothing to do with Coplen's candidacy and that I would back her in the election. She already knew that Steve Webb had passed Linda Coplen's petition, and she could identify every person who had signed— information from Charlie Hauenstein, who had been at the Board of Elections on filing day, monitoring petitions as they came in. Later, Todd Hey gave the pot a stir, phoning Hatcher and reminding her what her friends in Allen County had done.[10]

The pressure kept mounting. Hatcher called Jim Ruvulo, who called Sherrod Brown, who tried to talk Coplen into withdrawing her candidacy. Finally, a week after she had started the mess, Linda asked me what she should do. I declared that I was terribly unhappy, that her move against Hatcher was interfering with my effort to retain leadership of the party, and that I was supporting Jean Hatcher in the election. Confronted with this stand, Linda decided to withdraw her candidacy.[11]

Or, that is what she told me and Sherrod Brown. Coplen submitted a written withdrawal, all right, but turned she it in on March 1, one day too late for a candidate to withdraw from a primary race.[12] Apparently, Coplen had believed that she could have it both ways. By preparing a resignation of candidacy, she had technically complied with the pledge she had given me and Brown, but because she had presented it too late, the Board of Elections would have little choice but to keep her name on the ballot. Brown's office, had tried to protect itself against this dodge by calling Coplen on February 29, reminding her that she had until four o'clock that day to submit her withdrawal. Coplen had reassured Brown's office that she would.[13]

The day Linda Coplen waltzed into the Board of Elections, her letter of withdrawal in hand, happened to be my first day as a member of the board.[14] We were proceeding with routine organizational matters, and at first the board was willing to allow her resignation. But Charlie Hauenstein (who would continue to serve for another two years) raised a concern as to "whether there were any precedents to allow for late withdrawal." Faced with Charlie's challenge, the board postponed a decision until that Friday, March 4.[15]

By now, with Coplen's status as a candidate unclear, I was in trouble with the Democratic bigwigs downstate. Jim Ruvulo phoned and chewed me out. "I stuck my neck out for you guys—Webb and you—on the license bureau. So what's going on?"[16] I explained that I too was unhappy with the situation and that I had already bawled out Linda. Unfortunately, she had presented her resignation after the deadline, and it was doubtful that the Board of Elections would accept it. Ruvulo urged me to cut a deal with Republican Party boss Bob Holmes, who also chaired the board. I should explain to him that this was an internal party matter and stress that I needed his backing, just as he might need my support in some similar circumstance. Offer a quid pro quo, Ruvulo suggested—something like, "Agree to accept Coplen's resignation now, and I'll help you when you need it."

Ruvulo liked to give advice like this, but he did not understand the politics here. From Holmes's perspective, the "Linda Coplen Affair" exacerbated the feud between two Democratic factions, and the bigger the dispute, the better. There was absolutely no reason for him to cooperate with me. I also knew that I did not want to start my tenure on the Allen County Board of Elections by asking Bob Holmes for a favor. I rejected Ruvulo's advice and tried to defend Coplen's appeal, asserting that the law surely should not force a candidate, such as Linda, to run when she wanted to withdraw. It was a lame argument and prompted a scolding from Holmes, who reminded me that I should not let political matters get in the way of my legal obligations. Holmes was right. The law was clear, and the board voted to reject her request by a vote of three to one, with my vote providing the only dissent.[17]

Not long after the board had issued its decision, Sherrod Brown summoned Linda Coplen to his office and fired her. At least, that was Linda's story; Brown's version was that he had asked for and received a letter of resignation.[18] Either way, Linda Coplen was out of a job, and my followers were outraged. Steve Webb delivered the word of Linda's firing himself, storming into a DEP meeting and informing everyone that Sherrod had fired Linda, and then proceeding to "trash" Brown in highly vitriolic terms. Others at the meeting, roused by Webb's pique, added their own verbal blows to Brown and rhetorical sympathy for Linda. They wanted me to write a letter or issue a protest to Sherrod Brown, to the governor, to Jim Ruvulo, to anybody in high places who might listen.[19]

In the end, just to quiet the furor, I promised to pay Ruvulo a visit, mend fences, and detail the problem this whole sorry episode had created. Ruvulo was surprised that Coplen had been let go, declaring somewhat disingenuously that his role in the matter had been simply to "let Sherrod Brown know that two of his field workers were running against each other." Nevertheless, the ODP chief was unflagging in his support of Hatcher, proclaiming that she had always supported the party and him.[20]

I explained that the Coplen affair had stirred an immense ruckus. He needed to know, I said, that Jean Hatcher was not well liked in Allen County and that she had fomented dissension within my own Executive Committee. "We have people such as John and Mary Hevener who are on Linda's side in this dispute," I emphasized. "If I were you, I'd be concerned about being so supportive of someone the Heveners are against."[21] I continued that I found it distasteful to be in a situation where I have to discourage a candidate from running. "I hope we never get to the point where we close the political process, just because it's not convenient," I bristled. "Party offices are different," Ruvulo retorted sharply.

I let him have the final word and left Linda Coplen to her fate. A month later, Sherrod Brown would replace her with Rochelle Twining, an appointment that enhanced my access to the secretary of state's office.[22] Linda plugged ahead in her electoral contest with Jean Hatcher but in the end carried only 37 percent of the districtwide vote.[23] Embittered by the experience, she dropped out of politics altogether.

But I hadn't gone to Columbus that day just to defend Linda Coplen. I had a more important objective in mind and eased the conversation toward the prospect of Ruvulo endorsing me and Webb. I persuaded him to write a letter praising our leadership, with the understanding that we could use the message in the struggle against Todd Hey.[24] We would place Ruvulo's signed statement on sample ballots that highlighted the names of party-endorsed candidates for Central Committee. It complimented me and Webb for "doing all the right things"; in it Ruvulo declared, "I am certain your early preparation for the 1988 election, including the recruitment of highly qualified candidates, will pay dividends."[25] Uplifting words, but Todd Hey wasn't buying them.

The most remarkable feature about the "party fight" of 1988 was that it actually generated a dialogue. In 1986, the contest between the old guard and DEP had turned mainly on personal attacks and mean-spirited ploys—"Project Jabba the Hut" and the whole LaRouchie mess, for instance—but in 1988, Todd Hey's allies and mine actually presented competing visions of the party's future.

Hey formed a group called the "Grass Roots Campaign Committee" and launched a two-wave assault on the lean-slate issue, beginning with a fearsome letter-to-the-editor campaign. His candidates initiated the attack in early April, when Judy Humes (Lima, Seventh Ward) wrote the *Lima News*, "I have been defranchised [sic] by my own Allen County Democratic Party. . . . Instead of candidates, Mr. Angel gives us excuses."[26] Letters from former party treasurer Vern Eley (Auglaize Township) and Richard Groves (Lima, Seventh Ward) backed her up, arguing that I had fostered dissent and division within the party and that the lean-slate strategy was a reflection of my ineptitude.[27] Perhaps the most spirited letter came from Dan Kline (American Township), who declared, "Common sense tells me a lean slate does not elect Democrats. If you do not have a candidate on the ballot, you cannot win a race." Like the others, he challenged the competence of my leadership, claiming that I was "destroying the entire party."[28]

We did not let these letters go uncontested, but Hey's maneuver had caught us by surprise. Consequently, our responses—defensive appeals for patience—lacked force. Trying to rebut Judy Humes's attack, for instance, Deb Ioannidis of Shawnee Township wrote, "Common sense dictates that credible candidates cannot be created overnight," but her letter merely prompted Dan Kline's comeback.[29]

Three days before the primary, Charlie Hauenstein—who had been coaching Hey's group from the sidelines—provided the finishing touches when he laid out the choice facing Democrats: "And now we have the battle between Todd Hey's Grass Root Democrats and Bill Angel's D.E.P.S. [sic], over who will control the Allen County Democrat Party for the next two years." Charlie concentrated most of his fire on me, alleging that I had been "unsupportive" and "disruptive" when he had chaired the party. He too challenged my competence, claiming that under my leadership the party had frittered away its money, elected no Democrats, and recruited precious few to run in 1988. "There is only one way to go," he exhorted. "Support Todd Hey for chairman and return pride to the party."[30]

The second wave in Hey's strategy echoed the critical tone the letters had sounded. During the week before the primary, the Grass Roots Committee sent a two-piece mailer into contested precincts. One piece was a sample ballot that harped on the absence of Democratic candidates: "Don't you think it's time we do *something?*" it implored. Leaving nothing to chance, an arrow pointed to the name of Hey's candidate for Central Committee.[31]

The sample ballot was accompanied by a computer-produced broadside headlined, "Allen County Grass Roots Democrat '88 Campaign." Along the bottom appeared the names of Grass Roots Committee members, most of whom were Central Committee candidates. A block of "want ads" highlighted the middle of the page:

Lost—DEMOCRATS right to vote on a full slate of DEMOCRAT CANDIDATES.
Wanted—Pride in the ALLEN COUNTY DEMOCRAT PARTY.
Wanted—New ALLEN COUNTY DEMOCRAT leadership.

Old Machine: Cranks Up?

Old Machine: Cranks Up? Cartoon by David S. Adams; used with permission.

Needed—YOUR VOTE.

NOTICE—Remember to vote May 3rd and mark for: (name of candidate) as your candidate for Member of the County Central Committee.[32]

This was a clever piece, but when read in the context of Hey's two-wave strategy, with its tripe about "leadership," " "unity," and "restoring pride," the message offered no substantive reason why a voter should support any Grass Roots candidate.

More importantly, the negativism only highlighted the optimism of pronouncements from our side, that of the official Democratic Party. In addition to the sample ballot with Ruvulo's message, which we sent to all Democratic households, there was the *Democratic Voice,* a slick, four-page, newspaper-sized document printed on construction bond, trumpeting the virtues of the "New Democratic Party." This was the centerpiece of our campaign. My name appeared prominently on the front page—"Angel Blasts Republicans," went one headline—and the back page featured a political cartoon created by my colleague and friend David Adams. It depicted an overweight man (Charlie) sitting in the back seat of an old jalopy while a tall, skinny fellow with a moustache (Todd) tried to crank it, cursing, "This #@&# thing won't go anymore!" It was captioned "Old Machine: Cranks Up?" and the point was obvious even to the most casually informed Democrat.[33]

The *Voice* adorned its bright, substantive message with images of cheerful activism. Its handsome red, white, and black format contained photos, cartoons, another sample ballot, letters to the editor, and stories making the case for the lean slate. The *Voice* project was expensive, $1,425, plus presort services and postage, but it was a sound investment.[34] Its optimistic, can-do verve cast the impression of a party on the move, heading in the right direction.

To give substance to the party's newfound energy, our candidates worked their own precincts (which only a few of Hey's candidates did), hand-delivering literature, meeting and greeting Democrats in their own neighborhoods, and explaining the party's message. Melding our words with imagery and action, we lit candles every step of the way, while Hey and his crew wrote letters to the *Lima News,* cursing the dark.

· 16 ·

The Social Club

April 13, 1988

Everett Stemen had died. At least, that was the word I received from Smokey Hower. I checked the obituary page of the *Lima News,* and sure enough, there it was: "Everett Stemen, 66, of Elida died at 1 A.M. today at his residence."[1]

Everett had been a good guy, one of our Central Committee representatives from Marion Township, west of Elida. Also, he had been running for reelection, but that didn't matter anymore. He had been one of the faithful, signing on with DEP two years ago, and now he was gone.

I immediately phoned Evelyn Vanek, the party treasurer, and asked her to send a floral arrangement to the funeral home. The next evening I put on my best suit and went to the viewing to pay my own respects and those of the Democratic Party. It was the least we could do. Upon arrival, I signed the "friends and relatives" book and picked up a prayer card, gaving it a cursory glance before shoving it into my suit pocket. As I ambled toward the bier, I noticed the closed coffin; it had a beautiful walnut grain finish, a trifolded American flag at one end, and a picture of the deceased at the other. The photograph did not look much like Everett, but it was an old photo, one of those color-tints from the 1950s, showing a man much younger than Everett had been the last time I saw him.

As I stood near the casket, contemplating my next move, a woman in her mid-thirties approached. "It's so nice of you to come," she said, as if I were an old family friend. I started to introduce myself but she interrupted, "Oh, I know who you are. We see you on television. I'm Everett's daughter."

"We're sure gonna miss your dad," I managed to say. "He was a good Democrat. You have my sympathies and those of the Democratic Party." After a moment, I continued softly, "Say, we sure were shocked by Everett's passing. Was this a sudden illness?" Her eyebrows popped a notch, and she paused a moment before answering. "No ... he had cancer—lung cancer. Really started going downhill around the first of April."

"I'm really sorry. None of us knew." I was feeling guilty now—in fact, like I'd been kicked in the gut. I had more or less badgered Stemen into running for reelection. Everett had seemed reluctant to run even after Pickle Felter agreed to pass his petition for him. Small wonder. The man had been dying.

Breaking away from the daughter, I made my rounds, pausing to say a few words to various groups of mourners, telling them all how much Everett meant to the Democratic Party and how much he would be missed by all of us. Graciously, they thanked me, but they also kept exchanging quizzical looks among themselves, as if to say, "What's this guy doing here?"

Having offered my respects to Everett and his family, I headed to Democratic headquarters, where a task force was stuffing campaign packets with copies of the *Voice*. "Man!" I announced on entering the building, "I feel terrible. Everett died of cancer. The poor bastard was dying when I talked him into running for reelection, but he was too proud to tell me." Our volunteers looked up, collectively issued a blank stare, and went back to fixing campaign packs. We all had to move on.

Forty-five minutes later, Rochelle Twining picked up a packet of literature designated for Everett Stemen. "Bill, is Everett Stemen dead or what?" she asked irreverently. "Why, yeah. I went to the funeral home. Here's the prayer card," I said, reaching into my suit pocket.

"Read the name."

"Everett Stemen."

"The full name."

"Everett P. Stemen."

"Bill, our Everett is Everett *L*. Stemen."

"Holy shit." I murmured. "We sent flowers, too."[2]

Everett L. Stemen eventually won his Central Committee race—by one vote. The going had not been easy for him or for any of us, and in the days leading up to the primary, we began to get panicky. We had been through this struggle two years earlier, but in 1988 the roles had reversed. Now, the former DEP faction controlled the party's apparatus, while Todd Hey, Charlie Hauenstein, and the old guard were on the outside, battling us. We were the Democratic Party, no longer referring to ourselves publicly as DEP—and they, the instigators of rebellion.

Hey's forces didn't see themselves as rebels, however. Ever since their ouster two years earlier, Hey and Hauenstein and their followers had regarded themselves as "Democrats in Exile," occupying a place on the party's fringe and preparing for a comeback when the opportunity arrived. Hey had no qualms about casting himself as a representative of the Democratic Party if it meant getting his foot in the door. For example, making a trip around my precinct to register new voters, I discovered that "some tall guy with a moustache" had already been around the previous weekend. It was Todd, of course—just one of the party faithful, doing his duty for the voters of my precinct.

Similarly, Todd and Judy Hey paid a mid-April visit to Ida Kay Keller, who had no idea who they were or what they wanted. According to Keller, Todd never said anything against me personally, but he boasted of having been a Democrat all his life and stressed that he wanted to be party chairman, that he wanted to make various changes in the party structure, and that once Ida Kay became commissioner, he would meet with her every week to talk about issues.[3] Keller later called Rochelle Twining and the Heveners, who clarified the situation for her.

Hey's literature, along with those venomous letters to the editor, had distressed my followers, who feared that Todd was trying to foster a case of confused identity, blurring the distinction between his "Grass Roots Democrat" candidates and the ones who supported me and Steve Webb. In particular, Rochelle Twining, John Dornick, Bob Rowland, Cora Hamman, and a few others feared that average Democrats, nonactivists who paid minimal attention to the party's internal feuding, might receive the impression that Todd Hey represented the "true Democratic Party" and that we were the outsiders. This was a valid concern. Even though Hey's Grass Roots Committee had articulated a message that was completely opposite from the one the official party was promoting, Hey himself had deftly blurred the distinction between his faction and the regular party. His sample-ballot mailer, in particular, caused my allies to think that household Democrats might grab Hey's ballot on the way to polls and then cast votes for the opposition candidates without thinking the matter through.[4]

Consequently, on the day before the primary, Twining, Dornick, Elsie Crowe, and a few other loyalists staged a press conference emphasizing who was really in charge of the Democratic Party. Because Hey's group had been attacking me personally, we felt it wise to let surrogates carry the ball, delivering a statement that affirmed my leadership while demonstrating that the party had developed a proficient, pluralistic structure. Rochelle Twining gave an on-camera interview in which she emphasized that voters needed to understand that "the Democratic Party is led by Bill Angel and Steve Webb" and that they needed to vote for the party-endorsed candidates for Central Committee. "Any other vote," she declared, "is a vote for ancient history."[5] She also remarked in a newspaper interview, "The pro-Hey group has worked harder to get themselves elected than they ever did to get Democratic candidates elected in the fourteen years they controlled the party."[6] Of course, Charlie Hauenstein had issued a similar put-down of DEP's challenge two years' earlier. The roles had reversed, all right.

Given a chance to respond, Hey again denounced the lean-slate strategy and questioned my competence as party chairman. Then, voicing a charge we had not heard before, he accused me and an "elite group of Lima-ites" of running the party as "a social club" and closing it to most Democrats.[7] It was a curious comment. Coming one day before the primary, it probably had little impact on the outcome, but it did say a lot about the power struggle that had beleaguered the Allen County Democratic Party as far back as 1986. In referring to the party as "a social club," Hey was projecting his own feelings of exclusion, of being kept out of the central workings of the party apparatus, where he believed he belonged.

How could it have been otherwise? DEP's victory in 1986 had not been clean and convincing. We had not destroyed the will of the old guard to exert power, and we did not feel secure enough to invite, say, Todd Hey to sit with us to help manage the party. Speaking for myself, I could not confidently seek Charlie Hauenstein's advice on the thorny difficulties that my lieutenants repeatedly foisted upon me. So we went on alone, blundered into problems, and put ourselves in situations in which Todd and Charlie could highlight our mistakes. The current party fight was not a new struggle but an extension of the one of two years earlier. There were "two Democratic Parties" in Allen County, something Bryan Hefner had once observed publicly.[8] Until one faction could triumph overwhelmingly and force the other to submit to its leadership, the party would be burdened by factionalism.

April 26, 1988

Cora Hamman walked out of a DEP meeting. The tension of the campaign's closing days had pushed her into another of her tantrums. We had been considering whether to put an ad in the newspaper to counteract any press release Hey might issue over the weekend before the primary. "Who wants to put this together?" I asked. That was a mistake; Cora's hand shot up immediately. I ignored her upraised hand, turning instead to Deb Ioannidis, who agreed to help, as did Rochelle Twining. "What happened to that side of the table?" Ioannidis asked lightheartedly, gesturing toward Hamman, who was scowling. "Bill thinks we're incompetent," Cora muttered, seeing nothing funny in the situation. She stayed only a few more minutes, then sullenly gathered her papers, slung her jacket over her shoulder, and stomped out of the room, slamming the door behind her.

When John Dornick called Cora later that evening, she was still simmering. According to Dornick's report of the conversation, Hamman swore that she was dropping out of the party and not coming back. In particular, she was upset that I never paid attention to her, that I never called her, that I listened only to Rochelle Twining and the Heveners, and that I thought she was ignorant. Furthermore, she complained, she was "tired of doing all the work and not getting any recognition." Dornick persuaded Cora to think about her decision, and predictably, two days later she was back to her old self, telling John Hevener that the day after the primary she was going to "fire that damn Pearl Ward" at the license bureau.[9]

In fact, Cora's behavior over the previous three months had been erratic, sometimes damaging to my leadership, and the business with Pearl Ward was a particular example. Pearl had been one of Todd Hey's employees at the Lima Mall license bureau; Steve Webb had retained her even though she had been closely associated with Hey and Hauenstein when they had commanded the party. Politics dictated that choice: Pearl's husband Dick had become president of the Ford local of the UAW, and because we did not want to offend him or anybody in the UAW, Pearl stayed.

But bad blood quickly developed between Pearl Ward and Cora Hamman, spilling over in early February, about the time of the presidential-delegate caucuses. Cora and I were co-coordinators of Michael Dukakis's presidential campaign in the Fourth Congressional District, and Cora badly wanted to win election as a national delegate. However, Pearl also had declared herself a nominee for delegate, and word got out that the Ford local and other UAW affiliates in the district were going to pack the caucus to support the wife of their UAW brother. This was mostly bluff, for unlike in 1984, organized labor was not backing any particular candidate; in 1988 the unions were going in a number of different directions, mostly for Paul Simon, Dick Gephart, and Jesse Jackson, as well as for Dukakis.

Still, Cora believed that with union backing, Pearl Ward would edge her out as Dukakis's number-one female delegate in the Fourth District. Exploiting her position as manager of Webb's license bureau, Cora tried to intimidate Ward—making her life miserable, rebuking her publicly, and denying her breaks. She even threatened to fire Pearl unless she withdrew her candidacy. At one point, the two women got into a public shouting match. Still, Ward did not back down.

The whole controversy seemed to become moot after the caucus; Hamman finished first in the balloting for the two female delegate slots, drawing a few more votes than Ward, the runner-up. Cora thought she was all set to go to the National Convention in Atlanta—assuming, of course, that Dukakis took the district. Meanwhile, John Dornick and Steve Webb counseled Cora to take it easy on Pearl, and Cora, thinking she had won this skirmish, agreed.[10]

Cora Hamman was driving John Dornick crazy. He was staffing party headquarters, keeping track of the day's activities, and fielding nervous phone calls
from Cora. She finally showed up in person late in the morning, but after a few
hours of Cora's fretful behavior, Dornick had had enough and sent her home
to canvass her precinct one more time. Then, at 6 P.M., a crestfallen Cora called
Rochelle Twining and in a weepy voice moaned that her precinct was lost. She
knew it.[11]

Hamman had nothing to worry about. She would defeat her opponent by
forty votes. In fact, the DEP wing of the party took sixty of the ninety-eight
contested races; Rochelle Twining and Pickle Felter were the only core members of the party's leadership to suffer defeat. Steve Webb, Leonard Boddie,
Elsie Crowe, Mary Hevener, Tom Doyle, and I all convincingly won our races.

Meanwhile, core members of the old guard fell in a collective heap. Hey himself lost, as did former treasurer Vern Eley and former Board of Elections member Paul Prater. Charlie Hauenstein once again got pummeled in Bluffton by
Ray Hamman. The only bright moment for the Grass Roots Committee came
from Bill Johns's victory over Smokey Hower in the "American O" precinct.[12]

The local media trumpeted the news that Democratic voters had given victory to our side of the party and defeat to Hey. "Leadership of the Allen County
Democratic Party will remain the same," intoned Mark Byers, news anchor for
WLIO TV.[13] "Angel likely to retain control of Dem Party," headlined the *Lima
News.* "There comes a time in any organization when new leadership is required," I told Paul Smith. "The Democratic Party recognized the need for new
leadership two years ago, and that [leadership] was confirmed Tuesday."[14]

Despite the primary's positive outcome, I hoped the party could finally move
past the bickering and elect Democrats. Striking a unity theme, I extended an
olive branch to Hey and his side of the party, praising them for waging an important struggle. "They raised some issues that were worthy of being raised," I
observed, "and I will pay attention to those issues and improve the party."[15] Todd
Hey did not respond to this gesture. In fact, he was so startled by the election
results that he declined to give media interviews.[16]

Although his strategy had been a complete and utter failure, Hey remained
unwilling to admit defeat. A miracle might lift him back into contention—and
Cora Hamman almost handed one to him.

Michael Dukakis's victory in the Ohio primary seemed to have assured Cora
a berth in the state's delegation to the National Convention in Atlanta. However,

Dukakis delegates from the Fourth Congressional District, Governor's Mansion, Bexley, Ohio, July 1988. *Seated, from left:* Jack Obenour (Mansfield), Cora Hamman (Lima), and Bob Rowland (Lima). Bill Angel is standing behind them. From the collection of William Angel.

exactly one week after the primary, Anne Drake, coordinator for Dukakis's Ohio campaign, informed Cora that Dukakis's three delegates from the Fourth Congressional District would be Bob Rowland, Jack Obenour, and Pearl Ward.[17] All had ties to organized labor, an important consideration for the Dukakis organization. Cora might, however, be able to go to Atlanta as an at-large delegate. All she had to do was complete the required form, and the Dukakis campaign would seriously consider her.

Having to fill out this extra paperwork was not what Cora had expected. Furthermore, she felt humiliated, losing out to her archnemesis Pearl Ward, and she let Drake have a piece of her mind before phoning me and asking me to supply the form she needed. Those papers were at home, and I told Cora she could stop by my duplex that afternoon if she wanted the form right away. She wanted it immediately.

I arrived home in midafternoon, carrying an armful of books, dry cleaning, and groceries. Leaving the door to my apartment standing wide open, I moved through the living room to the kitchen, where I deposited my load on a counter. By the time I turned back to the door, Cora was standing in the middle of my living room, having traipsed in uninvited, as if she were Ethel Mertz. "Oh. Hi, Cora," I stammered, "You want that form, don't you? It's upstairs. I'll be right back." Cora fell in behind me as I rushed upstairs, making her way to my bedroom, where I hastily rummaged through a pile of mail on my desk. I retrieved the necessary paperwork, handed it to her, and ushered her quickly downstairs.

Every step of the way, up and down the stairs, Cora ranted about Pearl Ward, decrying the many problems the woman was supposedly creating at the license bureau. Intermittently, Cora vented self-pity—lamenting this calamity that would cause her to miss the National Convention—and raged at Anne Drake and the Dukakis committee, who in her view had deceived and betrayed her. After all the work she had done!

"Simmer down, Cora," I interrupted, managing to work a word in between diatribes. "This is not worth getting upset about. We are in a very delicate stage in our struggle. We have to play the end-game, and I don't want anything to mess us up. Specifically, I want you to stop ragging on Pearl Ward. That only causes trouble, and I don't want *anything* to happen to her." Cora turned on me. "Do you know what it's like to work with a whore?" she screamed. Then, in an astounding and bizarre move, she pulled up her blouse and rolled up her sleeves to display big splotches on her midriff and arms.

"She does this to me," Cora continued, more subdued but practically sobbing. "I'm a nervous wreck because of her. The problem is I really wanted to go to the convention," she persisted. "I didn't get to go last time [Cora had coordinated the Gary Hart campaign in 1984], and I really want to go." Trying anything to break her mood, I replied cheerfully, "You'll still be here in 1992. You're not planning on moving, are you?"

"I don't know, Bill," Cora sighed glumly, tears brimming as she mumbled something about a visit to her doctor. "I may not be here long," she said.[18] Affronted by this attempt to manipulate me, I responded coldly, "Yeah, well, hang in there. And remember this: Cool it with Pearl Ward. Nothing should happen to her."

"I'll try," Cora replied and left—mercifully.[19]

The next day, Cora phoned, practically singing. Overnight, sorrow had turned into joy. "Things are fine, Bill," she chortled. "Pearl agreed to resign [as Dukakis delegate]. She and I had a nice talk, and she said she didn't really want to go [to Atlanta], and since I did, she said she'd resign and let me go."[20] I was peeved: Cora had ignored the directive I had given her the day before to "cool it" with Pearl.

Like the Hatcher/Coplen brouhaha, the fighting between Cora Hamman and Pearl Ward had deep repercussions. Cora's verbal assaults on Pearl were affronts to the leadership of the Ford local and to the entire UAW—which, by the way, she had vulgarly insulted in one angry exchange. Because she was my ally, her attacks could be perceived as coming from me. Guilt by association could decide this struggle. Also, Cora's perky report offered a much-too-neat resolution to a complex problem. If Cora had given even the appearance that she was following through on her threat to fire Pearl Ward, her machinations could rupture the already tenuous relationship between me and the UAW, and they could jeopardize my efforts to retain control of the Democratic Party.

My unease proved justified a week later. Elsie Crowe called on May 18, expressing worry about a conversation with Nellie Burkholder, one of our committeewomen-elect. Elsie's account of that conversation went as follows: Nellie's son, Ron Burkholder, had called his mom to discourage her from voting for Steve Webb at the reorganization meeting. Ron, who was secretary of the Ford local and one of Todd Hey's committeemen-elect, told his mother to "think again" about supporting us. He asserted that Cora had threatened to fire Pearl Ward unless she resigned her position as a Dukakis delegate, and that Pearl had reluctantly complied. Ron did not like it; he declared that Webb and I were "a bad bunch." When Elsie's report neared its finish, she stopped abruptly, took a breath and said earnestly, "Bill, I think we've lost Nellie."[21]

Elsie agreed to talk to Nellie Burkholder again and try to give her our side of the story. But at this point I was not sure what our side of the story was, for Ron Burkholder's interpretation carried a grain of truth, especially given Cora's February threat to fire Pearl. Wanting another perspective on that "nice talk" between Cora and Pearl, I phoned Steve Webb and instructed him to look into the matter of Ward's sudden decision to resign her delegate's post. In the meantime, I lobbied Nellie Burkholder myself. So did Elsie Crowe and others in the party, including Webb, and thanks to our combined efforts, we retained her support.

Steve eventually reported that Cora and Pearl had simply had a friendly talk and that Pearl freely agreed to step down. "But Steve," I asserted, "Cora should *never* have talked to Pearl in the first place, especially after that row they had last February. Even if they did have a 'friendly talk,' as you say, there was this past threat hanging over their conversation."[22] I was steamed. I could no longer abide Cora Hamman's exasperating conduct, and I was not terribly happy with Webb for tolerating it. However, not wanting to force a confrontation—not yet, anyway—I decided to hold my fire until after the reorganization meeting.

About the same time the Burkholder crisis was unfolding, I received word from Becky Fox, a lawyer and one of our Central Committee representatives-elect, that she had had an intense face-to-face meeting with Todd Hey, in which he had itemized his objections against Webb's and my leadership. The list had included the business with Cora Hamman and Pearl Ward.[23] Losing Fox's vote was never an issue, but her report, when pieced together with the disturbance surrounding Nellie Burkholder, provided a picture of how Todd Hey's strategy was going to play out. Until the Nellie Burkholder flap, Todd's camp had not been heard from, and until I talked with Becky Fox, none of us had had the slightest inkling of what he was up to. In fact, his silence had left us wondering whether he was even going to bother us.

The Hamman/Ward dispute gave Hey an opening. By exploiting Cora's unpredictable conduct, he could pry at votes that had been committed to Webb, court our clearly identified supporters, and woo enough of them to his side to seize control of the party. If that was Todd's plan, he had a lot of front porches to visit. Even our worst-case scenario had Webb winning by a dozen votes; a more optimistic count saw the margin ranging to thirty votes and higher. Hey needed time—and lots of it—to rustle the votes of wavering Central Committee representatives.

His only hope was to stall the reorganization meeting, but he did not have control over that calendar. I did. Rather, I exercised that control according to Ohio's election code. On May 19 the Board of Elections would inspect the primary results and certify them as final. At the meeting when the board set the ground rules for this procedure, I put this question to my fellow members: "If I understand the law correctly, we have six to fifteen days to call our organization meeting once the election results are declared official. The clock starts then. Is that right?"

Charlie Hauenstein barely waited for the query to fly from my mouth when he pounced. "No, it doesn't, Bill. We have to settle recounts first. Results aren't declared until recounts are settled. Then, the clock starts."[24] We knew of no recounts, except for two Central Committee races that had ended in ties, and they could be resolved quickly. We board members sparred over Charlie's and my differing interpretations of the law but settled nothing.

Hauenstein—a bridge player, who normally held his cards close—had tipped his hand on this one. His overeager attempt to clarify the law let me know that he or Todd Hey would request eleventh-hour recounts in some of the Central Committee races in an attempt to delay our reorganization meeting until June.

I did not want to wait that long. I called Secretary of State Brown's office and talked with his elections counsel, Jonathan Marshall, who assured me that my interpretation of the law was correct. The clock started when the board declared the election official, and the holding of recounts for close races was not relevant.[25] With Marshall's reassurance, I again studied the appropriate sections of the election code, and just to make sure the party was not falling into any traps, I talked the issue over with John Hevener, Jim Ruvulo, and Rochelle Twining, now in place as Sherrod Brown's field representative. All agreed that if Jon Marshall said my interpretation of the law was accurate, then I could comfortably set the reorganization meeting.[26]

On May 19, 1988, the Allen County Board of Elections certified the 1988 primary and declared its results official.[27] That same day, I directed Elsie Crowe, secretary of the party's Central Committee, to send a letter to all Central Committee representatives scheduling a meeting on May 26, 1988, at 7:30 P.M. "for the purpose of organizing the party for 1988–1990."[28]

The clock was ticking.

May 23, 1988, Monday
Steve Webb phoned. Todd Hey had asked Becky Fox to file papers with Allen County Common Pleas Court petitioning for a temporary restraining order against the party's reorganization meeting. Fox had refused. I asked Webb to talk with Rick Siferd and Mike Bender—both had provided legal assistance to the party—and alert them to this development. Neither attorney took seriously the prospect of Todd filing suit against the party or asking for an injunction against our meeting. Neither did Rochelle Twining, who also was informed.[29]

That evening we held an orientation at the Alpine for all Central Committee representatives-elect. Bill Johns, husband of Board of Elections director Donna Johns, revealed his candidacy for Central Committee chair, running as Todd's stand-in. Johns's candidacy did not surprise us. As the only prominent member of the old guard to win a contested Central Committee race, he had worked hard to win his precinct, walking door to door, registering voters, and sending appeals for absentee votes.

Johns was touting a unity theme, claiming that only he could unify the party and get the various factions working together. On the surface, this seemed an ironic boast, considering Todd Hey's pending scheme to enjoin our meeting.[30] But then, Johns and his family had been unflagging in their support for the Democratic Party and its candidates. Together, he and Donna had coordinated Tony Celebreeze's campaigns in Allen County, first for secretary of state and later for attorney general. Bill Johns's loyalty to party outweighed his ties to any particular faction, and that circumstance afforded his candidacy considerable appeal.

When I spoke with Johns that evening, he seemed apologetic, almost as if he knew he could not win, implying that he was just a Democrat doing his duty on behalf of a friend. He was in a hard spot, and we knew it. By running, he was placing Donna's job in jeopardy. Her position would be safe as long as Hauenstein was on the Board of Elections, but if Johns lost this contest, my side of the party would name a replacement for Charlie in 1990. At that point, the party would have the opportunity to supplant Donna.

I didn't linger at the Alpine and arrived home at ten, to be greeted by a ringing phone as I walked through the door. It was Rochelle Twining. She had driven her usual route home, past Bill and Donna Johns's North Cole Street address, and had noticed a lot of cars parked in their driveway.

May 24, 1988, Tuesday

Donna Johns called to inform me that Todd Hey had filed requests for recounts in eight Central Committee races, all of which had been narrowly won by our candidates. She wanted to know when it would be convenient to schedule the procedure, and I suggested June 2.[31] Todd's plan was unfolding.

I stopped by Bender's office that afternoon, and we discussed arguments we could use against Todd should he proceed with an effort to enjoin our meeting. He and Siferd began building our case.[32]

May 25, 1988, Wednesday

Ben Rose called me at home early in the day and informed me that he was representing eight defeated candidates for "Democrat Central Committee," that on May 26 he would file a suit with Common Pleas Court, and that he planned to get a judge to issue a restraining order against our meeting. I told him that Mike Bender was our attorney, and Rose agreed to contact Bender.

But I called Bender first. "The shit's hitting the fan," I said.

So, Todd had found Waldo Bennet Rose to file the law suit against the Democratic Party. Rose was a bête noire for most county Democrats. He had been Bill Thompson's predecessor as state representative, serving the First District from 1973 to 1987 before making a futile challenge to the state auditor, Tom Ferguson, in 1986. During his time in the House of Representatives, Rose had climbed the Republican ladder, eventually reaching the post of assistant minority leader. It was in this position that he had caused the most aggravation for Democrats, constantly criticizing Governor Celeste and other state officeholders for their ethical lapses.

In 1986, Charlie Hauenstein had practically chortled at the news that Rose was not running for an eighth term. "I think it's time Allen County's people had a true representative in Columbus," he had said then.[33] Now, Rose had joined forces with Charlie's crony Todd Hey, working to file a lawsuit against the very Democratic Party Hauenstein had once led.

May 26, 1988, Thursday, 9 A.M.

The Board of Elections met to recount the two Central Committee races that had ended in ties. Candidates in these unresolved contests had already received letters notifying them of that evening's reorganization meeting, but with caveats explaining that they could participate only if the board declared them winners. The ties were broken, our side picking up one seat and Todd's faction the other.[34] The winning and losing candidates were informed later that morning.

It had been a tense session, and I had been barely civil to Charlie Hauenstein. I spent the rest of the day fidgeting and hanging out in various places—my office, Mike Bender's office, Rick Siferd's office. Our attorneys remained unperturbed, explaining to me and Steve Webb, who was as restless as I was, how difficult it was to prepare a case for a temporary restraining order. It was unlikely that a judge would restrain our meeting, they both stated confidently.

May 26, 1988, Thursday, 3:30 P.M.

Ben Rose filed his suit. He and Mike Bender met in Judge Robert Light's chambers regarding his request for a restraining order. Rose's brief did not dispute the right of the party to call the meeting when it had. But the meeting, he held, was in conflict with the section of the election code that governed recounts. He argued that if our eight committee members were permitted to vote before the recounts were "certified" (his term), his clients would be deprived of the right to participate in our reorganization meeting. Furthermore, Rose claimed, such an outcome would "obliterate" the constitutional rights of the voters, as well as "the sanctity of their voting franchise." He asked the judge either to stop the entire meeting or restrain the eight declared victors from voting.[35]

Neither option was acceptable, Bender argued. For one thing, it would be extremely costly and confusing to reschedule the meeting at this late date. More importantly, Bender saw no reason to consider the constitutional rights of the declared winners less important than those of the declared losers. Our meeting had been set as prescribed by Ohio's election code, and Rose's argument about "obliterating rights" rested on the thin and speculative assumption that recounts might overturn the results of an officially certified election. In Bender's view, the winners had a right to vote in the meeting because they had already been declared winners, and they should vote, and so should the remaining committee representatives.[36]

At 5:30, an hour and a half before our reorganization meeting, Judge Light decided neither to enjoin our meeting nor restrain the eight targeted representatives from voting.[37] The showdown was on.

May 26, 1988, Thursday, 7:30 P.M.,

Apollo Joint Vocational School

I had chosen the site. There was no door to shut. The meeting was held in an open assembly space just inside the entry to Apollo School, allowing folks who were not members of the Central Committee, including the media, to view the proceedings. Volunteers had cordoned off the area where the Central Committee itself would gather. Others were handing out credentials and directing members to the meeting space. Webb, Johns, and I were making our rounds, exerting nervous energy, mostly; we weren't changing any minds. Todd Hey and Paul Prater had driven some their representatives to the session, and Hey was hovering about, hustling to the end.

The outcome was not even close. The Central Committee gave Steve Webb eighty votes and Bill Johns forty-four; one representative abstained.[38] Attendance was down from 1986 (129 compared to 146), owing in part to the bitterness the controversy itself had engendered and in part to confusion over whether or not the meeting would be held at all. Webb gained only one more vote over his 1986 total, but his margin of victory was much larger than two years before, when he had defeated Hey by twelve votes.

Todd Hey had pushed for a court order to prevent our meeting from being held, and he had joined forces with Ben Rose to file a lawsuit against the Democratic Party. In a television interview immediately after the vote, I allowed my aggravation to show, declaring, "It's very discouraging for a fellow Democrat to hire a *Republican* attorney to stop a *Democratic* meeting."[39] But after a few days' reflection, my irritation subsided as I saw the irony in what Hey had done. Recounting the events to my friend Susan Gibler, I wrote, "We had been concerned about pounding a stake through Todd's heart. In the end, he did it for us."[40]

· 17 ·

No More Pressure

May 26, 1988, 9 P.M., Apollo Vocational School
Cora Hamman was fuming. The Central Committee had selected its vice chair, a ceremonial office that Cora had held during the previous term, but this time John Dornick had won the post, exactly as Steve Webb and I had planned.

Cora approached me. "I feel like I've been stabbed in the back," she muttered.

"What about?" I asked.

"Vice chair. I wanted that."

"No way, Cora. Not after the trouble and embarrassment you caused us at the license bureau. There was no way I could allow you to be vice chair."

"You can have the license bureau!" she yelled, then proceeded to gripe about Steve Webb, John Dornick, and John and Mary Hevener before stomping out. Cora Hamman did not show up for our victory party at the Alpine, which was probably for the best. We had one fine time.[1]

Although I made several changes during my second term, the most far-reaching had to do with Cora Hamman. According to party folklore, I "kicked her out of the party." I can live with that interpretation, but the truth is that I stripped her of any meaningful responsibility in party operations.

Shortly after the reorganization meeting, I summoned Cora to party headquarters, the old storefront office on West Spring Street in Lima. Steve Webb, John Dornick, and Elsie Crowe also were there.[2] I upbraided Cora, emphasizing that the repeated confrontations with Pearl Ward had embarrassed me and the party and that her conduct could have cost us our victory over Todd Hey. That said, I came to the point and pronounced judgment: She would no longer be a party officer, nor would she chair any party committee. She could continue to serve but only as a member of the Executive Committee, not in any role involving leadership. On hearing this, Cora bolted upright and headed for the door,

Bryan Hefner, talking with Helen Bolden, who was a Central Committeewoman and a Jesse Jackson delegate to the 1988 Democratic National Convention, at a Democratic Party picnic and rally, Lafayette, Ohio, June 1988. From the collection of William Angel, photograph by William Angel.

grumbling that she might just quit the party altogether. This behavior alarmed Dornick, who hustled after her and attempted soothing words—something like, "Aw, c'mon, Cora, you can still be part of things. You just can't be in charge, that's all." His words were of little comfort to Cora, who loved being in charge.

I did not see Cora for several days, not until mid-June, when Bryan Hefner and Keith Myers (Executive Committee member and Bryan's pal) held a victory rally for Democratic candidates in Lafayette's village park, near the eastern end of the county. Jean Hatcher was there too, speaking on behalf of Judge Alice Robie Resnick, who was running for Ohio Supreme Court justice. That spring Cora had befriended Resnick, throwing a reception for her, working her way into the judge's heart. Cora pulled me aside during the event, asking why Hatcher, and not her, was representing Resnick.

"Cora, we went over that last week," I answered. "I said I wanted you to stay involved only as a member of Executive Committee. No leadership positions. That means no campaign coordinator jobs."

"Well, I didn't think you meant I couldn't coordinate campaigns," she retorted.

"I did, Cora."

"I was loyal to you, Bill, and it hurts me to think that when people said I was antilabor and antiminority that you didn't speak up for me." That was a guilt trip, and I wasn't paying the fare. "I was loyal to you, too, Cora. When people were calling for your scalp, I stuck by you. But as I said last week, your behavior over the past three months had become intolerable. I was getting pressure from all sides."

"But think who the pressure was coming from."

"Cora, the strongest pressure was coming from our own committee, not from Todd and Charlie."

She took a big drag on her cigarette and looking away, announced sarcastically, "Well, I'll see you get no more pressure, Bill."[3]

Shortly after I trimmed Cora's political wings, Pearl Ward got laid off, but I did not learn about it until two weeks after it happened. Cora informed me, taking some delight in the telling.[4] The timing of Pearl's release may only have been coincidental, but it sure cast a smell, a smell that would not go away easily. On June 28, I had lunch with Ed Finn, who had once been president of the Ford local and who at the time was international representative for the UAW-CAP Council. I had been hoping to arrange the UAW's role in the fall campaign, but the firing of Pearl Ward—at least that's how it appeared—interfered with my agenda. Finn was angry, declaring, "I'll have nothing to do with the party until you take care of that situation you guys—that is, Webb—created out at the Lima Mall. It's one thing to take on one of our guys, but to take on his wife, that's pretty poor."[5]

I was as annoyed as Finn was—the party needed the UAW's help in the fall campaign—and I was irritated with Webb. By acceding to Cora's maneuvers against Pearl Ward, he had undercut my efforts to rein in Cora and had sent a confusing signal to loyal Democrats like Ed Finn.

In an effort to resolve the controversy, PC Wrencher, John Dornick, and I paid Webb a visit on June 30 to discuss the party's predicament. Steve was unhappy that we were meddling in his operation at the license bureau, sneering as I relayed the details of my conversation with Ed Finn. Webb defended his action against Pearl Ward, claiming that she had been evaluated and that her work had been found unsatisfactory. But after intense interrogation, he also admitted that Pearl had never been counseled about her alleged deficiencies, which caused Dornick to shake his head and declare, "I'd love to argue a grievance for Pearl on this one."[6] After considerable pressure from all three of us, Webb finally agreed to resolve the crisis. He eventually offered a settlement to Ward, who took a period of leave and didn't return.[7]

The entire episode made me even more resolved to hold the line on Cora Hamman. I could not control how Webb handled Cora or how he managed the license bureau, but I could restrict Cora's influence in party operations.

I would not find the going easy, however. Throughout the summer, Hamman persistently griped to anyone who would listen. According to one line, I had "used her, chewed her up, spit her out, knifed her in the back, and tap danced on her grave." I heard worse things too, but these recriminations were expected. More troubling were Cora's public rumblings that I was bullying her to resign from the Executive Committee, an accusation that was not true and that cast Cora as the victim.[8] This charge made the rounds and surfaced at an Operations Committee meeting in mid-August. "Is Cora still a member of the Executive Committee?" someone asked innocently. "Yes," I replied heatedly. "And I'm getting damn tired of Cora telling people that I want her to resign. I don't."[9]

I continued to receive intercessions from various party members who pleaded with me to relent and restore Cora Hamman to a leadership position, maybe just a small one. Folks were getting tired of her complaining about me.

These insistent efforts on Cora's behalf, however, amounted to nothing when compared to the interference I received from folks downstate. In June, I had tapped Delphos law director Clayton Osting to be Judge Resnick's Allen County coordinator and so informed Resnick's campaign director, Elaine Fortney. Yet throughout July I kept receiving word that Cora was operating as Resnick's local manager, or that at least she perceived herself as operating in that role, and that she was seething at my efforts to block her formal appointment. Finally, in late July, I checked into the matter with Fortney, who reassured me that Clay Osting—not Cora Hamman—was the judge's manager in Allen County.[10]

I was confident that my chat with Elaine Fortney had settled the matter, but it was a short-lived feeling. Shortly afterward, Jim Ruvulo phoned to inquire, "Do you have any objection to Cora Hamman being the Resnick coordinator?"

"Yes!" I shot back, flabbergasted that Ruvulo, of all people, would ask such a question. He knew about the Cora's feuding with Pearl Ward, because I had kept him apprised of the tumult it was causing. "That would create real problems," I insisted. "It's nothing against Cora personally, Jim. It's just that she has offended too many groups that we're going to need in November—most notably, the UAW."

"I'll see what I can do," Ruvulo responded, somewhat uncertainly.

"What do you mean?" I persisted. "I thought this problem was settled. I'm a little surprised it's still hanging fire."

"I'm not sure it is a problem."

"It sounds like Cora's been talking directly with Elaine Fortney," I conjectured, probing for information.

"No," Ruvulo said, "I think she's been talking to the judge."

A few days later, Ruvulo phoned and announced, "Osting is set."[11]

Not quite—Resnick's staff continued to talk with Cora, trying to set up fund-raising events. Nothing ever came of these endeavors, and eventually I gave up trying to head them off. In the end, there was little I could do about the shortsightedness of the Resnick campaign. So I shrugged and watched the judge capture her seat on the Ohio Supreme Court, while Cora Hamman gravitated to the periphery of party operations. Cora maintained her membership on the Executive Committee and stayed as a Central Committee representative, but as long as I remained chairman, she would never play a leading role in the party.

I could not escape mindless intrigue; it accompanied me even to Georgia on my brief foray into national politics. That July, I attended the Democratic National Convention in Atlanta as a nonvoting member of the Ohio delegation, and once there, I had to fight another skirmish, this one with the supporters of Jesse Jackson.

The previous spring, I had found myself in conflict with Jackson's effort locally when his statewide campaign had insisted on appointing Helen Bolden as the Allen County coordinator. At the time, Bolden had openly sided with Todd Hey and his "Grassroots Campaign," even though two years earlier I had appointed her to the Executive Committee. However, she had become estranged from my leadership and had stopped attending meetings, fund-raising events, and party activities. She had dropped out, or so I had thought, until I had begun hearing her name mentioned as Jackson's county coordinator, along with reports that she had been attending sessions with those who were laying plans to overthrow me.

This situation had caused a dilemma. While generally sympathetic to the inclusionist politics of the Jackson movement, I had become alienated from that campaign by its insistence on Helen Bolden as its representative in Allen County. She had allied herself with a group that would have undone the democratic procedures I had begun to establish in the Allen County Democratic Party. Yet she had been sponsored by the presidential candidate who was most true to the party's inclusionist ideals.

Once I had won reelection as party chair, I had determined not to reappoint Bolden as a member of the new Executive Committee. But I was not done with her. While at the convention, I had several run-ins with Helen, who was attending as a Jackson delegate and who sought every opportunity to plead for reappointment to the Executive Committee. "I guess somebody keeps voting me down," she sighed at one point.[12]

On the convention's final night, I met Jean Millet, an attorney from Columbus and Ohio's Jackson coordinator. "So, you're the one," she bristled when I introduced myself. "Helen has complained that she's been kicked off the Executive Committee." Millet then went on to emphasize the need for party unity and suggested that I sponsor Bolden's reappointment.

I tried to explain my side, but Millet was uninterested. She kept defending Bolden, claiming that she had done a good job for the Jackson campaign and insisting that Helen's dispute with me was more a matter of faulty communication. In Millet's eyes, I apparently was just some backwater hack standing in the way of a poor, defenseless black woman. And the pressure kept coming. On the morning I left Atlanta, my roommate John Ryan, an ardent Jackson delegate and labor activist (now the secretary of the Cuyahoga County AFL-CIO), also wielded the cudgel for Helen Bolden, emphasizing, as Millet had the night before, that we all needed to work together—for the good of the ticket.[13] Reluctantly and "for the good of the ticket," I endorsed Bolden's reinstatement on the Executive Committee, but that fall she would contribute little to advance the cause of Michael Dukakis or that of any other Democratic candidate.[14]

It was another instance of "not-all-politics-is-local." I was stung by Millet's unwillingness to listen to me and by her judgmental insinuation that I represented nothing more than an unenlightened, reactionary county politician. In truth, I was trying to build a local party that was consistent with the agenda promoted by Jackson's Rainbow Coalition. If I could be criticized, it would only be for defending my party from those, Helen Bolden included, who would pervert it for their own purposes. On the plane back to Ohio, I reflected on my relationship with Jesse Jackson's organization and wrote in my journal, "I'm dealing with people who don't understand the nuances of county politics."[15]

Maybe they were incapable of understanding. National political life does not connect easily with local political life; each responds to its own swirl of pressures and sees the other as an obstacle to its aims. In the eyes of Jean Millet, the spat between Helen Bolden and me was more than trivial squabbling. By pressuring me to show respect for Helen Bolden, Millet was waging a battle similar Jesse Jackson's own quest for honor within the National Democratic Party.[16] From my perspective, however, the dispute dealt with matters of power and direction of the local party. The one thing I wanted was simple comprehension of the job I was trying to do.

It never came.

Despite the "Helen Bolden episode," I had a good time in Atlanta. Watching and taking notes, I saw the whirl of the convention bring famous politicians down to the same status as courthouse hands, not much different from the ones I had been dealing with back home.

On the convention's second morning, for example, I watched John Glenn grab some breakfast at the fruit bar and pull up a seat next to some statehouse politicians, who were sitting around drinking coffee and reading newspapers. When Glenn sat down, they glanced up, murmured, "Hi, Senator," and went back to their reading. Glenn might have been Rick Siferd showing up late for a Policy Committee meeting—only taller.

If the convention cut politicians 'down to size, no one was struck down harder than Dick Celeste. In spring 1987, shortly after Donna Rice forced Gary Hart from the presidential lists, the governor had begun floating trial balloons about a possible presidential bid, but those balloons burst when reporters Brent Larkin and Mary Anne Sharkey of the Cleveland *Plain Dealer* released allegations that Celeste had had extramarital affairs of his own.[17] That ended any further talk of Dick Celeste becoming president.

Dick Celeste had become a politician without a following. He had no significant connection with the Dukakis organization, making him palpably inconsequential. One Ohio delegate noted, "For the first time, I sense he is a lame duck governor." Even Lieutenant Governor Paul Leonard piled on. Asked if Celeste would finally endorse Dukakis, he wisecracked, "Did you say 'endorsed' or 'indicted?'"[18] I noticed the same phenomenon, writing in my journal, "Normally a Democratic governor would get to speak from the podium, but not ours. He's really irrelevant here, an appendage to the Ohio delegation. Must be a blow to his ego."[19]

But if his ego was suffering, Celeste did not let it show. On the convention's last night, following Dukakis's acceptance speech, I headed back to the Pierremont Hotel, headquarters of the Ohio delegation, and drank a few beers in the hotel's bar. Toward midnight, I steered my way toward the elevator, where I encountered Dick Celeste and a few Celestials. "Hello, Governor," I said politely, trying not to slur my words.

He was upbeat—joyous, in fact. "Are we going to do it!" he yelled, pumping his fists, like a frat-house jock at Ohio State. "Yeah! Absolutely!" I responded, thinking that Dick Celeste had become not much different from me.[20]

Presidential years unsettle local parties: The jousting in the national arena resonates everywhere, but the county outfits are shadow players in this drama, more acted upon than acting.

For the Allen County Democratic Party, the 1988 presidential campaign re-sembled a summer thunderstorm in the country. Like a farm family standing on a front porch, we saw lightening, heard thunder, and watched showers hit a neighbor's field down the road. But the rain never fell on us; the storm swept over and disappeared. The whole phenomenon seemed remote and beyond our control, to everyone except for Allen County Republicans: they owned the farm down the road.

Ohio was a battleground state in 1988, but Allen County Democrats were only dimly aware of it. Michael Dukakis and his running mate, Lloyd Bentsen, focused on heavy urban areas, mostly along Ohio's "north coast," the Demo-cratic stronghold running from Toledo to Cleveland. The closest Dukakis ever came to Lima was a stopover in Dayton three weeks before election day.[21]

Generally speaking, Dukakis's effort in Ohio perplexed the state's Demo-cratic leaders. Campaign guru Gerald Austin, who had directed both of Celeste's gubernatorial wins and had managed Jesse Jackson's presidential bid in 1988, could not understand why Dukakis and his staff failed to consider the advice of Democratic officeholders like John Glenn and Dick Celeste, who had won statewide campaigns. Austin was particularly irritated by Dukakis's plan to visit South Dakota in the campaign's final week and dispatch Lloyd Bentsen to stump Ohio.[22] Similarly, Attorney General Tony Celebreeze was frustrated by Dukakis's refusal to respond to Vice President George Bush's advertisements casting himself as a defender of the environment, or to other ads—specifically the infamous Willie Horton spot—portraying Dukakis as soft on crime.[23] The state's top Democrats found themselves in the same position I had experi-enced as a county chair, wanting support from the party's higher-ups and not being listened to.

The Republican ticket, meanwhile, stumped the GOP strongholds in west-central Ohio, maintaining a constant and visible presence. Thunder, lighten-ing, and rain hit Republican territory at least once a week from September until election day. Bush visited the area twice. First came a September trip to Findlay, a half-hour north of Lima, where Bush took part in the city's flag festival. Then, two weeks before election day, he hit Lima, his second visit to the city in five months—he had already passed through in April.[24]

Although those were Bush's only personal calls in the area, they drew exten-sive of media coverage—three to four days' worth per visit—as did vice-presi-dential candidate Dan Quayle's mid-October tour through western Ohio, with stops in nearby Mercer, Van Wert, and Putnam Counties. President Reagan himself spoke at Bowling Green, sixty miles up Interstate 75, a few days after the Quayle visit. Supplemented by other surrogates, the "hits" kept coming, whipping up enthusiasm for the Republican ticket and encouraging a high turnout among the area's Republicans and Reagan Democrats.[25]

Meanwhile, we got Rob Lowe, the actor. He visited in late September, stopping by Lima Senior High School, where he touted Dukakis's "concern for humanity" to a student group and gave a live radio interview at WZOQ, a radio station that catered to a teenage audience. The interview created a traffic jam outside the station's parking lot, as cars packed with teenage girls snailed by, their occupants longing to catch a glimpse of Lowe. His visit gave us a couple of media hits, television and newspaper stories, but most of these portrayed the actor as a lightweight, highlighting the fact that he had registered to vote only two years before. "Governor Dukakis is a great guy," Lowe told the kids at Senior High. "He's like your best friend's dad."[26]

Two days later, the best friend arrived, only he was George W. Bush, the vice president's son, who described his father's virtues to another gathering of Lima Senior students. Claiming he was on hand just to boost the morale of local volunteers, Bush also turned to working the party phone banks, downplaying his ability to win over folks who hadn't made up their minds on the presidential race. "No, I'm not deluding myself to think that I'm going to switch somebody's vote," he said modestly.[27]

Despite the Republican presidential showers that swept Allen County, however, the local Democratic candidates ran surprisingly enthusiastic and upbeat campaigns. In midsummer, it looked like Paul Rizor had a chance to defeat his opponent, Dick Warren, in the judge's race, especially when a July poll showed Rizor leading 36 percent to 32 percent.[28]

Judges' races present tricky problems for political parties in Ohio. The candidates are nominated in partisan primaries, but they run on nonpartisan ballots, meaning that no party affiliation appears beside their names. Also, judicial candidates are ethically bound not to discuss matters of jurisprudence or specific cases; they confine their campaigns to listing their qualifications and to outlining reforms they might bring to the court system. A lot of energy goes into creating an image of solid judicial temperament.

The nonpartisan nature of the judicial race supplied Rizor an important benefit: He was able to build name recognition by campaigning in the heavy-turnout (predominantly Republican) precincts without emphasizing his Democratic affiliation. Rizor worked hard, canvassing neighborhoods door to door despite aggravating an old knee injury.[29]

In contrast, the Republicans made a concerted effort to link their guy, Dick

Warren, with the party. Congressman Mike Oxley made a radio ad endorsing Warren, and a television spot portrayed Warren shaking hands with Vice President Bush.[30] In addition, the numerous trips the Bush campaign had made through our area, plus the likelihood of a Bush victory, helped stimulate heavy turnout among Republicans. Rizor's campaign would matter little to the Republicans, as long as the party faithful stuck with the ticket.

Watching Rizor labor against Warren's obvious advantages, John Hevener once quipped that perhaps people were getting to know Paul "too well."[31] Rizor offered flash and dash in a race where voters really expected reserve and substance. A tall, handsome man with a sarcastic wit and a genuinely engaging laugh, he drove a Cadillac, acted in and occasionally directed community theatre productions, and liked to give orders to clerks and office personnel with a playful banter that still let them know he was in charge. Paul also was going through a divorce that summer, which didn't help his candidacy, since Dick Warren was a straight-arrow family man.

Rizor could be an irritatingly demanding candidate, particularly if things did not go his way. At the Allen County Fair, for instance, he and Warren maintained their fictions of nonpartisanship by setting up their campaign booths far away from the party tents, located near the grandstand. Rizor ended up in "Siberia," in a tent next to the Merchants Building, a space frequented by few fair-goers, while Warren landed right between a Belgian waffle stand and corn dog vendor; he set up a kiosk where the midway forked. Lots of fair visitors passed by Warren's booth daily, much to the chagrin of Rizor, who fussed and fumed over the situation.

At one point he demanded that I do something about Warren's volunteers, who, Rizor protested, were roaming the midway—"right smack in the middle of the goddamn midway"—passing out campaign literature. I walked down to check, only to find the Warren volunteers next to their kiosk, where they were supposed to be. I was not going to force a confrontation that would only have made the Democrats look petty, but Rizor kept nagging.[32] In the end, he found himself spending more time in the Democratic tent, where he could get more visibility—but as a Democrat.

Sometimes Rizor exuded so much confidence that he appeared arrogant. His television ads were highly theatrical, showing Paul alone on a set, bathed in light while everything around him was black, speaking directly and forcefully into the camera. Though dynamic spots, they accentuated Paul's ego and individuality, presenting a sharp comparison with his opponent's television spots, which showed Dick Warren in the company of other people—his wife

Dale Leppla, left, with Steve Webb at the Allen County Fair, August 1988. From the collection of William Angel, photo by William Angel.

and children, fellow Republicans, and colleagues. Consequently, Warren's presentation was one of a salt-of-the-earth candidate, a nice guy, as opposed to Paul Rizor, who came across as a fancy lawyer who like to talk about himself.[33]

In any case, Rizor's campaign was snakebit, it seemed. A week before the election, Pastor Leon Stutzman, a local television evangelist, gave his preelection endorsements on his weekly program on WTLW TV, the local Christian station. When he came to the Rizor/Warren race, he said, "Now, this Paul Rizor fella'—he's the incumbent—and he's the one who's been lettin' all those pornographers loose. So, we don't like him."[34] Rizor hit the ceiling. He called the station. He called me. I finally complained to the station manager, Bob Placie, who checked the tapes of the broadcast and found that Stutzman indeed had said those things. He asked the pastor to retract his statement, which Stutzman did, claiming that he had talked with Rizor, "who was very gentlemanly and had forgiven him." Maybe, but the pornography seed had already been planted, despite Stutzman's retraction.[35]

The incident's impact was probably minimal, in light of the decisiveness of Warren's victory. Warren trounced Rizor 26,710 to 16,798, securing 61 percent of the votes cast.[36] Nobody had expected Paul to lose so overwhelmingly, least of all Rizor himself.

Dale Leppla did not fare much better, though our summer poll had showed him in a dead heat with Don Reese for county commissioner.[37] In an issue-driven contest, Leppla argued ideas that either did not resonate with the voters or resonated badly. He made three topics the predominant focus of his campaign—the commissioners' quashing of the sales tax referendum, delays in starting the jail project that were increasing construction costs, and the commissioners' decision to purchase the Gregg's Building, a former department store, which the county planned to renovate as the Third District Court of Appeals Building. When Dale learned that renovation expenses would run over one million dollars, he hammered the commissioners, insisting that less costly downtown sites were available.[38]

Although Leppla's issues were important—they all emphasized the commissioners' failure to exercise sound fiscal management—our July poll showed that voters were not very interested in them, not even the tax issue.[39] Leppla kept pounding at them anyway, and late in the campaign he tried to open a new front, this one on annexation. In mid-October, the commissioners refused a request to annex Camp Woodhaven and its fifty-four acres to the city of Lima. The Appleseed Ridge Girl Scout Council, owners of the property, were planning a new multipurpose building on the site, and they wanted annexation in order to tie in to the city's water mains and secure cheaper water rates.[40]

Politics drove the commissioners' decision, however. When Gene Joseph became mayor of Lima in 1985, he had pursued a "hard water policy," a clumsy scheme to expand the city's fiscal base. As the policy stood in 1988, the city charged exorbitant water rates for out-of-city customers as a means of pressuring suburban property owners into petitioning for annexation. Almost two-thirds of the county's voters lived outside of Lima, however, and most chafed at the "hard water policy" as a form of blackmail.[41] By rejecting the Girl Scouts' request, the commissioners were playing to their suburban constituents.

Leppla ignored these considerations, and during the last week of the campaign he ran a radio ad castigating the commissioners for not annexing Camp Woodhaven, a decision that had, the commercial announced, "cost the Girl Scouts $30,000 a year [in water fees]."[42] Maybe so, but the commercial hurt Leppla by reminding all suburban voters of Dale's affiliation with Lima and lining him up on the wrong side of the county's political geography.

The ad also offended the Girl Scouts, who did not like being pulled into a political cross fire. On Friday, November 4, four days before the election, Leppla phoned, saying a lawyer from the Girl Scouts Council had called him, demanding that he pull the radio spot. He wanted to know what he should do. This was the first time Dale Leppla had ever sought my advice. I asked if he stood by the commercial. He said that he did, and I replied, "Well, then, I'll stand by you." I told him to keep running the commercial, and then I called Rose Marie Duffy, executive director of the Girl Scout Council, to give her the word.[43]

Duffy did not like this decision, nor did she like my attitude when I announced it. She later protested to Rochelle Twining that I had been arrogant and that I had not wanted to listen to her point of view.[44] Perhaps, but it had been a long campaign, and I was annoyed at the Girl Scouts for expecting a Democratic candidate to withdraw an ad because it ran afoul of their agenda. Leppla may have been on the wrong side of the issue, but his position already had been announced. For him to back down, to give in to pressure, would have made him look foolish.

Besides, there was something charmingly iconoclastic about Leppla's campaign. He ran on his own terms, not in the direction that polls and common sense provided. It was not that he objected to environmental concerns, which our polls indicated were uppermost on the minds of the voters; he simply cared passionately about fiscal issues, particularly about the commissioners' clumsy stewardship of the public trust. That's why he harped on the piggyback sales tax, the jail, the Gregg's Building, and annexation. Truthfully, Dale did the voters an immense service, joining a debate over matters that went against the grain of public consciousness. Leppla lost anyway, although he did finish with six thousand more votes than he had won two years earlier. Reese defeated him for a second time, taking 57 percent of the votes, 24,895 to 18,638.[45]

Leppla's focus on the ineptitude of county government helped energize Ida Kay Keller's contest for the other commissioner's post. Keller would produce the best showing of any of our candidates, although she displayed the least midsummer promise. Our July poll showed her badly trailing Commissioner Bob Mayer, 27 percent to 43 percent.[46] Worse, she also seemed uncertain of herself and hesitant to challenge the commissioners. She seemed unusually cautious and timid in social gatherings, unwilling to work crowds with much enthusiasm.[47] This was not the Ida Kay Keller I had witnessed leading the Dumpbusters.

In August, Rochelle Twining became Keller's coordinator and moved the campaign to a more aggressive track.[48] Her immediate task was to help Ida Kay break the common perception that she was a one-issue candidate, trumpeting only an environmental message. At Twining's urging, Keller challenged Bob Mayer to a debate. If she could draw him out into the open, went the reasoning, she could establish her general competence on public policy and draw the contrast between her candidacy and his. "I'm willing to meet him any time, any place," she declared, borrowing a line from Twining's own 1986 campaign.[49]

But Keller did more than call for a debate. She also accused the commissioners of making decisions before "weighing the facts," challenged their hasty decision on the Gregg's Building, and upbraided them for dragging their feet on creating a solid-waste-disposal district. Keller also compared their irresolute handling of these issues to their approach on the piggyback sales tax, proclaiming sardonically, "They didn't have any trouble making a decision on the piggyback sales tax without consulting the people."[50]

It was a combative proclamation, and it drew a sharp and ill-tempered rebuke from Mayer, who tried to put down both the challenge and the challenger the way Bill Thompson had disposed of Rochelle Twining's call for debate two years earlier. But this situation was different. For one thing, Keller did not carry any of Twining's feminist associations, nor did she exhibit Twining's strident demeanor. Ida Kay Keller was a known quantity to most people; she had proven her mettle in the battle with Waste Management, Inc., and her challenge to Mayer had been presented in a reasonable, albeit critical, tone.

Mayer dismissed Keller's challenge, observing, "She is a one-issue candidate who ranks low in the polls and is dropping. If it's a negative campaign she's after, I will have no part of it."[51] Three days later, Mayer again addressed Keller's attack, accusing her of waging a negative campaign. "She's had three news conferences," Mayer grumbled, "and out of these, she's not made one positive statement. The real issues that we face are the challenges of the future. What can we do to enhance the economy and bring more business and industry to Allen County? My pledge has always been to make Allen County a better place to live."[52]

The contrast was clear. Keller was the candidate who was offering real solutions to genuine problems, such as landfill, solid-waste disposal, and fiscal management, while Mayer provided only lofty generalities about "challenges of the future" and "making the county a better place to live." Keller was offering substance, Mayer pablum. She continued to concentrate her message on Mayer's unwillingness to face the sharp challenges confronting the county, and her campaign gradually picked up energy.

At one point, in fact, Dale Leppla grew so frustrated by the perception that Ida Kay was outdistancing him that he began complaining that she had stolen his issues on the Gregg's Building and the jail.[53] In fact, she was probably helping him as much he was assisting her. By melding these issues with her environmental focus, Keller underscored the commissioners' inability to lead on tough problems, which was a theme Dale wanted to stress too.

Despite the momentum Ida Kay gathered in the campaign's final month, the Bush sweep proved too strong.[54] She ended up losing to Mayer by less than four thousand votes—20,083 to 23,797.[55] Keller won 46 percent of the vote and came closer to winning office than any Democratic candidate had since 1976. Importantly, she held Mayer to the lowest vote total he had ever received, while she herself became the first Allen County Democrat in twelve years to crack twenty thousand votes.[56]

Ida Kay Keller took heart in her showing. While she was meeting reporters in the courthouse shortly after the final tallies were announced, Bob Holmes, the GOP county chair, approached, shook her hand, and congratulated her for running a good campaign. "I'll be back," Ida Kay quipped.[57]

At first glance, the 1988 campaign appeared a simple repeat of 1986, but a closer investigation showed that the infighting, scheming, plotting, and backbiting of that earlier campaign had been absent. Todd Hey was no longer in the picture, and Cora Hamman had been sent to the bench. Additionally, we had not targeted a particular candidate, as we had two years previously. The judicial candidate Paul Rizor had received slightly more funding from the party than did Leppla and Keller, but that decision was predicated by the July poll that showed him doing the best of any of the others.[58] Generally speaking, a unified spirit of camaraderie had prevailed.

I remained positive, despite the party's loss. Except for the Locker/Cupp race for state senate, which Cupp won overwhelmingly,[59] the Democrats had made a spirited and energetic fight. "I'm obviously disappointed," I admitted to Paul Smith of the *Lima News,* "but I'm heartened by the showing of the ticket, particularly Ida Kay Keller. . . . There's real reason for optimism."[60]

When Smith questioned the party's lean-slate strategy, wondering if our defeat challenged its wisdom, I simply observed, "I really don't know how we could have run a more effective campaign with more than three people on the ballot. If we would have run a full slate of nine candidates, it would have meant doom for the party." But I also promised, "We will not give Bill Thompson a bye again. We will have a larger slate [in 1990], and if we don't, I should be held accountable for it."[61] That statement made Rochelle Twining, John Hevener, and few of my compadres wince, but I wanted to demonstrate that my optimism signified more than empty words.

The Democrats had lost again, dropping every single race, but our party remained undaunted and in some respects it had become stronger. Shortly after Thanksgiving, Steve Webb confided to me that he planned to "resign from everything," including his post as chair of the Central Committee. His decision had been speeded along by passage, finally, of Governor Celeste's proposal to reform and depoliticize the license bureaus. Known as Senate Bill 1, the law had taken effect on November 28 and made it illegal for anybody to solicit political contributions from deputy registrars; furthermore, neither deputy registrars nor members of their immediate families could make political contributions totaling over one hundred dollars.[62] The license bureaus were out of politics, and so was Steve Webb.

The news came as no surprise—Steve's involvement in the 1988 campaign had been minimal—and his decision was not disabling. In fact, in John Dornick, who succeeded Webb, the party found a more resolute chairman of the Central Committee. Dornick was deeply respected by UAW hands like Ed Finn and Bob Gehr. He was always ready with a joke and generous in his compliments, and he played straight—no games, no hidden agendas. All Democrats trusted John, and he had a talent for inspiring people to work together.

Dornick had already proven his leadership skill during the election, having coordinated an aggressive get-out-the-vote drive. Taking an innovative approach to the GOTV assignment, he had begun by asking a friend, a retired telephone worker, to construct a phone board—a large plywood sheet, containing about a dozen or so receptacles that could be connected by a cable to the phone jack in party headquarters. It was a neat device that could be used election after election. John had also lined up volunteers, procured telephones, and stayed around the clock to encourage our workers and direct the phone bank when it was in operation. On election day, he had supervised a fleet of drivers who taxied Democratic voters to the polls on election day, and he had conducted "body pulls" in a few targeted precincts. Under Dornick, the GOTV program drew 13,712 votes to the Democratic ticket, over 1,500 more than the Mondale-Ferraro campaign had received four years earlier.[63] He would be a terrific Central Committee chairman, and our decision of the previous spring—choosing him instead of Cora Hamman to be vice chair of the Central Committee—turned out to have been more than ceremonial after all.

Though Cora Hamman remained in exile, she had left me something to ponder. During the summer of 1988, she had reportedly told Rochelle Twining that in 1990 I would realize how much I needed her, because Bill Johns—Todd Hey's stand-in candidate for Central Committee Chair—would be coming after me again.[64] I solved that problem. In July 1989, I met with Bill's wife, Donna, and promised that I would back her continued employment at the Board of Elections if she would support my leadership—meaning that she could neither participate in nor assist any effort to challenge my control of the party. It was understood that I expected Bill's cooperation, too. Donna, who was five years away from her state employee retirement pension, enthusiastically accepted the offer.

Not everyone liked this deal. Donna had offended a number of my DEP allies during the party fights of 1986 and 1988, using her position as director of the Board of Elections to favor Charlie Hauenstein's end of the dispute. At least, that was the view of some. Now, with the party structure safely in our hands, a few of my pals relished the opportunity to push Donna aside and appoint someone more loyal as board director. But I had grown weary of petty haggling, especially when someone's livelihood was at stake. Besides, gaining Donna's loyalty could provide immense dividends.

As events unfolded, I was proven right. Donna kept her end of the bargain, and I honored mine. In 1990, the party tapped Beverly McCoy to replace Charlie Hauenstein on the Board of Elections, and together Bev and I voted to reappoint Donna to another term as director of the board, where she served until her retirement in 1994.

Bereft of allies, Todd Hey was finished. He ran a paltry slate of Central Committee challengers in 1990, but the effort did not amount to much, and John Dornick won the Central Committee chair unopposed.[65]

Party peace had arrived, but something had been lost. My compromise with Donna Johns had been born out of a realistic desire to hold on to power. Without power—that is, without control of the party structure—I could never accomplish the kind of change I wanted our party to implement. But now that my position was secure, what would become of the party? The idealism of 1986 had been tempered by a more pragmatic approach to politics, replete with polls and concerns about not getting on the wrong side of the voters. If we were not careful, we could slip down a utilitarian path and away from the ideals that had brought us to this place.

Part Five

Questions of Faith

· 18 ·

Dancin'

*July 19, 1988, Ohio Dukakis Delegate
Meeting, Pierremont Hotel, Atlanta*
The orders were simple: "Vote no." Word had come down from Michael Dukakis himself, directing all his delegates to vote against a platform plank pledging no-first-use of nuclear weapons, to be offered that afternoon by Jesse Jackson's campaign.[1] Madeleine Albright, Dukakis's foreign policy adviser, made the case, claiming that the president needed to preserve the option to deploy nuclear weapons in the event of a Soviet attack in Europe.

Harry Meshel and Dennis Eckart were presiding over the Ohio caucus, and they had no patience with cerebral protests on the "no-first-use" proposal, which had drawn the sympathy of several delegates, including most notably Governor Celeste. We were to vote "No" because that is what Dukakis wanted. Eckart and Meshel were both veteran Ohio politicians, Eckart as a congressman from the First District and Meshel as minority leader of the Ohio senate and a state senator from Youngstown. "Remember who got us here and how we got here," admonished Eckart when faced with a smattering of grumbled opposition. "We got here because we *love* Mike Dukakis. We cannot turn our backs on him now."

Meshel was more emphatic. A barrel-chested Greek American, he had learned the trade of politics in Mahoning County, where the politicians are as hard-nosed as their rhetoric. "I've had to cast a lot of votes I didn't like," he thundered, thumping the podium. "And I've known senators from marginal districts who cast votes that were unpopular. But they voted with the team, because they knew they were part of the team!"[2] Meshel's pitch struck a nerve. He had been president of the Ohio senate in 1983 when my friend Steve Maurer had been one of seventeen Democratic senators to vote in favor of Governor Celeste's so-called 90 percent tax increase. The tax hike had passed seventeen to sixteen, and Maurer's action—sticking with the team—had cost him reelection the following year.

Teamwork—Remember how we got here—Dance with the one what brung you. It is easy for politicians to play the unity theme when it serves their own interests. Representatives of all three echelons of American party structure—national, state, and local—sat in the Pierremont Hotel the day Harry Meshel and Dennis Eckart gave us our marching orders, and it was clear who held the power and who was expected to bend to the will of the team.

It always worked that way, so it seemed. Throughout this narrative, you have encountered instances where the interests of the Allen County Democratic Party were either ignored or subordinated. We were under the hoof of higher and more powerful partisan interests, those at the state and national levels. County parties—especially marginal organizations like the one in Allen County—were kicked aside during the struggle. Even Jim Ruvulo, who was genuinely interested in helping local parties, was compelled to lend greater support to Governor Celeste and Ohio's state officeholders—the ones that had "brung him." The adage, "Not all politics is local" held firm.

It might seem easy to command teamwork, as Eckart and Meshel did that day in Atlanta, but command is a luxury unknown to most party leaders. Political parties bleed an inherent paradox. On the one hand, they rely on teamwork: Amateur and professional politicians work together, build a winning coalition, and pull for victory. Yet on the other hand, people are moved to take collective action—to become part of the team—to further their personal agendas. You will recall that when John Hevener and I formed DEP and launched the challenge to Charlie Hauenstein, we were successful because our coalition had a single, shared, common pursuit—getting rid of Charlie. But when Charlie was gone, other interests took over. People worked for the team when it served their needs, and when it did not, they went their own way.

Working out that paradox—melding self-interest with team spirit—is the primary job of party leaders, but matters of principle are also central to their struggles. They must grapple with what are called questions of faith, which define what is in the party's best interest and what it is supposed to represent, balancing that faith against the aims of others who have private agendas to pursue. The following two stories illustrate this problem. Although generating teamwork was an important part of each episode, the challenge for me lay in understanding what the party's stakes were, knowing where its values lay, and then working to protect the organization against forces that could have overwhelmed it.

January 30, 1987, 2:30 P.M.

When I arrived at the Yocum Real Estate building, John Coplen ushered me into a richly paneled office, where his boss, John Mongelluzzo, was standing behind a large oak desk. Mongelluzzo greeted me with pseudowarmth and twisted the louvered blinds tight, choking any natural light that might have passed through. I sank into a dark leather chair and watched the winter afternoon drift into twilight. Coplen, meanwhile, pulled the wooden door shut, grabbed a side seat, and began listening attentively.[3]

Talk turned immediately to the Spencerville landfill. The meeting had been prompted by public statements I had made, openly siding with the Dumpbusters and their campaign to resist the project.[4] Although I was acting partially out of environmental concern for Kendrick Woods Park, which lay adjacent to the landfill site, I also knew that the issue was loaded with political opportunity. The commissioners had waffled in handling the landfill crisis, demonstrating outward sympathy for the locals who were fighting the dump but refusing to offer any leadership in resolving the dispute. Reasoning that such indecisiveness might alienate voters in the Spencerville area, longtime Republican turf, I kept my oar in the debate, hoping that Democrats might benefit.

I was far out in front of the party this one—many of my Democratic friends were, at best, ambivalent on the controversy.[5] More importantly, my public opposition to the landfill piqued the concern of Mongelluzzo, a broker at Yocum Realty and a sometime backer of Democratic campaigns. As one of the option holders on the landfill site, he stood to make a lot of money if the Ohio Environmental Protection Agency granted Waste Management, Inc., its license, and he wanted the EPA to act quickly. Accordingly, working through John Coplen, he had arranged our little get-together.

Mongelluzzo opened with the familiar spiel about why the county needed a landfill, emphasizing that it would help economic development and improve livability. "It's got to go somewhere," he claimed. "I know," I replied, "and I don't completely agree with those folks who object primarily because it's headed for their backyard." I insisted that the commissioners should be held responsible for dumping the problem on the townships, and I outlined my worries about the ecological damage that the landfill could create.

Mongelluzzo listened until I had finished and then handed me a piece of paper. "Here's a letter Mayor Joseph has written to the governor. I'd like you to write one like it." I saw that Joseph had given unqualified support for a landfill at the Spencerville site. The clincher was a sentence Mongelluzzo wanted in any letter I might write: "I urge you to contact the Ohio EPA and urge the EPA to expedite its handling of this matter."[6] In other words, Mongelluzzo wanted quick action, before Dumpbuster opposition had a chance to build.

I said nothing after reading the letter, just looked up, which cued Mongelluzzo to make an offer: "If you write a letter to Governor Celeste—and by the way, one to the chairman of the Ohio Democrat Party—I'll make a sizeable contribution to *your* party."

I bit. "How much?"

"Five thousand dollars."

I drew a breath. "If you're asking for a letter like this one, I can't— not given the concerns I have. I have friends who back me on this issue and supporters whose loyalty I value."

Faced with resistance, Mongelluzzo changed his tack somewhat and appealed to my curiosity. "Bill, are you familiar with Waste Management's operation?" he asked. I wasn't. "How about if we go up to Toledo and see their facility up there? You can meet Jack Nichols [director of marketing for the northeast region of Waste Management Systems], and I'm sure you'll come away convinced they run a safe, reliable operation."

I accepted Mongelluzzo's offer to tour Waste Management's facility, saying that if my concerns about the park were satisfied, I might write a letter supporting the project, though it would not be as enthusiastic as Joseph's. Then, when our conversation was about to break up, I cautioned the realtor not to get his hopes up. "There's one more thing," I stressed. "I've taken a public stand on this issue. My credibility is at stake. I can't flip a '180' on this—not unless I truly believe I'm doing the right thing."

"Now, Bill," Mongelluzzo replied patronizingly. "The only people who will know will be the governor and the chairman of the Ohio Democrat Party and me."

"But I'll know," I whispered, and then again with emphasis, looking Mongelluzzo straight in the eye—"I'll know!" He rolled his eyes and looked to Coplen as if to say, "Who is this guy?" The meeting ended with Mongelluzzo reminding me that he'd let me know through Coplen the exact timing of our trip to Toledo.

Coplen and I walked out together and stood for a moment on the front porch of the Yocum Building. "What do you think, John?" I asked. "I'd have written the letter," Coplen advised reprovingly, lighting a cigarette. "That was a helluva offer." As I started to protest, he chuckled, waving away smoke. "Well, Bill, you know me."[7]

Throughout the week following that meeting, I kept my counsel, speaking to only a couple of party hands about the dilemma I was confronting. One of them, John Hevener, told me, "Don't worry about the money."

He was right. The money was not important, but my decision regarding what to do with Mongelluzzo's offer was. Still in my first year as chairman and lacking the confidence I would later acquire, I was concerned about John

Coplen's role in the matter. Mongelluzzo had dangled the promise of five thousand in exchange for my support on the landfill, and Coplen knew about it. If I didn't write the letter, he and Linda and their allies—Steve Webb, Bryan Hefner, Cora Hamman, and others who viewed politics more pragmatically—could undermine my authority for not accepting what Coplen had already dubbed "a helluva offer." But if I did write the letter, not only would my credibility be harmed, but I would forfeit the opportunity to build an alliance between the party and the community of Spencerville.

I ended up taking the trip to Toledo and writing a letter that backed the landfill. My support was conditioned on Waste Management's willingness to protect Kendrick Woods's ecosystem, but the letter did contain the magic words: "Please look into this matter and urge the Ohio EPA to expedite its handling of this issue."[8]

Even with my tempered support, Mongelluzzo had procured the main thing he wanted—my silence. When the permit came through, so would the promised contribution. Meanwhile, in an effort to honor my end of the deal, I stopped attending Dumpbuster rallies, and I ceased agitating Democratic opposition to the project. In late March, I issued my last public statement on the controversy, urging the commissioners to establish a solid-waste district and to exercise oversight of the landfill if it were to be located in Spencerville. When asked if I supported the Dumpbusters, I replied, "Not necessarily. Personally, I wish the landfill wasn't headed there, but I hate to take that position because I'm not aware of what other sites are available." With that, I stepped away from the Spencerville community, abandoning the residents to fight on their own.[9]

Ida Kay Keller and her fellow Dumpbusters, who noticed my withdrawal, assumed that someone had called me off.[10] They were right, of course. To her credit, Keller herself began attending Democratic events and establishing connections with the party, even as I was interposing distance between our two organizations. One event in particular stands out, a reception and ice cream social staged for Attorney General Tony Celebrezze. Keller was there, along with some Dumpbuster friends, which gave me my first opportunity to meet her personally. I took note when Celebrezze warmly praised Ida Kay in his remarks, and I watched with interest as he lingered afterward to talk with her about the latest news on the Dumpbuster front.[11]

As Keller initiated her overtures to the Democratic Party, I began rethinking my position. The turning point came at a Dumpbuster rally in late October 1987, the first rally I had attended in weeks. Keller and the Dumpbusters shared data they had gathered on the geology of the landfill site, warning that the location was not as safe as Jack Nichols and John Mangelluzzo had led me to believe. The data further supported the case for alternatives to landfill, including recycling and composting. Importantly, their concern was no longer focused solely on preserving property values or keeping an unsightly landfill out of their community. Rather, they now spoke of the connection between pollution and the entire ecosystem, between the human community and the earth itself.

I left that rally impressed by the Dumpbusters' sophisticated thinking and the quiet sense of urgency they communicated. I immediately wrote Governor Celeste a new letter and recanted my earlier commitment to the landfill project. After a reference to my February letter, I wrote, "At the time, I requested you to 'urge the Ohio EPA to expedite its handling of this issue.' I can no longer stand behind that letter or that request." Emphasizing my disillusionment with Waste Management's integrity and conduct, I urged, "Please advise the EPA to be very careful in handling this matter, paying close attention to Waste Management's previous track record and operating practices."[12]

I had ended up where I should have been all along, and when the word arrived three weeks later that Waste Management was withdrawing its request for a landfill permit, I could enthusiastically and genuinely share the Dumpbusters' joyous celebration.

Looking back at these events, I can see that the party should have sided with the Dumpbusters from the beginning, but at the time I found myself buffeted by a political swell, unable to steer the party in that direction. Lima City Council, proselytized by Mayor Joseph, had aligned itself on Waste Management's side that spring, and even local environmentalists had been called off.[13] For a time, John Mongelluzzo and his pal John Coplen had guided me and the Allen County Democratic Party away from the Dumpbusters' side, using the enticement of a political contribution.

But if I was supposed to dance with them what brung me, the dance initiated by Mongelluzzo and Coplen was one that undermined the interests of the Democrats and conflicted with the party's historical and philosophical preference for David in any battle with Goliath—in this instance, a community fighting to protect itself from a multinational corporation. Only at the last minute did I recognize that the Mongelluzzo's offer was fool's gold, that it would provide little or no benefit to the party. More important was the "social capital" held by Ida Kay Keller and the Dumpbusters.[14] The reevaluation of my February stance and my subsequent decision to recant that position kept the party's values intact. That decision also benefited the party in a more pragmatic way, giving the Democrats a narrow foothold in the community of Spencerville and allowing me to recruit Ida Kay Keller as a county commissioner candidate.

John Dornick, circa 1989. From the collection of Marge Dornick.

August 2, 1989

I charged into the Allen County Democratic Party's headquarters, newly located on North Main Street, and to the cheers of fifty members of the Lima Memorial Professional Nurses Association (LMPNA), I proclaimed the party's "enthusiastic" support for the nurses and their strike against Lima Memorial Hospital.[15] I accused hospital administrators of prolonging the strike by "digging in their heels and playing macho games." Asked whether the Democratic Party was politicizing a labor dispute, I replied, "Democrats have a responsibility to stand up for the community. We have a responsibility to take a position."[16]

The nurses had been on strike for almost two months and had been embroiled in conflict with Lima Memorial Hospital for longer than that. As far back as 1986, registered nurses at the hospital had pressed for improvements in work procedures and employment practices, carrying their concerns to nursing and hospital administrators, but nothing had changed. Morale deteriorated. A big problem was Greg Turner, Lima Memorial's president and chief executive officer. In fact, Turner's high-handed attitude and denial of professional respect for the nursing staff catalyzed the formation of a union. He ran the hospital as if he owned it, taking the attitude that if his nurses did not like the working conditions, they could leave. Many did. More were heading out the door, creating a situation that would have seriously jeopardized the quality of patient care unless something was done to improve the workplace.[17]

The drive to organize had been breathtakingly swift. Talks began with the

Ohio Nurses Association (ONA) in September 1988, and within two months over two-thirds of the nurses had signed union cards. Soon the LMPNA was formally organized, and in January 1989 the nurses took the final step, voting 342–114 to unionize and to authorize the LMPNA to negotiate a contract with the hospital.[18]

Rather than heed the decisiveness of this outcome, Turner and the hospital administration hired a consulting firm to help them break the union.[19] They unilaterally offered across-the-board raises to all nurses and nurse anesthetists, a violation of federal labor law.[20] They dragged their feet on scheduling bargaining sessions, playing "head games" with the nurses by agreeing to meetings and then abruptly canceling them. Between January 26 and June 1, less than eight hours of bargaining had been held, and according to one nurse, those sessions had accomplished nothing.[21]

On June 6, fed up with the hospital's refusal to negotiate seriously, the nurses walked out. When negotiations resumed late that month, positive media reports led the *Lima News* to predict a quick end to the strike,[22] but the grind was just beginning. The roadblock was the hospital's insistence on an open shop, giving nurses the right to work at Lima Memorial without joining the LMPNA. Hospital negotiators twice presented the union with contracts containing open-shop language, and each time the union's members overwhelmingly rejected the offer.[23] Each rejection upheld the principle of union security; the union did not want to be in a position of negotiating a labor contract for a workforce split between union and nonunion members.[24]

The hospital was playing out a cruel strategy. Its negotiators made concessions on peripheral matters but refused to negotiate fairly on the nurses' demand for union security. They called for votes on contracts that they knew would not win approval, thereby placing blame on the nurses for the inevitable collapse of negotiations. This maneuver was enhanced by the hospital's overly optimistic pronouncements, which the media echoed, claiming that progress was being made when really it wasn't. (Spokeswomen for the LMPNA were always more reticent about gains that they had supposedly made at the bargaining table.) When negotiations soured, the nurses felt the pressure. Anxiety rose among technicians and other hospital employees who had been laid off because of the strike. Outpatients who were being inconvenienced also lashed out.[25]

This was the situation when the Democratic Party and I entered the lists. John Dornick, in particular, was upset with Greg Turner and the hospital administration. John was a die-hard union man, and nothing made him angrier than unfairness; he was particularly incensed at the hospital for trying to cram an open shop down the nurses' throats. Dornick met personally with Jolene

Marshall, LMPNA president, and Fran Mauk, a spokeswoman for the union, arranging for them to appear before July's Executive Committee meeting. He tried to meet with Greg Turner and other hospital administrators to secure their point of view but was rebuffed.

On the evening of July 25, Marshall and Mauk spoke to the party, explaining the LMPNA's side of the dispute. I referred the matter to the Policy Studies Committee, chaired by Rick Siferd, who announced that the group would meet two nights later to prepare the party's response.[26] No one could have misinterpreted the significance of this development. Siferd's committee had been a force during my first term in office, investigating important issues and, through me as the spokesperson, pronouncing the party's viewpoint. The committee duly met with Mauk and Marshall to gather more facts and then formally ruled that the party should issue a statement supporting the union. Siferd, Dornick, and others suggested preliminary talking points, leaving it to me to design the press release.[27]

Had I confined my remarks on August 2 to a simple show of support for the union, my words might easily have been ignored as harmless bluster. But I did more. "The Allen County Democratic Party urges all Democrats to seek health services at hospitals other than Memorial until a settlement acceptable to the nurses is reached," I announced.[28] I threw down the gauntlet—the threat of a boycott. The Democrats were now the ones playing "macho games."

The hospital's vice president, John Weir, angrily denounced my statement, proclaiming the party's action "irresponsible." He was aghast at the prospect of a boycott, declaring, "It is regrettable that any political body would suggest to the public a restriction of their access to something as vitally important as health care." Finally, he defended the hospital's refusal to meet with party representatives to hear the administration's side of the controversy: "We will not politicize a labor dispute. We will not be part of this irresponsible action."[29]

Weir's public condemnation of the party was mild in comparison to what I personally received. At 5:30 A.M. on the morning after my press conference, I was awakened by a phone call from a technician who was working an early shift at the hospital. He berated me for not knowing what I was talking about and for ignoring his rights. I broke off in the middle of his harangue and hung up. He wasn't interested in hearing my side. Moments later, the phone rang again. I let the answering machine take this one. It was another hospital employee, a woman, angrily challenging me to come to the phone and wondering "which nurse I was sleeping with."[30]

The calls kept coming. I let my answering machine receive them; by nightfall over thirty messages, all negative, many abusive, had filled the cassette, and the machine shut itself off, causing my phone to ring incessantly and disturb my neighbors. I finally unplugged my telephone, just to get a little peace for myself and the neighborhood. I instructed friends and family that I would be incommunicado until the storm blew over. It lasted two weeks.

Letters arrived, too. Some were obscene, such as the card addressed sarcastically "Bill Angel, Mr. Democrat" and furtively dropped on my doorstep. Its cover was a frontal photograph of a pretty brunette with a sheepish smile—stark naked except for a pair of high heels. She was stooped awkwardly, her arms crisscrossed over her pubic area. A hand-drawn nurse's cap was perched on her head. The caption inside read, "I wish you'd stop sticking your nose where it isn't wanted." The anonymous sender had printed an addendum below the caption: "We righteous nonunion scabs are tired of it!"[31]

The newspaper's letter-to-the-editor pages were downright scathing. Karen Piercefield, a technician at the hospital who had previously written a letter criticizing the nurses' union, now castigated me for not considering the views of Democrats like herself. Resenting my "comments and endorsements," she angrily charged me with being either "misinformed or blind"; she asserted that the nurses were the ones "playing macho games."[32] In a strikingly similar letter that also disputed my right to stake out the Democratic Party's position, Sandra Clark, an antiunion RN, parroted: "Did Mr. Angel, as chairman, poll all Democrats in Allen County, asking if he could speak for them on this issue?" Like Piercefield, she proclaimed that my "allegations" were unjustified, observing that strike could be settled if not for the nurses' greed. "Is the Democratic Party so hard up for votes that it is willing to stoop to any depth to get them?"[33]

During the two weeks following my pronouncement, ten letters on the editorial page of the newspaper addressed the nurses' strike, and of these, eight were decisively against the nurses.[34] In addition, the *Lima News* itself editorialized against the LMPNA, claiming that the dispute had become one of "power" rather than "economics." The newspaper chastised the nurses for insisting on a "closed shop" and urged them to accept a right-to-work clause in the agreement. (The nurses actually wanted a union shop, not a closed one, but the *Lima News* seldom let details get in the way of a good argument.)[35]

These developments were disheartening, but not nearly as much as the written pronouncements I received from fellow Democrats, including a hand-delivered note from David and Estella Adams. Both were Democratic activists, and David would serve as the party's Central Committee chair in the mid-1990s. Estella directed the Cerebral Palsy Clinic at Lima Memorial Hospital, and the nurse's strike had shut down the clinic's services. The Adams's message expressed disappointment with the party's action.[36]

On the very day I had issued my statement and before the yowling had begun, Doris Miller wrote a two-page letter stating her consternation at the party's action. "I am afraid a terrible mistake has been made," she declared. Doris was a Central Committeewoman from the "old school," walking her precinct regularly, keeping in touch with the neighbors, and talking up the Democratic Party. The party and I could always count on her support whenever it was required. But not this time—Doris, whose precinct surrounded Memorial Hospital, expressed sympathy for her neighbors who worked at the hospital as cooks, orderlies, and technicians. Now they were laid off and angry at the Democrats, she said, and some were considering switching their politics because of what the party had done.[37] As a Democratic committeewoman, Doris Miller had been forced into the middle of the controversy, and she was uncomfortable with the position in which the party had placed her.

Eighth Ward city councilwoman Dorothy Riker also wrote me. I had circulated a nominating petition for her when she ran for reelection in 1987, but now she was one unhappy Democrat. Riker derided the nurses, condemned their demand for a union shop, and scolded me for sticking my nose into a nonpolitical issue.[38]

These were written protests. I also received vocal swipes from Democrats who bumped into me in public places. Some knew me only slightly, while others simply recognized my face from TV. No one applauded the party's stand, it seemed. Condemnation was the universal message. My declaration of August 2 seemed to have inspired a tilting contest throughout the county, and I was the quintain—the target for verbal lances directed against the party.

When the Executive Committee met again in mid-August, my nerves were fried. Facing a restless group of Democrats, anxious about the trouble I had stirred up, I reminded everyone of the Democratic Party's historical support for common people and their fight for justice, stressing the party's institutional voice in our community. It had, I said, an obligation to articulate a position on controversies like the one at Memorial Hospital.[39] Siferd echoed my remarks, as did John Dornick, who took particular aim at those who claimed, in his words, "'Angel don't speak for me!!'" Deeply disturbed by the flak I had been taking, John did not want to see my chairmanship hurt by the controversy. "We Democrats are proud of our right to disagree and vocalize it," he declared. "But let us not fall into the trap of letting others denigrate our leaders."[40]

In late August, the backlash began to subside. I reconnected my phone and revived my answering machine. Letters to the editor supporting the nurses replaced the recriminating ones.[41] But the strike continued. Negotiations were dead. The hospital's administrators clung to the belief that the furor I had stirred would eventually cause the nurses to give up, yet the nurses held fast.

Negotiations recommenced on September 6, and within two weeks the two sides hammered out a contract that provided the nurses' demand for union security. They won the union-shop clause. Greg Turner resigned. The strike was over.[42]

Some day, labor historians might analyze this struggle and conclude that the Allen County Democratic Party had blundered by entering the fray. But John P. Dornick never thought so. Toward the end of 1989, he and I were looking back on these events, and I asked him if he thought we had made a mistake by getting involved. "Hell, no!" John thundered, snapping a cigar out of his mouth and arching his back. Then, flicking ash off the end of the stogie, he leaned forward, gently narrowed his eyes, and said simply and reassuringly, "We did the right thing."

John Dornick understood that the Democratic Party had to do more than "register voters and elect Democrats."[43] It had to stand for ideas and have the courage to register its beliefs, especially when it was not convenient to do so. In his view, it was an essential part of the Democratic canon to support the rights of working people and their fight for political and economic justice. He could not have walked away from those striking nurses any more than he could have turned aside while a neighbor was being mugged. It was in his bones to help. And mine, too.

We had not been mindful, however, of the impact my statement would have on the entire community, and in that respect we can be judged foolhardy. We could have taken our stand in a more subtle, less antagonistic fashion. The party could have sent a donation to the nurses' strike fund, enlisted volunteers to initiate a letter-to-the-editor campaign, or recruited Democratic activists to join the union's picket line. Had we done so, I might have avoided the venomous abuse that fell directly on me.

But those would have been weak gestures. John Dornick, Rick Siferd, and I felt compelled to remind our fellow Democrats that the struggle of the nurses was our struggle too. True, the strike was causing tremendous inconvenience. Dialysis patients had to travel to Fort Wayne and back. Children with cerebral palsy could not get the therapy they needed. Cooks, therapists, and technicians at the hospital were laid off. A lot of people were paying a tremendous price. But Dornick, Siferd, and I believed that despite the resentment our action might kindle, Democrats needed to rouse themselves and answer the question evoked by that old labor ballad, "Which side are you on?"[44]

The predicament at the center of the hospital episode is different from the quandary represented in my story about John Mongelluzzo and the Spencerville landfill. In the earlier situation, I had been caught in a web of craven self-interest that blinded me to the party's philosophical bent to help communities in need. In the case of the nurses' strike, however, moral resolve had blocked consideration of practical politics, specifically the need to pay attention to the party's base—to cooks and orderlies tossed out of work by the nurses' action.

However, each experience taught important lessons about the place of values in politics. Regarding the Spencerville landfill, it turned out that ideals meshed nicely with pragmatism. It was astute to side with the Dumpbusters, and by ultimately sticking with principle I learned that philosophical standards and pragmatic concerns are not always in conflict. Even more pointedly, I discovered that when it comes to party operations, social capital is as important as, if not more important than, financial capital. But when pragmatism and ideals collide—as in the nurses' strike—it is probably best not to think too pragmatically. John Dornick, Rick Siferd, and I could have steered clear of the LMPNA, out of deference to Democrats who did not support the union, but that course would have directed the party away from "doing the right thing."

Both stories show that party organizations must stand for something substantial. A partisan value system—in this book, the beliefs defining what it means to be a Democrat—not only supplies important guidance for resolving conflict but shores up efforts to engage in dialogue, forcing a debate that is driven by something other than simplistic desire for political advantage.

In that respect, the nurses' strike supplied an awakening. Though dismayed by the public rancor I had stirred up, I was even more perplexed by the opposition that roared from fellow Democrats. It was one thing to dispute party strategy—questioning whether we should recruit a candidate for state representative, for example—but it was quite another matter to oppose principles that lay at the core of the Democratic Party's existence—to say that the nurses had to accept an open shop, as Dorothy Riker, a prominent member of the Democratic Party, had done. Could I reliably captain the team when some of its stalwarts showed such scorn for the striking nurses, rejecting the Democratic position I had pronounced? The negative reaction revealed fully what I was up against—an unrepentant conservative community that was steadfastly opposed to organized labor, and Democratic adherents who would flinch when the going proved disruptive.

Even the nurses, in whose cause we had enlisted, showed little appreciation for what the party had risked. The most thanks we received was a terse statement by Jolene Marshall at the time of my press conference. "The union appreciates that the Democratic Party is standing up for us," she said.[45] We never heard from the nurses' union again. When the party sent the LMPNA tickets to our fall dinner, they were unceremoniously returned, without explanation.

I began to comprehend why Ed Finn, Bob Gehr, and the boys in the UAW hall were so skeptical of the kind of leadership I could bring to the Democratic Party. They understood Allen County's conservative, antilabor climate much better than I did. Seeing me simply as some guy who was not a member of a labor union, they had to doubt my willingness to back the rights of labor. By September 1989, I realized what they and I were up against.

And I was starting to wear down.

· 19 ·

Dropping the Rope

Friday, August 31, 1990, 8 A.M.
I had just returned from my morning run, and the phone was ringing. It was PC Wrencher, John Dornick's good pal. "I got bad news, Bill," he said. "It's Dornick. Had a stroke early this morning. I'm at St. Rita's now, and it don't look good." I thanked PC and waited for a call I hoped would never come. A half-hour later, the phone rang again. "John's gone," was all I remember PC saying.

Yes, but he had left in characteristic style. Upon his arrival in St. Rita's emergency room, Dornick had faced a series of questions aimed to test his consciousness and orientation. "What year is it?" the attending physician asked.

"1990."

"What month?"

"August."

"What day?"

"Friday."

Then the doctor unwittingly posed a question that cut directly to John Dornick's partisan heart. "Who is president of the United States?" John stared up at him fiercely, as if he were confronting some impertinent voter, and declared, "George Bush—a fuckin' Republican."[1]

It was not a curse but a confession of faith.

Prior to John Dornick's death, our 1990 campaign had been guardedly optimistic. John had thrown himself into his Central Committee duties with considerable energy, fulfilling the promise that the party would finally assemble a coalition of hardworking precinct representatives. By midsummer, he had set Central Committee members to work preparing phone lists for voter contact in the fall. Thanks to John, "get out the vote" was under way, even in July.

In fact, it was because of Dornick that I had decided to run for a third term. From the beginning of my chairmanship, I had mused about stepping away from the post. But in 1989, a roller coaster of a year, my feelings about the job rose and fell, and the musings became more sincere. In March, faced with frustrations from Lima's mayoral campaign (see the next chapter), I openly mentioned not running, but I soon bounced back from that trough to cut my deal with Donna Johns. Then, the nurses' strike hit, and again I was ready to quit altogether.

That's when Dornick bucked me up and talked me into staying for one more run. "Nobody else can lead the party but you," he exhorted. I tried to tell him that Rochelle Twining could do the job, but he responded that while Twining was popular with some Democrats, she aroused resentment among others, especially remnants of the old guard. Twining herself shared this assessment, but she took my brooding at face value. She suggested a contingency plan whereby I would run again for chair and she would be appointed vice chair when the party reorganized. Then I could resign in midterm and turn the party over to her— that is, if I was of a mind to do so. In the meantime, she could begin shoring up her base. Dornick agreed to this scenario, though he hoped I would continue through a full term. In January 1990 I announced my intention to run again, never hinting that any design for my succession had been under discussion.[2]

As for the party's candidates in 1990, that spring's primaries had been active but not divisive. In the race for county commissioner, Ida Kay Keller, true to her word, was back, and this time she won the Democratic nomination, over former Republican Ron Pugsley.[3] I even found a candidate for state representative—Lorenzo White, an insurance agent who had become active in the party's minority caucus. He was an energetic, young, black Democrat whose family was active in the community and was well respected. His mother, Carlene, had been a longtime Central Committeewoman, and his brother William had been an all-American defensive back at Ohio State, later enjoying a successful career in the National Football League. White also had to navigate through a Democratic primary, where he was challenged by Ramon Moritz, a UAW Ford worker whom I had tried unsuccessfully to recruit for the slot two years earlier. It was a healthy contest, giving White a chance to establish a campaign message and to condition himself for the later battle against Bill Thompson. Lorenzo later acknowledged that the primary, in which he defeated Moritz with 55 percent of the vote, had been a positive "learning experience." I liked White's chances and praised his quick growth as a candidate, declaring confidently, "Bill Thompson will know he's been in a race."[4]

Although 1990 was shaping up to be a Republican year, with Republicans presenting strong challenges for several state offices long held by Democrats, I remained upbeat. Praising Keller and White as strong candidates who would fiercely challenge their opponents, I observed, "If voters are a mood to 'throw the rascals out,' that might work to the advantage of the Democrats in Allen County. The Republicans are the rascals here."[5]

If my outlook on the local races was bright-eyed, the condition of the state-wide campaign had become a source of concern. Attorney General Anthony Celebreeze was the party's candidate for governor. He had started out on the right foot in 1989 by making the rounds of Democratic chairmen, talking to us one on one, revealing his intention to run for governor. Over lunch he explained to me why he was taking on the gubernatorial race: he wanted to stay involved with state government. "That's where the action is going to be in the 1990s," I remember him saying.

Celebreeze's gesture—meeting with me personally rather than sending one of his field operatives—emphasized his difference from other state politicos I had encountered. He was a blue-collar politician—a man whose favorite sport was NASCAR racing and who in his spare time liked to work on his own car in his own back yard. If you were to meet Tony in a reception line, whether you were a county chair, a precinct committeewoman, or an ordinary voter, he would greet you warmly and sincerely listen—never pulling the politician's trick of shaking your hand while glancing out of the corner of his eye to see who's next in line. He comprehended the important work that local parties tried to accomplish and genuinely cared about grassroots activists like me.

This is why I took Tony at his word when he explained his shift on the abortion question. Throughout his political career, he had won elections as a pro-life Democrat, forging a coalition that united the party's Catholic, blue-collar base with its urban liberals—in effect, making the issue moot any time he ran for office. But on December 2, 1989, he declared that while he personally opposed abortion, he believed that as governor he could not stand in the way of a woman's access to such a procedure.[6] Seemingly overnight, Anthony Celebreeze had become a pro-choice Democrat. In explaining his change of position, he cited the U.S. Supreme Court's verdict in the *Webster* case, which the previous summer had awarded substantial power to the state governments to regulate abortion practices. That decision, Celebreeze said, "threw out the rule book on abortion."[7]

It was a remarkable turnabout, so much so that his announcement carried the traces of an election-year conversion. Dick Celeste had won elections in 1982 and 1986 by touting an unabashedly pro-choice position and taking advantage of a gender gap to seal his victories. Cynics who saw Celebreeze trying to pump the same formula challenged his sincerity. So did George Voinovich, the Republican candidate for governor, who continuously hammered Tony's "flip-flop" on abortion, seizing every opportunity to accuse him of switching his position out of political expedience.[8]

Never doubting Celebreeze's sincerity, I defended his move. On December 6, 1989, at a pre-holiday fund-raiser, I assured our rank and file that Tony had given the matter prayerful and introspective thought and that he had made his decision on the basis of his own conscience, not any crass desire to secure political advantage. I repeated my views a week later in introducing Tony when he came to Lima to celebrate the announcement of his candidacy.

I encountered my own share of resistance. Fr. Robert Sidner of St. Charles Parish sent me a handwritten note rebuking me for defending Celebreeze and reminding me that I did not speak for all Democrats. It was a throwback to remarks I had received the previous summer during the nurses' strike.[9] Then, Susan Stechschulte—Lima resident, state president of the Ohio Right to Life Society, and longtime local pro-life activist—contacted me, asking to address a party meeting regarding Celebreeze's switch on abortion. From my perspective, I owed Stechschulte nothing. She and her group had picketed Democratic events and agitated against Democratic candidates, even pro-life Democrats like Steve Maurer.

Even so, I took her request to January's session of the Executive Committee, where John Dornick moved—Ed Schwieterman (a strong pro-life Democrat) seconding—that a pro-life representative be invited to speak in February. A vigorous discussion ensued in which pro-life Democrats expressed their disappointment with Celebreeze; some even declared that they could not vote for him. They were countered by others who stressed party loyalty, arguing that we had to back Tony Celebreeze because he was going to be the party's nominee for governor and that we should not be distracted by single-issue groups that did not have the party's interests in mind. The motion was rejected. Pro-life Democrats had had their say, but I left that meeting sensing that Celebreeze had lost much of their confidence and good will.[10]

By late spring, gloom was enveloping Celebreeze's candidacy. In May, the Voinovich campaign began leaking stories about ethical improprieties in the attorney general's office, followed shortly by statewide polls that showed Celebreeze trailing substantially.[11] It looked like voters were going to punish Tony for the sins of Dick Celeste. Worse, local activists were not enthused about him. Celebreeze had assembled a young but spirited campaign staff led by a few veteran pols, including Tom Winters and Don Sweitzer, a Washington-based campaign consultant. On June 2, at a organizational meeting staged specifically for county chairs and local activists, Tony's campaign staffers enthusiastically promised victory in November. "We'll be there," several of them chimed, echoing each other's words as if they really believed them. But the house was not buying their fervor, a feeling picked up by Jim Ruvulo. "This race is winnable," he laconically observed, urging us not to give up hope.[12]

The general lethargy had not improved by September, when I attended the Ohio Democratic Party's biennial convention in Cleveland. In Allen County, we'd had trouble filling our slate of delegates, as opposed to 1986 and 1988, when spirited contests had prevailed. I later discovered that other county parties had experienced the same problem. As state conventions go, that one was godawful—a fake pep rally where speeches droned on, with no central message or theme. Halfway through the proceedings I stole away to the balcony of the Masonic Auditorium, which was barely half full—it had been completely filled in 1986, the last time the state convention had been held there. The speeches were tepid, delegates bored, and applause merely polite. At one point Sherrod Brown stopped for an applause line and was greeted, to his embarrassment, with dead silence—but then, all the speakers had awkward moments as they strained to generate enthusiasm from a house that was more concerned about lunch than politics. No one was taking much delight in this campaign.[13]

Truthfully, I was going through the doldrums myself. I had begun to redirect my attention to academic interests, temporarily setting aside my political duties during the summers of 1989 and 1990 to participate in a couple of seminars. When the 1990 seminar concluded, I headed for a vacation in Germany. In other words, I took off an entire summer, even though an important election was at stake.

There was another—and more acute—distraction. I was up to my gills in trying to organize a faculty union on the Lima Campus of Ohio State University. For over two years, bad blood had been building between the OSU/Lima faculty and Dr. James Countryman, the campus dean. The background to the dispute is complex and not particularly germane to this story, but it is sufficient to say that by spring 1990, the situation had worsened to the point that Lima's faculty were prepared to accept union representation—at least I thought so. Representatives from the American Federation of Teachers responded to an invitation I duly sent them, visited our campus, and initiated an organization drive. But when my colleagues were faced with the grim reality of forming a faculty union, I could not rally them, especially when Ohio State's central administration played the "tenure card," declaring that any collective bargaining agreement would effectively terminate tenure. Support for the union collapsed.[14]

Ensnared so deeply in this quixotic crusade to establish a faculty union, I was unable to provide the focused leadership the Allen County Democratic Party needed and deserved as it headed into that fall's campaign. I had been drifting, and so had the party. As long as John Dornick was at the helm we maintained course, but John's death changed the situation dramatically.

In particular, my absenteeism hurt Lorenzo White. Lorenzo had assembled an enthusiastic core of activists, but as an African American running a county-wide election, he was in for an uphill fight, a prospect perhaps even more daunting than the battle Rochelle Twining had faced four years earlier. White's campaign needed more forceful guidance than I had been able to offer. As the election moved into its final month, he needed financing to create television and radio spots, but unlike two years earlier, when the party had had a flow of cash every month from the license bureaus, the income had become more unsteady and tied to sporadic fund-raising events. The political party fund, which Governor Celeste had proposed in 1987 (see Chapter 10), had been established, but the money from that source did not make up for the revenues our deputy registrars had once contributed. Consequently, we had no money to run polls like we had in 1988, and the only financial help the party could supply was a donation to the White and Keller campaigns of a thousand dollars each. In the meantime, Lorenzo had overcommitted in buying billboard space, leaving his campaign short of funds for broadcast media. He voiced his frustration to me one evening in his campaign headquarters, saying that when I had recruited him, I had promised more financial help than he was receiving. There was nothing that I could do, although the party did end up giving his campaign a hundred dollars to help with GOTV expenses.[15]

I had let Lorenzo White down. Had I been less distracted and more attentive, I would have warned him not to invest in billboards—they have minimal impact on voters anyway—and encouraged him to set aside money for radio and television ads. I would also have been more direct in apprising him of party's financial condition and in helping him create a more pragmatic campaign budget. I would have had the energy to visit Speaker Vern Riffe's office, just as I had done for Rochelle Twining, to make a pitch for White's candidacy. Would have. Should have. But no, I didn't.

My AWOL status did not hurt Ida Kay Keller as much. Her 1988 run had made her an experienced candidate. By 1990, she was no longer shy about working a crowd and making one-on-one contacts with voters, and her public appearances were more confident and forceful. Also, she had a larger number of candidate forums where she could go head to head with her Republican opponent, Alberta Lee, and engage issues facing the community.[16]

But Keller was dogged by the charge that she was a "one-issue candidate," overrelying on the fame she had gained from her Dumpbuster days. In 1990, the problem was especially vexing, because voters were more focused on the formation of a county water district than on the environmental problems that had been at the center of Keller's earlier campaign.[17] Additionally, many residents still regarded Ida Kay Keller as a political newcomer, particularly when compared to Alberta Lee, who had been member of the Lima City school board since 1972 and county recorder since 1980.

Then, another blow. In mid-October, Rochelle Twining notified me that John Hevener had developed a malignant tumor in his lung and would soon undergo chemotherapy. His health had been deteriorating since 1988, a circumstance that had eventually forced his resignation from the Executive Committee, but none of us had anticipated this news. "Our party's fathers are leaving us," I remember Twining lamenting, a reference to the loss of Dornick's leadership and now Hevener's.

John Dornick was dead, John Hevener had cancer, and I had been absent from duty. At this point, I resumed a more spirited focus on my chairman's duties, beginning with a challenge to my Republican counterpart and rival, Bob Holmes. When Lima Municipal Court clerk Don Weideman, a Republican, retired from his post in late September, Holmes arranged things so that his own Central Committee would name him to serve the remaining year of Weideman's term.[18] The job paid $63,500 annually.

I condemned Holmes for engineering his appointment, labeling it a "move symbolizing both arrogance and hypocrisy." Attacking with years of pent-up fury, I denounced the way "high ranking Republicans [had] been riding roughshod over county residents." Galled by the double standard being applied in that fall's elections, I proclaimed, "Republican statewide candidates are currently criticizing Democrats for exploiting public office for partisan purpose when this is exactly what is happening here." Raking Holmes with rhetorical broadsides, I called his move a throwback to the days when party bosses nabbed the top jobs, "enriching themselves at public expense." I was angry, and I challenged voters to share my anger: "Isn't it time to put fresh leadership in the Court House?"[19]

Holmes, as expected, refuted my denunciation. "As usual, Bill hasn't done his homework," he replied. He defended his qualifications for the job and promised that he would not use his post to peddle influence in Lima City Hall; still, he had no effective response to the argument that lay at the core of my challenge, that his was "a backdoor appointment." Disingenuously claiming that "he was not aware that his interest in the job [had] scared off other candidates," he could only state that if he hadn't received the position, some other prominent Republican would have. In his view, my attack was unwarranted and unfair.[20]

My remarks drew a positive reaction from the party faithful. It was a necessary condemnation, one designed to galvanize all Democrats as we readied ourselves for the final push to election day. Even Cora Hamman, still a member of the Central Committee, sent me the newspaper clipping of my press conference. She had scribbled annotations in the margins with her views on the reportage, and then, in a gesture that I construed to be a peace offering, attached a warm handwritten note applauding my effort.[21]

Among the general public, however, my criticism of the Republican chairman produced only a shrug. The municipal clerk controversy quickly disappeared—a brief squall disrupting the Republicans' breezy sweep to election day—and I was left wondering whether the voters had been paying attention. But at least one man had noticed. Don Stratton, a well-respected inspector in the Lima City Police Department, wrote the *Lima News* endorsing my denunciation of the Holmes appointment. Proclaiming himself a Republican who was "not accustomed to agreeing with any Democrat since Harry Truman," Stratton took direct issue with Holmes's intention to serve as clerk of Municipal Court while continuing to operate as Republican county chairman. He urged Holmes to resign from one of the two posts, warning that unless he did so, Democrats could "soon gain a long sought foothold in county elected offices."[22]

I quietly welcomed Stratton's letter. Finally, someone was listening, and if Stratton was willing to express his views publicly, others—including independent-minded Republicans like him—must have been thinking the same thing. There was still hope.

Sunday, November 4, 1990, 4 P.M.

The day had begun miserably. The morning papers had published polls showing Tony Celebrezze losing by margins of from 7 to 14 percent.[23] His impending loss spelled doom for the ticket, particularly in the secretary of state's race, where two-term incumbent Sherrod Brown was caught in a dogfight with challenger Robert A. Taft III. For the past month, Taft's television ads had hounded Brown, one of them howling at a scheme that Brown had once proposed whereby Sherrod would take a sabbatical from his secretary of state's post to spend a few months in Japan. That had been a dumb idea, and the Taft ad lampooned it: "Say 'Sayonara' to Sherrod Brown."

The election of 1990 was less than forty-eight hours away. Yet despite the day's gloomy start, our volunteers had dutifully shown up at party headquarters to work their assigned shifts on the phone bank. Activity was proceeding routinely, though not enthusiastically, when Rochelle Twining strode into headquarters, a dark look on her face. She wanted to speak to me, *"privately."* Ron

Malone, Brown's volunteer coordinator, had ordered her to request that our phone bank immediately call all members of the Central Committee, asking them each to urge five voters in their respective precincts to vote for Sherrod Brown.

"What?" I shot back. "Our plan is set. We're calling as many voters as we can, trying to get out the vote, and now Malone wants us to stop everything we're doing and shift gears especially for the Brown campaign? It's not fair to our local candidates, and you know damn well that few of our people would respond to this shit." I paused a moment, slouching in a folding chair and letting my irritation subside. Finally, I asked, "Rochelle, what's really going on here?"

She didn't know for certain, but she theorized that Brown's own polls showed Taft winning. Malone had sounded scared, Twining said. I briefly pondered Twining's observation before muttering, quietly but emphatically, "Great. Sherrod Brown and Bob Taft run heavy media campaigns, trade salvos of thirty-second attack ads and undermine our efforts to engage a grassroots campaign. Now, Sherrod decides he needs us."

We left the matter there. I never directed our phone volunteers to call Central Committee members as Malone had wanted, although Twining, always the good trooper, mustered a few calls by herself. The phone bank continued, and we did tweak our script with a special plea for voters to "remember Sherrod Brown on election day." Brown lost, just as I had expected, along with Tony Celebreeze and our entire local ticket.[24]

It had been a frustratingly sad campaign, one beset by death, bad news, and miserable leadership from me. On election night, a half-hour or so after the last ballots had been tabulated, I sat slumped in a back corner of the Board of Elections office, far removed from the chortles and whoops echoing from the Republicans celebrating down the hall. A stringer for WLSR Radio found me and asked me to comment on the night's results.

Though I knew my words would hit the morning air waves, I spoke off guard, spilling my frustration and resentment. "This is a tough county, and I don't know what it takes for a Democrat to win," I growled. "We give the voters good candidates like Keller and White, and what to they do? Vote Republican just as they always have. . . . Well, people get the kind of leadership they deserve." It was an ill-tempered and intemperate response, and I realized as much the moment the reporter clicked off his tape recorder. Yet I didn't care.

March 19, 1991, 7:30 P.M.

Smiling broadly, I strolled briskly into party headquarters and began shaking hands and kibitzing with a cortege of Democratic friends. Bill and Donna Johns were there. So were pals of long standing—Rochelle Twining, Howard Elstro, Pickle Felter, Marge Dornick (John's widow, who had become the Central Committeewoman in John's old precinct), and the Heveners. My arrival was similar to any of my previous entrances to a meeting of the Allen County Democratic Party, except that on this occasion I had dressed up in my blue blazer and red paisley tie. The media was there, too, ready to report the news: I was leaving.

Four months had passed since my bitter pronouncement on the 1990 election results, and now I had to acknowledge publicly what I had intuitively understood then—that the party would be better served if somebody else were in command. I was no longer up to the job.

That had been made clear by my effort to recruit a candidate to challenge Bob Holmes in the 1991 election for municipal clerk. I had settled on Mel Woodard as the most logical candidate. Back in 1986, if you recall, Leonard Boddie had offered Woodard's name as a prospect for the county clerk's race. Now it was Mel's time, and I had believed that he was up to the task, even though I was fully aware of the challenges of sending another African American candidate into a county election—all county voters, not just city residents, can vote for Municipal Court positions. A candidate for county commissioner in 1984, he had come away from that campaign with a special resentment for Holmes, who, in Mel's view, had been both arrogant and patronizing in a conversation after the election.

Believing that Woodard could channel his rancor into a run at Holmes, I had met him at his insurance office in late January and put the question to him. Despite my ruminations about resigning as county chairman, I pledged full party support for his candidacy, stressing that his race would be the center of that fall's campaign and that the party really wanted to win it. Mel listened to me, then announced that he wasn't interested—though perhaps Edith, his wife, would be. With that, he jumped out of his chair and bounced to a work area in a far corner of the office, where Edith was at a copying machine. Mel told her that I was looking for a candidate to run against Bob Holmes, and before I knew it, I was giving her the same spiel. Though taken aback by the suggestion that she run for the clerk's post, Edith said that she would think it over. I had lost control of the process. The moment had moved too quickly, like the morning I had sat with Bryan Hefner while he bid party funds on a 1,500-pound steer, and again I lacked the good sense to halt the proceedings. The next day, Edith told me that she would run.

I did not want Edith Woodard to be the party's candidate for municipal clerk, but I lacked the resolve to say so. When I broke the news to members of the Operations and Candidate Recruitment Committees, they were stunned, aghast at idea of sending a black woman who lacked political experience against the chairman of the Allen County Republican Party. Immediately there were suggestions that we try to find someone else to run also, offering Democratic voters a choice in a competitive primary. But I was opposed to that. Having accepted Edith's candidacy and not wanting to seem to double-cross her, I discouraged recruitment of any additional candidates. I sternly reminded my colleagues that the party needed a candidate, and Edith Woodard had come forward. We needed to back her.

A few days before the filing deadline, Roger Rankin phoned and said that he had talked to Rochelle about the clerk's race. Twining was deeply troubled by the prospect of an Edith Woodard candidacy, as she should have been. As the party's vice chair, Rochelle would succeed me if I decided to resign and she would bear full responsibility for promoting Edith Woodard's campaign. At any rate, Rankin asked what I thought about his running for municipal clerk. He would have been a good candidate, eminently more electable than Edith Woodward, but I discouraged him, emphasizing once again that Edith was the party's candidate and that I did not want her to face opposition in the primary.

I had lost my way since 1988, when I told Dale Leppla, "If a guy wants to run, I can't stop him." Just a year earlier, commenting to the *Lima News* about the 1990 county elections, I had said that any Democrat who wanted to run "should go for it and let the voters decide."[25] I had even forgotten the words I had used when I castigated Bob Holmes for grabbing the clerk's post. Not only had I declared then that Democrats would present a credible candidate to challenge him, but I had promised, "There will likely be a healthy primary for the position."[26] It was a promise forgotten when the going proved "inconvenient."

Now I found myself perturbed by Rankin's offer to run and annoyed that Rochelle Twining was still trying to find a candidate. I felt cut off, alienated from fellow Democrats, Rochelle among them, who had once been so close to me, and I was worn down by intrigue against a decision that I thought deserved support. No longer possessing the energy to lead the party effectively, I had lost my bearings, unable to discern that Rochelle and my Democratic pals were working to save me and the party from a misguided decision.

By the time I came back to the surface and breathed in this reality, it was too late to salvage the clerk of court's race. Edith Woodard would become the party's nominee, only to lose substantially, as anticipated.[27] But I did recognize what I needed to do myself: resign and turn the party over to someone else. In late February, well after Woodard had filed her petitions of candidacy, I began conveying my decision to a few of my closest friends in the party, including Rochelle Twining, who agreed to take over.

I don't know if Charlie Hauenstein ever heard the news. He was in St. Rita's Hospital suffering from congestive heart failure when the information began to circulate. None of us knew how seriously ill Charlie was, and in an eerie coincidence, he died the morning after I formally announced my decision to the Operations Committee.[28] He had managed the party during tougher times than I had known, when the Democrats held few statewide offices and the party's money troubles were far greater than the ones our organization was experiencing. Charlie deserved more respect than I had given him while he was alive. Now, he was dropping his end of the rope, just as I was dropping mine, but he would never have done so willingly.

When members of the Executive Committee gathered on March 19 to hear the news they all knew was coming, I led the party in a moment of silent tribute for Charlie Hauenstein and delivered the baton to Rochelle Twining, encouraging my Democratic comrades to remember that "we are a good party, made up of good people committed to our cause."[29] Reflecting on the party's accomplishments during the previous five years, I stressed that Democrats had become more visible, more willing to point out "the ineffectiveness" of Republican stewardship over county government. In presenting the voters a strongly argued alternative, I declared, "We have made the electoral process work. . . . But in working hard ourselves, we forced our opposition to work just as hard."[30]

Bob Holmes later took issue with this latter point. Calling Hauenstein "a very good tactician and an excellent strategist," Holmes asserted. The Republicans had "worked very hard when Charlie was chairman. I wouldn't say we worked harder under Bill." He dismissed my efforts, saying that while I was more visible than Charlie, he was not sure the Democrats had "benefited from the change."[31]

As usual, Bob hadn't done his homework.

· 20 ·

Spading the Earth

Let's go back to the final day of November 1988. Despite the losses the party had experienced in that fall's election, I was in buoyant spirits. Ida Kay Keller had almost grabbed victory from a two-term incumbent, and she had already begun laying plans for 1990. Opposition from inside the party had melted. Even the UAW was coming around. My chairmanship was at its zenith.

Shortly after that election, the rumor had hit the streets that David Berger was running for mayor. If that was true, David's pathway into politics had come from a nontraditional direction. He had spent nine years in Catholic seminary, later abandoning plans for the priesthood to earn a bachelor's degree from Catholic University.[1] Berger had never run for political office, but his years of theological training had formed a sharp intellect, one that connected the philosophical tenets of seminary study with the earthy realities of urban life—the City of God and the City of Man—and Berger's public career reflected that connection. He had arrived in Lima in 1977 to run the Rehab Project, a nonprofit agency that refurbished residential housing in Lima's poorest neighborhoods. Under Berger's direction, the agency had engaged in community revitalization, arguing that by fostering pride of place, home ownership would help restore run-down neighborhoods. Importantly, the job required winning support from a variety of people who sometimes saw themselves as rivals—politicians, business executives, social-service professionals, and community activists. Berger had skillfully forged alliances among these diverse groups and had won assistance from both the public and private sectors to build Rehab into a successful operation.

By 1988, Berger believed that his work with Rehab had run its course. He had become frustrated by political obstacles beyond his control, most notably Lima's dismal record on minority hiring and its unwillingness to enforce its housing code, which city council had grudgingly adopted only in 1986. Berger was ready to leave Lima, particularly since he had received several job offers to work with nonprofits elsewhere. When he shared his frustration with members of Lima's business community, folks who had warmly backed Rehab, they suggested that he might like to run for mayor of Lima and try to fix the problems that Rehab couldn't correct by itself. David Berger was up to the challenge.[2]

He arranged a conference with me for the evening of November 30, agreeing to meet in my apartment, a few doors down from his family residence on Lima's west side. I was eager to talk to him. David was a fellow Democrat, and I figured that he wanted to reach out to the Democratic Party and learn my perspective on the mayor's race. But no. First off, he bluntly informed me that he had already started laying plans to run for mayor and that he had formed a committee, with Rick Siferd as treasurer. He clearly was not seeking my advice about whether or not he should run; he had already made up his mind.

Then, Berger fired a pair of explosive pronouncements. He said that he wanted to maintain a bipartisan flavor in his campaign. He had tapped Democrat James Meredith—brother of Dick Meredith, our Court of Appeals candidate in 1986—to be one co-chair. The other would be Ben Rose, the character who six months earlier had represented Todd Hey in that lawsuit against the Democratic Party. The very idea of Rose working as Berger's co-chair was a stunner.[3]

I bit my lip, allowing Berger to continue his statement and lob another bombshell. "I'd like you to do me a favor," my notes quote him saying. "I'd like you to promise not to take credit for my victory should I win. I want to keep the race a [bi]partisan one."[4] Say what? Here was a guy wanting to run for mayor—a Democrat, and good one, too—who was asking me and the party to stay out of his race. I was offended and told Berger so.

I forced the discussion back to the Ben Rose appointment, denouncing it as a move that "destroyed any possibility" of a bipartisan spirit. During Rose's career as a state representative, I reminded Berger, his partisan assaults on Democratic officeholders had received glowing publicity in the local media, permeating county politics and feeding the general perception that Democrats were "scum." In making Rose his co-chair, Berger had inadvertently brushed himself with the same tar that had splattered Todd Hey six months earlier.

Berger, who clearly was not thinking of such matters, had extended the invitation in a spirit of pragmatic bridge-building. He had heard that Rose had wanted to run for mayor himself, and so David had visited him to share his plans and discover Ben's intentions. Rose had made no commitment one way or the other at the time, but shortly afterward he had told David that he had decided against becoming a candidate. Delighted by this news, Berger had asked him on the spot to become his co-chair. Rose accepted.[5]

Berger's decision to tap Ben Rose as a co-manager was an incomprehensible miscalculation. He had never considered how offensive that choice would be to local Democrats. It sent the message that Berger valued Rose's ability to open doors to Republican power brokers more than any help he might receive from me. I was indignant at Berger's stubborn insistence that he was forging a bipartisan campaign by making Ben Rose one of the principals. Behind the bipartisan rhetoric, the real message was that Republicans would occupy front row seats on the Berger bus and Democrats would be directed to the rear. I had endured condescension from Republicans. I expected better treatment from a fellow Democrat.

Fuming, I admonished Berger: "I wanted to become party chairman because I hoped the party could make a positive difference in our community. Finally, we get a good, visionary Democrat to run for public office, and he wants to the party to lay off. That hurts!"[6] Berger responded that city races in Lima were nonpartisan and that if he hoped to be an effective mayor and encourage coop-eration among the various factions within the city, he would have to hold him-self apart from partisan politics. The best way to accomplish this result, he be-lieved, was for Republicans and Democrats to coalesce behind his campaign. Consequently, he could not be seen as a candidate beholden to one political party or the other.[7]

We talked for forty-five minutes, reiterating our respective positions and talking past one another. When Berger left he was just as adamant about run-ning a so-called bipartisan campaign as he had been when he walked through the door, and I was still seething.

My mood was not helped when I later discovered who had been pushing Berger's candidacy. One of his most prominent mentors was A. D. "Sandy" MacDonell, the president of Met Bank—a Republican, a well-known patron of the arts, and one of key players in Lima's business establishment. MacDonell was generally regarded as the central figure in a growth coalition—bankers, retailers, and developers—that wanted to improve city infrastructure, clear space for new development, and revitalize the community. He saw Berger's design for neighborhood regrowth as part of the mosaic. Although MacDonell's focus was primarily downtown, he worked behind the scenes for Berger, open-ing doors and providing access to monied interests.

However, Wes Runk was Berger's most visible and most enthusiastic advo-cate among the city's business elite. Runk was a stand-out activist in Lima's Rotary Club and owner of CSS Publishing, a vanity press located around the corner from one of Rehab's greatest successes—the renovated Eureka Street neighborhood, where houses had been restored through skills learned and applied by inmates from Ohio's female penitentiary in Marysville.[8] Operating as Berger's campaign coordinator, Runk revered Berger's intellect, once reportedly calling him the most brilliant man he had ever met. More importantly, he admired Berger's ability, demonstrated by the Rehab Project, to make pragmatic contributions to the community. Consequently, he gave him unqualified backing, despite David's Democratic affiliation.

Still, Berger's Democratic ties bothered Runk, Rose, MacDonell, and the other members of the campaign committee, and they had begun pressuring David to put distance between himself and the Democratic Party. Fearing the prospect of a Democratic endorsement of Berger's candidacy, the Republican-dominated group urged him to call me off.[9] My public profile had angered many Republican voters; intervention by the Democrats, reasoned Runk and the others, would drive away Republican volunteers and Republican money. Berger had acceded to their judgment, and the result was that unfortunate meeting of November 30.[10]

To be fair, Berger does not now recall asking me not to take credit for his victory, but it is in my notes, written down within days of our get-together. Clearly, I had perceived that he had made such a statement, and that perception guided my attitude toward his campaign.

January 6, 1989, 8 A.M.

I made the short trek from my apartment on State Street to the Berger residence, where David would formally announce his candidacy. I stepped inside the house, still decorated for Christmas, only to be treated as if I were carrying some horrible disease. Berger and his family welcomed me, but David's Republican chums were decidedly stand-offish. One of them, who didn't notice me standing within earshot, whispered grimly to a pal, "What's Angel doing here?" He glanced toward me when his friend poked him, then looked away, glowering. I stayed for the announcement, congratulated David on his remarks, then left quickly, stalking back to my place, where I felt compelled to take my second bath of the morning.

The principal obstacle to Berger's crusade would not come from the incumbent mayor, Gene Joseph. By late 1988, the mayor's political credibility had totally evaporated. Not only had he feuded with the townships over his administration's "hard water policy," but basic services were not being delivered. Potholes went unrepaired; sidewalks and curbs crumbled. In the fall, leaves piled up in the streets, damming water run-off and forming ponds for cars to navigate. In the winter, snow lay unremoved, turning neighborhood avenues into toboggan runs. Parks were unmowed, decrepit, and unsafe. Crack cocaine—and the gangs that

Lima mayoral candidates socializing at a candidates forum, April 1989. *From left:* Rolland Smith, Harry Moyer, Jerry Winkler, Paul Mullenhour, Mayor Gene Joseph, and David Berger. *Lima News* photo from the collection of the Allen County Historical Society.

marketed it—had invaded the city in the mid-1980s. Meanwhile the police force remained understaffed, powerless to deal with a crime rate that had catapulted 19 percent in 1988 alone.[11] Additionally, Joseph's administration had signed extravagant contracts with the city's firefighters and the other city unions, apparently hoping to buy their favor.[12] But no support coming from city workers would be enough to save the mayor. Gene Joseph was a lame duck, and opposition candidates, like a flock of turkey vultures, were circling.

In addition to Berger, four candidates had lined up to oppose Joseph, but only one of them was contender. The "pretenders" were Rollie Smith and Paul Mullenhour, both Republicans, and Democrat Jerry Winkler, a former City Council president whose last political foray had been a failed run for county commissioner in 1978. None of these guys stood a chance.

The genuine challenge would come from Lima's former mayor, Harry Moyer, who had lost to Joseph in 1985 by only four votes. Moyer had served three terms before that debacle, in which he had taken his victory for granted, thinking that the people of Lima would never be so foolish as to elect Gene Joseph. But they had. Hubris had gotten Harry Moyer that time, and he was not going to let it get him again. With three mayoral campaigns under his belt, Moyer had forged an electoral machine that could canvass precincts, erect yard signs, and mobilize voters with unparalleled ease. His machine had made its energy available to

Furl Williams in 1979, 1983, and 1987, helping Furl win three successive terms as city council president. Now it was ready to roll once again, geared up and well oiled for Harry's comeback. It would be his last hurrah.

Harry Moyer looked like a mayor. Although seventy-one years old, he did not appear a day over sixty. Tall, trim, handsome, sporting a healthy shock of silver hair combed straight back, Moyer had a pleasant grin and an easy banter. He liked people, looked voters straight in the eye when he talked with them, and possessed an uncanny ability to remember names and find appropriately personal bits of information to work into conversation, just to convince voters he really was their friend. As mayor, he had successfully initiated downtown redevelopment, his most notable achievement being the Veterans Memorial Civic Center, which had opened in 1984. During his last term, however, Moyer had begun feuding with a conservative faction on city council, spearheaded by Gene Joseph, then the Seventh Ward's representative, and he had failed to win support for other projects that could have enhanced the Civic Center's effectiveness, most notably a downtown hotel and parking garage.

Sandy MacDonell and the city's growth coalition had backed Harry's efforts in those days, but that was then. Moyer's time had passed. In this race they were supporting Dave Berger, and it was serious, high-stakes politics. There were risks in losing. Despite Harry Moyer's outwardly genial manner, he was a remarkably thin-skinned politician who bore grudges against people to whom he had been loyal and who later spurned his loyalty. If Moyer were to defeat Berger, it would be hard for the downtown boys to reestablish a working relationship with a potentially hostile Moyer administration. So Berger had to win, and in their view, the most viable route to victory required minimizing the candidate's contact with the Democratic Party.

Today, in telling this story, I understand why Berger took the course he did. It was in his political self-interest to keep us Dems at a distance. But during the winter of 1989, watching the candidates line up and listening to Berger tout his message of "bringing together every segment of the city,"[13] I stewed. I was chafing under Berger's righteous claim that city elections were nonpartisan. I'd show him "nonpartisan." I began publicly searching for a Democrat to oppose First Ward councilman Gene Anspaugh, a Republican.[14] Announcing the party's intention to the *Lima News*, I declared, "The nonpartisan nature of the [city] charter works against the Democratic Party."[15]

My stance was sternly rebuked. I was defying tradition. Anspaugh deemed it "very inappropriate for the Democratic Party to get involved in a nonpartisan race."[16] Mayor Joseph disapproved. So did my counterpart Bob Holmes, warning that if the Democrats became active in city politics, the Republican

Party would also.[17] It turned out, in fact, to be an unwise, ill-fated skirmish. Anspaugh did end up with an opponent, but it was a fellow Republican, John Nixon—and the Democratic Party was unable to recruit a candidate. I accomplished nothing. My proclamation on the First Ward race—the result of my sulking over the Berger campaign—had pushed the party into taking a position that proved embarrassing.

I continued to brood as I watched close Democratic friends, both mine and Berger's, drift to the Berger cause. Howard Elstro, for one, was closely involved. He and Berger had been fellow seminarians, and when Berger took over Rehab, he had hired Elstro to be his second in command. They were also close friends, and to a great degree Elstro's zany humor and earthy spirit lightened Berger's ordinarily serious personality. Pickle Felter, likewise, began working hard for Berger. That was no surprise. For years, Berger, Elstro, and Felter had organized the annual "Derby Day," a springtime festival in which a cross-section of Democrats, Rehab supporters, and west-end Catholics gathered to grill hamburgers ("ponyburgers") and hot dogs, bet in a Kentucky Derby pool, swill soda and beer, and dance until early the next morning. Other Democrats jumped on the Berger bandwagon, as well—the Heveners, Bev McCoy, Frank and Jean Winegardner, Rochelle Twining, John Dornick, Roger Rankin and his wife Leslie Rigali—though they all knew my fundamental objections to Berger's candidacy.

From my perspective as party chairman, Dave Berger was doing harm to Democrats. He had told me that he didn't want our organization to participate in his campaign or share in any victory he might achieve, but he was more than willing to poach the party's social capital to help him achieve that victory. In the meantime, he was captive to a Republican-dominated committee, listening to and accepting advice from Ben Rose and Wes Runk while ignoring Democratic activists—Rochelle Twining, for instance—who tried to crack Berger's inner circle and provide leadership to a campaign that at times seemed clueless.

In late March, for example, Berger staged a "beach party," a fund-raiser in the Lima Civic Center, complete with a dance band and refreshments. Charging only twenty dollars per ticket, the campaign had not coordinated any follow-up on ticket sales. Consequently, fewer than a hundred people attended, hardly enough to cover the overhead expenses. The financial debacle could have been avoided had Wes Runk and the boys listened to Rochelle Twining, who had warned them of the impending calamity.[18]

Then, there was the goofy, gentrified quality of Berger's campaign. His organization established a Hollywood connection through a film company called Mayfield Productions, which had been talking with the Rehab board for over two years about doing a show on the agency's work. Tony Dow, who had played

Wally in the old *Leave It to Beaver* series, was a principal investor in Mayfield; so was his wife, Lauren, who had visited Lima twice to confer with the agency. Although the program had never appeared, this personal connection brought the Dows to the Berger campaign. Mr. Dow and Barbara Billingsley, better known as June Cleaver in the series, both endorsed David in a television spot that included the *Leave It to Beaver* theme and ended with the tag, "Leave it to Berger!"[19] This ill-advised testimonial ad caused a number of eyebrows to pop, as voters and candidates alike wondered how Berger could afford to hire "movie stars" to cut commercials for him.[20]

The heart of my objection to Berger's campaign, however, lay in words Mayor Joseph used on the day he announced his own candidacy. Trenchantly characterizing David Berger as a candidate of "the power structure," the mayor pronounced that the Joseph campaign would represent everybody, "not just a few rich and famous individuals."[21] Jerry Winkler, another candidate, followed up Joseph's criticism of Berger's campaign, sneering, "There is always a controlled candidate supported by unlimited funds and campaign help."[22]

Wounded, Berger touchily reasserted his intention to run "a broad-based campaign drawing on every segment of the community" and lamely referred to his "bipartisan campaign committee" as evidence of that intent.[23] This defense would not wash. Berger took out two loans that spring from Huntington Bank, one for $4,000 and another for $4,500, to finance campaign expenses.[24] In mid-April, Berger's fellow candidates and the local media received documentation regarding "an extensive line of credit with a local bank." Berger tried to deflect accusations that he was receiving financial favors from the city's economic elite, asking rhetorically, "If the campaign were as well-funded as critics say, why would it need a loan?"[25] The fact remained that he had been able to secure a loan; I knew well the difficulty of prying capital from a bank to fund a political campaign. Local banks had refused credit to the Democrats in 1986, when we had had a reliable source of income in the license bureaus. Now, through Sandy MacDonell's pull, Berger had wangled a loan tied to pledges from the business community. That's the way it looked.[26] The power-structure charges made sense.

I continued to condemn Berger to anyone who would listen. On several occasions, Rochelle Twining—an avid Berger supporter—took issue with my attitude, She said she had difficulty understanding my anti-Berger stance. In her view, it was "an ego thing," that Berger had challenged my manhood and that I resented him for it. "No," I declared, "it's his continuous failure to keep in touch with the party, to bring good folks like you into the center of his campaign. It's his acceptance of Ben Rose's advice and the rejection of Democrats who know how to run a campaign. It's his creation of a Yuppie, west-side Republican coalition. All these things bug me."

Twining listened quietly to my peroration, and by the time I had wound down, she was a bit more sympathetic to my stance, though still perplexed. "Look," I said, making what amounted to a peace offering, "I don't care where my friends in the party stand. If they choose to side with Berger, fine. I'll bear them no ill will, but I do hope they offer me the same consideration."[27]

Neither Rochelle nor most party hands were fully aware of the depths of my hostility to Berger's campaign. I was so bitter that I dallied in erratic behavior that could have brought real harm to the party. I had been spending a lot of time at Murphy's, an Irish-style pub directly across from the courthouse, drinking stout, listening to live music, and meeting local politicians who drifted through. It was a "clean, well-lighted place," and I enjoyed my evenings there.[28] One night during spring break, I was perched on bar stool, drinking a beer and sharing political gossip with Mike Bender. An attractive woman, twenty-something, petite with auburn hair and large brown eyes, walked by us and sat on the stool next to Bender, who recognized her and asked, "Kim, do you know Bill Angel?"

With that I was introduced to Kim Shearn, secretary to Mayor Joseph.[29] Bender left shortly after the introductions, and I took over his stool and began swapping conversation and beers with Kim. She was pretty—a former cheerleader, I later discovered—and I had been a bachelor for over three years, devoting myself almost completely to politics. I was intrigued by her presence and what appeared to be her genuine interest in me. As our conversation shifted to the mayor's race, she began assuring me that Gene Joseph was a "wonderful guy" who really understood the people of Lima, that he had done a terrific job in his first term, and that he deserved a second one. When I let down my guard— too much beer will do that—and let slip my frustrations about Dave Berger, she pressed her case, coaxing me to come over to Gene's side and support him.

I finally relented, blurting, "I'll say this: If the election were held today, I'd vote for Gene." Even considering my deep resentment of Berger, that was indeed a bizarre admission. Joseph was a Republican, and aside from the sweetheart contracts with public employees' unions, he had done nothing even remotely consistent with my party's philosophy. Shearn forged ahead, having received what must have sounded like a breakthrough commitment, and tried to coax me into going public. Regathering my wits, I told her that I could not do that—the party had decided to stay out of the mayor's race.[30] I was not issuing any endorsements, certainly not from a bar stool at Murphy's.

Then things got steamy. We began openly flirting with each other, sharing kisses in full view of the patrons of the bar. She gave me her phone number. We walked out together but went home separately.

I called Kim the next day and arranged a dinner date. We had a good time—dinner, dancing, good conversation, a little more drinking—but nothing more than that. I did end up working a stint at Joseph's campaign office in the Yocum Building, which housed John Mongelluzzo's office, stuffing envelopes for the mayor. My backing of Gene Joseph extended little farther,[31] and while Shearn and I continued to be friends, we never dated again. The idea of the chairman of the Democratic Party dating the secretary of Mayor Joseph was volatile. We both knew that and backed off.

It had been a close call, one that could have severed ties between me and my Democratic supporters. By late April, my mood began to thaw, and I started to see Berger in a different light. Rochelle Twining, who had been working on me for over three months, reminded me that Berger had always been a Democrat and argued that he would continue to be a Democrat.[32] "He is one of us," I recall her saying. Howard Elstro, who feared permanent harm to both our friendship and the party, expressed regret at the way Berger had treated me but asked me to "rise above it."[33] I even sat down with Ed Finn and Bob Gehr of the UAW, who weren't at all bothered by the Republican tenor of Berger's campaign. In their view, he was the candidate most interested in job creation and capable of delivering on his commitments.[34]

But it was Berger himself who turned me around. At the League of Women Voters Candidates Forum—the most highly publicized and most closely watched of all the mayoral forums—the candidates were asked this question: "How do you plan to be more responsive to the minority community so that their involvement will be a more integral part of community life?" Berger's opponents largely disdained the question and turned their answers into attacks on minority hiring. "I won't beg anyone, minority or not, to work with the city," blathered Jerry Winkler. Rollie Smith stuck to a position he had articulated a week earlier, that people should be hired on the basis of civil service qualifications, not race. Mullenhour echoed this view. Moyer condescendingly declared that he would offer educational services to instruct minorities on how to apply for jobs with the city. Joseph shrugged in denial: "Things are fine as they are," he said.[35]

Berger stood up to the field. Bringing himself to his full height and speaking with an emotion I seldom heard from him—his normal delivery style was dryly professorial—he bristled, "This community has never faced up to the issue of race, and we've got to consider it." He lambasted the Joseph and Moyer administrations for neglecting racial issues, for ignoring black neighborhoods, and for excluding African Americans from participation in city politics.[36] I was moved. Berger had not only courageously challenged his opponents but had faced them down, speaking from the heart—a heart that understood and communicated clearly what it meant to be a Democrat. He had espoused the idea that individual achievement is the product of a strong, caring community that allows all citizens an opportunity to participate, regardless of gender, race, religion, or family background. This concept had been invoked by every Democratic presidential campaign since Franklin Delano Roosevelt, and that night in April 1989 I heard it from David Berger. Yes, he was one of us.

I congratulated Berger for his statement and later took an additional and very important step: I apologized. On the next to last weekend before the primary, I encountered Berger at the "Debutantes for Christ Cotillion," sponsored by the Shiloh Missionary Baptist Church.[37] I was circulating through the house shaking hands and greeting church members—the Shiloh Church had become familiar turf—when I spotted Berger sitting at a table with several of his supporters. There was an empty chair next to him, and I sat down. "I'm sorry," I began, "for anything that I've personally said or done to hurt your campaign. I was embittered by some things Republican members of your committee had said about me and the way they had treated the party. I took things a bit too personally."[38]

Berger was taken aback by my declaration. In his view, I had done nothing to apologize for.[39] "I appreciate that," he replied, reiterating once again that he thought creating a "bipartisan" coalition was the right thing to do.[40] Berger apparently still didn't understand my frustration with his campaign, but he managed to call Howard Elstro the next day, expressing surprised pleasure at my remarks.

David Berger placed first in the primary, collecting one-third of the vote and pulling four hundred votes more than Harry Moyer, the runner-up. The rest of the field trailed—including incumbent Mayor Joseph, who finished fourth, nearly two thousand votes off the lead.[41]

When I had offered my apology at the "Debs for Christ" cotillion, I was "in neutral mode," still weighing my options but leaning toward Berger.[42] Finally, I had gulped hard and voted for him, reporting my action and change of heart to the May meeting of the Executive Committee. Party secretary Elsie Crowe, a strong backer of the Berger campaign, was especially pleased by this announcement. She momentarily paused in her note taking as I issued my "personal reflections on the mayor's race" and smiled glowingly.[43]

With Harry Moyer confirmed as his opponent in the general election, David Berger would desperately need his Republican allies, who now covered the op-ed pages of the *Lima News* with erudite letters extolling the virtues of David's candidacy. Still, the critical element was money. Over thirty-six thousand dollars ultimately ended up in Berger coffers, much of it supplied by the Republican benefactors whom I had scorned so bitterly during the primary season. According to published reports, 461 donors fed the campaign, with twenty-one Allen County residents supplying $10,370 in donations of two hundred dollars or more. Two-thirds of this "Group of 21" were Republicans or Republican-leaning independents.[44] No Democratic campaign in Allen County had ever been able to amass a campaign treasury of the size David Berger assembled in 1989. By comparison, the Moyer campaign accumulated $15,697, a hefty sum but less than half the amount Berger raised.[45]

Harry Moyer, a Republican, tried to counter Berger's financial clout by forging his own bipartisan coalition, this one built on elected Democratic officials, such as Furl Williams. Williams had endorsed Moyer prior to the primary, a move that shocked and dismayed Berger. Furl had been such a staunch supporter of housing reform and so cooperative an ally of Rehab that Berger had fully expected his endorsement. But Williams had turned him down.[46]

Berger should not have been surprised, and it was a mark of his political naivete to think that Furl might endorse anyone but Harry Moyer. At Moyer's urging, Williams had made a risky decision in 1979 to leave a safe seat on city council and run for council president at a time when many local pundits had believed that Lima's voters would never elect a black man to a citywide office. Harry Moyer's own political machine had campaigned relentlessly for Williams, however, and when the last ballot had been counted, Williams had found himself with a fourteen-vote edge over opposition candidate Gene Joseph, then a city councilman. Reelection by larger margins had followed in 1983 and 1987, and each time Moyer had directed his political operatives to assist Furl's campaign. Williams owed his council presidency to Harry Moyer, and now he had to return the favor. It was a matter of loyalty, he told Berger.[47]

In a press conference following the primary, Moyer, a Republican himself, unveiled his bipartisan coalition. Council members Leonard Boddie, Keith Cunningham, Tom Sciranka, and Dorothy Riker, all Democrats, had jumped on board, as had city auditor Harry Vorhees, also a Democrat. All praised Moyer's experience. Moyer "could make things happen in the entire city," Boddie said. Furl Williams agreed, calling Moyer the "right person" to make city government move. Dorothy Riker, who was not present, sent her written endorsement: "When I look for a candidate to support, I have to look at the experience within the city," she pronounced stiffly. "I am not looking for change at this time."[48] By the time this little love fest had concluded, Moyer held a fistful of endorsements, including backing from First Ward councilman Gene Anspaugh (R) and former mayoral candidates Rollie Smith (R), Jerry Winkler (D), and Paul Mullenhour (R). (Mayor Gene Joseph declined to give any endorsement in the mayor's race.) "This a *truly* nonpartisan campaign," Moyer crowed, waving his achievement in Berger's face.[49]

Dave Berger needed help, more help than his Republican compatriots and their money could provide.

A front-page photograph in the *Lima News* on May 3, the day after the primary, showed Berger "consulting" with Wes Runk and Ben Rose regarding the vote tabulations. No Democrat was in sight, except the victorious candidate himself. In the end, however, Berger's own growth as a candidate would hone the edge of his campaign. Berger had started out wanting to run a positive, upbeat campaign, but he learned quickly that politics is a rugged trade, and he forged his own tough style, posing gutsy questions about Moyer's "experience." During the primary campaign, he got under Moyer's skin when he condemned the former mayor for being hostile toward housing, charging that as mayor Harry Moyer had blocked grant applications and put Rehab six years behind in its plans for renovating neighborhoods.[50] Moyer immediately refuted Berger's charges, and he was still grousing a week later, denouncing Berger as a "single-issue" candidate.[51]

Berger had drawn blood, demonstrating how prickly Moyer could be when his record as mayor was challenged. Moyer liked to present himself as the wise leader who had built the Civic Center and renovated the downtown, who had kept corporate employers like Westinghouse and General Dynamics in the community, and who had been tough on criminals and a strong backer of safety services.[52] Berger relentlessly contested all these claims, countering that while Moyer had supported downtown renovation, he had done very little for neighborhoods where ordinary people lived, that he had allowed the police department to fall below its authorized strength, and that he had no vision for maintaining jobs in an economic climate in which international market pressures threatened local financial stability.[53]

Late in the campaign, Berger brought these messages into voters' homes with an ingenious series of newspaper ads—comic strips entitled *Dave and Harry*. The strips, drawn by David Adams, poked fun at Moyer's pronouncements and presented Berger in favorable contrast. For instance, the "Neighborhoods" strip showed a caricature of Harry Moyer pronouncing, "When I was mayor, I demolished hundreds of homes." In the next panel, a balding, middle-

Dave and Harry: Neighborhoods, paid political advertisement for the 1989 Berger mayoral campaign. Cartoon by David S. Adams; used with permission of David S. Adams and David Berger (for the Berger campaign committee).

aged homeowner envisioned a steam shovel gnawing at his house. "If Harry keeps this up, we won't have a neighborhood," the man mused. Moyer was a dominant, scowling presence in the series, while Berger was represented by an assortment of talking "critters"—dogs, birds, and cats—who barked, chirped, and purred the virtues of their buddy "Dave."

Dave and Harry burrowed under Moyer's skin, and as election grew closer he looked like a petulant candidate who was about to come unglued. At the League of Women Voters Debate, for example, five days before the election, he openly protested the cartoon strips, huffing, "In twenty years of politics, I have never been as ridiculed or demeaned by an opponent as I have by this one."[54] One of the enduring images of that debate—and of the entire campaign, for that matter—was Harry Moyer shaking his head at one of Berger's charges and clucking, "David, David, David." He meant to produce a sound bite like Ronald Reagan's "There you go again," but it didn't work. It only made Moyer look humorless and tired, a politician whose time had passed.

Indeed. Berger's win was so convincing that the *Lima News* headline blared, "Berger eases to mayoral victory." He had defeated Harry Moyer by 1,800 votes.[55]

I attended the inaugural, where I was acknowledged as an honored guest. Berger had not forgotten that Democrats had participated in his achievement, albeit in the shadows. Harry Moyer had poached flashy endorsements from local Democrats who brought their names and little more, but for Berger the Democratic Party itself had provided organizational muscle and deep commitment.

Unlike 1987, when the party had openly sided with Leonard Boddie and Furl Williams, this time the party's assistance was more oblique, less tangible.

John Dornick led Berger's get-out-the-vote effort that fall, helping him set up a phone bank and installing the "phone board" the party had used in 1988. When Berger needed a pollster, Rochelle Twining suggested Odesky and Associates, who had done polling for the Democrats in 1988. The firm's head, Stan Odesky, would not work for Berger without my approval. I sanctioned the arrangement, which Twining finalized, and Odesky began running polls for Berger's campaign.[56]

"When it came down to it," Rochelle Twining later reflected, "it was the Democrats who did the grunt work in that campaign." Ben Rose, Wes Runk, and Sandy MacDonell may have held forth at meetings, but Tom Doyle, Mary Hevener, Rick Siferd, Pickle Felter, Evelyn Vanek, Roger Rankin, Leslie Rigali, and other Democrats did the bulk of the foot-soldiering, carrying Berger's message into the precincts and working long stints on his phone banks.[57] I walked my precinct for Berger, thanks to a bit of good-natured cajoling from John Dornick, who, having settled into his job as Central Committee chairman, began encouraging precinct representatives in the city to get behind Berger.

We Democrats who backed Berger shared one dominant characteristic: We were "DEP-ers," core members of Democrats for an Effective Party, the organization that had brought change, reform, and new leadership to the Allen County Democratic Party in 1986. We were supporting Berger now because he shared our vision. If he won, we won.

Under our leadership, the party had projected itself as an catalyst for change. We had challenged Democrats to cast off old leadership, and we had convinced the rank and file to keep us in charge when the old guard mounted a counter-revolt. Democratic candidates themselves—from Rochelle Twining, who presented herself as "not one of the boys," to Ida Kay Keller, Ed Schwieterman, Dale Leppla, and Paul Rizor—mirrored the party's more activist identity. They all vocally and vehemently urged the voters to examine critically their Republican ties and vote Democrat for a change. Even Leonard Boddie, who backed Moyer in 1989, had won his council seat by promoting himself as a young leader with fresh ideas.

The call for change had been accompanied by a plucky spirit, as witnessed in my news conferences where I had confronted the local power structure, urging citizens to accept a new vision of community. This quality appeared in my statement on behalf of the nurses' strike at Lima Memorial Hospital, which occurred as the mayoral election was in progress. It was also to be found in a successful campaign that Bob Routson, Dale Leppla, and other Democrats initiated that summer to organize a referendum against a five-dollar surcharge on license-plate fees, which the commissioners imposed in June. Although the Democratic Party was not involved directly in that effort, the dispute was evidence of a feisty atmosphere that had entered county politics through an enlivened group of Democratic activists.[58]

Throughout his campaign, David Berger's rhetoric strongly paralleled the party's own challenge to community. On the night of his victory in the primary, he announced, "Lima is really interested in a change."[59] As Harry Moyer continued to emphasize his own experience and point to Berger's lack of it, David hammered out his message that the city needed a fresh approach if it was to surmount adversity and promote progress. "We need to have a new style of leadership that . . . moves us forward," he stated in an interview with the *Lima News*. He promised to focus as mayor on "long-term benefits rather than short-term problems," and he constantly emphasized that "people who want a change of leadership" were the force behind his coalition.[60] "Change" was the clarion call of the Berger campaign.

David Berger was thirty-four years old when he announced his intention to run for mayor. In a way, he was the kind of "warm body" Vern Riffe would have loved to send against a multiterm incumbent—ballot fodder in a meaningless race. Berger had never managed an election campaign, had never held public office, and was relatively unknown outside a small group of insiders. Somewhat owlish in appearance and not particularly charismatic on the stump, he could trade on neither looks nor persona to secure votes. In fact, he was shy and stand-offish in public gatherings. His professional background was in neither law nor business, two traditional roads to a political career; instead, his expertise lay in running a nonprofit agency that relied considerably on government funding and private grants for survival. Here he was, facing a twenty-year veteran of local politics, someone whose name and face were familiar to even the most casual citizen. When he declared his candidacy, David Berger was not exactly on the fast track for political success. Yet he won.

"Dave wouldn't have become mayor had it not been for the Democrats," once declared my friend and colleague Nancy Wyche, an associate professor of social sciences at Lima Technical College. She was also a longtime observer of local politics, as well as a friend of David Berger's wife Linda. I was surprised by Wyche's observation, offered when I expressed my frustration at the story of a party that had never won an election.

"What about Dave Berger?" Nancy replied. She then proceeded to lay out what I now call the "Wyche thesis." Her interpretation does not imply that I or the Democrats caused Dave Berger's election. Other forces—Republican backing, David's skills as a campaigner, the message of his campaign, the bipartisan strategy—all exerted a far more direct impact on Berger's success. Rather, her thesis holds that the Democrats under my leadership had caused the political culture in Allen County to shift in such a way that Berger's election became possible. The party's new leaders had, in effect, nudged the community in a progressive direction and made voters receptive to a candidate calling for change.[61]

David Berger identified with this dynamic, and we, the core leaders in the Democratic Party, identified with him. He had made no secret of his Democratic ties, and he had been cordially supportive of my leadership, despite our spat during the winter of my discontent. The DEP coalition, as Howard Elstro later pointed out, "brought a new wave of Democrats who hadn't been involved in politics because they couldn't break in."[62] Berger was part of that wave, and when he laced his Democratic boots with Republican money, a synergy developed that made his campaign hard to beat. The altered political culture was an important element in that synergy, and had it evaporated or never developed, Berger would have had no chance. Harry Moyer, campaigning with an armload of endorsements from old-school politicians, would have pummeled him in that 1989 election.

I ran this interpretation by Dave Berger himself, by that time in his third term as mayor of Lima. Although he questioned whether data were available to support the idea, he gave it serious thought, and then admitted that it made sense. "When you were the chairman," he observed, "you stimulated a fair amount of controversy, which the Republicans didn't like, and spaded the earth, breaking ground on why new leadership matters."[63]

The Wyche thesis lays claim to the principal point of this book: the value of parties transcends their impact on elections. In ways that cannot easily be measured, local parties engage their communities in dialogue, raise issues, and focus citizen attention on matters that need to be discussed. In other words, they challenge voters to take responsibility for their government.

Importantly, they are keepers of values and represent those values in public discourse. Why did I ultimately support David Berger despite my resentment of his uncharitable treatment of the Democratic Party? It was not because I sensed he was going to win. Far from it. The connection between us—between him and the party I represented—was so strong that deserting him and supporting some other candidate would have meant betraying the values I had been fighting to preserve and energize in Allen County.

Berger was true to the faith. He increased minority hiring, especially in the city's fire and police departments, and he signaled a new trend in city employment generally by appointing an African American budget director. Working with church groups, Berger helped to organize "study circles" among black and white congregations, building bridges of understanding between the city's neighborhoods. Under Berger's administration, the police force grew, and the city began a more concerted effort to combat the drug and gang epidemic that had infested it. The city finally constructed the parking garage and downtown hotel that had never passed the blueprint stage under Harry Moyer, but Berger also showered attention on residential neighborhoods, enforcing the housing code, refurbishing streets, renovating housing, and upgrading parks. Perhaps his most important achievement was preserving the jobs endangered by British Petroleum's decision to close down its refinery in Lima. Berger doggedly pursued back channels to the oil industry, trying to find a purchaser for the refinery and finally persuading Clark Oil to buy the facility.[64]

David Berger has never seen himself a political boss who could inspire voters and officeholders to march to the beat of a Democratic drum. Although he has recognized the general weakness of the Democrats in Allen County and the inability of a two-party system to function effectively there, he also has acknowledged that he is not the one to fix that problem. "I couldn't succeed at the polls doing that," he told me, "and I couldn't succeed on the job doing that.

"It's the job of others."[65]

· Epilogue ·
Not All Politics Is Local

September 1992

Though still serving on the Board of Elections, I was long gone as party chair. So was Rochelle Twining, my successor, who had resigned on election day 1991 to accept a civil service job with the Ohio attorney general, Lee Fisher. One month later, the Executive Committee tapped Dick Meredith to take the helm. But Meredith came on board too late to lead a candidate-recruitment drive, and the party was bereft of nominees to run for any local office, much to the chagrin of some local Democrats.[1]

Facing two leadership changes in less than eight months, our organization was stressed and disoriented, and county residents had only one local contest, the race for county sheriff.[2] Charlie Harrod, the Republican incumbent, was running for his fifth term. He was a gregarious, hardscrabble politician who took tremendous pride in the fact that he had worked his way up through the ranks in the sheriff's department, joining as a deputy in 1968 and finally winning the head job in 1976. Harrod had a reputation for hard living, but when opponents questioned his moral character, the sheriff cast himself as a victim, blaming all allegations on "mud slinging."

That was how he responded in 1984. Ted Wade, his Democratic challenger that year, somehow had gained possession of a Lima city police report from January 1981 in which Harrod was described as creating a disturbance in "an extreme state of intoxication" at an apartment complex on Lima's west side. One of Wade's supporters leaked the report to the press, giving Wade the chance to make an issue of Harrod's reputation for hard drinking and womanizing. (Allegedly a girlfriend was involved in the 1981 incident.) "It's shocking," Wade declared during the campaign's final week. "It's not leadership by example." A perplexed Harrod tossed off the charges. So did the voters, who handed him a runaway victory.[3]

Bill Angel presiding at the Allen County Democratic Party's fall fund-raiser, October 1989. From the collection of Malcolm and Beverly McCoy, photograph by Beverly McCoy.

It was Harrod's lackadaisical approach to law enforcement—not his moral character—that bothered police professionals. In 1987 at a Democratic fund-raiser in Shelby County, Sheriff John Lenhart approached me to plead that I find a candidate to run "against that sheriff up there in Allen County." Lenhart had grown frustrated, running investigations on drug trafficking and prostitution rings, only to see the trail go cold at the Allen County line. Ted Wade himself had hinted at such problems in his 1984 campaign.[4] By 1992, the crime situation in Allen County had worsened, especially an escalating drug epidemic, which Harrod curiously shrugged off as a problem "we're [not] going to conquer overnight."[5]

Charlie Harrod, who had not run in a contested election in eight years, ended up facing two consecutive opponents in 1992. First, he had to get past Joe Bowsher in the Republican primary. Bowsher was a retired lieutenant from the Lima City Police Department, a twenty-five-year veteran of the force taking the unusual step of challenging a four-term incumbent from his own party. The fact that intraparty opposition had surfaced, especially in the person of a well-respected police officer, itself signaled doubt in Harrod's ability to do the job, and Bowsher said as much during the campaign. "My race for sheriff is the result of frustration with the lack of leadership in that agency," he declared.[6]

Bowsher assembled a strong coalition of independent voters and progressive-minded Republicans; he even induced Democrats to cross party lines and vote in the Republican primary. The result was a tremendous turnout that saw almost seventeen thousand voters taking GOP ballots—five thousand more than usual. Bowsher threw a real scare into the Republican organization, which put on a last-ditch push during the campaign's final weekend, enough to ensure Harrod's survival by a little over 150 votes, or 50.4 percent of the total.[7] Bob Holmes's machine had pulled Harrod through—barely.

With Bowsher turned aside, Dan Beck entered the ring. He had filed petitions to run as an independent candidate, and in June the Allen County Board of Elections certified his candidacy. He had been a Republican,[8] a fairly conservative one, with twenty-one years' experience in law enforcement—sixteen with the Fort Shawnee Police Department in Allen County, where he had also served as deputy chief. Beck had begun organizing his candidacy more than a year earlier, showing up in venues where his voice mattered—water policy hearings, meetings on environmental permits, sessions of the regional transportation authority, and so forth—getting to know the community. Now he had an excellent opportunity to build on Republican disaffection with Sheriff Harrod, to combine that disaffection with backing from independent voters and Democrats, and to win in November.

In early September, questions surfaced about Beck's credentials—specifically, whether he had accumulated the requisite supervisory experience in the Fort Shawnee department.[9] Sam Crish raised "a formal objection" to Beck's candidacy, submitting a written protest to the Board of Elections. Crish was at it again. Five years earlier, he had started the informal inquiry into petitions circulated against the piggyback sales tax. Now, he was a lieutenant in the sheriff's department, as well as treasurer for Charlie Harrod's campaign—but his affiliation with Harrod had nothing to do with his action, or so he protested. "[I'm] acting only as a resident of the county and a registered voter," he claimed.[10]

Paul Schulien, deputy director of the Board of Elections and an operative in Republican organization, took Crish's letter directly to the county prosecutor, David Bowers, and not to the Board of Elections, as protocol required. This was a political move that alerted Bowers to the case. Upon finally receiving Crish's letter, the board declared that it had already reviewed Beck's credentials, as affirmed by Judge Michael Rumer, and it instructed Schulien to request that the prosecutor drop the matter.[11]

But it was not dropped. The board chair was Charles Rossfeld, a jovial but pliant Republican loyalist who had succeeded to the post when Bob Holmes resigned to become clerk of Municipal Court. Four days after the Board of Elections decided to dismiss the Crish protest, Rossfeld reversed course and insisted that because a protest had been filed, the Board of Elections had to reconsider Beck's qualifications to run for sheriff. According to Rossfeld, the board needed "to discuss the matter openly and maintain its credibility with the voters." He set a special hearing for September 17 and subpoenaed Beck's personnel records as well as testimony from Judge Rumer and the Fort Shawnee police chief, Gene Sharp.[12]

A dark undercurrent was at work, but I had other plans. Working with fellow board member Bev McCoy and several Democratic lawyers—including Mike Bender, Rick Siferd, and Dick Meredith—I prepared a written motion, filled with series of "whereases" that justified the action I wanted the board to take. The motion chronicled the Board of Election's own evaluation of Beck's candidacy and cited appropriate sections in Ohio Revised Code regarding the board's responsibilities for evaluating protests and assessing the qualifications of candidates, but its essence was this: The Allen County Board of Elections had no authority to hold a hearing in response to Sam Crish's protest, because the protest had been filed too late. In other words, I wanted the hearing to be canceled.[13]

On the morning of the inquiry, I briefed my fellow board members on the motion, and I pointedly told Rossfeld and "Peg" Moles (the other Republican member): "Everyone knows why this hearing has been called; Republicans want to see Dan Beck's candidacy disappear." Of course, Rossfeld and Moles objected to this interpretation, insisting that the board wanted only to verify Beck's qualifications, but they could not budge Bev McCoy or me from our belief that the hearing's subtextual purpose was to throw Beck off the ballot, paving the way for Charlie Harrod to win a fifth term.

That exchange occurred in-house, but the hearing itself was staged in the open, in a room filled with witnesses ready to testify, along with a cortege of principals and interested bystanders—including Dan Beck, Bob Holmes, Sam Crish, and a bevy of Beck supporters. County prosecutor Bowers was set to lead the inquiry, but before he had a chance to start I introduced my motion, which McCoy seconded. The board debated for forty-five minutes and settled nothing, splitting two to two on the motion.

Our positions were clear. Republicans Rossfeld and Moles opposed the motion, firm in their belief that the board had the right to hold the hearing. They saw the board as fulfilling a gate-keeper role in which it monitored the electoral lists, closing them to unqualified contenders. That was beside the point, McCoy and I countered: While the board did have gate-keeper responsibilities, they were not unlimited. "Deadlines are there to allow elections to take place," I said. Once the deadlines are past, the people must decide whether a candidate is qualified. The hearing adjourned while Rossfeld, Moles, McCoy and I voted several more times, trying to break the impasse, but neither side would give ground.[14]

At that point, each faction sent letters to Secretary of State Bob Taft summarizing its arguments, and we waited. Less than a week later, Taft settled the dispute, siding with McCoy and me: he "could find no statutory or case law authority which would allow a board of Elections to entertain a protest past the statutory deadline."[15]

Taft's decision did not end the matter. The day after that ruling, Judge Michael Rumer ordered a grand jury to investigate whether Beck had "falsified" his application. David Bowers, in turn, requested the appointment of two special prosecutors, Mark Spees of Auglaize County and Daniel Gerschutz of Putnam County, to conduct the inquiry.[16] Grand jury. Special prosecutors. This was no ordinary probe into Beck's qualifications or a simple effort to deny him access to the ballot. Dan Beck was facing possible criminal indictment.

Even the normally easygoing Dick Meredith was alarmed. Although Meredith normally preferred to exercise low-key leadership, he did not hesitate to challenge this new attack on Beck's candidacy. "There appears to be a decided effort to prevent the voters from being the ones to decide who shall serve this county as sheriff," he charged, expressing concern that the grand jury investigation could undermine "the integrity of the election process."[17] For his part, Bob Holmes denied any Republican responsibility for the grand jury move. "We are not involved in that, one iota," Holmes claimed several times in response to criticism that his party was pushing the process. "Going to the grand jury was strictly the judge's decision."[18]

Not many people bought this line, least of all Beck's supporters, who saw Republican intrigue, an attempt to tear down their man's candidacy. Condemning the latest challenge as "bovine excrement," Beck's campaign manager John Brentlinger roared, "These guys are trying awful hard to make sure the sheriff has no opposition."[19] Others agreed. At a public rally on the morning of the grand jury session, John Murray, a Beck volunteer and a Republican from Elida, called it "dirty politics," singling out Bob Holmes for particular vilification. "I think it's partly Holmes and the whole Republican party," Murray alleged. "They don't want new blood in there, new ideas." Another Beck supporter—fifteen-year-old Trisha McKinney, a sophomore at Elida High School—was so angry that she skipped her morning classes to show solidarity with Beck. "All the Republicans are making him out to be a bad person," she declared. "They don't want him elected, but he's the best person for the job."[20]

As Dan Beck entered the Allen County courthouse to testify to the grand jury, he paused to greet a rally of over seventy supporters near the front steps. "Mama said there'd be days like this," he quipped.[21] He didn't need to worry. The grand jury cleared him, deciding neither to issue an indictment nor to challenge his right to be a candidate. The only public statement came from Special Prosecutor Spees, who said simply, "There was no probable cause to believe he [Beck] committed any criminal offense."[22] Beck would remain on the ballot, and there would be no further challenges to his qualifications, except those raised in the campaign itself.

That inquiry could have damaged if not destroyed Dan Beck's candidacy, but instead it provoked an outcry that transcended the sheriff's election, supplying a towering platform from which Beck's defenders could condemn "old guard Republicans" and decry the perils of one-party government. Charlie Haskins—a Democrat from Spencerville, a friend of Ida Kay Keller, and a Beck supporter—charged, "It's the same old stuff. They [the Republicans] not only don't want a two-party system, they don't want a one-party system unless they can name the candidate."[23]

Haskins's cry was an echo. During my chairmanship, I had warned voters about the danger of one-party government; so had our candidates. Now, the "matter of Dan Beck" had brought our concerns sharply into focus. The hegemony of the Republican Party had become so strong and the camaraderie among its various players—Crish, Schulien, Bowers, Rumer, Rossfeld, Holmes, and the rest—so compelling that the Beck case was pushed forward in reaction. The lines of power between the Allen County Republican Party and county officials—between partisanship and public authority—had blurred to the point that it was hard to determine where party activity stopped and governmental process began.

The Allen County Republican Party had become a victim of its own dominance—and its own history. During the previous six years, county voters had seen Republican commissioners impose tax increases in election off-years. They had seen Republican county officials quash a legitimate attempt to referend a tax increase. They had seen the prosecutor, sheriff, and auditor, all Republicans, dispatch deputies to question petition signers. They had seen the head of the Republican Party wangle his own appointment to one of the most lucrative electoral billets in the county. Now, in the grand jury proceedings against Dan Beck, they saw "the same old stuff." However much Bob Holmes might swear that his party was not involved in the Beck inquiry, no one, except the most myopic Republican, could have found such an argument credible.[24]

People do get the kind of government they deserve. One month after the grand jury probe, over forty-three thousand Allen County citizens cast votes in the sheriff's race. The sheriff's election and the controversy surrounding it had inspired a remarkable public dialogue regarding the quality of local political life. In the end, the voters determined that Dan Beck was qualified to be their sheriff; they gave him 57 percent of their ballots and a six-thousand-vote victory over Charlie Harrod, who became the first GOP candidate in sixteen years to lose a county election.[25] Though not shattered, the Republican lock on the courthouse door could be seen dangling on the latch.

December 1992

John Hevener lived just long enough to see Charlie Harrod lose and Bill Clinton win. John's cancer had returned, and by autumn, housebound and under hospice care, he knew he was dying. I went to see him a few days before Christmas, and as I sipped coffee in his living room—the very place where he and Mary and I had once laid plans to take over the Democratic Party—we chatted about the election, especially Clinton's victory, and rehashed old times. Months earlier I had sent him some preliminary chapters for this book—ones that I later abandoned because they were too pessimistic, too petulant. He gently handed the manuscript back, still in its manila envelope, apparently unread, apologizing for not being able to work his way through it. But John may have read farther than he was willing to admit. Encouraging me not to worry about the party's electoral failures, he reminisced about why we had needed to move Charlie Hauenstein aside. "It was worth it," he declared.

John Hevener died five days after Bill Clinton was inaugurated president of the United States. Mary had forgotten to line up pallbearers—too many details to arrange—and following the service, the funeral director began seeking volunteers to move John's casket to the hearse, all set to carry him to Pocohantas County, West Virginia for burial in the family plot. Tom Doyle, Howard Elstro, Pickle Felter, and I stepped forward, grasped the rails of the casket, and together we lifted John up over the church steps, toward home.

Why does anyone, Republican or Democrat, devote to partisan politics the kind of energy I have described in this book? Why did we do it? Perhaps the answer lies in one final story, in the events surrounding our 1987 fall dinner, back in the days when we called it an "ox roast."[26] The party had lined up Senator Howard Metzenbaum as the guest speaker; with presold tickets and walk-ups combined, we were aiming to top the previous year's attendance of 550, quite an achievement for an off year. Furthermore, Rochelle Twining had organized a special reception for the senator, extending special invitations to union activists in an attempt to shore up the party's relationship with organized labor.

At 9:30 on the morning of the event, George Dunster, news director at WLIO TV, called with information that threatened to dash these plans. "What do you know about Metzenbaum going to the hospital with chest pains?" Dumbstruck, I could only manage to say, "George, I haven't heard anything about that."

"Well, as soon as you hear, let me know what you're going to do with the ox roast."

"We'll not cancel," I replied.

As I began to digest this information and ponder its validity, Paul Smith from the newspaper phoned, wanting to know what I'd heard about Metzenbaum. In fact, I'd heard nothing, not a word from the senator or his office. Finally, I got in touch with Sherry Sweitzer, his scheduler in Washington, D.C., who told me that Metzenbaum had indeed gotten sick—"flulike symptoms"—and was returning to the capital. In the meantime, she promised, an aide from the senator's office in Columbus would help us find a replacement speaker. Later that morning, Metzenbaum himself called me, sounding healthy and sincerely apologetic. "I'll be there next year, Bill. You can count on it," he said—making a promise that we held him to.

I did not wait for Metzenbaum's man in Columbus to help us but went directly to Jim Ruvulo, who helped resolve the crisis. Within a half-hour I was speaking with the state treasurer, Mary Ellen Withrow, who called me at Ruvulo's request and agreed to attend our dinner and pitch her "link deposit" investment policy.

Seven hundred Democrats showed up to hear Mary Ellen Withrow talk about link deposits.[27] It was not a scintillating speech, but that didn't matter. As the celebration was about to end, I reminded the crowd: "Yes, Howard Metzenbaum couldn't make it here tonight, but you did. . . . You did." That's what counted.

Local activists do count, a point that politicians in the larger arena sometimes forget. In our activism, we prod ourselves and others into becoming members of the civic community. We may snarl and snap at each other, like quarrelsome teenagers, but in the final analysis, our behavior mirrors our passion: We care about political life and want to connect with leaders—Metzenbaum, for instance—who fight for us in places where the stakes are higher and the publicity more intense.

Seven hundred Allen County Democrats cared enough to show up that night in October 1987. They didn't know if they would hear a guest speaker or not, but they came anyway. A year later, fifty volunteers came out on the Saturday before the presidential election and worked all day in the pouring rain, distributing literature for Michael Dukakis—knowing well that he was going to lose. I'd say they cared. So have the countless volunteers who replaced yard signs the opposition tore down, managed campaigns for crotchety local candidates, staffed phone banks, or dished out potato salad at the party dinners. They were doing their part, connecting their lives with the larger arena of political life.

In 1992 I returned to Democratic headquarters, on another rainy preelection weekend—this time as an ordinary Democrat—to distribute literature for Bill Clinton. Dressed in my "political uniform"—fatigue jacket and a Greek fisherman's cap (which I had owned before I'd even heard of Michael Dukakis)—I was assigned to one of Lima's most Democratic, yet poorest precincts, in the city's south side. Trooping between the row houses, abandoned buildings, burnt-out factories, and carry-outs that dominated the precinct's landscape, dripping wet, I felt like a member of this community—where voters, black and white alike, took my literature, smiled, and responded with something like, "Yeah. We're gonna get 'em this time."

Campaign politics still comes down to the voter, a truth often noted by Tip O'Neill, the late Speaker of the House, who lost his first campaign. Running for city council in Cambridge, Massachusetts, three-quarters of century ago, he didn't campaign among his neighbors—a failure that cost him their support and the election. Afterward, his father pulled O'Neill aside and reminded him, "All politics is local. Don't forget it."[28]

Not all politics is local, but the most important part of it is. When campaigns are stripped of their sound bites and media events, their polls and thirty-second spots, their overpaid gurus and "spin doctors," they still come down to the moment when one voter extends a hand and quietly says, "Friend, we need you on Tuesday."

· Glossary of Characters and Terms ·

Adams, David: Cartoonist; associate professor of sociology (emeritus); Ohio State University at Lima; activist in Democratic Party.

AFSCME: American Federation of State County and Municipal Employees.

Allen County Democratic Women's Club: Club associated with and sanctioned by the Allen County Democratic Party; provided space for Democratic women (and men) to gather and discuss politics; raised money for Democratic campaigns.

Alpine Village Restaurant: Restaurant on Lima's west side; gathering place for Democrats; owned and managed by "Little Joe" Guagenti.

Angel, Bill: Chairman of Allen County Democratic Party, 1986–91.

Beck, Dan: Independent candidate for Allen County sheriff in 1992; reelected in 1996 and 2000, again as an independent.

Bender, Mike: Attorney; DEP activist; member of Democratic Central and Executive Committees.

Berger, David: Executive director of Rehab Project, an organization that rebuilt dilapidated housing in Lima; ran for mayor of Lima in 1989.

Board of Elections: Bipartisan office consisting of two Democrats and two Republicans; charged with supervising elections within each county; clerks and office workers, even temporary workers, must be equally divided between the two parties.

Boddie, Leonard: African American politician, Sixth Ward base; DEP activist; headed the Allen County Democratic Party's minority caucus.

"Body pull": Party volunteers going door to door in targeted precincts on election day, encouraging residents who have not voted to do so. A more aggressive body-pull operation would include driving admitted nonvoters to the polls and making sure that they voted.

Bolden, Helen: Central Committeewoman in Allen County Democratic Party, member of Executive Committee; supported Todd Hey's grassroots campaign in 1988; Jesse Jackson delegate to 1988 Democratic Convention in Atlanta, Georgia.

Bowers, David: Allen County prosecutor, Republican; central figure in the controversy over the piggyback sales tax, 1987.

Brown, Roger: Democratic candidate for Allen County clerk of courts, 1986.

Brown, Sherrod: Ohio secretary of state, Democrat; lost reelection bid in 1990, currently member of Congress, serving Ohio's Eleventh District.

Budget Committee: One of several committees organized under Angel chairmanship; set the budget for the party and authorized spending of funds; chaired by John Dornick.

Campaign Committee: A committee set up during election years to coordinate among various campaigns within the county. Headed by the party chair. Local candidates and their managers meet with party leaders and coordinators of statewide campaigns to set strategy and share information. In Allen County, the meetings were held biweekly during the summer, shifting to a weekly schedule in September and continuing through election day.

Candidate Recruitment Committee: Another committee under Angel chairmanship; spearheaded recruitment of candidates; chaired in Angel's first term by Cora Hamman and later by John Hevener.

CAP (Community Action Program) Council: Coordinates political activities for the UAW within a UAW district. Works with active and retired UAW members to help elect candidates favored by the UAW, also builds public support for issues favored by the union.

Celebreeze, Anthony: Democratic gubernatorial candidate in 1990; Ohio attorney general during the Celeste years.

Celebreeze, Frank: Chief justice of the Ohio Supreme Court, Democrat; lost reelection bid in 1986 to Republican Thomas Moyer.

Celeste, Richard: Governor of Ohio, 1983–91, Democrat.

Central Committee: The official controlling committee for the party organization at both the county and state levels; members are elected in partisan primaries for two-year terms; reorganized every two years; in some counties, reorganization occurs on a four-year cycle; generally delegates responsibility for managing party operations to the Executive Committee.

Coordinated Campaign Committee: Also known as the Campaign Committee (q.v.); operated under both the Hauenstein and Angel chairmanships; active during election years when several partisan candidates were campaigning, including candidates in statewide races; coordinated events and share information, providing a smooth flow to the campaign.

Coplen, John: Former Democratic county commissioner; lost reelection bid in 1980; lost attempt to regain seat in 1984; DEP activist during the formative years (1986 and before); member of Executive Committee; married to Linda Coplen.

Coplen, Linda: President of Allen County Democratic Women's Club; field representative for Secretary of State Sherrod Brown; member of Democratic Central Committee; married to John Coplen.

Coleson, Ray: Allen County clerk of courts, Republican.

Crish, Sam: Administrative assistant to Allen County sheriff Charles Harrod; worked in the civil division; Harrod's main political operative.

Crowe, Elsie: Secretary to Allen County Democratic Party; DEP activist; member of Democratic Central and Executive Committees.

The Democratic Voice of Allen County (or the *Voice*): A publication of the Allen County Democratic Party; published semiannually in a newspaper format, it announced events and supplied political analysis of interest to the county's Democrats.

DEP: Democrats for an Effective Party; political committee organized in 1985 for the purpose of overthrowing Charlie Hauenstein; John Hevener, Bill Angel, and Steve Webb were the principal leaders of this effort; continued to operate as a political committee even after Angel became chairman.

Deputy registrar (DR): Director of a license bureau; responsible for processing drivers' licenses and vehicle registrations; once a patronage appointee of the governor, but in 1988 the office was depoliticized.

Ditto, Richard: Allen County treasurer, Republican; also served as state senator from the Twelfth District and as Allen County auditor.

Doyle, Tom: DEP and social activist; member of Central and Executive Committees; known as "yard sign czar" for his prowess at coordinating sign placement.

Dornick, John: Labor activist; chairman of Democratic Central Committee, 1988 to 1990; DEP activist.

Dumpbusters: Group organized in 1987 by Ida Kay Keller to prevent Waste Management, Inc., from placing a landfill in Spencerville area.

Dunster, George: News director of WLIO TV.

Eley, Vern: Treasurer of Allen County Democratic Party when Charlie Hauenstein chaired the party; old guard activist.

Elstro, Howard: David Berger's deputy at Rehab Project; DEP activist; member of Executive Committee.

Engle, Joe: Ran in Democratic primary for county commissioner in 1988, losing to Dale Leppla.

Executive Committee: Controls party operations at the state and county levels, as delegated by the Central Committee; reorganized every two years; in come counties, reorganization occurs on a four-year cycle; members are appointed: Chair of the Executive Committee is chair of its party.

Falk, Carol: Secretary to Allen County Democratic Party when Charlie Hauenstein chaired the party; later served as secretary during Bill Angel's third term as chair; clerk at Board of Elections.

Felter, Jerry "Pickle": DEP activist; member of Central and Executive Committees; member of Policy Committee.

Field representative: Patronage appointee by state officials (e.g., secretary of state); purpose was twofold—to manage business for the office in various regions of the state and to raise funds, and to serve as a political operative for the state official; political duties were to be kept separate from official functions.

Finn, Ed: UAW activist; former president of the Ford local; international representative for UAW CAP Council (q.v.).

French, H. Dean: Allen County auditor, Republican; central figure in the controversy over the piggyback sales tax, 1987.

Fuqua, Johnnie Mae: Ran in Democratic primary for state senate in 1988, losing to Dale Locker.

Gehr, Bob: UAW activist, president of UAW CAP Council (q.v.).

GOTV: "Get out the vote"; campaign specifically designed to stimulate voter turnout on election day; targets voters who are expected to vote for party's candidates.

Grass Roots Campaign Committee: Political committee which appeared in 1988; purpose was to restore old guard leadership; headed by Todd Hey.

Guagenti, "Little Joe": DEP activist; owner of Alpine Village Restaurant, a meeting place for Democrats until it closed in 1988.

Hamman, Cora: DEP activist; member of Democratic Central and Executive Committees; chaired Candidate Recruitment Committee during Bill Angel's first term as chair; married to Tim Hamman.

Hamman, Tim: Attorney; Democratic candidate for prosecutor in 1980 and for state representative in 1984; party activist; married to Cora Hamman.

Hamman, Ray: Central Committee representative from Bluffton; defeated Charlie Hauenstein in 1986 and 1988 in Central Committee elections for their precinct; father of Tim Hamman.

"Hard water policy": Initiated by Lima mayor Gene Joseph (1985–89) to induce outlying communities to annex themselves to the city. As originally established, the policy had required property owners adjacent to the city to annex before they could receive water services. In August 1988, city council modified the policy somewhat, substituting exorbitant water fees for out-of-city customers as a means of pressuring suburban property owners into petitioning for annexation.

Harris, Otha: President of Allen County NAACP; Charlie Hauenstein's main connection with the county's African American community.

Harrod, Charles: Sheriff of Allen County, Republican; lost reelection bid for a fifth term in 1992 to Dan Beck.

Hatcher, Jean: Democratic state committeewoman from Fourth District; field representative for Sherrod Brown.

Hauenstein, Charlie: Chair of Allen County Democratic Party from 1972 until 1986; head of the party's old guard.

Hefner, Bryan: DEP activist; farmer; member of Democratic Central and Executive Committees; loyal supporter of Democratic candidates.

Henderson, Charles: DEP activist; member of Central and Executive Committees; member of minority caucus.

"Hens and chicks strategy": A communications strategy created by Democrats for an Effective Party (DEP) during the 1986 party fight; core DEP activists (the hens) would keep in touch with less active Central Committee candidates (the chicks), coordinating DEP strategy and planning.

Hevener, John: DEP activist; helped orchestrate overthrow of Charlie Hauenstein in 1986; chaired Patronage Committee; married to Mary Hevener.

Hevener, Mary: Democratic activist and DEP supporter; member of Democratic Central Committee; married to John Hevener.

Hey, Todd: Central Committee chairman under Charlie Hauenstein; deputy registrar of Lima Mall license bureau; prominent leader of the party's old guard.

Holmes, Bob: Chair of the Allen County Republican Party; chaired the Board of Elections.

Horne, Henry: Lima's Sixth Ward city councilman, 1979–87.

Hower, "Smokey": DEP activist; loaned twelve thousand dollars to Democratic Party for 1986 campaign.

Johns, Bill: Democratic activist with the old guard; ran for Central Committee chairman in 1988; married to Donna Johns.

Johns, Donna: Democratic activist; director of Board of Elections; retired in 1994; married to Bill Johns.

Joseph, Gene: Mayor of Lima, 1985–89.

Keller, Ida Kay: Democratic activist from Spencerville; county commissioner candidate in 1988 and 1990; leader of the Dumpbusters, a group that prevented approval of a landfill near Spencerville.

"LaRouchies" (or LaRouche Democrats): followers of Lyndon LaRouche, political extremist and presidential candidate; received prominent attention in 1986 when LaRouche Democrats won nominations in Illinois's Democratic primary.

Lee, Alberta: Allen County recorder, Republican; later, county commissioner.

Leonard, Paul: Ohio lieutenant governor, 1987–91.

Leppla, Dale: Democratic activist; county commissioner candidate in 1986 and 1988; member of Central and Executive Committees.

Lima News: Most prominent daily newspaper in Allen County; part of the Freedom chain of conservative newspapers.

Locker, Dale: Democratic candidate for state senator, 1988; from Shelby County; former member of Ohio House.

MacDonell, A. D.: President of Met Bank; strong advocate of David Berger's candidacy for mayor of Lima in 1988.

Maurer, Steve: State senator from the Twelfth District, which included Allen County, 1981–85, Democrat; lost reelection bid in 1984; later became Ohio director of agriculture.

Mayer, Bob: Allen County commissioner, Republican.

McCoy, Beverly: DEP activist; member of Board of Elections; member of Executive Committee and the minority caucus.

Meredith, Richard: Attorney; Democratic candidate for Court of Appeals in 1986; chair of Allen County Democratic Party, 1991–97.

Mihlbaugh, Robert: Attorney; Democratic activist; ran for Congress in 1964 and 1966.

Minority caucus: Committee created to provide voice for minorities within the Allen County Democratic Party; organized under Angel chairmanship; chaired by Leonard Boddie.

Mongelluzzo, John: Realtor and businessmen; in 1987, held option on the land proposed as the site for Spencerville landfill.

Moritz, Ramon: Democratic activist; ran in 1990 Democratic primary for state representative, losing to Lorenzo White.

Moyer, Harry: Former mayor of Lima; lost narrowly in 1985 to Gene Joseph; David Berger's opponent for mayor in 1989 general election.

Nominating petition: Must be filed by all candidates running for political office; candidate designates address, office being sought, date of the election, and other information as specified on the petition; candidates must collect signatures from registered voters of the precinct, county, or district where election will be held; number of signatures required varies, depending on the office being sought.

ODOT: Ohio Department of Transportation; repaired and maintained Ohio's roads and bridges; source of patronage appointments to permanent positions or to summer jobs.

ODP: Ohio Democratic Party.

Old guard (or "party regulars"): Those members of the Allen County Democratic Party whose personal allegiance was to Charlie Hauenstein and Todd Hey—the leaders who immediately preceded the Angel chairmanship.

Operations Committee: Another committee organized under Angel chairmanship; consisted of secretary, treasurer, chair of the Central Committee, all vice chairs, and other members the chair might appoint; served as an advisory body to the chair and helped manage party activities and plan party operations; an "executive committee" of the Executive Committee.

Patronage: Practice of appointing political supporters to jobs on the public payroll.

Patronage Committee: Committee that made recommendations on patronage appointments; chaired by John Hevener.

Piggyback sales tax: A sales tax levied by county government on top of the state sales tax, county's portion of sales tax going to the county government; may be imposed by an ordinance of the county commissioners or by a popular vote.

Pitts, Jerry: Attorney; activist in the African American community and in the Democratic Party.

Policy Studies Committee (or Policy Committee): Established under Angel chairmanship; studied political issues facing the county and recommended a party position to chair, who would issue a statement or state a position on behalf of the party; chaired by Rick Siferd.

Prater, Paul: Democratic activist; supporter of Charlie Hauenstein; member of Board of Elections.

Quinn, Janet: Democratic activist; DEP supporter; member of Allen County Democratic Women's Club.

Rankin, Roger: DEP activist; managed Rochelle Twining's race for state representative in 1986.

Reese, Don: Allen County commissioner, Republican.

Rehab: Also known as Rehab Project; organization directed by David Berger; rebuilt slum housing in Lima.

Riffe, Vern: Speaker of Ohio House of Representatives, Democrat.

Rizor, Paul: Attorney; Democratic candidate for state representative in 1986; in 1988 ran for judge of Common Pleas Court.

Rose, Ben: Attorney; Republican; state representative from First District, which includes only Allen County; Republican candidate for state auditor in 1986.

Rossfeld, Charles: Republican member on Allen County Board of Elections; became chair of the board in 1990.

Routson, Bob: Leader of piggyback sales tax referendum campaign in 1987; Democrat.

Runk, Wes: Lima businessman; managed David Berger's mayoral campaign in 1989.

Ruvulo, James: Chairman of the Ohio Democratic Party during the Celeste years.

Schulien, Paul: Deputy Director of the Allen County Board of Elections, became director of the board when Donna Johns retired in 1994.

Schwieterman, Ed: Democratic candidate for county commissioner in 1986; member of Executive Committee.

Shepherd, J. Vane: Third Ward councilman in Lima; ran for city council president in 1987.

Sheeter, John: Democratic activist in Delphos; mayor of Delphos; deputy registrar of Delphos's license bureau.

Siferd, Rick: Attorney; DEP activist; chair of Policy Committee and member of Central and Executive Committees.

Smith, Paul W.: Political reporter for the *Lima News*.

Spin control: Any attempt to influence media coverage of an election, a political campaign, or an issue; object is to make sure that media coverage of a story or event is beneficial to the candidate or the political organization.

Street money: Money spent to stimulate turnout in minority precincts; individuals are paid to distribute sample ballots at polls, contact voters, and drive voters to the polls; money is spent through a group or an individual, often with minimal reporting or accountability.

Taft, Robert: Ohio secretary of state, Republican; defeated Democratic incumbent Sherrod Brown in 1990; elected governor in 1998.

Thompson, Bill: State representative for First District, Republican; successor to Ben Rose.

Townsend, Bob: Allen County commissioner, Republican.

Twining, Rochelle: DEP activist; member of Central and Executive Committees; ran for state representative in 1986; field representative for Secretary of State Sherrod Brown; in 1991, succeeded Bill Angel as chair of Allen County Democratic Party.

Vanek, Evelyn: Treasurer to the Allen County Democratic Party; DEP activist; member of Central and Executive Committees.

Voinovich, George: Republican candidate for governor in 1990, defeating Anthony Celebreeze.

Ward, Dick: UAW activist; president of Ford local; married to Pearl Ward.

Ward, Pearl: Democratic activist; supporter of old guard leaders; married to Dick Ward.

Waste Management, Inc.: Corporation that in 1987 attempted to build a landfill near Spencerville, Ohio.

Webb, Steve: Labor activist; union representative for AFSCME (q.v.) locals; DEP activist; chairman of Democratic Central Committee, 1986–88.

White, Lorenzo: Democratic candidate for state representative in 1990.

Williams, Furl: President, Lima City Council; activist in Lima's African American community; Democrat.

Winters, Tom: Executive assistant and counsel to House Speaker Vern Riffe in 1986.

Withrow, Mary Ellen: Treasurer of the state of Ohio; Democrat.

WLIO TV: Main television station in Allen County; later joined by WTLW TV, a religious station.

Woodard, Edith: Democratic candidate for municipal clerk of courts in 1991; married to Mel Woodard.

Woodard, Mel: Pastor and insurance executive; Democratic candidate for county commissioner in 1984; member of minority caucus; married to Edith Woodard.

Wrencher, PC: DEP activist; member of Central and Executive Committees and the minority caucus; UAW activist with the Ford local; served as interim Democratic chair between Rochelle Twining and Dick Meredith.

· Notes ·

Introduction

1. Samuel J. Eldersveld, *Party Conflict and Community Development: Postwar Politics in Ann Arbor* (Ann Arbor: Univ. of Michigan Press, 1995).

2. Isaiah Berlin, "Political Judgement," in *The Sense and Reality: Studies in Ideas and Their History*, ed. Henry Hardy (New York: Farrar, Straus and Giroux, 1996), 44–45.

3. "County to City: Jail Is Going Up and You Can't Stop It," *Cleveland Plain Dealer,* Mar. 12, 1999, 1A.

4. Among the most important circumstances was that Bill Clinton was at the head of the Democratic ticket. Strength at the top of any ticket raises the morale of local parties and of voters at the grassroots. The Democratic commissioner candidate, Jack Rex, was former president of the Ford local of the UAW, thus giving him a following and an organization that was ready to work on his behalf. His opponent, Keith Cunningham, was president of the Lima city council and was, therefore, hopelessly identified with Lima and its politics. Rex, who was from the village of Lafayette, a farming community east of Lima, built upon the resentment of county voters, who distrusted any politician from Lima; at the same time, he exploited the solid Democratic base that Lima provided for his candidacy. As for the engineer's race, James Schmenk was the Democratic candidate and defeated Clayton Bacon, the incumbent, who earlier that year had faced charges of "honest graft." That is, he was accused of making decisions on subdivision development to benefit a private engineering firm he owned. Bacon was found not guilty of corruption, but the controversy left an odor that helped Schmenk.

5. Robert Putnam has written about the decline of social capital in American politics, the tendency of modern Americans to turn away from civic activity. He defines social capital as "features of social life—networks, norms, and trust—that enable people to act together more effectively to pursue shared objectives." Robert Putnam, "The Strange Disappearance of Civic America," *The American Prospect* (Winter 1996): 34. See also his "Bowling Alone: America's Declining Social Capital," *Journal of Democracy* 6 (Jan. 1995): 65–78.

6. In other words, local parties help stimulate "civic engagement," which Robert Putnam has defined as "people's connections with the life of their communities, not only to politics." What is happening to party organizations may offer some clue to the questions Putnam has explored. My interest, of course, runs in a somewhat different direction from his. Where Putnam has explored reasons for the decline of social capital,

I am interested in how political organizations, county parties in particular, serve to augment social capital and stimulate civic engagement. Indeed, a more proper concern is whether parties have any impact at all on these variables. Putnam, "The Strange Disappearance of Civic America," 34 ff.

7. William Riordan, *Plunkitt of Tammany Hall* (New York: Dutton, 1963), 25.

8. "Editorial," *Dayton Daily News,* Nov. 4, 1990, 18.

9. Tip O'Neill, *All Politics Is Local.* (New York: Random House, 1994), xv.

10. Tape recorded interview with Lima mayor David Berger, City Hall, Lima, Ohio, Apr. 16, 1999, William Angel, interviewer.

1. Charlie, Mary, and John

1. Notes of meeting of Mar. 12, 1986, personal files of author; William Angel to Susan Gibler, Mar. 16, 1986, personal files of author.

2. "March Regular Meeting," memo to Executive Committee members from Charles Hauenstein, Mar. 4, 1986, personal files of author. "It should be an interesting meeting," Hauenstein wrote. "There are questions about fund raising, our candidates, our executive committee and this election year that need to be answered by all of our committee." The memo closed with this ominous pronouncement: "This will be an executive session, open only to members of the committee."

3. Celeste, however, had considerable support from other quarters, including the Speaker of the Ohio House, Vern Riffe, and Representative C. J. McClin of Dayton, a longtime civil rights activist who had organized the Black Elected Democrats of Ohio (BEDO). Celeste also had the editorial endorsement of the *Plain Dealer,* as well as extensive backing among organized labor. See Tim Miller, "The Celeste Era," in *Ohio Politics,* ed. Alexander Lamis (Kent, Ohio: Kent State Univ. Press, 1994), 142–44.

4. John Coplen and Jim Schaffer each won county commissioner seats that year.

5. Hauenstein's wife and son worked for the Ohio Department of Transportation, and his daughter held a job with the office of the state auditor, Thomas Ferguson. Other members of Hauenstein's entourage held positions with the Bureau of Motor Vehicles, Office of Liquor Control, and the Department of Transportation.

6. Until the 1990s, distilled spirits were sold only in state liquor stores, run by the Ohio Department of Liquor Control. When George Voinovich became governor in 1991, he moved quickly to take the state out of the liquor business; although a few state stores still exist, most distilled spirits today are sold by private merchants.

7. Mary [Hevener] Kahal to William Angel, Nov. 14, 1996, personal files of author. This letter describes the circumstances surrounding the intraparty fight in 1982. News coverage of this event was minimal.

8. Ibid.

9. Ibid.

10. Consider the following documentation. In December 1986 I received two separate statements from Ohio Democratic Party headquarters. One announced that there were 13,484 "Deputy Registrar transactions" for November, itemizing them bureau by bureau. The other was our assessment, accompanied by a cover memorandum from party chair Ruvulo, who cautioned, "As you know it is within your discretion to raise these funds as

you deem appropriate. There is no requirement that these monies come from any particular source." But we all knew that Allen County's DRs would provide funding for our assessment, which for November 1986 was $674.20. Ohio Democratic Party, memorandum to Bill Angel, "For Your Information," Dec. 8, 1986; assessment 003215, Dec. 8, 1986, to Bill Angel, personal files of author. See also Evelyn Vanek, Treasurer, "Political Party Finance Report, Allen County Democratic Party," Dec. 12, 1986, personal files of author.

11. Information regarding the financial operation of the license bureaus came from Frank Winegardner, who operated the Eastgate bureau in Lima during the Celeste administration. Telephone interview with Frank Winegardner, Aug. 14, 1998, William Angel, interviewer.

12. The third bureau was in Delphos, where John Sheeter, then a Delphos councilman, had the support of the Heveners and Charlie Hauenstein.

13. Mary (Hevener) Kahal, telephone interview by William Angel, Aug. 12, 1996 (hereafter Kahal interview).

14. Charles Weidel, interview by William Angel, Lima, Ohio, Aug. 9, 1996 (hereafter Weidel interview); Kahal interview.

15. Weidel interview.

16. Beverly McCoy, interview by William Angel, Aug. 15, 1996, Lima, Ohio (hereafter McCoy interview).

17. Kahal interview.

18. Ibid.

19. Ibid.

20. William Wells, "Eulogy for John Hevener," typescript, Jan. 1993, personal files of author.

21. Kahal to Angel, Nov. 14, 1996. Mary later told me that John himself actually used the label "Calvinist" to describe fellow activist Tom Doyle, who worked relentlessly on behalf of candidates and causes. When Mary heard this description, she thought, "It takes one to know one." Mary [Hevener] Kahal to Bill Angel, Sept. 11, 1997.

22. Rochelle Twining interview, by William Angel, Lima, Ohio, Aug. 13, 1996 (hereafter cited as Twining interview). Charlie expressed these views to Twining during a long election recount in November 1989.

23. Kahal interview; Kahal to Angel, Nov. 14, 1996.

24. Ibid.

25. Weidel interview.

26. Martin Glazier, interview by William Angel, Lima, Ohio, Aug. 6, 1996.

27. McCoy interview.

28. McCoy interview; Mary (Hevener) Kahal, telephone interview by William Angel, Sept. 16, 1996.

2. Power of the Chair

1. In Ohio's 1984 Democratic presidential primary, delegates were elected by congressional district. Seventy-five days before the primary, each presidential campaign held nominating caucuses, assembling by district to select delegates according to rules laid down by the Ohio Democratic Party (ODP). In the primary, only the presidential

candidates' names appeared on the ballot; afterwards, delegates were allocated according to the proportion of votes each candidate had received in the district. Additional at-large delegates were appointed later, along with so-called superdelegates, who were state officials and officers of ODP. These procedures were followed again in 1988.

2. The Community Action Progam (CAP) Council is the political arm of the United Auto Workers. The UAW is organized into twelve regions, and each region has several CAP Councils, which educate local citizens about issues important to the organization (e.g., globalization). CAP Councils also become involved in electoral politics and work to elect candidates sympathetic to the UAW's agenda. Gehr was president of Lima-Troy CAP Council in Region 2B.

3. Mary [Hevener] Kahal to Bill Angel, Sept. 11, 1997 personal files of author; Beverly McCoy, telephone interview by William Angel, Sept. 17, 1997 (hereafter McCoy interview); "First Campaign: The Party," unpublished manuscript, 1992, personal files of author, 18–22. Descriptions and conversations, however, are reconstructed from my recollection of the event.

4. Kahal to Angel, Sept. 11, 1997; McCoy interview.

5. Kahal to Angel, Sept. 11, 1997.

6. Ibid.

7. McCoy interview.

8. In 1983, Celeste requested that a temporary 50 percent tax increase, as ordered by Governor Rhodes, become permanent. He also asked for a 40 percent surcharge on top of that, hence the "90 percent tax increase." In the November 1983 election, the tax survived a statewide repeal effort.

9. For a description of events in this meeting, see my "Politics in the Real World: Rebellion and Change in the Allen County Democratic Party, 1984–1987," paper presented at the 1987 meeting of the American Political Science Association, Chicago, Sept. 1987, mimeo, 18–19.

10. Ibid., 20. In reality, the candidates ended up with eight hundred dollars each; the party retained two hundred dollars to help pay for the mailing of sample ballots. Also, Todd Hey and Charlie Hauenstein later claimed the contribution to be much larger, somewhere between seven and fourteen thousand dollars; I have no idea how they came up with these figures (see chapter 6). My figures derive from my notes on the event and from Tim Hamman's financial report, specifically, Earl R. Eastman, Treasurer, "Campaign Committee Finance Report, Committee to Elect Timothy C. Hamman State Representative," Oct. 25, 1986, personal files of author. I also have a copy of the Allen County Democratic Party's financial report for 1985, which shows that the party borrowed $5,366.05 from the Bluffton Citizens National Bank for election expenses. These figures reflect a five-thousand-dollar principal, paid back at 7.32 percent interest. This item must be the money the party gave to the candidates for the 1984 campaign. See Vern Eley, Treasurer, "Political Party Finance Report, Allen County Democratic Party," Dec. 20, 1985, personal files of author.

11. As I recall, Charlie complained, "You should have talked to me first. We do our own campaigning here." I took the scolding and apologized, "Sorry. I'll get some brochures for you, if that's what you want."

12. Johnson relayed to me an accounting of this conversation on Oct. 28, 1984.

13. For a description of events in this meeting, see my "Politics in the Real World," 21. The dialogue is based on my memory of the event itself and conversations with others who were there.

14. See Angel, "Politics in the Real World," 22; descriptions and dialogue from this encounter are as I remember them.

15. In Allen County the figures break down this way: white 96,326, African American 12,235, total 109,755. African Americans are concentrated in Lima, where the racial division is as follows: white 34,043, African American 10,914, total 45,549. U.S. Department of Commerce, Bureau of Census, *1990 Census of Population, Social and Economic Characteristics, Ohio* (Washington, D.C.: GPO, 1993), 37:24, 51, tables 6 and 7.

16. I have no copies of the party's 1984 postelection report to verify whether GOTV money came into Allen County from some outside organization. (The Allen County Democratic Party would have filed a campaign finance report with the Board of Elections, but those reports are retained for only six years.) Rumor had it that the party received a large donation from C. J. McLin's black caucus in the state legislature. In fact, no one would acknowledge how much money actually entered the county—ten thousand dollars, by one account—or how it was spent. After the campaign, I asked Vera Gales, Maurer's coordinator in the black community, and Otha Harris if they knew what the money had been used for. They both confirmed that funds had helped with election expenses, but when I asked how it was spent, I received vague answers like "food for the workers" and "rent for a sound truck." I even talked to staff in the black caucus but again received evasive replies.

17. Beverly McCoy, interview by William Angel, Lima, Ohio, Aug. 15, 1996.

18. In Allen County, Walter Mondale took 12,176 votes to 33,506 for President Reagan. The local races went as follows: Bob Mayer (R) beat Mel Woodard in one county commissioner's race, 30,821 to 13,791; Ed Peyton defeated Coplen in the other commissioner's contest, 24,650 to 19,952. In the sheriff's race, incumbent Charles Harrod defeated his Democratic challenger, Ted Wade, 26,879 to 18,721. Republican Herb McElwain beat Frank Winegardner in the treasurer's contest, 27,426 to 17,586. In the Ohio House Race, First District, longtime state representative Ben Rose defeated Tim Hamman, his Democratic opponent, 28,781 to 16,548. In the senate race, Twelfth District, Bob Cupp, retook the seat for the Republicans, defeating Steve Maurer, 80,427 to 51,395. *Ohio Election Statistics, 1983–1984* (Columbus: Office of the Ohio Secretary of State, 1985), 151, 164, 168, 197.

3. Democrats for an Effective Party

1. Twining interview, Aug. 13, 1996.

2. William Angel, "Politics in the Real World: Rebellion and Change in the Allen County Democratic Party, 1984–1987," paper presented at the 1987 meeting of the American Political Science Association, Chicago, Sept. 1987, mimeo, p. 27.

3. William Angel to Susan Gibler, Mar. 3, 1986, personal files of author.

4. Ibid.

5. DEP financial records, 1986, personal files of author; Angel, "Politics in the Real World," 47.

6. See Angel, "Politics in the Real World," 37.

7. Ibid., 39–40.

8. Charlie Hauenstein made a veiled reference to these shenanigans in a letter to members of the 1986 Democratic Central Committee (see chapter 6). Hauenstein to Democratic Central Committee representatives, "Dear Committeeperson," June 5, 1986, personal files of author. The story of Cora's "undercover assignment" came directly from John Hevener, who witnessed the conversation between Hamman and Harris. Although he repeated the tale on numerous occasions, I heard it for the first time in 1983.

9. Angel to Gibler, Aug. 25, 1985. Description of my phone conversation with Cora is based upon my recollection of the event. This story is also highlighted in Angel, "Politics in the Real World," 37–39.

10. See Angel, "Politics in the Real World," 39.

11. The previous summer, while I was attending a seminar in Boston, Hauenstein had asked John Hevener about meetings I was holding in the Alpine. When John told him that I was on the east coast and couldn't hold any meetings, Charlie backed off the interrogation, but both he and Todd continued to hassle Hevener and others connected with our movement as if they knew something was afoot. Angel to Gibler, July 22, 1985; Angel to Gibler, August 5, 1985; Angel to Gibler, August 20, 1985.

12. Angel to Gibler, Feb. 15, 1986.

13. Our fruitless courtship with Delphos continued for another three months. In April, Webb and I attended a meeting of the Delphos/Marion Township Democratic Club, where we withstood a barrage of criticism by Todd Hey, Charlie Hauenstein, and Paul Prater. Wegesin, Youngpeter, and Sheeter attended, along with Jane Goergens, a committee member from Delphos. The only person clearly aligned with us was Stanley Carder, who had grown up in Delphos and was running for a Central Committee post in American Township. Webb and I found ourselves constantly on the defensive; no one from the Delphos community rose our aid or even tried to defuse or redirect the attacks. The meeting ended with Jane Goergens flinging a large manila envelope in Carder's face. It was no mean feat, as the envelope was heavy, containing enough DEP literature for Goergens to distribute in her home precinct, and it had to bounce past several rows of chairs to get to Stan. As she threw the package, Goergens declared, "Here's your envelope, Mr. Carder. I've made up my mind. I'm stickin' with Charlie." Sheeter and Wegesin appeared embarrassed by this outburst, but I don't believe we received their votes. Almost certainly, no committeeman or committeewoman from Delphos voted for us. See Angel, "Politics in the Real World," 49.

14. Angel to Gibler, Feb. 26, 1986.

15. Ibid.; Angel to Gibler, Mar. 16, 1986.

16. Angel to Gibler, Feb. 26, 1986.

4. Protest

1. The description of the meeting, including Holmes's comments, comes from witnesses, notably Pickle Felter and Bryan Hefner, who were there and reported it to a DEP meeting on the evening of February 27. Characterizations and descriptions that appear here and elsewhere in this chapter are based upon my own eyewitness observations of

board meetings and my experiences with the characters involved. "Petitions Rejected for Primary," *Lima News,* Feb. 28, 1986, D1; minutes, Allen County Board of Elections, special session, Feb. 27, 1986, Office of the Allen County Board of Elections, Court of Appeals Building, Lima, Ohio. See William Angel, "Politics in the Real World: Rebellion and Change in the Allen County Democratic Party, 1984–1987," paper presented at the 1987 meeting of the American Political Science Association, Chicago, Sept. 1987, mimeo, 42–43.

2. See Angel, "Politics in the Real World," 41.

3. Ibid.

4. "Democrats for an Effective Party, Press Conference, 2/21/86," typescript, personal files of author, 1; "Group Eyes Change in Democratic Hierarchy," *Lima News,* Feb. 21, 1986, D1.

5. "Group Eyes Change in Democratic Hierarchy."

6. Angel to Gibler, Feb. 26, 1986.

7. "County Democratic Chairman Responds to Ouster Attempt," *Lima News,* Feb. 22, 1986, A5.

8. Ibid.

9. See Angel, "Politics in the Real World," 46; Howard Elstro, interview by William Angel, Lima, Ohio, Aug. 17, 1996.

10. The counting of absentee ballots was a particular source of apprehension. At the time, absentee voters penciled in their selections on their ballots before mailing them to the board office. Prior to the election, clerks would transpose the selections from the mailed-in ballots to regular ballots by punching the choices. This procedure, Hevener and I warned, could open the opportunity for fraud. Where no choice had been made in a Central Committee race, the clerk (whom Charlie would select) could simply punch in the choice for Hauenstein's candidate. Kindt promised that a representative of the secretary of state's office would be on hand to view the processing of absentee ballots. Angel to Gibler, Sept. 17, 1985; Angel to Gibler, Sept. 22, 1985; Marie Von der Embse, "memo" to William Angel, n.d. (ca. Dec. 1, 1985), personal files of author.

11. Angel to Gibler, Sept. 17, 1985; Angel to Gibler, Sept. 22, 1985.

12. Ohio Revised Code, Elections, (ORC) 3501.38.

13. These candidates included Todd Hey, Willie Denson, John Davenport, Charlie Camper, Norman Davis, Lula Jackson, and Claude Godsey, all being protested under ORC 3501.38. Others were Mary Finn, James McClendon, Louis States, and Klor Newland, all being protested for miscellaneous irregularities in their petitions.

14. Angel to Gibler, Mar. 3, 1986.

15. Marilyn Jones, Reporter, "Meeting of the Board of Elections, Lima, Allen County, Ohio, Transcript of Proceedings," Mar. 13, 1986, Jones Reporting Services, Lima, Ohio, 1986, mimeo, personal files of author, 5.

16. Ibid., 6. The Board of Elections minutes show that a protest was brought against Loggi and that it was sustained. This is a misinterpretation of what happened. Minutes of special hearing of Mar. 13, 1986, Office of the Allen County Board of Elections, Court of Appeals Building, Lima, Ohio.

17. Meeting of the Board of Elections, 9.

18. ORC, 3513.262.

19. Meeting of the Board of Elections, 13.

20. Ibid., 19.

21. Ibid., 20

22. Ibid., 21.

23. Ibid., 22.

24. Ibid., 23–24.

25. Ibid., 24.

26. Siferd had dated his declaration of candidacy "2d day of February, 1986," but the board interpreted the date to read "24 day of February," four days after the filing deadline. The board accepted his explanation that a groove in his kitchen table had caught his pen as he recorded the date, leading to the confused interpretation. Donna Moore had typed the pertinent data onto the petition paper, using a typewriter with a well-worn ribbon; she seemed to have omitted the date of the election from the petition. The date appeared on photocopies, however; and the board easily recognized its mistake and granted Moore's candidacy, as well as Siferd's. "Meeting of the Board of Elections," 38–44.

27. "Elections Board Hears Petitions Protest, *Lima News,* Mar. 14, 1986, B6.

28. Ibid. The "rebel Democrat" line came from WLIO TV's *News Journal;* it was used by the 11 P.M. news anchor on March 3, 1986.

29. William Angel to Sherrod Brown, Mar. 14, 1986, personal files of author.

30. Jonathan Marshall to Donna Johns, Apr. 7, 1986, personal files of author. Marshall's language was less precise regarding the board's handling of Dorothy Loggi's petition. "As a practical matter only those petitions protested are required to be given the scrutiny provided for in the hearing," he wrote, "and other petitions not protested need not be reviewed in a hearing."

31. Angel to Gibler, Feb. 26, 1986.

5. LaRouchies

1. William Angel to Susan Gibler, Apr. 2, 1986, personal files of author. Mihlbaugh is John Coplen's uncle.

2. Angel to Gibler, Apr. 2, 1986.

3. Angel to Gibler, Apr. 20, 1986.

4. Ibid.

5. Ibid. There was just enough truth to this rumor to give it credibility. I was getting a divorce and was living in a poor, mostly African American neighborhood.

6. Lyndon LaRouche has perennially run for president, first in 1976 as candidate of the U.S. Labor Party; in 1980, 1984, 1988, and 1992 he sought the Democratic Party's nomination. In 1987, a federal grand jury indicted him for obstruction of justice in a case stemming from phony fund-raising tactics used by his organization. In 1988, LaRouche was found guilty and sentenced to fifteen years in prison. Even today he takes pride in the fact that he has been the only U.S. presidential candidate "to have been convicted in a Federal criminal case," which he offers as proof of the conspiracies against him. See the LaRouche Website, http://larouchepub.com/resume.html (Aug. 1, 1998).

7. See William Angel, "Politics in the Real World: Rebellion and Change in the Allen

County Democratic Party, 1984–1987," paper presented at the 1987 meeting of the American Political Science Association, Chicago, Sept. 1987, mimeo, 53–54.

8. See Angel, "Politics in the Real World," 54.

9. See ibid., 49–50; Charles Hauenstein, "Dear Committee Member," letter to Executive Committee members, Apr. 8, 1986, personal files of author.

10. See Angel, "Politics in the Real World," 50, 54; Angel to Gibler, Apr. 20, 1986.

11. As recorded in Angel to Gibler, Apr. 27, 1986.

12. Angel to Gibler, May 5, 1986.

13. Allen County Democrat Party, sample ballot, May 1986, personal files of author.

14. Angel to Gibler, Aug. 5, 1985.

15. See Angel, "Politics in the Real World," 57.

16. "Dem Club Endorses Shift in Party," *Lima News,* May 2, 1986, D1. Linda Coplen herself contacted the *Delphos Herald* to give it the following message: "Creative ideas are needed to revitalize the party. This can only occur under new leadership. The party can once again become a vital force using the diversified talents within the Democratic community of Allen County." *Delphos Herald,* May 3, 1986.

17. Angel to Gibler, May 5, 1986.

6. Taking Over

1. "Reorganization Group Claims Control," *Lima News,* May 7, 1986, B1.

2. Ibid. Under party rules, Hauenstein could have been elected without being a Central Committeeman. The same was not true for either Todd Hey or Steve Webb, but both of them won their races.

3. Three contests ended in ties, two of which were decided in DEP's favor by a coin flip.

4. "Angel Predicts Brighter Future for Allen Democratic Party," *Lima News,* May 8, 1986, B1.

5. Ibid.

6. At this point "Yuppie" did not have the negative connotation it later acquired. The word came out of Gary Hart's 1984 presidential campaign, which at first gathered considerable support from young, urban professional workers who were disenchanted with Walter Mondale, whom they saw an uninspiring captive of organized labor.

7. See William Angel, "Politics in the Real World: Rebellion and Change in the Allen County Democratic Party, 1984–1987," paper presented at the 1987 meeting of the American Political Science Association, Chicago, Sept. 1987, mimeo, 50–52.

8. Ibid., 52; minutes, Allen County Board of Elections, May 17, 1986, and May 22, 1986, Office of the Allen County Board of Elections, Lima, Ohio.

9. William Angel to Susan Gibler, May 23, 1986, personal files of author; Twining interview, Aug. 13, 1996.

10. Twining interview, Aug. 13, 1996.

11. Ibid.

12. The Board of Elections had certified the primary results on May 22, and according to statute, the reorganization meeting had to be called no earlier than six and no later than fifteen days from the day of certification. Accordingly, the earliest date for the

meeting would be May 28, the latest June 6. Hauenstein interpreted the rule differently. For him, the "reorganization clock" did not start ticking until May 28, the day the Board of Elections held a recount of the Republican contest for Third District Court of Appeals. Ohio Revised Code, Title 35, Elections, 3517.04; Angel to Gibler, June 4, 1986.

13. William Angel, "Steve Webb to Friend," June 4, 1986, personal files of author; Todd G. Hey to fellow Democrat, June 2, 1986, personal files of author.

14. Charles Hauenstein to committeeperson, June 5, 1986, personal files of author.

15. Ibid.

16. Ibid.

17. Ibid.

18. Notes from conversation with Tom Thompson, June 16, 2000.

19. Linda Coplen and Steve Webb, "Timothy Hamman, Mel Woodard, Paul Rizor, and John Coplen to Fellow Democrats," June 6, 1986. Hamman had been a candidate for state representative in 1984 and for county prosecutor in 1980. Coplen had run for county commissioner three times (1976, 1980, and 1984), winning in 1976. Mel Woodard had been a candidate for county commissioner alongside Coplen in the 1984 campaign, and Rizor had run for state representative in 1982. See also Angel, "Politics in the Real World," 61.

20. "Fellow Democrats." Letter, June 6, 1986. Emphasis is included in the original.

21. Todd G. Hey to fellow Democrat, June 6, 1986, personal files of author.

22. This story is Pickle Felter's, told many times during the planning sessions for the 1986 takeover.

23. The party's constitution and bylaws were ambiguous as to exactly who should appoint a temporary chairman: "A temporary chairman and secretary shall be chosen, and the Committee shall proceed to organize." We took it to mean that the Central Committee—and not Todd Hey—should choose a temporary chair. *Constitution and By-Laws of the Democratic Party of Allen County, Ohio,* article 3, sec. 2, mimeo, ca. 1986.

24. The following dialogue and descriptive details come from my letter to Susan Gibler, June 10, 1986. Dialogue appears as recorded in the letter.

25. See Angel, "Politics in the Real World," 83.

7. Not Like the Old Bunch

1. The Operations Committee finally consisted of Central Committee chairman Steve Webb, Executive Committee secretary Elsie Crowe, Executive Committee treasurer Evelyn Vanek, and myself, along with the following additional vice chairs—Rochelle Twining, Leonard Boddie, Cora Hamman, Ellen Wright, and PC Wrencher. Steve Webb was also elected as first vice chairman of the party. See William Angel, "Learning Lessons," unpublished manuscript, ca. 1992, personal files of author; Hullinger to William Angel, June 23, 1986, personal files of author; and Rosemary Geiger, Acting Secretary, "Allen County Democratic Party Executive Committee Minutes," June 25, 1986, personal files of author.

2. See Angel, "Learning Lessons," 6.

3. Ibid., 9.

4. Bender was a funny guy, very glib and excellent with a quip. He "zinged" me at a fund-raiser in an adjacent county where I had appeared in a new outfit—blue blazer, tan slacks, and bright scarlet galluses. As I strolled among the tables, I paused occasionally to display my new duds, spreading open my jacket at the waist to make sure folks noticed my snappy suspenders. That was not all they noticed. I was unzipped, much to the horror of Rochelle Twining, who asked Bender if someone ought to tell me. "Naw," Bender wisecracked, "He's trolling."

5. Angel to Gibler, Sept. 18, 1986; Angel to Gibler, Sept. 26, 1986.

6. Todd Hey, "Dear Fellow Democrats," letter to members of Allen County Democratic Central Committee, Aug. 12, 1986, mimeo, personal files of author. Hey opened by thanking all of those "who have helped the Democrat Party in so many ways" during his tenure as Central Committee chair. Then followed three short paragraphs, each reflecting on Hey's accomplishments, friendships, and personal growth. Finally, in the last paragraph, Todd got around to issuing the support statement I had demanded: "In order to keep the Democrat Party alive and active, I urge you to support and cooperate with the new leadership. I feel working together we can and will elect Democrats."

7. See Angel, "Learning Lessons," 10.

8. Vern Eley, Treasurer, "Political Party Finance Report, Allen County Democratic Party," Dec. 20, 1985; Evelyn Vanek, Treasurer, "Political Party Finance Report, Allen County Democratic Party," Dec. 12, 1986; assessment 003215, Dec. 8, 1986, to Bill Angel; all in personal files of author.

9. Angel to Gibler, June 17, 1986.

10. Conversations and discussion regarding the Susan Ward appointment are recorded in ibid.

11. Angel to Gibler, June 29, 1997.

12. The deputy registrars helped underwrite our expenditures for the Junior Fair Auction. Frank Winegardner (Eastgate Mall) contributed $150, as did Todd Hey (Lima Mall), while John Sheeter (Delphos) chipped in fifty dollars. Political Committee Finance Report, Allen County Democratic Party, personal files of author, Oct. 23, 1986.

13. Description of the Democratic Party's participation in the 1986 Junior Fair Auction is found in Angel to Gibler, Aug. 26, 1986.

14. The party sold most of its livestock to meat buyers, leaving only the "premium," the difference between the bid price and the net sale (market) price, to be paid. Of course, the party bore the full expense for the hog it donated, at Bryan Hefner's behest, to the El Karan Grotto, and for the rabbits, whose fate was never discovered. Political Committee Finance Report, Allen County Democratic Party, Oct. 23, 1986, personal files of author; miscellaneous buyers vouchers, Allen County Junior Fair Sales, ca. Aug. 1986, personal files of author; Elsie Crowe, Secretary, "Allen County Democratic Party, Executive Committee Minutes," Sept. 17, 1986, personal files of author; and Angel to Gibler, Aug. 26, 1986.

15. Although it seems grotesque, the carcass show has purpose. It demonstrates how well meat judged on the hoof bears up when it has been dressed and placed under scrutiny in the showcase.

1. William Angel to Susan Gibler, June 17, 1986, personal files of author.
2. Angel to Gibler, June 29, 1986.
3. Ibid.
4. Ibid.
5. Ibid.; "1986 Election Abstract," Allen County Board of Elections, Lima, Ohio.
6. Judgeships in Ohio are elected on nonpartisan ballots in the general election, giving the illusion that judges are above partisan politics. However, each party nominates judicial candidates in a partisan primary.
7. Angel to Gibler, July 27, 1986.
8. Angel to Gibler, Aug. 19, 1986.
9. Ibid. The fifteen-day window applied to the Republican Party's decision to appoint a successor to Dunlap, but both parties were required to select their respective nominees within ten days.
10. *Ohio Election Statistics: 1983–1984* (Columbus: Office of the Ohio Secretary of State, 1985), 197.
11. Angel to Gibler, Aug. 19, 1986.
12. A civil rights activist from Dayton, McLin had served in the Ohio House as one of Speaker Vern Riffe's most trusted floor leaders. He helped found BEDO, and under his leadership, the group became a powerful organizing force for black politicians. Also, McLin's early endorsement of Dick Celeste's gubernatorial bid in 1982 was instrumental in helping Celeste win the Democratic primary and go on to capture the governorship. Tim Miller, "The Celeste Era," in *Ohio Politics*, ed. Alexander Lamis (Kent, Ohio: Kent State Univ. Press, 1994), 143.
13. Angel to Gibler, Aug. 21, 1986.
14. Angel to Gibler, Aug. 19, 1986.
15. Description of this meeting, including quotations, and events leading up to it are contained in Angel to Gibler, Aug. 19, 1986. Also, see Angel, "Learning Lessons," unpublished manuscript, ca. 1992, personal files of author, 31–33.
16. Angel to Gibler, Aug. 21, 1986.
17. Description of this meeting, including quotations, come from Angel to Gibler, Aug. 21, 1986.
18. Ibid.
19. Angel to Gibler, July 27, 1986. Cora's husband, Tim, ran for county prosecutor in 1980 and for state representative in 1984, the same year Cora coordinated Gary Hart's presidential campaign in the Fourth Congressional District.
20. Ibid.
21. Ibid.
22. Evelyn Vanek, Treasurer, "Political Committee Finance Report, Allen County Democratic Party," Dec. 12, 1986.
23. Angel to Gibler, Sept. 6, 1986.

1. Donna Kauffman to Bill Angel, "Memo: Schweiterman Campaign," Aug. 26, 1986, personal files of author. Kauffman was a lecturer in the Sociology Department at OSU/Lima.

2. See William Angel, "Politics in the Real World: Rebellion and Change in the Allen County Democratic Party, 1984–1987," paper presented at the 1987 meeting of the American Political Science Association, Chicago, Sept. 1987, mimeo, 70.

3. The plan worked this way. Using its bulk mailing permit, Ohio Democratic Party sent sample ballots to all Democratic and independent voters residing within a county. The local party bore a small portion of the total expense for mailing the ballots, which were tailored for each participating county.

4. William Angel, "Learning Lessons," unpublished manuscript, ca. 1992, personal files of the author, 18.

5. Angel to R. V. Hower, Sept. 2, 1986, personal files of author. In retrospect, twelve thousand dollars seems like a paltry amount, especially when compared to the size of campaign war chests of the late 1990s, but the Allen County Democratic party in 1986 was barely able to meet its monthly operating expenses, and this figure seemed awfully large to us.

6. Elsie Crowe, Secretary, "Allen County Democratic Party, Executive Committee Minutes," Aug. 13, 1986; Evelyn Vanek, Treasurer, "Political Committee Finance Report, Allen County Democratic Party," Oct. 23, 1986; Angel to Gibler, Aug. 5, 1986; all personal files of author.

7. Twining's pro-choice views were not extreme, however. In a candidates' forum she stated that she opposed state funding for abortions: "Abortion is a personal, moral, and religious issue. Nobody should be forced to pay for something they don't believe in." *Lima News*, October 2, 1986, B3.

8. "Twining Against Further Tax Reduction," *Lima News*, Oct. 25, 1986, A12; "Twining announces proposals to protect the elderly in Ohio," *Lima News*, Oct. 14, 1986, B1.

9. Angel to Gibler, Oct. 27, 1986, personal files of author. The "Dear Friend" letter was published by the Thompson for State Representative Committee, 1986.

10. Angel to Gibler, Oct. 27, 1986.

11. Angel to Gibler, Oct. 26, 1986.

12. "Education Crucial to Revitalizing the State," *Lima News*, Sept. 4, 1986, B1.

13. This exchange occurred in early September 1986 and is reported in William Angel, "First Campaign: The Candidates," unpublished manuscript, ca. 1991, personal files of author.

14. "Twining Seeks Debate with Thompson," *Lima News*, Sept. 19, 1986, B3.

15. "Thompson Declines Debate Invitation," *Lima News*, Sept. 20, 1986, A1.

16. "Twining Says Challenge Unanswered," *Lima News*, Oct. 1, 1986, B1.

17. Ibid.

18. "Not One of the Same Old Boys" brochure, published by the Rochelle Dennis Twining for State Representative Campaign Committee, 1986, caricatures by Lima artist David Adams, personal files of author.

19. A Rashomon quality has infused this anecdote, and I hesitate to mention specific names in telling it. On election night, November 4, 1986, a reporter told Rochelle Twining and me the following story: Shortly before the ballot count began, someone in the press room at the Court House quipped that Allen County was so Republican that its voters would elect Adolf Hitler if he were on the GOP ticket. A prominent Republican, who was standing nearby, took offense and launched an expletive-filled diatribe that denounced Rochelle as, among other things, "a man-hating, ball-busting bitch." Years later, I crossed paths with this same reporter, who is no longer a journalist, and asked if he remembered telling me the story of that election-night tirade. He said that yes, he did, but he also added some clarifying detail. He was in the press room when he heard the activist rant about Twining and make some profanely crude remarks about her size. The reporter asked him to leave the press room, saying that no one wanted to hear that kind of language. The Republican complied but later returned and apologized. As for the "ball-busting bitch" comment, the reporter has since admitted that he personally did not hear the activist use those words. Those remarks were passed to him by second reporter, who now denies having witnessed the incident. Information from notes on conversation with former reporter regarding Republican activist, Aug. 14, 1999, personal files of author; telephone interview with Rochelle Twining, William Angel, interviewer, Aug. 20, 2001; telephone interview with second reporter, William Angel, interviewer, Aug. 20, 2001.

20. Thomas Suddes, "Panorama of Ohio Politics in the Voinovich Era, 1991–" in Alexander Lamis, editor, *Ohio Politics* (Kent, Ohio: Kent State University Press, 1994), 166.

21. Ibid, 166, 169.

22. Thomas Suddes, "Vernal G. Riffe, 1925–1997: He Helped Rule Ohio for 20 Years," *Cleveland Plain Dealer,* Aug. 1, 1997, 8A.

23. William Angel, "Not One of the Boys," unpublished manuscript, ca. 1992, personal files of author, 30.

24. This part of the exchange between me and Winters appears as recorded in Angel to Gibler, Oct. 2, 1986.

25. Ibid. See also Angel, "Not One of the Boys," 31. Angel to Thomas Winters, Sept. 30, 1986, WordStar disk files of author.

27. Twining telephone interview, Aug. 20, 2001; Angel to Gibler, letter, Oct. 12, 1986.

28. Angel to Gibler, July 22, 1986.

29. Angel to Gibler, Aug. 15, 1986.

30. Ibid.

31. Angel to Gibler, Sept. 18, 1986.

32. Ibid.

33. Ibid.

34. "Political Committee Finance Report, Allen County Democratic Party," Oct. 23, 1986, personal files of author. Although I am uncertain of the reasoning behind our decision to award Schwieterman and Meredith more money than Brown and Leppla, I believe it had to do with our Operations Committee's belief that Meredith had an outstanding chance of winning and that Schwieterman had a highly energized campaign— and so it appeared in September. Although Brown was performing a mighty service to the party by running as a late entrant into the campaign, no one gave him much of a

chance. As for Leppla, he hadn't exactly endeared himself to party leaders and was at the same stage of organization as Brown, who had been nominated only a month before.

35. Angel to Gibler, Sept. 18, 1986.

36. Ibid.

37. Ibid.

38. Angel to Gibler, Sept. 24, 1986.

39. Angel to Gibler, Sept. 18, 1986.

40. Angel to Gibler, Sept. 24, 1986.

41. Angel to Gibler, Oct. 20, 1986.

42. Angel to Gibler, Oct. 26, 1986.

43. "First Campaign," 10–11.

44. "Schwieterman Press Conference," mimeo transcript; Oct. 26, 1986, personal files of author.

45. "First Campaign," 11–12.

46. Angel to Gibler, Oct. 26, 1986; "Schwieterman Press Conference"; "Candidate Seeks Annexation Plans," *Lima News,* Oct. 27, 1986, D1.

47. Donna Kauffman to Angel, "Memo: Schweiterman Campaign."

48. Angel to Gibler, Nov. 4, 1986.

49. Ibid.

50. Ibid.

10. Down the Tubes

1. William Angel, "Next Year in Jerusalem," unpublished manuscript, ca. 1992, 1–2, personal files of author.

2. Notes from "Official Abstract of Votes Cast in Allen County, Ohio, on November 4, 1986," Allen County Board of Elections, Lima, Ohio, personal files of author. Also, "Thompson Snares Ohio House Seat," *Lima News,* Nov. 5, 1985, A1, A2.

3. William Angel to Susan Gibler, Nov. 11, 1986, personal files of author.

4. Ibid.

5. Angel to Gibler, Oct. 12, 1986.

6. Angel to Gibler, Nov. 11, 1986.

7. See Angel, "Next Year in Jerusalem," 3.

8. Ibid., 3–4.

9. Angel to Gibler, Jan. 14, 1987.

10. Angel to Gibler, July 29, 1986, "Environmental Issues in Forefront of Future Legal Debate: Celebreeze," *Lima News,* October 29, 1986, B1.

11. See, for instance, Ohio Citizens for Decency and Health Political Action Committee, Bill Steensland, chairman, "Why Homosexuals Support Celeste," advertisement appearing in the *Lima News,* Oct. 24, 1986, A3.

12. Tim Miller, "The Celeste Era" in Alexander Lamis, ed., *Ohio Politics* (Kent, Ohio: Kent State Univ. Press, 1994), 152–53; "Ad Campaign Becomes Issue in Ohio Gubernatorial Race," *Lima News,* Oct. 22, 1986, D3; "Celeste, Rhodes Swap Criticism over Issues," *Lima News,* Nov. 3, 1986, A1, A5; Bill Steensland, "Dear Pastor," letter, Ohio Citizens for

Decency and Health, personal files of author; Ohio Citizens for Decency and Health, "Why Homosexuals Support Celeste," paid political advertisement, *Lima News,* Oct. 24, 1986, A3.

13. Mary Anne Sharkey, "This Time Celeste Blamed Himself," *Cleveland Plain Dealer,* July 6, 1986; Miller, "The Celeste Era," 151–53.

14. "Jim Rhodes: 25 Years of Witch-Hunting, an Annotated Historical Guide to Modern Political Witch-Hunts by the Grand Old Party of Ohio," Columbus, Ohio, mimeo, 1986. This document was mailed to county chairs by Jim Ruvulo the day after the Conrad/McCartney indictments were announced. Its message was that Rhodes had used grand jury indictments to fuel his previous campaigns.

15. Angel to Gibler, Aug. 19, 1986.

16. Michael Curtin, ed., *The Ohio Politics Almanac* (Kent, Ohio: Kent State Univ. Press, 1996), 59.

17. The proposal ultimately would open license bureau franchises to competitive bidding, thus denying county chairmen the right to recommend appointments, and it would call for mail-in registration, a reform that would dry up the revenues produced by the local license bureaus themselves. See David Sturrock et al., "Ohio Elections & Political Parties in the 1990s," in *Ohio Politics,* ed. Lamis, 346.

18. Miller, "The Celeste Era," 153.

19. Angel to Gibler, Jan. 21, 1987.

20. Ibid.; Sharkey, "This Time Celeste Blamed Himself."

21. Angel to Gibler, Jan. 21, 1987.

22. Ibid.

23. Treasurer Evelyn Vanek's end-of-year report showed a cash balance of $2,421—not a lot perhaps, but considerably more than the $489.33 that had been left at the end of 1985, according to the end-of-year report that Hauenstein's treasurer, Vern Eley, submitted. "Political Party Finance Report, Allen County Democratic Party," Dec. 20, 1985; "Political Party Finance Report, Allen County Democratic Party," Dec. 12, 1986; both in personal files of author.

24. "Two Candidates for House Seat Meet at Forum," *Lima News,* Oct. 2, 1986, B3.

25. Angel to Gibler, Dec. 2, 1986; Elsie Crowe, Secretary, "Allen County Democratic Party Executive Committee Minutes," Dec. 1, 1986.

11. Gestapo Politics

1. Richard E. Siferd to Policy Studies Committee, "Minutes from December Meeting," Jan. 13, 1987, personal files of author.

2. "Candidates Focus on Landfill, Finances," *Lima News,* Oct. 29, 1986, B1; "Incumbent Eyes Revenue Sharing at Top of Agenda," *Lima News,* Nov. 2, 1987, B2.

3. "Incumbent Republican Enjoys Job of County Commissioner," *Lima News,* Nov. 2, 1986, B2.

4. "Republicans Townsend, Reese, Easily Retain Commission Seats," *Lima News,* Nov. 5, 1986, A1.

5. See "Democrat Cites Experience in Bid for County Post," *Lima News,* Nov. 2, 1986, B2, for Ed Schwieterman's view on county finances, and "Democrat Sees Need for

Balance on All-GOP Commission" *Lima News,* Nov. 2, 1986, B2, for Dale Leppla's perspective. Also, "Candidates Focus on Landfill, Finances," and "2 Challengers Take on Reese during Forum," *Lima News,* Oct. 29, 1986, B1, B3.

6. "County Sales Tax Increase Faces Minimal Opposition," *Lima News,* Feb. 4, 1987, A1.

7. Siferd to Policy Studies Committee, "Minutes of January 16 Meeting," sent Jan. 19, 1987, personal files of author.

8. William Angel, "Taxation and Representation," unpublished manuscript, ca. 1992, personal files of author, 4–5.

9. Ibid., 6.

10. "County Tax Hike Timing Questioned," *Lima News,* Jan. 30, 1987, B1.

11. WLIO TV, *Perspective,* Jan. 24, 1987. This quote is based on notes from the broadcast.

12. "Remarks by William Angel, Chair, Allen County Democratic Party, Press Conference on Proposed Increase in County Sales Tax," Jan. 29, 1987, typescript, personal files of author.

13. "County Tax Hike Timing Questioned," *Lima News,* Jan. 30, 1987, B1.

14. "County Sales Tax Faces Minimal Opposition."

15. Ibid.

16. Ibid.

17. William Angel to Susan Gibler, Feb. 17, 1987, personal files of author.

18. Ibid.

19. Ibid.

20. Ibid.

21. Angel to Gibler, Feb. 17, 1987. I do not know why Elsie changed her position. Along with the Heveners, she was among my strongest supporters in the party, and perhaps she wanted to spare me from taking a position against Hamman, Webb, and the others who wanted the party to wage a more active fight against the tax. Elsie died on June 21, 1998; I never got a chance to interview her.

22. Ibid.

23. "Local Group Eyes Referendum on Tax," *Lima News,* Feb. 19, 1987, late edition, C1.

24. Bob Routson, interview by William Angel, Oct. 2, 1998, Elida, Ohio (hereafter Routson interview). The interview was not recorded, at Routson's request.

25. Ibid.

26. See Ohio Revised Code 305.31. Eventually Routson did form a committee; the members were W. Don Fetter, Norm Kettleman, Larry Miller, and Buddy Feaser. Petition paper filed on Allen County Resolutions 87–92 and 87–93, County Auditor Dean French's office, Allen County Court House, Lima, Ohio.

27. Because a referendum election would not occur until November, the county would be unable to collect revenues from the tax increase and could not certify its share of the jail-construction grant. "Commissioners OK Sales Tax Hike," *Lima News,* Feb. 10, 1987, A1, A3; "Local Group Eyes Referendum on Tax."

28. "Local Group Eyes Referendum on Tax."

29. "County Auditor Gains Vote of Confidence," *Lima News,* Nov. 5, 1980, B3.

30. Dean French, interview by William Angel, Allen County Court House, Lima, Ohio, Sept. 18, 1998 (hereafter French interview). This portion of the interview was unrecorded.

31. "Drive May Hit Snag," *Lima News,* Mar. 11, 1987, D1; Routson interview.

32. "Drive May Hit Snag."

33. French interview.

34. Routson interview; "Future of Attempt to Referend Tax Remains Uncertain," *Lima News,* Mar. 12, 1987, D3; "Petitions Filed to Put Tax Hike before the Voters," *Lima News,* Mar. 13, 1987, D1.

35. Routson interview.

36. The following Central Committee or Executive Committee members circulated referendum petitions—Bryan Hefner, Loren Keith Myers, James Harrod, Ann Schneidhorst, Howard Greene, Frieda Hire, T. Forrest Bassinger, Richard Hullinger, Todd Hey, Cora Hamman, John Boyd, Joyce Badertscher, Walter Hawk, Kathy DeLuca, Mark Binklely, Ray Hamman, William Fricke, Helga Keith, and John Dornick. Miscellaneous petition papers filed on Allen County Resolutions 87–92 and 87–93, County Auditor Dean French's office, Allen County Court House, Lima, Ohio.

37. "Tax Hike Petitions Thorough," *Lima News,* Mar. 19, 1987, B3; "Sales Tax Referendum Effort Step Closer to Vote on Issue," Mar. 27, 1987, D4.

38. "Allen County Auditor to Inspect Tax Referendum Petitions," *Lima News,* Mar. 28, 1987.

39. French interview; Routson interview; petition paper filed on Allen County Resolutions 87–92 and 87–93, signed by Dr. L. Y. Soo, County Auditor Dean French's office, Allen County Court House, Lima, Ohio.

40. French interview.

41. "Deputies Check Legality of Tax Move Signings," *Lima News,* Apr. 2, 1987, A1.

42. "Angel Blasts County for Petition Queries," *Lima News,* Apr. 2, 1987, B3.

43. Angel to Gibler, Apr. 6, 1987.

44. "Tax Referendum May Be off Ballot," *Lima News,* Apr. 4, 1987, A8.

45. "Reese Backs Probe of Tax Petitions," *Lima News,* Apr. 7, 1987, B1.

46. French interview.

47. French interview; Routson interview; Maj. Larry Van Horn, interview by William Angel, Allen County Sheriff's Department, Jan. 20, 1999.

48. French interview.

49. French interview. See also "Deputies Check Legality of Tax Move Signings," and "Reese Backs Probe of Tax Petitions."

50. Routson interview.

51. Ibid.

52. Ibid

53. Ibid.

54. "Tax Referendum Backers Ready to Give Up the Fight," *Lima News,* Apr. 8, 1987, A1.

55. French interview.

56. Ibid.; Routson interview; "Tax Referendum May Be off Ballot," *Lima News,* Apr. 4, 1987, A8.

57. French interview.

58. Routson interview.

59. French interview.

60. "Tax Referendum Backers Ready to Give Up Fight"; Routson interview.

61. Meeting of the Policy Studies Committee, Apr. 9, 1987. Dornick's quote is based upon personal recollection of the author, plus that of Rick Siferd.

62. "Unseemly Factor Added to Tax Vote," *Lima News,* Apr. 5, 1987, F1.

63. "County Receives Written Request to End Tax Issue," *Lima News,* Apr. 10, 1987, D1.

64. See Carla Coleson, "Progress Hindered by Constant Negativism," Feb. 23, 1987, B2; Rena Scarberry, "New Jail Facility Is Imperative" Feb. 23, 1987, B2; Jack Somerville, "New Jail Is Investment in the Future" Feb. 26, 1987, B2; all *Lima News,* letters to the editor.

65. Routson interview.

66. Angel to Gibler, Mar. 9, 1987; "Tax Petition Drive 300 Short," *Lima News,* Mar. 10, 1987, B3.

67. French interview.

12. *Steering a Course*

1. William Angel to Susan Gibler, June 30, 1987. This letter contains the complete account of our meeting with the Heys and of the conversation between Webb and me that followed.

2. Angel to Gibler, May 26, 1987.

3. My description of this meeting is found in Angel to Gibler, Mar. 9, 1987.

4. At the time, political forces were stymieing legislation on the license bureau issue. See "Why No Auto-Tag Bill?" *Toledo Blade,* June 4, 1987, 14.

5. Angel to Gibler, May 26, 1987.

6. Ibid.

7. Angel to Gibler, June 1, 1987.

8. Angel to Gibler, June 30, 1987.

9. Ibid.

10. Ibid.

11. Angel to Gibler, July 6, 1987; "Webb to Head License Bureau," *Lima News,* July 1, 1987.

12. Angel to Gibler, July 6, 1987.

13. Angel to Gibler, June 30, 1987.

14. Angel to Gibler, July 20, 1987.

15. Angel to Gibler, Aug. 11, 1987.

16. Angel to Gibler, July 20, 1987.

17. Ibid.

18. Ibid.

19. Elsie Crowe, Secretary, "Allen County Democratic Party, Executive Committee Minutes," Sept. 15, 1987.

20. Angel to Gibler, July 20, 1987.

21. My letters from this period are filled with stories detailing Cora Hamman's exasperating conduct. The following represents one of the more humorous ones. Angel to Gibler, May 11, 1987.

22. Angel to Gibler, May 11, 1987. Also, my interview with Twining, Jan. 26, 1999, Lima, Ohio, confirms this version of the story.

23. Angel to Gibler, Mar. 9, 1987.

24. Twining interview, Jan. 26, 1999.

25. Angel to Gibler, Sept. 14, 1987.

26. Ibid.

27. Angel to Gibler, July 20, 1987.

13. Boddie/Horne

1. Discussion of this meeting is found in Angel to Gibler, letter, 26 May 1987, personal files of author. Vorhees, Sciranka, and Cunningham later became Republicans.

2. "Williams Defeats Joseph in Presidency Race," *Lima News,* Nov. 7, 1979, A1, A3; "Williams Says Election Win Vindicates Stand on Issues," *Lima News,* Nov. 9, 1983, A1; Official Abstract of Votes Cast in Allen County, Ohio, November 6, 1979, Allen County Board of Elections, Lima, Ohio; Official Abstract of Votes Cast in Allen County, Ohio, November 8, 1983, Allen County Board of Elections, Lima, Ohio.

3. Minutes of the Executive Committee of the Allen County Democratic Party, Jan. 21, 1987.

4. Angel to Gibler, May 26, 1987.

5. Ibid.

6. "Nominating Petition for Leonard W. Boddie," Leonard W. Boddie File, Allen County Board of Elections, Lima, Ohio.

7. Elsie Crowe, Secretary, "Allen County Democratic Party, Executive Committee Minutes, Feb. 18, 1987" ; Angel to Gibler, Apr. 13, 1987.

8. Molly Ivins, *You Got to Dance with Them What Brung You: Politics in the Clinton Years* (New York: Random House, 1998), xxii.

9. Angel to Gibler, Apr. 6, Apr. 13, 1987.

10. Angel to Gibler, May 26, 1987.

11. Ibid. Boddie's financial reports show that Hey contributed only twenty-five dollars to the Boddie campaign, doing so on June 12, 1987. Leonard W. Boddie file.

12. Angel to Gibler Aug. 11, 1987.

13. Angel to Gibler, Aug. 17, 1987.

14. Ibid.

15. "City Employees Question New Residency Policy," *Lima News,* June 18, 1987, A1; "Residency Policy Has 3 Aims, Mayor Says," *Lima News,* June 19, 1987, D1.

16. "Residency Policy Has 3 Aims, Mayor Says."

17. Angel to Gibler, Sept. 1, 1987.

18. Following a meeting with union leaders at which he had encountered their adamant opposition, Joseph finally withdrew his proposal for a residency requirement. "Mayor to Talk with Unions before Deciding on Residency," *Lima News,* Aug. 6, 1987, B1; "Joseph Shelves Residency Plan," *Lima News,* Aug. 14, 1987, A1.

19. Angel to Gibler, Sept. 1, 1987.

20. Angel to Gibler, Sept. 14, 1987.

21. Executive Committee minutes in 1990–91 show an active minority caucus under Dobbins's direction, even though Boddie technically was still president of the organization. See Carol Falk, Secretary, "Minutes of the Allen County Democratic Party," Oct. 16, 1990; Jan. 15, Feb. 19, Mar. 19, 1991; typescript, personal files of author. See also Dollie

Taylor, Secretary, "Minutes, Democratic Minority Caucus Meeting," Leonard Boddie, acting chairman, typescript, personal files of author.

22. William Riordon, *Plunkitt of Tammany Hall* (New York: Dutton, 1963), 25.

23. "Challenger Raps Incumbent in City Race," Oct. 5, 1987, B3; "Boddie Responds to Horne," Oct. 12, 1987, B1; "Sixth Ward Candidates Exchange Barbs," Oct. 28, 1987, D1; all *Lima News.*

24. "Councilman Responds to Challengers' Charges," *Lima News,* Oct. 8, 1987, D3; "Sixth Ward Candidates Exchange Barbs."

25. "Boddie Responds to Horne"; "Campaign Literature Defended by Horne," *Lima News,* Oct. 31, 1987, A4.

26. Leonard W. Boddie to John Dornick, chair, Allen County Democratic Party Budget Committee, June 11, 1987, personal files of author; "Report of the Budget Committee," Oct. 20, 1987, John Dornick, Chairman, personal files of author; Evelyn Vanek, Treasurer, "Political Party Finance Report, Pre-election, Allen County Democratic Party," Oct. 22, 1987, personal files of author; Elsie Crowe, Secretary, "Allen County Democratic Party, Executive Committee Minutes," Oct. 20, 1987, personal files of author.

27. Angel to Gibler, Oct. 17, 1987.

28. "Challenger Raps Incumbent in City Race," *Lima News,* Oct. 5, 1987.

29. Williams's decision to endorse Boddie was apparently taken independently of any advice from his campaign staff. Both Harry Hale, his campaign manager, and Dale Leppla, one of Furl's principal advisers, later reprimanded him for doing it. Angel to Gibler, Oct. 27, 1987.

30. As recorded in Angel to Gibler, Oct. 17, 1987.

31. Ibid.

32. In 1989 Victory Village was torn down and replaced by the Steiner/McBride Apartments, a public housing project consisting a single-story rowhouses.

33. Boddie/Horne debate, videotape, personal files of author.

34. Ibid.

35. Ibid.

36. Ibid.

37. Boddie's campaign finance reports show that Webb donated three hundred dollars to the campaign, including a $250 contribution during the week before the election. Angel to Gibler, Nov. 4, 1987; "Campaign Finance Report, Leonard W. Boddie for Sixth Ward City Council," B. Lamont Monford Chair, Dec. 7, 1987, Leonard W. Boddie File, Allen County Board of Elections, Lima, Ohio. As of Feb. 1999, Boddie's 1987 campaign showed an outstanding loan; hence, the file was still active and still being maintained by the Allen County Board of Elections. Normally, the board holds files for only six years, which is why Horne's finance reports were not available.

38. "Three Incumbents Ousted from Council," *Lima News,* Nov. 4, 1987, A3; Angel to Gibler, Nov. 4, 1987.

39. "Campaign Finance Report, Post-Election," Leonard Boddie for Sixth Ward City Council, B. Lamont Monford, Treasurer, Dec. 7, 1987; and "Campaign Finance Report, Pre-election," Leonard Boddie for Sixth Ward City Council, B. Lamont Monford, Treasurer, Oct. 20, 1987; Leonard Boddie File, Allen County Board of Elections, Lima, Ohio.

40. "Candidate Opposes MHA Plans," *Lima News,* Sept. 30, 1987, D1; "Cutting City's

MHA Link Might Be Complex Task," *Lima News,* Oct. 1, 1987, B1; "Shepherd, Daley Clash over MHA," *Lima News,* Oct. 27, 1987, B1.

41. "Warning," paid political advertisement, Charles Brogee, Treasurer, J. Vane Shepherd Committee, *Lima News,* Oct. 29, 1987, A5; Angel to Gibler, Nov. 4, 1987.

42. "Williams Criticizes Shepherd," *Lima News,* Oct. 1, 1987, B3. See also "Williams Kicks Off Campaign," *Lima News,* Sept. 3, 1987, B1; "Keeping Council in Good Hands Williams' Goal," *Lima News,* Nov. 1, 1987, B1.

43. "Williams Swamps Shepherd," *Lima News,* Nov. 4, 1987, A1.

44. Angel to Gibler, Sept. 28, 1987.

45. Actually, the party gave $620 to Williams—five hundred directly to the campaign itself and $120 to Democrats for Furl Williams. Williams ended up with $925 altogether from Democratic sources. See "Political Committee Finance Report," Democrats for Furl Williams Committee, Steve Webb, Treasurer, Dec. 1, 1987; and "Political Party Finance Report," Allen County Democratic Party, Evelyn Vanek, Treasurer, Oct. 22, 1987, both in personal files of author.

46. Todd G. Hey, "Blaming the Party Is Inappropriate," letter to the editor, *Lima News,* Nov. 15, 1987, E6.

14. Warm Bodies

1. William Angel to Susan Gibler, Jan. 12, 1988, personal files of author.

2. Ibid.

3. I did talk to two other prospects. Shortly before Christmas I tried to recruit Randy Reeves, a young attorney who in 1986 had run in the Democratic primary for county commissioner against Dale Leppla. Reeves had law enforcement background, I had been told, but he also had a young family and could not take the time away from developing his law practice. I also asked Ted Wade, 1984's Democratic candidate for sheriff, to run, but Wade was still burned out by that campaign.

4. Angel to Gibler, Jan. 12, 1988. Quotes as reported by Rochelle Twining.

5. Angel to Gibler, Jan. 12, 1987.

6. The following offices were up for election—state representative (First Ohio House District), sheriff, county prosecutor, county clerk of courts, county recorder, county treasurer, coroner, county engineer, and two seats on the county commission. The senate seat was for the Twelfth District.

7. Official Abstract of Votes in Allen County, Ohio, 1990 primary election, Allen County Board of Elections, Lima, Ohio. Voter lists are maintained for four-year cycles, and partisan figures may vary slightly from year to year, but the 1990 figures are typical for the time frame of this analysis.

8. Angel to Gibler, Dec. 19, 1987.

9. Stanford Odesky and Associates, "Allen County Base Line Study," mimeo, personal files of author, Dec. 1987, 8.

10. Angel to Gibler, Jan. 28, 1988.

11. Ibid.

12. Ibid.

13. Ibid.

14. Angel to Gibler, Nov. 12, 1987.

15. Ibid.

16. Angel to Gibler, Jan. 28, 1988.

17. Ida Kay Keller, interview by William Angel, Spencerville, Ohio, Feb. 13, 1999 (hereafter Keller interview).

18. Angel to Gibler, Dec. 28, 1986, Feb. 10, 1987.

19. "Group Seeks Help in Landfill Battle," *Lima News,* Jan. 30, 1987, B3.

20. Keller interview.

21. "Area Landfill Opposition Continues," Feb. 24, 1987, A1.

22. "Nichols Attacks Statement by Geologist on Landfill Site," *Lima News,* Feb. 27, 1987, D1; Keller interview.

23. Keller interview.

24. Ibid.; "EPA Assessment Nixes Proposed Landfill Location," *Lima News,* Nov. 17, 1987, A1.

25. "Village Gives Shank Hero's Welcome," *Lima News,* Nov. 19, 1987, A1. Headline refers to Richard Shank, director of the Ohio EPA.

26. Keller interview.

27. Odesky and Associates, "Allen County Base Line Study," 7.

28. Angel to Gibler, Jan. 28, 1988; Twining interview, Feb. 11, 1999; Keller interview.

29. Angel to Gibler, Jan. 28, 1988.

30. "Locker Announces Senate Candidacy," *Lima News,* Feb. 2, 1988, B1.

31. "Fuqua Running for Ohio Senate," *Lima News,* Feb. 18, 1988, D1.

32. Judge Michael Rumer of Allen County Common Pleas Court had appointed Twining to the post, much to the chagrin of most Republican activists. They feared that Twining might use the post to launch another run at political office. Rumer, to his credit, recognized that Twining had the interpersonal skills needed to make this office function efficiently and ignored the political pressure.

33. Angel to Gibler, Feb. 25, 1988.

34. Ibid.

35. Ibid.

36. Ibid.

37. This confrontation occurred on the doorstep of the Allen County Board of Elections, on Feb. 25, 1988. Steve Webb and I were inside watching the board inspect candidates' petitions when Leppla arrived and called me outside. It was an unforgettable conversation.

38. Credit must go to Judith Viorst, *Alexander and the Terrible, Horrible, No Good, Very Bad Day* (New York: Atheneum, 1972). Even politicians have days like Alexander's.

39. Angel to Gibler, Feb. 25, 1988. This letter mentions only my "horrific day" trying to recruit candidates on Saturday, Feb. 13, but I remember that day vividly.

40. Ibid. Here, I wrote only that the "Speakers office called," not mentioning Marsh specifically. I remember the caller as Ty Marsh, however, and at some point in studying the letter I scribbled his name in the margin of the page describing this controversy.

41. Ibid.

42. Elsie Crowe, Secretary, "Allen County Democratic Party, Executive Committee Minutes," Feb. 17, 1988.

43. Twining interview, Feb. 11, 1999.

44. Speeches and comments are reconstructed from Allen County Democratic Party, Executive Committee Minutes, Feb. 17, 1988, personal files of author.

15. Lean Slate

1. "Democratic Party Boss Not Worried about Lean Slate in '88," *Lima News,* Feb. 20, 1988, A1.

2. Ibid.

3. E. E. Schattschneider has discussed power in terms of the ability to manage conflict, stressing at one point, "The definition of the alternatives is the supreme instrument of power." This was a lesson I had absorbed and applied in this specific situation. See Schattschneider, *The Semi-Sovereign People: A Realist's View of Democracy in America* (New York: Harcourt, Brace, and Jovanovich, 1975), 66.

4. William Angel to Susan Gibler, Mar. 29, 1988, personal files of author.

5. Angel to Gibler, Feb. 23, 1987.

6. Angel to Gibler, May 11, 1987.

7. Ibid.

8. Angel to Gibler, Mar. 2, 1988.

9. Twining interview, Jan. 26, 1999.

10. Angel to Gibler, Mar. 2, 1988.

11. Ibid.

12. *Ohio's Election Laws, Annotated* (Columbus: Banks-Baldwin, 1988), Ohio Revised Code (ORC), 3513.30; Angel to Gibler, Mar. 2, 1988.

13. Twining interview, Jan. 26. 1999.

14. In Jan. 1988, the Executive Committee elected me to succeed Paul Prater, whose term expired on Feb. 29. Elsie Crowe, Secretary, "Allen County Democratic Party, Executive Committee Minutes," Jan. 13, 1988.

15. Angel to Gibler, Mar. 2, 1988.

16. Angel to Gibler, Mar. 29, 1988.

17. Minutes of Mar. 4, 1988, board meeting, Donna Johns, director, Allen County Board of Elections, Lima, Ohio.

18. Angel to Gibler, Mar. 29, 1988.

19. Twining interview, Jan. 26, 1999; Angel to Gibler, Mar. 29, 1988.

20. Angel to Gibler, Mar. 29, 1988.

21. Ibid. As a protest on Linda's behalf, the Heveners did not buy tickets to the 1988 Ohio Democratic Party dinner, prompting a phone call from Sherrod Brown himself, who attempted to explain his side of the story.

22. "Twining Resigns Support Agency Post," *Lima News,* Apr. 29, 1988, B1.

23. "Parties Pick Committee Reps," *Lima News,* May 4, 1988, B3.

24. Angel to Gibler, Mar. 29, 1988.

25. James M. Ruvulo to William Angel, Apr. 1, 1988, personal files of author; also, Allen County Democratic Party, "Allen County Democrat Endorsed Candidates," issued and paid for by Allen County Democrat Executive Committee, Evelyn Vanek Treasurer, May 1988, personal files of author.

26. Judy Humes, "Leadership in Question," *Lima News,* Apr. 5, 1988, B2.

27. Vernon Eley, "Self-Exposure More Important," *Lima News,* Apr. 9, 1988, A12; Richard Groves, "Isn't It Time to Take Action?" *Lima News,* Apr. 15, 1988, B8.

28. Daniel J. Kline, "Members Need to Know Truth," *Lima News,* Apr. 25, 1988, D1.

29. Deborah Ioannidis, "Angel's Efforts Commendable," *Lima News,* Apr. 9, 1988, A12. See also Katherine DeLuca, "Time to Step Up to the Future," *Lima News,* Apr. 18, 1988, D1; Clementina DePalma, "Current Dem Leaders Working Diligently to Strengthen the Party," *Lima News,* Apr. 20, 1988, D2.

30. Charles Hauenstein, "Support Hey, Return Pride to the Party," *Lima News,* Apr. 30, 1988, A10.

31. Grass Roots Campaign Committee, "Grass Roots Sample Ballot," mimeo, 1988, personal files of author.

32. Grass Roots Campaign Committee, "Want Ads," 1988, mimeo, personal files of author.

33. *Democratic Voice of Allen County* 1, no. 1 (Spring 1988).

34. Allen County Democratic Party, "Political Party Finance Report, Post-Primary," June 9, 1988, Evelyn Vanek, Treasurer, personal files of author.

16. The Social Club

1. "Everett Stemen Obituary," *Lima News,* Apr. 13, 1988, A4.

2. Angel to Gibler, Apr. 19, 1988, personal files of author. This incident became part of party folklore. Mary Hevener later checked the deceased Everett's registration, and sure enough, he was a Democrat. The Stemen family sent a card thanking the Democratic Party for the floral arrangement. For the record, Everett L. Stemen died in April 1993, almost five years to the day after Everett P. Stemen passed away.

3. Ida Kay Keller, interview by William Angel, Feb. 13, 1999.

4. "Allen Democrats Struggle over Party Leadership Roles," *Lima News,* May 2, 1988, C5.

5. WLIO *News Journal,* May 2, 1988, tape, personal files of author; "Allen Democrats Struggle over Party Leadership Roles."

6. "Allen County Democrats Struggle over Party Leadership Roles."

7. WLIO *News Journal,* May 2, 1988; "Allen Democrats Struggle over Party Leadership Roles."

8. The occasion was the 1987 ox roast, when Bryan received the first-ever Gerry Tebben Democrat of the Year Award. Angel to Gibler, Oct. 17, 1987.

9. Angel to Gibler, Apr. 30, 1988.

10. Angel to Gibler, Feb. 25, 1988.

11. Angel to Gibler, May 6, 1988.

12. Democrat County Central Committee, "Allen County Board of Elections Tally Sheet," May 3, 1988, personal files of author.

13. WLIO *News Journal,* May 4, 1988, tape, personal files of author.

14. "Angel Likely to Retain Control of Dem Party," *Lima News,* May 4, 1988, B1.

15. WLIO *News Journal,* May 4, 1988.

16. Ibid.

17. Dukakis won 28,378 votes in the Fourth Congressional District, compared to Jesse Jackson's 7,368, meaning Dukakis won three delegates from the district, Jackson one. *Lima News,* May 4, 1988, A5.

18. Sometime previously (my notes say fall 1987), Cora had had surgery.

19. This episode, including characterization and dialogue, is presented as recorded in my letter to Susan Gibler, June 6, 1988.

20. Ibid.

21. Ibid.

22. Ibid.

23. Ibid. Notes from conversation between Becky Fox and Bill Angel, ca. May 18, 1988, personal files of author.

24. Angel to Gibler, June 6, 1988. I was citing Ohio's Election Laws Annotated, ORC 3517.04, which stated, "In case of a county Central Committee, the meeting shall be held not earlier than six nor later than fifteen days following the declaration of the results by the board of elections."

25. Angel to Gibler, June 6, 1988; Jonathan W. Marshall to Bill Angel, May 18, 1988, personal files of author.

26. Angel to Gibler, June 6, 1988.

27. Allen County Board of Elections minutes, May 19, 1988, Allen County Board of Elections, Lima, Ohio.

28. Elsie Crowe to Central Committee representative, May 19, 1988, personal files of author.

29. Angel to Gibler, June 6, 1988.

30. Ibid.

31. Ibid. The recount was eventually set for June 1. The victors being challenged were Dean Diehl, Lima 1E, five-vote margin; Charles Brown, Lima 4E, one-vote margin; Evelyn Vanek, Lima 4I, one-vote margin; Everett L. Stemen, Marion East, one-vote margin; Raymond Doyle, Lima 8F, one-vote margin; Gary Hoffer, Shawnee A, three-vote margin; Paula Shrader, Shawnee C, three-vote margin; and Louis C. Daley, Sugar Creek East, one-vote margin. *Bendele et al.* v. *Webb et al.,* summons filed in Allen County Common Pleas Court, 88-Civ 253, May 27, 1988, personal files of author; Democrat County Central Committee tally sheet, May 3, 1988, personal files of author.

32. Angel to Gibler, June 6, 1988.

33. "Rose-less Race for House Seat Cheers Democrats," Feb. 19, 1986, B1.

34. Donna Johns, Secretary, "Allen County Board of Elections Minutes," May 26, 1988, Allen County Board of Elections, Lima, Ohio.

35. *Bendele et al.* v. *Webb et al.,* complaint for injunction with attached motion for temporary restraining order and affidavit, Allen County Common Pleas Court, 88-Civ-253, May 26, 1988; Angel to Gibler, June 6, 1988.

36. Ohio's Election Laws Annotated, ORC 3517.04, "Meetings and Organization of Major Party Central Committees"; Angel to Gibler, June 6, 1988.

37. Despite Judge Light's order, we would have remained subject to Hey's lawsuit had recounts changed outcomes of any of the races at issue. On June 1, those eight Central Committee races were counted again, and not a single outcome was changed.

Allen County Board of Elections minutes, June 1, 1988, Donna Johns, director, Allen County Board of Elections, Lima, Ohio.

38. Elsie Crowe, Secretary, "Minutes, Allen County Reorganization Meeting," May 26, 1988; tally sheets for Allen County Democratic Party Central Committee chairman, Mary Hevener (chief teller), PC Wrencher and Rose Madonia (assistant tellers), May 26, 1988, personal files of author; "County Dems Organize," *Lima News,* May 27, 1988, B1.

39. *WLIO News Journal,* May 26, 1988, videotape, personal files of author.

40. Angel to Gibler, June 6, 1988.

17. No More Pressure

1. Allen County Reorganization meeting, minutes, May 26, 1988, personal files of author; William Angel to Susan Gibler, June 6, 1988, personal files of author.

2. I have no notes or detailed descriptions of this meeting. As far as I know, written records of this confrontation no longer exist. But I do make reference to the meeting in my letter to Susan Gibler, June 25, 1988, in which I reiterate things that were said at that confrontation.

3. Dialogue reported in Angel to Gibler, June 25, 1988.

4. Ibid.

5. Angel to Gibler, July 8, 1988.

6. Ibid.

7. Phone conversation between author and Pearl Ward, Mar. 8, 1999. Angel to Gibler, July 8, Angel to Gibler, July 14, 1988.

8. Angel to Gibler, Aug. 18, 1988.

9. Ibid.

10. Ibid.

11. Ibid.

12. William Angel, "Journal, 1988 Democratic National Convention, Atlanta, Georgia, July 18–22, 1988," handwritten notebook, personal files of author, 9.

13. Ibid, 43–50.

14. Elsie Crowe, Secretary, Allen County Democratic Party, Executive Committee Minutes, Aug. 16, 1988, personal files of author.

15. Angel, "Journal, 1988 Democratic National Convention, 50.

16. Going into the convention, Jesse Jackson and his adherents felt snubbed by the Dukakis organization. Never seriously considered for the vice-presidential nomination and insulted by Michael Dukakis's cavalier treatment of his candidacy, Jackson had to fight for respect from Dukakis, who condescendingly allowed Jackson's name to go into nomination and reluctantly permitted debate on three of Jackson's platform planks. Jack Germond and Jules Witcover, *Whose Broad Stripes and Bright Stars? The Trivial Pursuit of the Presidency, 1988* (New York: Warner Books, 1989), 336–50.

17. Brent Larkin and Mary Anne Sharkey, "Celeste Womanizing Worries Aides," *Cleveland Plain Dealer,* June 3, 1987, 1A, 15A. There were other problems with a Celeste presidential bid, most notably the string of scandals that had affected his administration; Joe Hallett of the *Toledo Blade* saw Celeste's marital infidelity as the final straw. Joe Hallett,

"Statehouse Notebook," *Toledo Blade,* June 7, 1987, A3. Also, Tim Miller, "The Celeste Era, 1983–1991," in *Ohio Politics,* ed. Alexander Lamis (Kent, Ohio: Kent State Univ. Press, 1994), 154.

18. Mary Anne Sharkey, "Celeste Left on Sidelines," *Cleveland Plain Dealer,* July 20, 1988, A13.

19. See William Angel, "Journal, 1988 Democratic National Convention, Atlanta, Georgia," 21.

20. Ibid., 52.

21. "Dukakis to Focus on Economic Issues in Ohio Visit," *Lima News,* Oct. 14, 1988, B3.

22. "Aide Raps Duke's Ohio Bid," *Lima News,* Nov. 2, 1988, A1; also, "Dukakis Needs to Pay Attention to Ohio: Dems," *Lima News,* Sept. 3, 1988, B1.

23. "Dukakis to Focus on Economic Issues in Ohio Visit."

24. "Bush Promises No Tax Increase," *Lima News,* Sept. 17, 1988, A1; "Bush Warms Lima Area GOP," *Lima News,* Oct. 26, 1988, A1.

25. "Quayle Touts Education to Students in Ottawa," *Lima News,* Oct. 11, 1988, A1; "Quayle Visit Designed to Get Out GOP Vote," *Lima News,* Oct. 11, A5; "Quayle Blasts Dukakis in Swing through the Area," *Lima News,* Oct. 12, 1988, B1; "Reagan: Democrats out of Touch," *Lima News,* Oct. 20, 1988, A1, A2; "Bush Stand on Pledge Earns Praise: HUD Chief Speaks at Ohio Northern," *Lima News,* Oct. 6, 1988, B1; and "Maureen Reagan Urges GOP to Keep Working," Oct. 26, 1988, D1.

26. "Humanitarian Ideals Fuel Actor's Politics," *Lima News,* Sept. 28, 1988, A1.

27. "Bush's Son Campaigns to Buoy Party Workers," *Lima News,* Sept. 30, 1988, B1.

28. Stanford H. Odesky and Associates, "Allen County Pre-election Poll," July 1988, mimeo, personal files of author, 10.

29. Angel to Gibler, Aug. 18, 1988.

30. Angel to Gibler, Nov. 15, 1988.

31. Warren was the more seasoned of the two candidates. Although both had extensive legal experience, Warren had practiced law for twenty-two years, eighteen as an assistant county prosecutor. Rizor, by contrast, had only twelve years' experience as a practicing attorney, none in a prosecutorial capacity.

32. Angel to Gibler, Aug. 24, 1988.

33. Angel to Gibler, Nov. 15, 1988.

34. Ibid.

35. Ibid.

36. "Warren Wins Gavel in Allen Judge Race, *Lima News,* Nov. 9, 1988, B1.

37. Stanford Odesky and Associates, "Allen County Pre-election Poll," 9–10.

38. "Challenger Says Tax Payers Have Paid for Poor Leadership," *Lima News,* Nov. 6, 1988, B1; "1.15 Million Estimate Put on Gregg's Work," *Lima News,* Sept. 2, 1988, B1.

39. Only 8 percent of respondents listed taxes as a "major problem facing residents of Allen County." By contrast, the landfill drew 25 percent, waste disposal 24 percent, and water 23 percent. Residents outside Lima had stronger attitudes about environmental issues than did Lima residents. Odesky and Associates, "Allen County Pre-election Poll," 6.

40. "County Rejects Annexation of Camp Woodhaven," *Lima News,* Oct. 18, 1988, B1.

41. "Townships Find Voting Clout Strong in Allen," *Lima News,* Apr. 29, 1988, B1.

42. Angel to Gibler, Nov. 15, 1988.

43. Ibid.

44. Ibid.

45. "Republicans Maintain Hold on County Commission," *Lima News,* Nov. 9, 1988, A1. In 1986, Reese drew 17,775 votes; Leppla, 12,672; and Joan Petty, an independent candidate, 3,155. *1986 General Election Abstract,* Allen County Board of Elections, Lima, Ohio.

46. Stanford Odesky and Associates, "Allen County Pre-election Poll," 10.

47. Angel to Gibler, June 25, 1988.

48. John and Mary Hevener had originally agreed to direct Ida Kay's race, but the Heveners had to relinquish their responsibilities to Twining when John was diagnosed with postpolio syndrome. Angel to Gibler, Aug. 24, 1988.

49. "Keller Challenges Mayer to Debate," *Lima News,* Sept. 16, 1988, B1.

50. Ibid.

51. "Debate Considered," *Lima News,* Sept. 17, 1988, A8.

52. "Mayer Says He'll Debate Keller Only during Public Forum Series," *Lima News,* Sept. 19, 1988, B3.

53. Angel to Gibler, Nov. 15, 1988.

54. Bush took 30,991 votes in Allen County, compared to Dukakis's 13,712, a 69 percent to 31 percent victory for the vice president. Dukakis's showing was comparable to Carter's 1980 total of 13,140 (30 percent) and well ahead of Mondale's 12,176 (27 percent). *Ohio Election Statistics, 1979–1980* (Columbus: Office of the Ohio Secretary of State, 1980), 158; *Ohio Election Statistics, 1983–1984* (Columbus: Office of the Ohio Secretary of State, 1985), 151; *Lima News,* Nov. 9, 1988, A5.

55. "Republicans Maintain Hold on County Commission," *Lima News,* Nov. 9, 1988, A1.

57. In 1980 Mayer won 25,217 votes, defeating Democrat James Shafer, who drew 13,938 in a multicandidate race. Four years later, Mayer took 30,821 votes, more than doubling Mel Woodard's total of 13,791. In the 1984 election, John Coplen came close to the twenty-thousand-vote barrier, winning 19,952 in his loss to Ed Peyton, who drew 24,650. *Ohio Election Statistics, 1979–1980,* 203; *Ohio Election Statistics, 1983–1984,* 197.

57. Angel to Gibler, Nov. 15, 1988.

58. Rizor ended up with $2,000, Leppla with $1,700, and Keller with $1,600. "Political Party Finance Report, Pre-election," Allen County Democratic Party, Evelyn Vanek, Treasurer, Oct. 27, 1988; "Political Party Finance Report, Post-election," Allen County Democratic Party, Evelyn Vanek, Treasurer, Dec. 13, 1988; both personal files of author.

59. Cupp nearly doubled Locker's vote total in defeating him, 83,249 to 44,503, winning 65 percent of the vote. Locker never seemed to find direction. In a one-week period in July, the senate caucus informed him that he would not receive any media money, and the Ohio Education Association (OEA) endorsed Bob Cupp. Those two blows sent Dale into a funk, from which he never recovered. Angel to Gibler, July 14, 1988, and Aug. 18, 1988; and "Cupp Clobbers Locker," *Lima News,* Nov. 9, 1988, A1.

60. "Allen Democratic Chief Optimistic Despite Losses," *Lima News,* Nov. 11, 1988, D1.

61. Ibid.

62. "Celeste Expected to OK Auto Registration Reforms," *Lima News,* Nov. 18, 1988, C3; memo from James M. Ruvulo to county chairs, Dec. 8, 1988, personal files of author.

63. *Lima News*, Nov. 9, 1988, A5; *Ohio Election Statistics, 1983–1984*, 151.

64. Angel to Gibler, July 8, 1988.

65. Hey managed to contest only thirty-eight of our loyal Central Committee representatives, losing twenty-nine of those races. Dornick won his Central Committee chairmanship without opposition. "New County Democrat Leaders Optimistic about Fall Prospects," *Lima News*, June 1, 1990, A4; William Angel, personal journal, entry for May 31, 1990, personal files of author. List of candidates in Democratic Central Committee races, undated but ca. Mar. 1990, compiled by the Allen County Board of Elections, personal files of author; John Hevener, untitled, notes handicapping 1990 Central Committee races, personal files of author.

18. Dancin'

1. Actually, two of Jackson's planks were at issue before the Ohio delgates, and both required "no" votes. The other one proposed a fairer tax system and was known as the "tax-the-rich" plank. Unlike the no-first-use plank, it drew little support from the Ohio delegates. Dukakis wanted to stress "responsible fiscal management," and he did not want to go on record as "raising taxes." Of course, Bush would hammer him on this one anyway—"Read my lips" and all that. William Angel, "Journal, 1988 Democratic National Convention, Atlanta, Georgia, July 18–22, 1988," 15–16.

2. Ibid.

3. Description of this meeting, including dialogue, comes directly from my letter to Susan Gibler, Feb. 2, 1987, personal files of author.

4. See William Angel, "Construction of Landfill Would Be Detrimental to Entire County," *Lima News*, Jan. 1, 1987. I also attended and spoke at several Dumpbuster rallies.

5. Rick Siferd's firm, for instance, did legal work for Waste Management, Inc., the firm that was spearheading landfill development. Howard Elstro, who at the time worked as David Berger's assistant at Project Rehab, was concerned that Rehab would have to haul its waste to landfills outside the county, adding expenses to the organization's tight budget.

6. This quote is taken from my notes on Joseph's letter, as stated in my letter to Susan Gibler, Feb. 2, 1987.

7. Angel to Gibler, Feb. 2, 1987.

8. William Angel to Governor Richard Celeste, Feb. 16, 1988, personal files of author; Angel to Gibler, Feb. 10, 1987.

9. "Commissioners Urged to Re-establish County Landfill District," *Lima News*, Mar. 26, 1987, D1; "Statement by Bill Angel," press conference on the Spencerville landfill, Mar. 26, 1987, personal files of author.

10. Ida Kay Keller, interview by William Angel, Feb. 13, 1999.

11. William Angel, "Dumpbusters," typescript, unpublished manuscript, ca. 1992, 15–16.

12. William Angel to Governor Celeste, Oct. 30, 1987, personal files of author. The rally was held on Oct. 31, and I mistakenly dated the letter October 30.

13. During the week after my meeting Mongelluzzo and Coplen, I met with Kevin Haver, director of the metro-park district, and Carol Decker, president of the TriMoraine

Audubon Society. I discovered that their original opposition to Waste Management's plan had cooled considerably and that the park district had been negotiating an agreement with the company. "City Council OKs Ordinance on Area Landfill, *Lima News,* May 5, 1987, D1; "Council Action No Surprise to Dumpbusters," *Lima News,* May 5, 1987, D1. For environmentalists' views, see Angel to Gibler, Feb. 10, 1987, and "Landfill Official in Agreement with Park Plan," *Lima News,* Feb. 20, 1987, D1.

14. Robert Putnam, *Making Democracy Work* (Princeton, N.J.: Princeton Univ. Press, 1993), 167–71; and Robert Putnam, "Bowling Alone: America's Declining Social Capital," *Journal of Democracy* 6 (Jan. 1995): 65–78.

15. Our headquarters had moved to the Union Centre on North Main Street in Lima prior to the 1988 election.

16. "Boycott of LMH Solicited: Democratic Chairman Urges Nurses' Support," *Lima News,* Aug. 2, 1989, A1.

17. Letters to the editor provide critical insights into conditions at LMH prior to the strike. Although the nurses at LMH were underpaid relative to other hospitals in the area, the letters from LMPNA members and their advocates focused primarily on noneconomic issues, among which were problems caused by understaffing. See Winnie Pickering, MS, RN, "Nurses Taking Stand for What They Believe," *Lima News,* Jan. 25, 1989, B2; Karen Melhaus, RN-C, "Nurses Want Some Control over Their Futures," *Lima News,* Jan. 25, 1989, B2; Pamela Winkle, "Nurse Shares Frustrations of Profession," *Lima News,* Feb. 6, 1989, C2; Terri Shaw, RN, Phylis Turrentine, RN, and Julie Hattery, RN, "LMH Ignored Nurses' Plea for Help," *Lima News,* June 3, 1989, A10; L. Hunter, RN, BSN, "LMH Nurses Don't Want a Strike," *Lima News,* June 1, 1989, D2; Ann Muhler, RN, "Quality of Caring Should Be Extended to LMH Nurses," *Lima News,* June 2, 1989, D2; Kathy Hunnaman, "Nurses Seek Wages, Benefits Competitive with Other Facilities," *Lima News,* June 2, 1989; Vonda Rempfer, RN, "Nurses' Proposals Are Not Unreasonable," *Lima News,* June 11, 1989, E4; Beverly Krouskop, "LMH Nurses Deserve Better Treatment," *Lima News,* June 12, 1989; Linda Goodwin, RN-C and Robin Woolenhaupt, RN-C, "Nurses Only Seek Compensation Proportionate to Skills Rendered," *Lima News,* Aug. 13, 1989, A8; and Anita Klausing, "Nurses Put Their Careers on Line to Guarantee Quality Health Care," *Lima News,* Aug. 21, 1989, B2. Also, Rick Siferd, who chaired the Policy Studies Committee at the time of the strike, has provided his recollections of the conflict from the Democratic Party's perspective; Rick Siferd, interview by William Angel, Apr. 15, 1999, Lima, Ohio (hereafter Siferd interview).

18. "Memorial Nurses Consider Pitch for Unionization," *Lima News,* Sept. 21, 1988, B1; "Nurses at Memorial Select Union Officers," *Lima News,* Nov. 10, 1988, B1, B3; "Memorial Nurses OK Union," *Lima News,* Jan. 27, 1989, A1, A5.

19. "Hospital, Nurses Hold Negotiations," *Lima News,* Apr. 3, 1989, D1.

20. "Progress in Contract Minimal between Nurses, Lima Memorial," *Lima News,* May 19, 1989, D1.

21. Muhler, "Quality of Caring Should Be Extended to LMH Nurses."

22. "Memorial, Nurses Make Some Progress in Talks," *Lima News,* June 21, 1989, B1; "Striking Nurses, Hospital Negotiate for 2nd Day," *Lima News,* June 30, 1989, D1; "Strike Issues Settled," *Lima News,* July 6, 1989, B1; "Hospital, Nurses Continue Negotiations," July 13, 1989, B1.

23. "Nurses to Vote Monday on Contract," *Lima News*, July 20, 1989, B1; "Nurses Cast Ballots on Memorial Offer," *Lima News*, July 24, 1989, B3; "LMH Nurses Nix Contract," July 25, 1989, B1; "LMH Nurses Cool to Contract Offer: Key Elements Unresolved Union Says," *Lima News*, Aug. 1, 1989, A1; "Nurses Ready to Resume Bargaining," *Lima News*, Aug. 4, 1989, A1.

24. See Mancur Olson, *The Logic of Collective Action* (Cambridge: Harvard Univ. Press, 1965). Olson argues that if individuals can receive all benefits an interest group might achieve and not actually be dues-paying members of the group, then most people will opt not to join. For example, if I can listen to public radio without paying a membership fee, then I will choose not to pay. This is the problem unions confront when companies try to force open-shop conditions into contracts. If nonunion workers can receive union-negotiated benefits and wage gains, then most workers will choose not to join the union, membership will decline, and the union will lose power in its dealings with the company.

25. Norm Ketteman, "LMH Situation Is Difficult for Patients," *Lima News*, July 28, 1989, D2.

26. Allen County Democratic Party Executive Committee minutes, July 25, 1989, personal files of author.

27. John Dornick, "Memorandum to All Members, Allen County Democratic Central Committee: Lima Memorial Nurses Strike," Aug. 14, 1989, personal file of author.

28. William Angel, "The Nurses Strike at Memorial Hospital," prepared statement for press conference, Aug. 2, 1989, Union Centre, Lima, Ohio, typescript, personal files of author.

29. "LMH Exec Call Democrat Stand 'Irresponsible,'" *Lima News*, Aug. 3, 1989, A1.

30. Angel to Gibler, Aug. 23, 1989.

31. "Stop Sticking Nose" (White Plains, N.Y.: Brazen Images, 1989), inscribed anonymously, personal files of author.

32. K. Piercefield, C.R.T.T., G.R.T, "Not All Democrats Support the Nurses's Strike," *Lima News*, Aug. 7, 1989, C2.

33. Sandra Clark, "Angel's Allegations Are without Justification," *Lima News*, Aug. 9, 1989, B2.

34. In addition to the two letters previously cited, these remonstrations appeared: Carl Wehri, MD; James Bagenstose, MD, David Steiner, MD; officers of the Academy of Medicine of Lima and Allen County, "Physicians Urge LMH, Nurses to Agree to Back to Work Plan," *Lima News*, Aug. 7, 1989, C2; Robert Stern, MD, "Sympathy for Striking Nurses Wanes," *Lima News*, Aug. 8, 1989, B2; Sharon Argo, "Commitment Is Vital to Nursing," *Lima News*, Aug. 9, 1989, B2; W. V. Bucher, "Let Negotiators, Mediators Iron Out Agreement," *Lima News*, Aug. 12, 1989, A10; Bruce Brondes, "Demanding Closed Shop Is Bad Move," *Lima News*, Aug. 13, 1989, A8; and A. Napier, "Strike Is Hard on Patients," *Lima News*, Aug. 16, 1989, D2. Two letters backing the nurses appeared ten days after my announcement. Neither referred to the party's action. Goodwin and Woolenhaupt, "Nurses Seek Compensation Proportionate to Skills Rendered," and Doris Steiger, "Administration Is Doing Disservice to the Community," *Lima News*, Aug. 14, 1989, B2.

35. "Closed Shop Is Morally Wrong," *Lima News*, Aug. 7, 1989, C2. My old adversary

Ed Finn admonished the *Lima News* for incorrectly using the term "closed shop." As Finn pointed out, the Taft-Hartley Act of 1947 had outlawed the closed shop, which required employers to hire only union members in good standing. The union shop, by contrast, allows employers to hire nonunion employees, but after a probationary period, say sixty days, they must join the union. Ed Finn, "Closed Shop Is Not Correct Terminology," *Lima News,* Aug. 24, 1989, A14. See also Jay M. Shafritz, ed., *The Dorsey Dictionary of American Politics* (Chicago: Dorsey Press, 1988), 107, 561.

36. I have been unable to locate my copy of this card, although it left a distinct impression because the Adamses had been such strong supporters of my leadership.

37. Doris L. Miller to Bill Angel, "Wednesday Eve," Aug. 2, 1989, personal files of author.

38. Dorothy J. Riker to William Angel, Aug. 9, 1989, personal files of author.

39. My remarks to the Executive Committee were first articulated in a letter I wrote to Doris Miller, a response to hers of August 2. William Angel to Doris Miller, Aug. 4, 1989, personal files of author; Allen County Democratic Party, Executive Committee minutes, Aug. 17, 1989, personal files of author. Also, Siferd interview.

40. John made this statement that night; the quote derives from a memo he had sent to all Executive Committee and Central Committee members explaining the party's rationale for supporting the nurses. John Dornick, "Memorandum to Central Committee," Aug. 14, 1989. Also, Executive Committee minutes, Aug. 17, 1989.

41. Susan Clum, RN, Cindy Newcomer, RN, and Linda Meredith Winters, RN, "Contract Will Be Basis for Future Agreements," and Anita Klausing, "Nurses Put Their Careers on Line," and Stanley E. Kollars, "Avoidable Lawsuits Also Raise Costs," all in *Lima News,* Aug. 21, 1989, B2; Ed Raines, "Nurses Worth Their Weight in Gold," and Clarence C. Roller, "A Strong Union Is Essential to the Security of Employees," both in *Lima News,* 31 Aug. 31, 1989, B4.

42. The LMPNA won the union shop but in a slightly modified form. Nurses already employed at the hospital had the right not to join the union, but all nurses hired in the future were required to become union members as a condition of their employment. "Hospital Talks Resume," *Lima News,* Sept. 6, 1989, D1; "Lima Memorial Nurses OK Contract, End Strike," *Lima News,* Sept. 21, 1989, A1; "Nurses Pact Covers Range of Issues," *Lima News,* Sept. 23, 1989, A1.

43. Todd Hey had once said this during an interview with WLIO TV. WLIO *News Journal,* May 2, 1988, video tape, personal files of author.

44. John Hevener used this song, written by Florence Reese, as a title for his book on the United Mine Workers' organizing campaign Harlan County, Kentucky. John W. Hevener, *Which Side Are You On?* (Chicago: Univ. of Illinois Press, 1978), x.

45. "Boycott of LMH Solicited," *Lima News,* Aug. 2, 1989, A1.

19. Dropping the Rope

1. Marge Dornick, John's widow, told me this story, and it has become part of the folklore of the Allen County Democratic Party.

2. William Angel to Susan Gibler, Mar. 26–27, 1989, personal files of author; Elsie

Crowe, Secretary, "Minutes of the Allen County Democratic Party Executive Committee," Jan. 17, 1990, personal files of author.

3. The final tally showed Keller defeating Pugsley 4,895 to 2,025. Keller's eventual opponent, Alberta Lee, had a much more difficult time, winning her race by only twenty-one votes. Final, official vote totals showed Lee with 4,204 votes, Bath Township School Board member Bob Tomlinson with 4,183 votes, and American Township Trustee Merle Miller with 3,803 votes. "Lee Slips by Tomlinson," *Lima News,* May 9, 1990, A1, and "Lee Picks Up 3 More Votes," *Lima News,* June 1, 1990, B1.

4. "White to Face Thompson," *Lima News,* May 9, 1990, B1. The final tally showed White defeating Moritz 3,528–2,869.

5. "Democrats Hope to Crack GOP's 'Courthouse Gang,'" *Lima News,* May 22, 1990, D1, D3.

6. "Celebreeze Still Taking Heat on Abortion," *Lima News,* Dec. 11, 1989, B1; "Celebreeze Makes It Official," *Lima News,* Dec. 12, 1989, B1; and "Celebreeze Against Role of State in Abortion," *Lima News,* Dec. 14, 1989, A1.

7. In *Webster v. Reproductive Health Services,* the Court upheld a 1986 Missouri law forbidding the use of public facilities for abortions, ruling that a state may use its power to allocate public resources, hospitals, and medical staff, in order to impose "a policy favoring childbirth over abortion." See Planned Parenthood, "Major U.S. Supreme Court Rulings on Reproductive and Health Rights: *Webster v. Reproductive Health Services,* 1989," http://www.plannedparenthood.org/ABOUT/NARRHISTORY/court-23.html, Mar. 1999; "Celebreeze Against Role of State in Abortion."

8. "Gubernatorial Debate Highlights," *Lima News,* Oct. 23, 1990, B3.

9. I no longer have Father Sidner's note. I was so angry at its tone and content that I threw it away shortly after I received it.

10. Carol Falk, Acting Secretary, "Minutes for Meeting of January 17, 1990," Allen County Democratic Executive Committee, personal files of author.

11. In mid-May, a *Columbus Dispatch* poll showed Voinovich defeating Celebreeze by a 14 percent margin, 53 percent to 39 percent. Furthermore, Voinovich's lead had grown from a December poll that showed him with only a 7 percent lead. "Voinovich's Lead Growing," *Lima News,* May 21, 1990, B1.

12. See William Angel, personal journal, June 3, 1990, 3–4.

13. William Angel to Mary Anne Sharkey, *Cleveland Plain Dealer,* July 31, 1994, personal file of author. I wrote this letter—in which I relay my story about the 1990 state convention—in response to Sharkey's article, "Death of the Ohio Democratic Party," which had appeared in that morning's magazine section of the *Plain Dealer.*

14. I have an extensive file on this episode, which includes the following: "OSU Lima Faculty Takes Initial Steps toward Forming Union," *Lima News,* July 5, 1990, A1; Jim Degan, Faculty Secretary, "Minutes of Closed Faculty Meeting," Sept. 18, 1990; "Lima Prepares to Vote on Faculty Union," *onCampus,* Sept. 27, 1990, 5; and "OSU Lima Faculty to Cancel Union Vote," *Lima News,* Oct. 11, 1990, A1.

15. Political Party Finance Report, Allen County Democratic Party, Evelyn Vanek, Treasurer, Oct. 24, 1990, personal files of author; Political Party Finance Report, Allen County Democratic Party, Evelyn Vanek, Treasurer, Dec. 14, 1990, personal files of author.

16. Ida Kay Keller, interview by William Angel, Feb. 13, 1999 (hereafter Keller interview).

17. "Water, Environment Seen as Priorities," *Lima News,* May 6, 1990, D1; Keller interview.

18. "Holmes Appointed Court Clerk," *Lima News,* Oct. 5, 1990, D1.

19. William Angel, "Statement by Bill Angel," Press Conference, Oct. 10, 1990, WordStar files, personal files of author; "Angel Criticizes Holmes for Taking Job with Court," *Lima News,* Oct. 10, 1990, B3.

20. "Angel Criticizes Holmes for Taking Job with Court."

21. Cora Hamman to Bill Angel, Oct. 12, 1990, enclosing annotated copy of "Angel Criticizes Holmes," personal files of author.

22. Don Stratton, "Holmes Can't Properly Tend 2 Positions," *Lima News,* Oct. 21, 1990, C9.

23. A *Columbus Dispatch* poll showed George Voinovich, leading Celebreeze 55.5 percent to 44.5 percent; a *Plain Dealer* poll had Voinovich leading 50.7 to 41.9; the University of Akron Poll, published by the *Beacon-Journal,* showed Voinovich winning by a narrower margin, 51.5 to 44.2. The Ohio Poll, sponsored by the University of Cincinnati, the *Cincinnati Post,* and the *Dayton Daily News,* showed Voinovich winning by nearly 14 percent, 52.3 to 38.5. "Celebreeze Trails GOP's Voinovich in 4 Ohio Polls," *Lima News,* Nov. 5, 1990, B1.

24. Both Keller and White fell convincingly. Keller lost to Alberta Lee 15,424 to 20,399, drawing five thousand fewer votes than she had in 1988 and winning only 43 percent of the vote. More disheartening was the realization that even if Keller had polled the same number of votes she had obtained two years previously (20,083), she still would have lost to Lee. Lorenzo White drew 31 percent, receiving only 10,411 votes to Bill Thompson's 22,561. "Allen County General Election, November 6, 1990, Final Report," Nov. 20, 1990, personal files of author.

25. "Democrats Try to Seize Chance as Townsend Exits," *Lima News,* Jan. 8, 1990, C1.

26. "Angel Criticizes Holmes for Taking Job with Court."

27. Woodard fared well, drawing almost 39 percent of the vote, 10,388 votes to Holmes's 16,472. "Holmes Breezes to Victory in Municipal Court Clerk Race," *Lima News,* Nov. 6, 1991, B7.

28. "Former Allen Dem Chief Dies," *Lima News,* Mar. 15, 1991, A15.

29. William Angel, "Message to the Allen County Democratic Party," Mar. 19, 1991, presented at Democratic headquarters, 718 North Main Street, Lima Ohio, personal files of author. Also, "Twining Replaces Angel as Democratic Leader," *Lima News,* Mar. 20, 1991, C1.

30. William Angel, Message to the Allen County Democratic Party, Mar. 19, 1991.

31. "New Party Chief Says Democrats Will Succeed," *Lima News,* Mar. 3, 1991, A4.

20. Spading the Earth

1. "Berger Pledges Change in Style of Leadership," *Lima News,* Nov. 5, 1989, A2.

2. Mayor David Berger and Howard Elstro, Lima public works director, interview by William Angel, City Hall, Lima, Ohio, Apr. 16, 1999 (hereafter Berger/Elstro interview). Berger contributed this information.

3. William Angel to Susan Gibler, Dec. 13, 1988, personal files of author.

4. Ibid. My notes show that Berger used the terminology "bipartisan" and "nonpartisan" interchangeably. Berger, however, has insisted that his intention was to create a campaign in which Democrats and Republicans both participated, hence "bipartisan." Berger/Elstro interview, information from Berger's commentary; tape and field notes from interview are in possession of author.

5. Berger/Elstro interview, Berger's contribution.

6. Angel to Gibler, Dec. 13, 1989.

7. Ibid; Berger/Elstro interview, Berger's contribution.

8. Rehab had received national attention when the Eureka Street project was featured on CBS *Sunday Morning*. "Lima Rehab Project May Go Hollywood," Lima News, Feb. 23, 1989, B1.

9. Berger/Elstro interview, Berger's contribution.

10. Ibid.

11. "Chief Blames Drug Problem for Lima Crime Rate Increases," *Lima News*, Apr. 17, 1989, C1.

12. "Williams Backs Moyer, Blasts Joseph's Support," *Lima News*, Apr. 18, 1989, B1; "Union Leaders Rebut Claims by Williams," *Lima News*, Apr. 19, 1989, B1.

13. Captioned photograph showing David Berger filing his petitions of candidacy, *Lima News*, Jan. 26, 1989, A3; "Candidate Says He's Not Controlled," *Lima News*, Feb. 2, 1989, B1.

14. Elsie Crowe, Secretary, "Minutes of the Allen County Democratic Party Executive Committee," Jan. 17, 1989, personal files of author.

15. "Council Candidate Search Breaks Tradition," *Lima News*, Jan. 27, 1989, B1.

16. Ibid.

17. "Joseph Stresses Continuity in Re-election Bid," *Lima News*, Jan. 31, 1989, B1.

18. Angel to Gibler, Apr. 2, 1989.

19. "Lima Rehab Project May Go Hollywood"; Angel to Gibler, Apr. 2, 1989.

20. Angel to Gibler, Apr. 2, 1989.

21. "Joseph Says Good Times Lead to Crowded Mayoral Race Field," *Lima News*, Jan. 25, 1989, B1; also, "Joseph Stresses Continuity in Re-election Bid."

22. "Candidate Says He's Not Controlled."

23. Ibid.

24. "Candidate Campaign Finance Report, Berger for Mayor Committee, Report for Post-election Primary," Rick Siferd, Treasurer, June 9, 1989, personal files of author.

25. "Candidate Says Stolen Letter Debunks Myth," *Lima News*, Apr. 13, 1989, B1.

26. Berger/Elstro interview, Berger's contribution; Angel to Gibler, Apr. 23, 1989.

27. Angel to Gibler, Apr. 2, 1989.

28. Ernest Hemingway, "A Clean, Well-Lighted Place," in *The Complete Short Stories of Ernest Hemingway*, Finca Vigia edition (New York: Charles Scribner and Sons/ Macmillan, 1987), 291.

29. The incident that follows is described in Angel to Gibler, Mar. 26, 1989.

30. Elsie Crowe, Secretary, "Minutes, Allen County Democratic Party Executive Committee Meeting," Feb. 22, 1989, personal files of author; "Democrats Nix Endorsement," *Lima News*, Feb. 24, 1989, D3.

31. I did send a twenty-five-dollar contribution to the mayor's golf outing, an an-

nual fund-raiser, but I mailed the check after Joseph was eliminated in the primary, intending it as a gesture more on behalf of Kim Shearn than her boss. I did not attend the event. William Angel to Kim Shearn, May 12, 1989, personal files of author.

32. Angel to Gibler, Apr. 23, 1989.

33. Berger/Elstro interview, comments by Elstro; Angel to Gibler, Apr. 23, 1989.

34. Angel to Gibler, Apr. 23, 1987.

35. "Lima Mayoral Candidates Field Questions at Forum," *Lima News*, Apr. 13, 1989, B1; "Candidates: Area Needs Harmony," *Lima News*, Apr. 19, 1989, A5; Angel to Gibler, Apr. 23, 1989.

36. Angel to Gibler, Apr. 23, 1989; "Candidates: Area Needs Harmony."

37. The Debutante's for Christ Cotillion is an important fund-raiser for the church, celebrating the commitment of young black women to accept a life of Christian fulfillment. It's a banquet with speeches, and not much dancing, aside from a waltz performed by the debutantes and their escorts.

38. Angel to Gibler, Apr. 23, 1989.

39. Berger/Elstro interview, Berger's comments.

40. Angel to Gibler, Apr. 23, 1989.

41. Berger ended up with 3,036 votes (32.5 percent) and Moyer with 2,667 (28.5 percent). Rollie Smith came in third with 1,391 votes (15 percent), followed by Joseph (1,233 votes, 13 percent), Mullenhour (624 votes, 7 percent), and Winkler (402 votes, 4 percent). *Lima News*, May 3, 1989, A1.

42. Angel to Gibler, Apr. 23, 1989.

43. Elsie Crowe, Secretary, "Minutes, Executive Committee of the Allen County Democratic Party Meeting," May 9, 1989, personal files of author. Not everybody agreed with my decision, however. Dale Leppla, a Moyer supporter, needled me briefly after the meeting adjourned.

44. Published records show that thirty-eight contributors made donations of two hundred dollars or more, for a total of $16,080 coming in large contributions. The "Group of 21" includes Allen County residents only, not donors from outside the county, nor does it include a thousand-dollar contribution from the Ohio Realtors PAC. The Republican-leaning independents were not Republican voters at the time they wrote their checks to Berger but later voted in a GOP primary. The Group of 21 also included four Democrats or Democratic-leaning independents. "Moyer, Berger Total More than $32,000 in Campaign Funds," *Lima News*, Oct. 30, 1989, C3; voter files, Allen County Board of Elections, Lima, Ohio.

45. "Moyer, Berger Total More than $32,000 in Campaign Funds," C1, C3; "Campaign Report Discrepancy Found," *Lima News*, Nov. 2, 1989, B1, B3. Moyer's campaign was funded by 127 contributors. Half of the Berger total came in bank loans, which were paid off through pledges of support.

46. "Williams Backs Moyer, Blasts Joseph Support"; Berger/Elstro interview, information from Berger.

47. "Looking for Leverage," *Lima News*, Nov. 4, 1979, C1, C3; "Philosophy of Leadership Key in Council Presidency Race, *Lima News*, Nov. 4, 1979, C1; "Williams Defeats Joseph in Presidency Race," *Lima News*, Nov. 7, 1979, A1, A3; "Williams Says Election Win Vindicates Stand on Issues," *Lima News*, Nov. 9, 1983, A1; "Williams Swamps Shepherd," *Lima News*,

Nov. 4, 1987, A1. Official Abstract of Votes Cast in Allen County, Ohio, Nov. 6, 1979, Allen County Board of Elections, Lima, Ohio; Official Abstract of Votes Cast in Allen County, Ohio, Nov. 8, 1983, Allen County Board of Elections, Lima, Ohio; Official Abstract of Votes Cast in Allen County, Ohio, Nov. 3, 1987, Allen County Board of Elections, Lima, Ohio; Berger/Elstro interview.

48. "Six Councilmen, Ex-Candidates to Back Moyer," *Lima News,* June 1, 1989, D1; "2 More Councilmen Throw Support behind Moyer," *Lima News,* Apr. 2, 1989, B3. Sciranka and Cunningham, who were chagrined by the support that Democrats had given Berger, later became Republicans.

49. Ibid. Italics added.

50. "Berger Lashes Out at Former Mayor," *Lima News,* Apr. 21, 1989, C1, C3.

51. "Moyer Criticizes Joseph," *Lima News,* Apr. 26, 1989, B1, B3.

52. "Armed with Endorsements, Moyer Stumps," June 3, 1989, A1, A4; "Housing, Drug Control Key to Future: Moyer," July 13, 1989, B1; "Moyer Believes Past Experience Key to Success," Nov. 5, 1989, A1, A2.

53. "Berger Disputes Criticism of Non-Profit Housing Efforts," July 13, 1989, B3; "Berger, Moyer Debate Park, Housing Issues," Oct. 11, 1989, C1, C3; "Mayoral Candidates Face Off in First Televised Debate," Oct. 31, 1989, B1; "Mayoral Candidates Haggle over Campaign Statements," Nov. 3, 1989, A1; "Berger, Moyer Trade Charges," Nov. 3, 1989, A1; "Berger Pledges Change in Style of Leadership," Nov. 5, 1989, A1, A2; all *Lima News.*

54. "Berger, Moyer Trade Charges."

55. Berger won 57.5 percent of the ballots. *Lima News,* Nov. 8, 1989, A1.

56. Twining interview, July 28, 1999.

57. Ibid.

58. "Angel Denies Party Backing of License Fee Referendum," *Lima News,* July 26, 1989, B3; "Allen County Voters Reject License Plate Fee Increase," *Lima News,* Nov. 8, 1989, A1.

59. "Berger, Moyer to Vie for Mayor," *Lima News,* May 3, 1989, A1, A6.

60. "Berger, Moyer Trade Charges"; "Berger Pledges Change in Style of Leadership."

61. William Angel e-mail to Nancy Wyche, Apr. 20, 1999; Nancy Wyche e-mail to William Angel, Apr. 22, 1999, confirming this interpretation.

62. Berger/Elstro interview, Elstro's contribution.

63. Ibid. Also Berger/Elstro interview. I did not bring Nancy Wyche's name into this discussion but referred to her interpretation as the "synergy thesis."

64. For an excellent portrayal of the BP controversy, see Marc Cooper, "A Town Betrayed: Oil & Greed in Lima, Ohio," *The Nation,* July 14, 1997, 11–15. Also, "Oil Refinery Rescued," *Lima News,* July 2, 1998, A1.

65. Berger/Elstro interview, Berger's contribution.

Epilogue

1. In March 1992, Jerry Winkler wrote a scathing letter to the editor denouncing the Democratic leadership for not enlisting any local candidates. Jerry Winkler, "Where Are the Democrats?" *Lima News,* Mar. 9, 1992, C2.

2. There was a write-in candidate for state representative, Charles Hamilton, but he

presented only pro forma opposition to Bill Thompson, who won with 35,585 votes. Also, Marty Hess, a Democrat from Urbana, faced Bob Cupp for the senate seat in the Twelfth District, eventually losing with only 30 percent of the vote. "Incumbent Republicans Fare Well in House Races," *Lima News,* Nov. 4, 1992; "Cupp, Gilmore Win Ohio Senate seats," *Lima News,* Nov. 4, 1992, A8.

3. "Document Makes Waves in Campaign," *Lima News,* Nov. 1, 1984, D1; "Harrod Easily Wins Re-Election with Margin of 8,000-Plus Votes," *Lima News,* Nov. 7, 1984, B1.

4. "Wade Urges Visibility in Sheriff's Post Bid," *Lima News,* Nov. 1, 1984, D1 (except for Lenhart's statement).

5. "Incumbent Sheriff Pledges Continuation of Community Service," *Lima News,* May 31, 1992, A1.

6. "Bowsher's Goal: Responsiveness in Local Government," *Lima News,* May 31, 1992, A1.

7. "Harrod Holds Off Bowsher Charge for Allen Sheriff: Incumbent Wins by a Whisker in GOP Contest," *Lima News,* June 3, 1992, A1.

8. Prior to 1992, Beck had voted in Republican primaries. In the 1992 primary, however, he took a nonpartisan ballot, voting on issues only, a practice he has continued since. Beck has maintained his status as an independent candidate and has not affiliated with any political party. Allen County Board of Elections, voter registration data, Lima, Ohio.

9. Section 311.01 of Ohio Revised Code lays out specific qualifications for sheriff candidates, including the requirement that they submit employment histories and submit to background checks regarding employment credentials. In Beck's case, Judge Michael Rumer had conducted the investigation and ruled that he was eligible to run for Allen County sheriff. Among the requirements, and the one brought into play in Beck's case, was the specification in section B(9) of the law requiring a minimum of two years' experience in a supervisory role. Beck's opponents cited payroll records allegedly showing that although Beck had served as deputy chief in the Fort Shawnee Police Department, he had not accumulated the requisite hours on the job in a supervisory capacity. Beck countered that he had been paid as a supervisor only for time he actually spent on patrol, not for time doing administrative work. The deputy chief position, he insisted, was a full-time job. ORC 311.01; "Sheriff Candidate Lashes Back after Credentials Questioned," *Lima News,* Sept. 15, 1992, A3; "In the matter of Daniel W. Beck, Application for candidacy of Sheriff of Allen County Ohio," certified by Judge Michael Rumer, May 6, 1992, typescript copy, personal files of author.

10. "Sheriff Candidate Lashes Back after Credentials Questioned." See also Samuel J. Crish to Allen County Board of Elections, Sept. 8, 1988, typescript copy, personal files of author.

11. Minutes, Allen County Board of Elections, Sept. 10, 1992, Office of the Allen County Board of Elections, Court of Appeals Building, Lima, Ohio.

12. "Sheriff Candidate Lashes Back after Credentials Questioned."

13. Minutes of special meeting, Allen County Board of Elections, Sept. 17, 1982, Allen County Board of Elections, Lima, Ohio.

14. The core of Moles's and Rossfeld's argument was a ruling by Ohio Supreme Court in May 1992, *Shumate v. Portage County Board of Elections.* The Court had ruled

that "the duty to determine the qualifications of candidates rests solely on Board of Elections," effectively removing the power of judges to certify the qualifications of prospective sheriff's candidates. However, *Shumate* applied only to candidates for the primary, not the general election. According to the secretary of state's office, there was "no method to remove an unqualified candidate from the general election ballot after the primary." This latter interpretation formed the heart of Beverly McCoy's and my argument. *The Taft Report*, a publication from the office of Secretary of State Bob Taft, vol. 2, no. 8 (Aug. 1992): 105; "Taft to Break Election Board Tie on Sheriff Hopeful's Credentials," *Lima News*, Sept. 17, 1992, A2; William Angel and Beverly McCoy to the Honorable Robert Taft, Sept. 17, 1992, typescript copy, personal files of author; and Charles Rossfeld and Doris E. Moles to the Honorable Robert Taft, Sept. 17, 1992, typescript copy, personal files of author.

15. Bob Taft, secretary of state, to Donna Johns, director, Allen County Board of Elections, Sept. 23, 1992, typescript copy, personal files of author.

16. "Beck's Petition Examined," *Lima News*, Sept. 29, 1992, A1, A6.

17. "Dems Blast Beck Grand Jury Probe," *Lima News*, Oct. 1, 1992, A3.

18. Ibid.; "Beck Supporters Rally outside Court House," *Lima News*, Oct. 2, 1992, A1; "Grand Jury Gives the Go-Ahead to Beck Bid," *Lima News*, Oct. 3, 1992, A2.

19. "Dems Blast Beck Grand Jury Probe"; "Beck's Petition Examined."

20. "Beck Supporters Rally outside Court House."

21. Ibid.

22. "Grand Jury Gives the Go-Ahead to Beck Bid."

23. "Beck Supporters Rally outside Court House."

24. I asked Bob Holmes to be interviewed for this book, but he refused. Bob Holmes voice-mail to author, Sept. 3, 1998.

25. Beck received 24,847 votes to Harrod's 18,749. By comparison, 47,320 votes were cast in the presidential contest. While turnout for the presidential race may have stimulated turnout, a more important factor was the attention focused on the sheriff's election. It is worth noting that Harrod was able to increase his primary total by only about 10,000 votes. If one assumes that Beck would have gathered the bulk of the primary support that had gone to Bowsher in the Republican primary—a pretty safe assumption—Beck was able to augment Bowsher's total by more than 16,000 votes. Abstract of Votes Cast in the General Election, Allen County, Ohio, November 3, 1992.

26. Descriptions and conversations regarding the 1987 ox roast are found in William Angel to Susan Gibler, Oct. 17, 1987, personal files of author. Also, "State Treasurer to Substitute for Metzenbaum at Ox Roast," *Lima News*, Oct. 12, 1987, B1, and "Ox Roast Survives Canceled Speaker," *Lima News*, Oct. 13, 1987, B1.

27. "State Treasurer to Substitute for Metzenbaum at Ox Roast."

28. Tip O'Neill, *All Politics Is Local* (New York: Random House, 1994), xv.

· Index ·

National Association for the Advancement of Colored People (NAACP), 28, 34, 162, 163

Obenour, Jack, 21, *206*
Ohio Democratic Party, 12, 19, 59, 86, 120, 150, 160, 176, 192, 193, 236, 295*n*.1, 305*n*.3. *See also* Ruvulo, James; State Central Committee
Ohio Department of Transportation (ODOT), 37, 86, 151, 152, 156, 160, 175
Ohio Secretary of State, 48, 54, 139, 192, 193, 196, 210, 254, 281, 299*n*.10, 331*n*.14. *See also* Brown, Sherrod; Taft III, Robert A.
Ohio State University at Lima, 5, 14, 251
O'Neill, Thomas ("Tip"), 285
Osting, Clayton, 217, 218
Oxley, Congressman Michael, 60, 182, 223

Patronage, 8, 9, 37, 77, 85–87, 151–53, 156, 160, 294*n*.5. *See also* Allen County Democratic Party; License bureaus
Piggyback sales tax increase, 130–37, 145, 146; referendum on, 134–41, 143–46, 149, 177, 225, 226, 309*n*.27. *See also* Routson, Bob
Pitts, Jerry, 48, 94–97, 162, 176–78, 182
Prater, Paul, 26, 34, 45, 51, 52, 68, 72–78, 178, 205, 213, 298*n*.13, 316*n*.14
Presidential delegate nominating caucus, 19–23, 204, 295*n*.1

Quinn, Janet, 23, 34, 58, 78, 81, 84, 91

Rankin, Roger, 68, 99, 108, 183, 257, 265, 273
Reese, Don, *100*, 106, 130, 133, 134, 138, 141, 176, 183
Rehab Project, 32, 259–61, 265, 270, 271, 322*n*.5
Resnick, Judge Alice Robie, 215, 217, 218
Rhodes, Governor James, 6–8, 120, 121, 296*n*.8, 308*n*.14
Riffe, Vern, 104–6, 119, 176, 183, 186, 187, 252, 274, 294*n*.3, 304*n*.12
Riker, Dorothy, 157, 243, 245, 270, 271
Rizor, Paul, 72, 173, 188, 224, 228, 273, 302 *n*.19, 320*n*.31, 321*n*.58
Rose, Waldo Bennet (Ben), 67, 105, *130*, 211–13, 260–62, 265, 266, 271, 273, 297*n*.18
Rossfeld, Charles, 45, 50, 51, 78, 279–82, 331*n*.14
Routson, Bob, 137–46, *140*, 174, 177, 273, 309*n*.26
Rowland, Bob, 108, 111, 188, *206*
Rumer, Judge Michael, 133, 279–82, 315*n*.32, 331*n*.9
Runk, Wes, 133, 261, 262, 265, 271, 273

Ruvulo, James (Jim), 12, 13, 77, 83–85, 121–23, 149, 150, 175, 188, 194–96, 210, 217, 218, 234, 284, 308*n*.14. *See also* Ohio Democratic Party

Schmenk, Jim, 175, 293*n*.4
Schulien, Paul, 279, 282
Schwieterman, Ed, *100*, 111–14, 116, 117, 124, 125, 130, 176, 177, 183, 184, 250, 273, 306*n*.34
Sciranka, Tom, 40, 157, 270, 312*n*.1
Shaw, Steve, 91, 116
Shearn, Kim, 267, 268, 329*n*.31
Sheeter, John, 43, 295*n*.12, 298*n*.13, 303*n*.12
Shepherd, J. Vane, 169, 170
Shiloh Missionary Baptist Church, 40, 93, 269
Siferd, Rick, 45, 49–53, 66, 73–76, 99, 129, 131, 144, 145, 174, 210–12, 220, 241, 243, 244, 273, 280, 300*n*.26, 322*n*.5
Smith, Paul W., 47, 133, 141, 190, 205, 228
Smith, Rolland, *263*, 268, 271
Social capital, 238, 245, 265, 293*nn*.5, 6
Soo, Dr. Dixie, 153, 154
Soo, Dr. L. Y., 140–42, 144, 153
Spencerville, 178, 282; Dumpbusters, 178–81, 235, 237, 238, 245; landfill controversy, 178–81, 235–38, 320*n*.39
Stemen, Everett L., 200, 201, 317*n*.2, 318*n*.31
Street money, 28, 29, 34, 98

Taft III, Robert A., 120, 254, 255, 281
Tefft-Keller, Kathy, 28, 121
Thompson, Bill, 99, 101–4, 114, 115, 117, 124, *130*, 176, 183, 185–87, 227, 228, 248, 327*n*.24, 331*n*.2
Townsend, Robert (Bob), *100*, 112–14, 130, 134, 136, 159
Turner, Greg, 239, 240, 244
Twining, Rochelle Dennis, 31, 82, 83, 110–12, 152, 154–56, 174, 177, 178, 181, 183, 188, 201–5, 211, 226–28, 248, 253, 257, 258, 277, 284, 302*n*.1, 321*n*.48; and Berger mayoral campaign, 265–68, 273; as candidate for state representative, 67–70, 89, 91, 99–106, 108, 114–19, 124, 187, 226, 252, 305*n*.7, 306*n*.19; as field representative for Secretary of State, 196, 210, 254, 255

United Auto Workers (UAW), 6, 9, 19–23, 36, 47, 86, 87, 118, 137, 157, 178, 186, 204, 208, 216, 217, 229, 246, 259, 268, 296*n*.2
UAW Hall, 19, 21–23, 70, 72, 74

Not All Politics Is Local

was designed and composed by Christine Brooks

in 10/13.5 Minion

on a Macintosh G4 using PageMaker 6.5;

printed on 55# Supple Opaque stock

by Thomson-Shore, Inc., of Dexter, Michigan;

and published by

THE KENT STATE UNIVERSITY PRESS

Kent, Ohio 44242